Black Gotham

Black Gotham

A Family History of African Americans in Nineteenth-Century New York City

CARLA L. PETERSON

Yale
UNIVERSITY PRESS
New Haven and London

Yale University Press books may be purchased
in quantity for educational, business, or
promotional use. For information, please e-mail
sales.press@yale.edu (U.S. office) or
sales@yaleup.co.uk (U.K. office).

Designed by Sonia Shannon.
Set in Caslon type by
Tseng Information Systems, Inc.
Printed in the United States of America.

Library of Congress Cataloging-in-Publication Data
Peterson, Carla L., 1944–
Black Gotham: a family history of African Americans in
nineteenth-century New York City / Carla L. Peterson.
p.   cm.
Includes bibliographical references and index.
ISBN 978-0-300-16255-4 (alk. paper)
1. African Americans—New York (State)—New York—
History—19th century. 2. African Americans—New York
(State)—New York—Social conditions—19th century. 3. African
Americans—New York (State)—New York—Biography.
4. White, Philip, 1823–1891. 5. Guignon, Peter, 1813–1885.
6. Peterson, Carla L., 1944–   —Family. 7. New York (N.Y.)—
Biography. 8. New York (N.Y.)—History—19th century. 9. New
York (N.Y.)—Social conditions—19th century. I. Title.
F130.N4P47 2011
305.896′0730747—dc22   2010039306

A catalogue record for this book is
available from the British Library.

This paper meets the requirements of
ANSI/NISO Z39.48-1992 (Permanence of Paper).

10 9 8 7 6 5 4 3 2 1

Contents

Acknowledgments

THIS BOOK WAS LONG IN the making, but I was fortunate enough to receive help from many different quarters at every step of the way. Historian friends and acquaintances encouraged me throughout the years. Ira Berlin, Jim and Lois Horton, David Waldstreicher, Leslie Harris, David Blight, and Richard Rabinowitz taught me the historian's craft. Craig Wilder, Graham Hodges, Shane White, Craig Townsend, and Barney Schechter answered every question put to them, large or small. Martha Jones passed on invaluable archival material. Through careful editing, my agent Sam Stoloff showed me how to transform the data I had collected into narrative form.

Archivists went out of their way to help. I owe a special debt of gratitude to staff: at the Schomburg Center for Research in Black Culture, especially Diana Lachatanere and Steven Fullwood in the Manuscripts and Rare Books Division, Mary Yearwood and Antony Toussaint in Prints and Photographs, and Christopher Moore, curator and research coordinator; at the New York Public Library Schwartzman Building, especially Matthew Knutzen in the Map Room, Virginia Bartow at the Arents Collection, and librarians in the Local Historical and Genealogical Room; librarians at the New-York Historical Society. I also wish to express thanks to Gwynedd Cannan at the Trinity Church Archives; Wayne Kempton at the St. John the Divine Archives; David Ment at the New York Municipal Archives; Phil Lapsansky at the Library Company of Philadelphia; and Elaine Grublin at the Massachusetts Historical Society.

Generous support from various institutions gave me the opportunity to devote full time to the project. Fellowships from the University of Maryland, the Cullman Center for Scholars and Writers at the New York Public Library, the National Endowment for the Humanities, and the Gilder Lehrman Institute were invaluable.

Researchers Christine McKay, Robert Swan, Reginald Pitts, Valerie Idehen, and Jeremy Fain provided important help in identifying and double-checking facts.

Finally, I owe my greatest debt of gratitude to my family: my father and mother, whose memory provided a continued source of inspiration; my sisters Jane and Danna, my husband David, and my daughters Sarah and Julia, whose faith encouraged me to the end.

A Note on Language

THROUGHOUT THE NINETEENTH CENTURY, blacks referred to themselves variously as African, colored, colored American, Negro, and black. Statements by men and women during that period, and my own associated comments, follow this usage. Otherwise, I use the terms black, black American, and African American interchangeably in my narrative.

Black Gotham

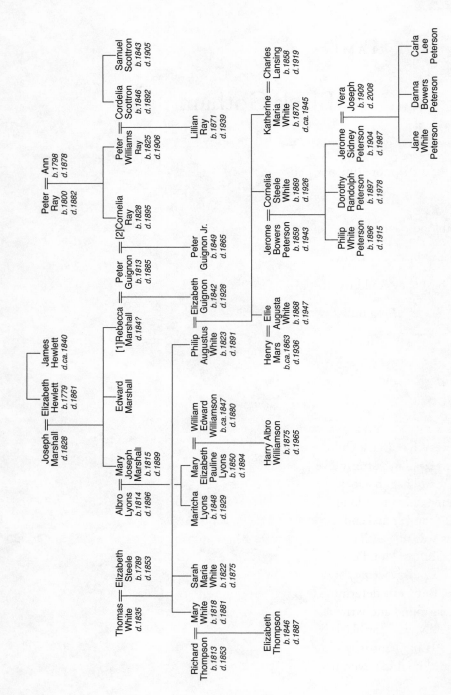

Family tree (Courtesy John Norton)

Prologue

FAMILY, MEMORY, HISTORY

Denver was seeing it now and feeling it—through Beloved....

And the more fine points she made, the more detail she provided,

the more Beloved liked it. So she anticipated the questions by giving

blood to the scraps her mother and grandmother told her—and a

heartbeat.... Denver spoke, Beloved listened, and the two did the

best they could to create what really happened, how it really was,

something only Sethe knew because she alone had the mind

for it and the time afterward to shape it.

—Toni Morrison, *Beloved*

I ENTERED THE MANUSCRIPT room of the Schomburg Center for Research in Black Culture with some trepidation. It was brightly lit, un-cluttered, and utterly silent. The archivists politely asked me to store my coat and bag in a locker outside the door, and then directed me to a seat facing them at a long, low, bare wooden table. They provided me with paper and pencil and left to retrieve the material I had asked for. Clearly, this was not a place for dilettantes. No chattering allowed, and please refrain from loud exclamations or emotional outbursts.

You're looking for a needle in a haystack, my historian friends warned me. But I was determined to find out more about my family's New York background and write as best I could about "what really happened, how it really was" for black New Yorkers in the nineteenth century.

Like Morrison's Denver, I had no memories of my own. Beyond that, I couldn't even rely on scraps I'd been told. All I had was a single name, that of my paternal great-grandfather Philip Augustus White, and a story about him that eventually proved false: that he was born Philippe Auguste Blanc, a "white Haitian" who fled to Paris at the time of the revolution in Saint-Domingue (Haiti), became a pharmacist, and then emigrated to New York, anglicizing his name to Philip Augustus White.

It made sense to me to begin with a trip to the Schomburg Center, which houses the city's largest collection of archival material on black New Yorkers, to see what I could find. Going through the manuscript division's finding aid, I came across a listing for the Rhoda G. Freeman Manuscript and Research Collection. I'd already read Freeman's book, *The Free Negro in New York City in the Era Before the Civil War*. Although written in the 1970s, it was chock-full of good information, so I decided to take a look at her papers.

The collection consisted of hundreds of note cards and folded pieces of paper stuffed into approximately twelve files the size of shoeboxes. I went through them methodically, taking notes on economic conditions, political rights, community institutions, and the like until I came to a box labeled "biography." And that's when I found them: two pages torn from an unidentified scrapbook on which newspaper clippings had been carefully pasted.

The first page was made up of several different items. What caught my eye was the long skinny column on the right containing the obituary of P. A. White clipped from the February 21, 1891, issue of the *New York Age,* the city's major post–Civil War black newspaper. On the left side, there was an assortment of poems that, judging from the varied print size, had been taken from different sources. On the second page I found a three-column obituary of Peter Guignon cut from the January 31, 1885, issue of the *New York Freeman,* the predecessor of the *Age.*[1]

I couldn't let out a whoop, so I just sat there quietly, my heart racing, and read through Philip White's obituary line by line, devouring every word.

According to the obituary, White had been born sixty-eight years earlier. Doing a quick calculation, I figured out that the year of his birth must have been 1823. After the untimely death of his father, White was "thrown upon his own resources." He attended one of New York's

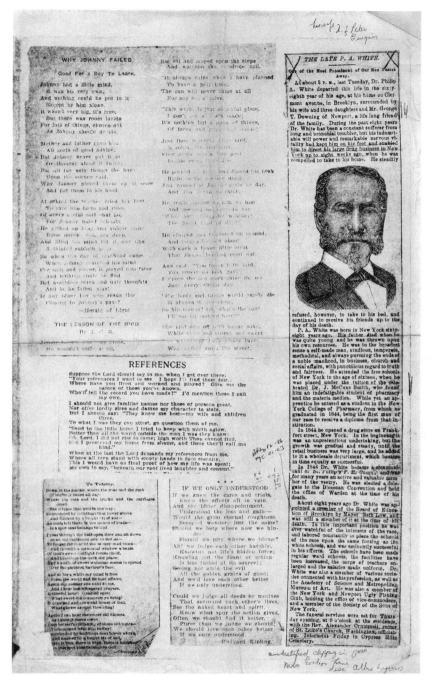

Obituary page for Philip White, with clippings from unidentified newspapers (Rhoda G. Freeman Manuscript and Research Collection, MG 313 Box 7, Schomburg Center for Research in Black Culture, The New York Public Library)

African Free Schools until the age of sixteen and then began an apprenticeship in the pharmacy of James McCune Smith, one of the first black doctors in the United States. While still an apprentice, White attended the College of Pharmacy of the City of New York, from which he graduated in 1844, "being the first man of our race to receive a diploma from that institution." That same year he opened his own drugstore in Lower Manhattan. Initially an unpretentious endeavor, it grew into a large retail business to which White eventually added a successful wholesale department.

The obituary intimated that White was a reserved, perhaps even staid, man. It was this sobriety that made him so successful in business. "He was in the broadest sense a self-made man," the writer opined: "studious, temperate, methodical, and always pursuing the ends of a noble manhood, in business, church, and social affairs, with punctilious regard to truth and fairness." Even though it's blurry, the photograph that accompanies the obituary suggests as much: a long severe face, piercing eyes that stare directly out, a thin aquiline nose, and a tidy goatee over which hovers a full, bushy mustache carefully swept to each side off the chin and cheeks. White's steady comportment served him equally well in both his church life and his activities outside the black community. A longtime communicant at St. Philip's Episcopal Church, one of the city's earliest black parishes, he served for many years as vestryman and then senior warden. Over time, he gained admission to the city's major professional pharmaceutical societies and became a member of both the Academy of Sciences and the Metropolitan Museum of Art. Impressively, in 1883, Mayor Seth Low appointed him to the Brooklyn Board of Education. Occupying the colored seat on the board, White successfully lobbied for the improvement of education for African American children. He held this position until his death in 1891. Alexander Crummell, the most eminent African American Episcopalian clergyman of the nineteenth century, to whom W. E. B. Du Bois devoted an entire chapter in *The Souls of Black Folk* in 1903, officiated at White's funeral.

Feeling amply rewarded, I idly picked up the second obituary. The name "P. A. White" caught my eye, and once again I became absorbed in reading. The subject of this obituary, Peter Guignon, had a daughter, Elizabeth, who had married Philip White. So Guignon was White's father-in-law and my great-great-grandfather! Once again, I suppressed a whoop and studied the obituary closely. Its author was none other than Alexander Crummell. A close friend of Guignon's since childhood, Crummell offered a poignant portrait of the deceased. Making no reference to Guignon's father, Crummell noted that his mother had come from the West Indies to New York City, where her only child was born in 1813. As a youngster, Guignon attended the old Mulberry Street School for colored children. He was, Crummell wrote,

> the contemporary at that school from about the year 1828 of the most celebrated pupils which ever were enrolled upon its records. His school-mates were George Allen, Thomas Sidney, the two Moores (Isaac and George), the three Reasons (Eliver, Patrick, and Charles L.), Isaiah Degrasse, J. McCune Smith, Henry Highland Garnett, George T. Downing. His standing and character in his school days can be seen that he was the friend and intimate companion of every one of these eminent boys, not only in their boyhood, but afterwards in their manhood and maturity.

I recognized these names, Crummell's included, as a roll call of prominent northern black leaders, and was astonished to learn that my great-great-grandfather had been their friend.

As a schoolboy, Guignon was, according to Crummell, a paradoxical mix of gravity and hilarity. Even the obituary illustration of Guignon as an older man with his broad face and full head of curly hair suggests a much less severe and reserved man than his son-in-law. In adult life, tragedy tempered without destroying the lighter side of his character. His first wife, a former schoolmate named Miss Marshall (my great-great-grandmother) died early, leaving him with young Elizabeth. Guignon subsequently married Cornelia Ray and, like White, became a pharmacist and respected businessman. But tragedy struck again some years later when his only son, a student at Oberlin College who had not yet reached his seventeenth birthday, was killed in an accident. Guignon's lasting grief over his son's death, Crummell wrote, strengthened his religious convictions. Like White, Guignon became an active mem-

ber of St. Philip's and a frequent member of the vestry. He engaged in
many acts of charity. When he became ill during the last years of his life,
he accepted his suffering with forbearance. Upon his death in 1885, "society," Crummell averred, "lost a unique and singular character, which
it is impossible to replace."

This book is about Philip White and Peter Guignon. It's not exactly
a family memoir, but neither is it traditional social history. It is a narrative that lies somewhere in between. It records my search to find my
father's New York family; my success in uncovering many documents
about these two men but my frustration in discovering only faint traces
of other relatives, particularly women; my determined effort to tell their
story despite the little I had. Peter Guignon's and Philip White's lives
shape the contour of my narrative, yet they also serve as a pathway to a
larger public history: the history of social movements, political events,
and cultural influences in which my great-great-grandfather and great-
grandfather were participants and witnesses.

We still hold certain truths about African Americans to be self-evident:
that the phrase "nineteenth-century black Americans" refers to enslaved
people; that "New York state before the Civil War" denotes a place of
freedom; that "blacks in New York City" designates Harlem; that the
"black community" posits a classless and culturally unified society; that
a "black elite" did not exist until well into the twentieth century. The
lives of Peter Guignon and Philip White belie such assumptions. They
were born free at a time when slavery was still legal in New York state.
They lived in racially mixed neighborhoods, first in Lower Manhattan
and then after the Civil War in Brooklyn, at a time when Harlem was
a mere village. They were part of New York's small but significant black
community, and specifically its elite class.

In 1820, the city counted approximately 10,300 black inhabitants,
and their numbers never reached above 16,300 until after the Civil
War.[2] They were concentrated in the city's Fifth, Sixth, and Eighth
Wards that ran from Bowery Road west to the Hudson River. In the
harsh and competitive environment that was New York City, blacks suffered from the additional burden of deep and pervasive racial discrimination. Most remained mired in the ranks of unskilled and illiterate

laborers. But a minority prospered, among whom were my great-great-grandfather, many of the "eminent boys" of his school days, including James McCune Smith, George Downing, Henry Highland Garnet, Charles and Patrick Reason, among others, and, in the next generation, my great-grandfather. They received the best education available to black children at the time. In adulthood, some became tradesmen—carpenters, shoemakers, or tailors—while others gained a foothold in the professions as schoolteachers, ministers, or pharmacists. A number emerged as leaders of the city's black community; several achieved national prominence. They founded newspapers, literary societies, political associations, and schools. They engaged in political resistance, holding conventions and mass meetings, and lobbying city and state legislators.

Although their tactics often differed, these young men shared similar values and goals. Much like white middle-class Americans, they placed emphasis on education, a Protestant ethic of hard work, and strict adherence to a code of respectability. Like them, they strove for socioeconomic advancement and security. Yet, given their second-class status, they needed to fight for rights that many of their white counterparts already took for granted: the acquisition of citizenship in the country of their birth, the attainment of all the privileges and obligations that came with being an American. They sought, as W. E. B. Du Bois later wrote, "ultimate assimilation *through* self-assertion, and on no other terms."

Following the example of New York's reigning literati, members of the black elite proudly referred to the place where they lived as Gotham and themselves as Gothamites.

Theirs was a pre-Harlem world. The early presence of men like Peter Guignon and Philip White in the city overturns the commonly held notion that New York's black intellectual and cultural life began in Harlem with the New Negro Renaissance of the 1920s. In fact, many of the Harlem Renaissance figures familiar to us were not native New Yorkers but came to the city as young adults from places as close as New Jersey, Pennsylvania, and Washington, D.C., and as far away as Jamaica and Guyana. But Peter, Philip, and their friends were New York born and bred. They lived downtown in the midst of the city's white population, not in a segregated black neighborhood. They were not bohemians or rebels; to the contrary, they held values remarkably similar to white middle-class norms.

Men like Peter and Philip were, Du Bois admitted, "exceptions." But he took umbrage with "the blind worshippers of the Average" who "cried out in alarm: 'These are the exceptions, look here at death, disease and crime—these are the happy rule.'" Du Bois never disputed the existence of the "happy rule," but he blamed it on a "silly nation" and insisted that the exceptional needed to be nurtured as the "chiefest promise" of the race. I follow his call.[3]

Remembering

So many questions swirled around in my head. How did a black elite emerge in early nineteenth-century New York? What were the educational opportunities for its members? How were they able to enter professions like pharmacy? Which city neighborhoods did they live in and what were their living conditions like? How did they relate to white New Yorkers, and to less privileged blacks for that matter? I was even more bothered by another set of questions. Why have histories of New York City ignored the presence of this nineteenth-century black elite until quite recently? More puzzling still, why did African Americans, my family included, forget this history? Why did they not hold on to their memories of the past, instead believing, as Toni Morrison wrote in the last pages of *Beloved*, that this was "not a story to pass on"? Why did I have to go to the archives to reconstruct my family's history?

Perplexed, I turned back to the Morrison quote with which I began this chapter and thought about how Denver so desperately wished to give "blood to the scraps her mother and grandmother told her—and a heartbeat," and how she and Beloved "did the best they could to create what really happened, how it really was, something only Sethe knew because she alone had the mind for it and the time afterward to shape it."

The need to remember and preserve the past is one of the most powerful of all human impulses, powerful for individuals and groups alike. In Morrison's novel, Denver is convinced that knowledge of her mother's past will help shape her own identity. Not too differently, nations and other communities also hold on to memories of people and events they deem historically significant; these memories lay the groundwork for group identity, inviting each and every member to connect with one another through a shared history and a common set of values. They establish a sense of "who we are as a people."

Morrison insisted that Denver and Beloved were trying to "create what really happened, how it really was." This I knew to be impossible. Just as Denver and Beloved possess only "scraps" of Sethe's life, so communities don't always have all the facts they need to reconstruct past realities, and sometimes can't even agree on what those realities are. There's also the question of whose past is being remembered. Much like Denver and Beloved's efforts to re-create their mother's past, societies often seek to hold on to memories of earlier generations that they themselves never experienced. So we need to think of remembering—whether undertaken by individuals or collectivities—as a dynamic process, an act of imagination. Remembering shapes and reshapes the past as it reinterprets this past from the perspective of the present, assesses how it affects the present, and reflects on how it might influence the actions of future generations.

Rituals help preserve memories of the past. Denver and Beloved's conversation is an example of how family members turn to storytelling to honor past people and events that have shaped the lives of later generations. Nations, too, make use of rituals, setting aside specific days of the year to commemorate past events and reaffirm a sense of group identity. Every July 4, for example, Americans pause to remember the war of independence and the birth of the United States as a nation founded on principles of freedom and equality. Every Thanksgiving they gather together to pay tribute to the hospitality of Native Americans to the newly arrived Pilgrims. Yet national rituals also exclude, failing to take into account the omission of African Americans and other minorities from the "men" honored in the Declaration of Independence as well as the horrific acts of violence perpetrated against Native Americans after the first Thanksgiving. Religions, much like nations, also rely on commemorative rituals. Every Easter, Christians throughout the world re-affirm the central values of suffering and redemption as they pause to remember Christ's sacrifice for humankind.

But the lifespan of rituals may be tenuous. If not carefully maintained, rituals fade into oblivion. In the face of such dangers, societies often turn to more material forms of remembering, hoping that these will leave a more permanent physical mark. They record events in writing. They create objects—monuments, statues, tombstones, plaques—and preserve places as embodiments of memories. Old, disused buildings may become living testaments to the past.

Throughout the nineteenth century, black New Yorkers worked hard both to preserve memories of a past history of oppression and resistance *and* to create new memories of current events they wanted future generations to hold on to. Early in the century, they held celebrations every January 1 to mark the end of the United States slave trade in 1808, and every August 1 to remember West Indian emancipation in 1834. Along with the rest of the nation, northern blacks commemorated Independence Day, but many chose to celebrate July 5th rather than the 4th to remind themselves and the nation of their continued exclusion from full political and civil equality. As devout Christians, black Americans repeatedly turned to the Bible to cast their history of oppression and yearning for deliverance through Old and New Testament stories. They interpreted their history of New World suffering through the lens of the passion of Christ; they gave the title of Moses to leaders like Harriet Tubman who willingly risked their lives to free the enslaved.

Forgetting

At the same time, societies forget. Sometimes they simply choose to abandon memories of events that retrospectively strike them as insignificant or unworthy of commemoration. Or they may have the will, but not the resources, to remember. Communities can hardly hope to enshrine past memories when funds are not available to erect a monument, when literacy is not assured, or when writing is an expensive luxury rather than a common daily practice. Even if created, without the means to preserve them written texts will eventually crumble at the touch, monuments and buildings fall into disrepair or vanish entirely.

Despite their best efforts, nineteenth-century black New Yorkers were often unable to create long-lasting memories to pass on to future generations, a sober reminder that memorializing can never be taken for granted. Financial woes forced early newspapers like *Freedom's Journal* or the *Colored American* to stop publication after only a couple of years. At century's end, black leaders failed in their plans to create a memorial in honor of Peter Guignon's former schoolmate Henry Highland Garnet, a Presbyterian minister and radical reformer who had called for slave insurrection as early as 1843, actively recruited black soldiers during the Civil War, and later served as a United States minister to Liberia, where he died in 1882. Over time, many issues of later newspapers like the *New York Freeman* have simply disappeared as have entire years of its successor, the *New York Age*.

All too often, underfunded communities lose ownership of their memorials—whether written texts or physical monuments—or the authority to preserve them. City officials may heedlessly, or perhaps deliberately, destroy such memorials in order to make way for the new or to erase reminders of a history deemed worthless or best forgotten. Consider the fate of the Negroes Burial Ground. Part of the City Commons, at the beginning of the eighteenth century it was the only cemetery in which black New Yorkers could bury and honor their dead. By century's end they were helpless in preventing New York's wealthy landowners from repossessing the land and carving it into lots as part of the real estate frenzy that had overtaken Lower Manhattan. All memory of this African American sacred place was lost until 1991 when the General Services Administration (GSA) announced plans to build a vast federal office complex on the site. In excavating the area, archaeologists found many human remains. Black communities in New York and throughout the nation galvanized to prevent the GSA from proceeding with construction. They held public meetings and organized commemorative ceremonies at the site in honor of their dead ancestors. After a two-year struggle the activists prevailed. In 1993, the federal government designated the burial ground a National Historic Landmark, and in 2006 a National Monument, the African Burial Ground Memorial Site. Since 2005, the Schomburg Center in conjunction with different federal agencies has celebrated the preservation of the burial ground in annual "reinternment ceremonies."[4] In 2010, a museum opened on the site.

Forgetting may also have deeper roots. If a group's history has been one of violence and oppression, of physical and psychological wounding, later memories may result in cultural trauma. As with Morrison's Sethe, remembering the past simply becomes too painful, creating a festering wound that will not heal, a shame that burns and scars the soul. Such were the reactions of many black New Yorkers after the Civil War. Alexander Crummell, for example, worried out loud about how black Americans should handle their prewar history, insisting that the constant recollection of the slave past was a pernicious habit, a morbid obsession, a form of mental enslavement. "For 200 years," Crummell declared in 1885, "the misfortune of the black race has been the confinement of its mind in the pent-up prison of human bondage. The morbid, absorbing and abiding recollection of that condition—what is it but the continuance of that same condition, in memory and dark imagination?"[5]

History

Browse through the shelves of books about nineteenth-century New York history at your local library and here's what you're likely to find: at one extreme, rags-to-riches stories about how men like John Jacob Astor came to New York from Germany with nothing in his pockets, built a fabulous fortune, and helped turn the city into a great metropolis; biographies of famous mayors like the upstanding Philip Hone or the corrupt Boss Tweed; and accounts of the growth of Wall Street, the creation of Central Park, or the building of the Brooklyn Bridge. At the other extreme are tales of poverty-stricken Europeans fleeing to New York in search a better life, such as Irish peasants escaping the potato famine of the 1840s; descriptions of the deplorable conditions of the slums in which they huddled together; and tales of the criminal activities of neighborhood gangs. Bringing the two extremes together are meditations on the disparities of wealth and poverty that resulted in a highly combustible mix and frequently erupted in violence.

Yet a sense of incredible optimism often seems to pervade these histories. The Statue of Liberty and Emma Lazarus's poem engraved on its base best sum up this can-do spirit. "Give me your tired, your poor, your huddled masses yearning to breathe free, the wretched refuse of your teeming shore," Lady Liberty cries out in welcome: "I lift my lamp beside the golden door." With few exceptions and until fairly recently, however, historians have tended to turn a blind eye to the degree to which the "yearning to breathe free" of black New Yorkers has so often been thwarted, if not actively resisted. Historians were once reluctant to acknowledge that slavery existed in the state until 1827, that the city's commercial ties to the slave South and the Caribbean persisted until the Civil War, and that its wealth was founded in large part on slave labor. They also refused to recognize the highly qualified nature of black freedom after emancipation and the many acts of violence perpetrated with stunning regularity against black New Yorkers. Such admissions would have blatantly contradicted the ethos of liberal individualism that, we've been told, laid the foundation of New York's emergence as a world metropolis.

It's only in the past couple of decades that New York historians have undertaken serious study of the city's early black population. They have focused on New York's dependence on slave labor and the systemic discrimination that maintained blacks in an underclass status. At the same time, they have emphasized the presence of an early black elite that counters racist notions of black Americans' inferiority and incapacity to be civilized.[6] Yet to this day few nineteenth-century black New Yorkers figure in history books: Alexander Crummell; James McCune Smith, Philip White's mentor, a highly respected doctor, writer, social activist, and ally of Frederick Douglass; radical reformer Henry Highland Garnet. Others receive a bare mention: Charles Reason, professor of belles lettres; his brother Patrick Reason, an early African American artist and engraver; George Downing, abolitionist and close friend of

Charles Sumner. As minor actors on the stage of history, men like Peter
Guignon and Philip White are altogether absent.

Family

Despite his admonition not to give in to morbid recollection, Crummell
knew that it was impossible fully to suppress memories of the past. So
he urged his contemporaries—Peter Guignon and Philip White among
them—to avail themselves of "hope and imagination" in order to transform their memories into a "stimulant to high endeavor" and memorialize their history as one of dignified struggle for future generations to
build on.[7]

So what happened to my family's memories? Did my great-great-
grandfather and great-grandfather disregard Crummell's advice? Or
had they tried to pass memories down to future generations, but failed?
If so, why?

In the absence of any concrete information, I've tried imagina-
tively to reconstruct why and how this process of forgetting happened.
Philip White's middle daughter, Cornelia, was my grandmother; she
married Jerome Bowers Peterson shortly after her father's death. Both
had come of age in the waning years of the nineteenth century, shared
the same ethical values and moral sensibility as the older generation,
cherished the same collective memories, and attended many commemorative celebrations with their elders. I believe it was the next generation,
that of my father Jerome Sidney Peterson and my aunt Dorothy Ran-
dolph Peterson, who turned their backs on the nineteenth century's collective memories. Neither ever volunteered much information about our
family, and I never bothered to ask. I have no idea whether they would
have answered my questions, but in any event my aunt died in 1978 and
my father in 1987 after a twelve-year illness that severely impaired his
memory.

Maybe an unbridgeable generation gap had opened between my
grandparents' and my father's generations. My father and aunt reached
adulthood in the 1920s. I'm guessing that as the Harlem Renaissance

got under way, accounts of nineteenth-century black New Yorkers held little meaning for them. They had had no direct experience of this earlier history and could not fit it into their new twentieth-century context. Listening to stories about their forebears, they might well have dismissed them as hopelessly old-fashioned. They did not believe that their future lay in preserving the tight-knit community, time-honored traditions, and deeply felt values of respectability that had guided earlier generations.

More troubling, it's also possible that since they had *not* participated in the struggles of the nineteenth century, this younger generation felt their traumatizing effects to a much greater extent. They might well have felt the degradation that accompanies humiliation and violence, but none of the pride and empowerment that come from determined resistance. They might have felt only shame about family members or acquaintances who had been slaves, domestic servants, or victims of racial violence. Such feelings might have convinced them that this was not a story to pass on.

Psychologists also remind us that memory crises are often brought on by personal family traumas. I thought back to a story in our family's more recent history that my father and aunt *had* mentioned, though briefly and reluctantly. They had a much beloved older brother, Philip, named after his grandfather. He drowned at sea one summer day, eerily at almost exactly the same age as Peter Guignon Jr. half a century earlier. I turned to my oldest sister for details. The three children had gone to the beach unaccompanied. A strong undertow caught them by surprise. My aunt attended to her baby brother, assuming that Philip would be strong enough to swim to shore on his own. When she turned around, he was gone. His body was never recovered. Grievances festered under the surface, never to be brought up, aired, and much less resolved. According to my sister, either my aunt blamed her mother for not being present, or Cornelia blamed her daughter for not saving Philip. Or maybe it was both.

Either way, my aunt rebelled and engaged in behavior that her family considered highly unrespectable. She moved out of Brooklyn and up to Harlem on her own where she became a schoolteacher. She hung

Jerome Bowers Peterson, circa 1900

out with the newcomers of the Harlem Renaissance. She became an actress. Exerting a powerful influence over her baby brother, she took my father with her. For better or for worse, they loosened their ties with the past to become New Negroes in Harlem, Greenwich Village, and abroad in Paris and other places. They imagined themselves as modern cosmopolitans, as citizens of the world, eager to encounter and experience other cultures. As an adult, my father worked in the field of international public health and our family spent years abroad in Beirut, Lebanon, and Geneva, Switzerland. He never said much about his own experiences growing up.

I now realize that what my father had passed on to me was a legacy of silence. Psychoanalysts who study family histories might well con-

Cornelia White Peterson with her two older
children, Philip and Dorothy, circa 1900

clude that my father and his generation had unconsciously transmit-
ted their unfinished business to mine. They were unable to put to rest
whatever "shameful" family secrets they possessed, so these lingered on
to haunt the younger generation like ghosts, leaving my sisters and me
feeling empty and unsettled.

I'm hoping to put these ghosts to rest. On a personal level, I want
to claim a form of belonging I've never had. On a broader social level,
I've become so frustrated by the lack of historical accounts about the
black elite prior to the Harlem Renaissance that I'm determined to fill
this void. I can no longer ask questions of the older generation who have
long since passed. But I want to recover a family history to pass on to
the younger generation.

Quest

I began my quest with empty hands.

There was that one story my aunt had told about the Haitian Philippe Auguste Blanc, but it turned out to be false. There were the innuendos of dinnertime conversation: our ancestors had probably come from the Caribbean; who knew whether there had been slaves in the family. And there were silences.

Where had my family stored its memories?

I tried to think back to household rituals that I could interpret as commemorations of the past—special food preparations or holiday meals, the wearing of jewelry, prayers, sayings, or maxims—but nothing came to mind. Whatever special rituals my family might have once practiced had been assimilated into northern urban culture and become unidentifiable.

Perhaps my parents' home was an archive that secretly housed memories of the past. In the summer of 2001, I helped my mother "break house" and move into a retirement community. The last room I tackled was my father's study, which had been left undisturbed since his death. The room was dominated by one piece of furniture: a heavy desk with a roll-down top and many small drawers and compartments. I remembered that it had followed my father overseas and home again. It was in fact an archive. A small round label pasted on the bottom of one of the drawers informed me that the desk had belonged to Philip White. Looking further, I came across some items tucked away in one of the back compartments that my father had never shared with us: a photograph of Peter Guignon and one of Philip White; some books, copies of Dante and Shakespeare, with Philip White's name inscribed on the frontispiece page; a family Bible. But that was all.

I wanted to ask relatives, but there were none. My father's brother, Philip, died before reaching adulthood, my aunt never married. There was a cousin, also unmarried, but she too was long dead and had left no children. I contacted a collateral descendant in Brooklyn but he too knew nothing, and wasn't interested. Another descendant found me through the Internet, but she was hoping that *I* would be the one to provide her with family information.

My dilemma was compounded by the fact that my family's nineteenth-century neighborhoods had long since broken up. Over time, members of their original social circle had moved away and their descendants had disappeared. A request for members of early St. Philip's families to step forward yielded no results. In dispersing, they had taken whatever memories they had with them. And most of the places that had once embodied these memories, that had borne witness to human lives and human events, had also vanished or been emptied of meaning. What places remained needed an interpreter to bring them alive.

I began haunting the city's streets hoping to find some trace of my family's nineteenth-century past. But time and "progress" had obliterated so much. Court buildings now stand on the original site of St. Philip's. Vandewater Street, the location of White's last Manhattan home, has disappeared and given way to One Police Plaza. A Pace University building has replaced his drugstore at the corner of Frankfort and Gold Streets. But here and there I did catch glimpses of the past. Philip White's last home still stands at 312 Clermont Avenue in Brooklyn. The family graves still lie in Cypress Hills Cemetery; Philip and his family are nestled in a quiet grove; Alexander Crummell is close by, as is James McCune Smith; and Peter Guignon rests at the top of a small hill in the plot of his second wife's family, the Rays.

Archives

Having reached a dead end, I turned to the archives, those storehouses of memories that have been painstakingly preserved on scraps of paper or in other forms, from paintings and photographs to digital images. Archives are man-made. Not all communities have the power to establish them since they require material resources—money, buildings, technologies of writing and preservation—as well as cultural resources, including literacy and historical knowledge. Those who have the means assemble, classify, and deposit what *they* deem worth preserving, discarding what *they* consider trivial, irrelevant, or even threatening to their way of life. They create history, determining what can be forgotten, and what must be remembered and passed on to future generations. Even after archives have been assembled, they never remain static monuments but are imbued with a sense of impermanence. Materials get damaged, lost, sold, removed from their original site and forgotten, destroyed through political upheaval or just sheer carelessness.

What would I find? Not find? How would I be able to put together the scraps that I found? What could I make out of those I didn't find?

I visited the Schomburg Center time and again, and haunted the city's many other libraries, museums, historical societies, and memorials. I gradually realized that although much of New York's black history was irretrievably lost, some of it was still there, buried but waiting to be found. I also discovered that despite any personal or cultural traumas nineteenth-century black New Yorkers might have suffered, many had made determined, if sometimes futile, efforts to commemorate their history.

In the nineteenth century, black New Yorkers lacked the means to create their own archives. New York's white elite had them. In 1804, wealthy merchant John Pintard joined forces with ten friends to form the New-York Historical Society. Pintard had been intimately involved in the great events that shaped the city's history. During the revolutionary war, he was commissioned to help alleviate the lot of American prisoners held captive by the British. He later became a merchant, accumulating a considerable fortune in the East India trade (before losing it by taking over a friend's debt). He served in the state legislature and the New York City Corporation, while many of his colleagues were lawyers and politicians. According to Pintard and the other founders, the New-York Historical Society's mission was "to collect and preserve whatever may relate to the natural, civil or ecclesiastical History of the United States in general and of this State in particular." Acutely aware of the fragility of historical records, Pintard insisted that their first step must be "to rescue from the dust and obscurity of private repositories such important documents, as are liable to be lost or destroyed by the indifference or neglect of those into whose hands they may have fallen. For," he continued, "without the aid of original records and authentic documents, history will be nothing more than a well-combined series of ingenious conjectures and amusing fables."[8]

Pintard maintained that the society would limit itself to "collecting and preserving whatever may be useful to others in the different branches of historical inquiry." What was Pintard's definition of "useful"? Who were the "others" who would find the preserved documents useful? We can get a sense of the answers to these questions by perusing the advertisements that the founders placed in local newspapers in which they requested donations of biographical memoirs, newspapers, magazines, accounts of imports and exports, and material related to early Indian settlements. They made no mention of the experiences of New York's black population. This doesn't mean, however, that black history is entirely absent from the society's archives. True, its founders didn't seem particularly interested in it, undoubtedly finding it "useless," hardly worthy of historical inquiry, or perhaps even inconveniently contradictory to the history of the city they envisioned. Nevertheless, traces of black life do surface, albeit couched within a white context, located on the margins of white history, and presented from a white perspective.

Yet black Americans never countenanced abandoning the preserving and telling of their history to white elites. Due to their straitened circumstances, the older generation could only engage in sporadic and scattershot efforts—newspapers that were short-lived, annual commemorations that were eventually abandoned, planned memorials that never came to fruition. It would be left to members of the next generation—those born in the postwar nineteenth century and endowed with greater financial resources, levels of formal education, cultural sophistication, and broader social networks—to begin the work of preserving, institutionalizing, and committing to print the collective memories of early black New Yorkers.

Take James Weldon Johnson, for example. Born in Jacksonville, Florida, in 1871, Johnson spent many childhood summers visiting family in Brooklyn. Educated at Atlanta University, he lived in the southern United States and Central America for several years before moving permanently to New York. Once there, Johnson quickly advanced to the forefront of black political activism as a high-ranking official with the NAACP and contributor to the *New York Age*. A prolific writer, in the early 1930s he published a memoir, *Along This Way*, and the seminal history *Black Manhattan*.

In the book's preface, Johnson insisted that his ambitions were limited. He was not attempting to compile "in any strict sense a history" but simply to "etch in the background of the Negro in latter-day New York, to give a cut-back in projecting a picture of Negro Harlem." Yet fully one-third of *Black Manhattan* concentrates on early black life in the city, before the emergence of Harlem as a neighborhood and a cultural movement. I wonder whether Johnson's turning back to the distant past might not have been impelled by his own failure to learn anything about his father's family. "Here I am again confronted with my lack of foresight," Johnson lamented in his memoir; "I know nothing of my father's early life and of his background, aside from the meager facts just stated. I never heard him speak of his childhood and what lay back of it and beyond it; and I never questioned him."[9]

Despite his humble disclaimers, Johnson was in fact something of a historian. At the end of his preface he thanked all those who had helped him, eyewitnesses, research assistants, and last but not least he added: "I wish also to acknowledge my indebtedness for source material to THE ARTHUR A. SCHOMBURG COLLECTION." Johnson was referring to the energetic bibliophile who had devoted his life to establishing a library and archive of black history and culture. Born in 1874, Schomburg came to New York from Puerto Rico in 1891. He quickly integrated himself in the city's black community, meeting Johnson in 1905. Some six years later, Schomburg helped establish the Negro Society for Historical Research. Like Pintard a century earlier, the society's founders resorted to the word "useful" to describe their mission. They were "to collect useful historical data relating to the Negro race, books written by or about Negroes, rare pictures of prominent men and women, . . . letters of noted Negroes or of white men friendly to the Negro, African curios of native manufacture, etc., etc." This material would be useful, indeed indispensable, to writing the history of the black race and teaching it to black people. Within a year, Schomburg had amassed some three hundred books and documents, and with Johnson's help compiled a *Bibliographical Checklist of American Negro Poetry*. When the 135th Street branch of the New York Public Library decided to create a separate space to house its material on black history and culture, they enlisted Schomburg and Johnson's help. Soon thereafter, Schomburg agreed to add his library to this initial effort. In 1927, the Schomburg Collection was born. It contained approximately three thousand books, eleven hundred pamphlets, and many prints and manuscripts.[10]

Like Johnson, I too must acknowledge my debt to Arthur Schomburg. After mining the Schomburg archives, I came to two conclusions: first, that I could actually find documents pertaining to my family; and second, that despite the lapses of my parents' generation, there had been a powerful impulse to memorialize New York's black history, embodied in Arthur Schomburg and his collection. What gave me the courage to pursue my quest was my early discovery of the scrapbook pages containing the obituaries of Peter Guignon and Philip White. The *New York Freeman* and *Age*, I realized, had cared enough about these two men to memorialize them in print; an individual, still unknown to me, had cared enough to create scrapbook pages commemorating their lives and deaths; historian Rhoda Freeman had cared enough to preserve these pages in her research collection; and the Schomburg Center had cared enough to house her collection in its archives.

The Harry Albro Williamson Papers

At the Schomburg, I found an even more valuable cache, the Harry Albro Williamson Papers, preserved on a number of microfilm reels, which I'd been told was one of the few nineteenth-century family collections held at the center. I had no idea who Williamson was or who his family might be, but I started systematically working my way through his papers. Born in New York in 1875, Williamson seems to have dedicated his entire life to freemasonry, amassing volumes of material to compile a comprehensive history of black lodges in the United States. But Williamson was also interested in family history, and in plowing through his genealogical notes I made a serendipitous discovery just as astonishing as the earlier obituaries. Neatly typed on a piece of paper was the following line: "Rebecca was married to Peter Guignon in 1840; she was his first wife." When least expected, I had found one more

Double ambrotype portrait of Albro Lyons Sr. and Mary Joseph Lyons,
circa 1860, by an anonymous photographer (Photographs and
Prints Division, Schomburg Center for Research in Black Culture,
The New York Public Library)

link to my family! Rebecca was none other than the Miss Marshall
who Alexander Crummell had named in the obituary of his old friend.
Her parents were Joseph and Elizabeth Marshall. The Marshalls had an
older daughter, Mary Joseph, who married Albro Lyons, also in 1840.
One of the Lyons's daughters married William Edward Williamson,
and Harry was their son. If you're still with me, Harry Albro Williamson is my grand-uncle.

It was clear to me that Williamson was determined to preserve as
much of his family history as possible. He compiled genealogical lists.
He jotted family stories he had heard down on paper, beginning with
comments like "I often listened to the story of how" or "I can recall
my grandfather telling me." He put together a nine-page typed document titled "Folks in Old New York and Brooklyn" in which he explicitly warned of the dangers of historical forgetting: "The various items
which shall follow are intended for the present generation (1953) of citizens of color who have little or no knowledge pertaining to members of

their race whose identities have now completely disappeared from local records because the old have been replaced by the new."[11]

In Williamson's papers I uncovered an even more telling example of the will to record the history of nineteenth-century black New Yorkers in a memoir written by another daughter of Albro and Mary Joseph Lyons, Maritcha Lyons (Williamson's aunt and hence my great-grandaunt). Born in 1848, Maritcha composed her memoir for publication in the late 1920s but died before completing a final draft. In reading through it, I was amazed at how deep the commitment to preserve family and community history ran in the Lyons family. In her introduction Maritcha noted that her father had hoped to write a book about his life and times but never got further than the title, "The Gentlemen in Black." Given that he had been one of Peter Guignon's schoolmates at the old Mulberry Street School and later his brother-in-law, I can only lament that Lyons was never able to fulfill his writerly aspirations. Lyons asked his daughter to carry on his legacy. Although Maritcha was convinced that her "literary nephew" was better suited to the task, she dutifully complied, working from "the vast output of fugitive scraps" that Williamson had gathered over the years. The very title of her memoir, "Memories of Yesterdays, All of Which I Saw and Part of Which I Was—An Autobiography," suggests just how eager she was to preserve the memories of her father's generation.[12] Now it's up to me.

Had my grandparents, Cornelia White and Jerome Bowers Peterson, tried to emulate the example of their contemporary, Harry Albro Williamson? I'll never know.

Scrapbooks

"Colored men! Save this extract. Cut it out and put it in your Scrapbook, and use it at a proper time." So reads the caption of an article titled "Black Heroes" published in the March 10, 1854, issue of *Frederick Douglass' Paper*, the major black newspaper of the mid-nineteenth century. In writing these lines the author was exhorting his readers to save his article in a scrapbook as a way of keeping alive for possible future action memories of black soldiers who had bravely fought on the side of the Republic during the revolutionary war. The lines reminded me of the scrapbook pages in the Rhoda Freeman collection on which an anonymous owner had pasted Peter Guignon's and Philip White's obituaries as a memorial to these two men. It made me wonder whether even the small, personal act of keeping a scrapbook could also be a form of public history making.

Scrapbooking is a household art with a long, time-honored tradition, popular to this day. Scrapbooks memorialize, preserving in physical form significant experiences the owner wishes to remember, savor, and maybe even leave as a testament to loved ones. What gets put in scrapbooks varies tremendously from owner to owner: flowers, locks of hair, ticket stubs, postcards, handwritten notes, clippings from newspapers or other publications. Items may range from public issues to community affairs to family and personal matters. In pasting these items in their scrapbooks, owners create their own versions of history, composing new narratives out of old recycled material. And since scrapbooks are not meant for publication, owners are not obliged to follow any particular set of rules but are free to create as they please.

Thus, scrapbooks run the gamut from private musings to forms of history making that address a public need. For nineteenth-century black Americans, scrapbooks became a way to write their history, one in which they were the central protagonists, not the marginalized, despised, or forgotten. Telling their history from their own perspective, they allowed multiple voices—sometimes in harmony, sometimes in tension with one another—to emerge. Whatever their content, their scrapbooks, much like archives, reflected a sense of the evanescence of experience, a fear of forgetting, and a determination to preserve past events for posterity.

Williamson's family collection is a scrapbook of sorts. It's filled with cards, letters, genealogical charts, newspaper clippings, and recollections from him and others written down by hand or in typescript—what Maritcha tellingly referred to as the "fugitive scraps" from which she composed her memoir. Following in their footsteps, I imagine this book as a kind of scrapbook that memorializes my nineteenth-century forebears, their friends, and acquaintances. I haven't been able to account for all facets of their lives, so my narrative is made up of what I found and what I didn't find in the archives, of what was remembered and what was forgotten.

Like Morrison's Denver, I've tried to endow the few scraps of memories I possess with blood and a heartbeat. But, unlike Denver, my memories are not those of a still living parent and grandparent but of distant ancestors who have bequeathed to me even less than Sethe and Baby Suggs gave her. This absence of memory has weighed heavily on me.

Reflecting on her method for writing *Beloved,* Toni Morrison explained how "I must trust my own recollections. I must also depend on the recollections of others. Thus memory weighs heavily in what I write, in how I begin and in what I find to be significant. . . . But memories and recollections won't give me total access to the unwritten interior life of these people. Only the act of the imagination can help me."[13]

I'm not a novelist, however, and I can't compensate for my family's silences by writing fiction. Instead, I've turned to the archives. On a personal level, my research in the archives has been a form of memory work for me. Professionally, I've operated like a historian, working to make sense of the scraps I've found, selected, and brought together. I uncovered few personal documents that could give me insight into the feelings, psychological states of mind, or motivations of family members. Instead, I found information primarily in public documents: black newspapers such as New York's early *Freedom's Journal* and *Colored American;* Frederick Douglass's *North Star* and *Frederick Douglass' Paper;* the short-lived *Weekly Anglo-African;* and the postwar *New York Globe* (later the *Freeman* and *Age*), as well as white ones, notably Horace Greeley's *New York Daily Tribune* and the *Brooklyn Daily Eagle;* records of meetings of the Philomathean Society, the Brooklyn Literary Union, and other organizations; proceedings of black conventions such as the state convention held in Albany in 1840; and acts of incorporation like that of the New York Society for the Promotion of Education Among Colored Children.

Putting these scraps together, I'm hoping to fulfill my family's legacy and write the history of the "gentlemen in black."

Concentric Worlds

This book is a partial history: partial because it tells only one part of nineteenth-century New York history; because it favors family history as a point of departure; because it is made up of fragmentary parts; because I am part of it as descendant, researcher, and narrator; because I have allowed my quest to find lost family memories to become part of my story.

Each chapter title contains a date, a place, or an event of some importance to my great-great-grandfather, my great-grandfather, or one of their close associates. Similar to a clipping or a snapshot, that is the scrap I've chosen to paste in my scrapbook. I then let the work of memory, history, and archival discovery guide me through my narrative.

Bit by bit, I widen my lens. I see Peter Guignon and Philip White as living within several circles, each wider than the last. The first was what Crummell called "the wide circle of the leading citizens of New York and vicinity." Bound together by more than family ties, Guignon and White were part of a small class of educated blacks; pharmacists by profession, they were comparatively wealthy; they worshiped together at St. Philip's Episcopal Church, often joined the same organizations, and fought for the same political causes; they turned to the same group of friends, many of them Guignon's former schoolmates, for succor and counsel. Taken together, these men, their wives, and their children constituted New York's black elite, a social circle so tightly knit that they could almost think of themselves as a "family." I have to confess that I see Guignon as an unremarkable member of this group. In contrast, Philip White's individual achievements were quite amazing; he qualifies as "the first" in so many of his endeavors. Yet he could not have accomplished what he did without the help of Guignon's former classmates, Patrick and Charles Reason, James McCune Smith, George Downing, Alexander Crummell. In his youth, they were his mentors. As he grew older, they became his intimate friends just as they were his father-in-law's.

The second circle was the black community. New York City's African American population was never very large. In 1810, it numbered 7,470 free persons and 1,446 slaves out of a total population of 91,660. In

1830, the city's slave population had dwindled to 17 while the number of free blacks stood at 13,976 out of approximately 202,600 inhabitants. In 1840, the black population peaked at 16,358 (out of 312,700), and then it slowly declined to 12,574 (out of 813,700) in 1860.[14] In Brooklyn the numbers were even smaller: in 1860, there were 4,900 blacks out of a total of 266,000 inhabitants. They lived, as social historians like to say, in the black community that cohered around a number of institutions: the African Society for Mutual Relief; the Mulberry Street School; churches like St. Philip's or Mother Zion; newspapers like *Freedom's Journal,* the *Colored American,* the *New York Globe, Freeman,* and *Age;* and the annual conventions of colored people.

Neither Peter, Philip, nor their friends remained confined to the black community, however. They inhabited a third circle, the city itself as well as its "vicinity" (Brooklyn). In a time before residential segregation hardened, they and other black New Yorkers lived and worked in racially mixed neighborhoods next to people of differing ethnicities and, at least in the early years, of different classes. In these neighborhoods, blacks interacted on a daily basis with whites of all classes—poor Irish and German immigrants as well as upper-class whites. Despite their differences, they were all subjected to the same indignities of metropolitan life: filth, epidemics, disease. Beyond the geographical confines of their neighborhoods, Peter, Philip, and others who worked in trades or professions had a wide variety of contacts with whites throughout the city—as colleagues, employers, or customers. As political reformers, they worked alongside white activists. During their leisure hours, they mingled with whites in public venues like the Crystal Palace. My most fascinating discovery was that of the Lorillard family—tobacco merchants, tanners, city officials, cultural power brokers—whose lives intersected with those of my family over several generations in surprising ways.

The fourth circle was that which lay beyond the "city and vicinity." The black elite interacted with relatives, friends, and fellow activists in other cities—Philadelphia, Boston, Rochester, for example. But in addition, frustrated by the racism that pervaded the city of their birth, many chose to go into self-imposed exile—to other cities, to upstate New York, or across the Atlantic to England or the African continent.

Yet with few exceptions these men and women returned to New York, almost as if the city held them in thrall. It was, I think, the chance of beating the odds, the intellectual ferment, the social activism, and the political energy of the city that brought them home.

The last circle was the cosmos itself. As they struggled to define what it meant to be a black American, members of the elite rejected any narrow and parochial definition of themselves. I was astonished to discover that one hundred years before my father and my aunt, many among them had acquired a cosmopolitan sensibility. Reading, study, work, and travel abroad gave them an opening onto a new world of culture, taste, and aesthetic appreciation that extended far beyond their racial group, their city, and even their nation. The more they read and traveled, the more determined they were to expand their identity beyond that of "colored American" to include "citizen of the world."

Over the course of my narrative I deepen my lens as more archival material about my great-grandfather's life became available to me from the 1850s on. As a consequence, Philip White emerges as the hero of my book. Nevertheless, I've been frustrated in my efforts to gain access to what Morrison called "the unwritten interior lives" of nineteenth-century black Americans. My most intimate glimpses of my great-great-grandfather and great-grandfather have come ironically enough from their scrapbook page memorials. I learned to read between lines and between items. I came to realize that four of the poems placed to the left of Philip White's obituary were in fact indirect commentaries on what my great-grandfather had cared about so passionately in life. "Why Johnny Failed, Good for a Boy to Learn" speaks of the difficulty of educating black children. "To Trinity" is a paean to the mother church that gave birth to St. Philip's. "References" pays homage to a dead man whose life had centered not so much on public affairs as on the "little home . . . and wife and children three." And "If We Only Understood" is a mysterious plea not to judge a person's external appearances "knowing not life's hidden forces." The scrapbook page, I realized, memorializes both a public and private life.

I've written *Black Gotham* out of a sense of obligation to the dead, to give a face to those left faceless by acts of trauma and erasure. I also feel I owe something to my family and my community—not only black

Americans but Americans nationwide. In writing a new and different version of African American history that challenges the ones we're so used to reading, I'm hoping to find a usable past for a nation that 150 years after emancipation still has a long way to go in solving its racial problems. *Black Gotham* is meant to be an act of reparation, an act to repair the tears of memory—tears in the sense of both sorrow and rupture.

PART ONE

Lower Manhattan

1795–1865

CHAPTER ONE

Collect Street

~ CIRCA 1819 ~

WHERE TO START? I STARED at the two obituaries and settled on
that of the older man, my great-great-grandfather Peter Guignon, hoping to find information about *his* parents. But Alexander Crummell's
references to his friend's background were circumspect. "Peter's mother,"
he wrote guardedly, "was a native of the West Indies and came thence
to the city of New York and resided there until her death." The sentence
raised more questions than it answered. What part of the West Indies
did Peter's mother come from? Who was his father and what was his
racial identity? Further information came to me in stages and to this
day remains woefully incomplete. I uncovered a brief notice of Peter's
death in the *Brooklyn Eagle*. The deceased, it noted, "was born in Bayard
Street in 1814, his parents having come from Hayti."[1] Although I now
knew Peter's parents' place of origin, the obituary prompted even more
questions. Why and how had they come from Haiti? Were they living
together on Bayard Street? Were they the household listed in the 1820
census as composed of the free white James Guignon residing in the
Sixth Ward with a free white woman and male child under ten? But
Peter was not white, so his mother couldn't have been either. Was James
Guignon living with a light-skinned black woman? Were they married?
Was he passing her and their son off as white? Why did Crummell make
no mention of him?

A chance introduction to a historian at a conference led to a discussion of my dilemma. To my astonishment, some months later I

Peter Guignon

opened my email to find that she had sent me copies of records she had happened upon in the archives of St. Peter's Church in Lower Manhattan. The most significant document was a bann of marriage dated February 1811, which read in part:

> Alexis Duchesne has been born at Laon in champain, & Sophie Guignon Was born in the Ile of St Domingue. This marriage was celebrated after Three Successive publications of the bans. Witnesses have been the Following, who have signed their names, Viz: Jean Baptist Gunian, Joseph Pierre Bérard, Pierre Guignon, Jacques Guignon Et autres.[2]

The bann placed the Guignon clan in the same social circle as the Bérards, who are well known in the historical record as *grand blanc* slaveholders forced to flee Saint-Domingue at the time of the revolution. The Bérard family arrived in New York in the late 1790s with their slaves but without the great fortune they had amassed.[3] I don't know who Sophie Guignon was or which Guignon might have fathered Peter — Pierre, Jacques (the French name for James), or yet another. But this man was clearly the "white Haitian" that my family had referred to so vaguely when I was a child. Peter's mother was undoubtedly a mulatto woman who had come with the Guignons from Haiti, as a slave, a servant, or perhaps a free woman. The deafening silence around their relationship and the father's absence from Peter's life suggested to me that they were not married.

Having reached a dead end, I decided to shift tactics and approach Peter through his in-laws, who I knew from Williamson's genealogical notes were named Elizabeth Hewlett Marshall and Joseph Marshall. They are the starting point of my story, shadowy figures in the background urging me forward to compose a picture in black and white of early social life in New York City.

The Black Families of Collect Street

Armed with a new family name, I went to the municipal archives and plowed through city directories, tax assessment records, and minutes of the Common Council. Here's what I found.

In 1818, the City of New York sold at auction land on Lower Manhattan's Collect Street to one George Lorillard, a wealthy tobacco merchant and real estate speculator. Among the lots purchased were numbers 17, 18, and 19, also 39 and 40, 51 and 52, and 80 through 83. Lorillard promptly turned the properties around and leased or sold several to a group of black New Yorkers. In 1819, the African Episcopal Society — soon renamed St. Philip's Episcopal Church — acquired a sixty-year lease on numbers 17, 18, and 19. That same year, George DeGrasse became the owner of lots 79 and 80. In 1820, Boston Crummell acquired lot 51, and Joseph Marshall lot 40. After a house was built on his lot, Marshall's property was valued at $900. When Collect Street was renamed Centre Street, Marshall's house was renumbered 72. In 1829, its value was listed at $1,200. After his death, the property passed to his widow, Elizabeth Hewlett Marshall, who built a rear house on the premises. By 1838, the total value of the property had risen to $2,000.[4]

Who were the parties to these real estate transactions? Let's begin with the black families, the DeGrasses, Crummells, and Marshalls. What were their backgrounds? How were they able to become property owners—or freeholders—in early-nineteenth-century New York? Much earlier, under Dutch rule, the director general of New Netherlands had given farmland north of the city to some thirty Africans in order to create a buffer protecting the Dutch from attacks by Native Americans. But after the slave insurrection of 1712, the New York Assembly passed "An Act for preventing suppressing and punishing the Conspiracy and Insurrection of Negroes and other Slaves." Among other things, this act prohibited blacks from owning property. Not until 1809 would they once again be allowed to inherit or bequeath property.[5]

I searched for the names of the three men in African American history books and found some information on both Crummell and De-Grasse. Boston was Alexander Crummell's father. An amazingly prolific writer, Peter's childhood friend has left us with many letters, essays, speeches, and sermons, some published in collected volumes during his lifetime, others still stored in manuscript form in the Schomburg Center archives. Alexander maintained that his father was born in Africa "in the Kingdom of Timanee" (now Sierra Leone); some even claimed that Boston was descended from Temne chiefs. It was Alexander's belief that his father "was stolen thence at about 12 or 13 years," arriving in the United States around 1780. Boston eventually became the slave of Peter Schermerhorn, a member of an old and prominent Dutch family, who had increased the family's wealth through the shipping industry and speculation in Manhattan real estate. Legend has it that Boston "was never emancipated," but simply told Schermerhorn one day that "he would serve him no longer" and "notwithstanding all remonstrations and intimidations could not be got back." Proud of his father's act of resistance, Alexander frequently referred to himself as "the boy whose father could not be a slave."

Boston married Charity Hicks, a free woman from Long Island, who was reported to have been brought up in "the same family that produced the celebrated Quaker, Elias Hicks." Hence, his "*maternal* ancestors," Alexander asserted, "have trod American soil, and therefore have used the English language well nigh as long as any descendants of

Alexander Crummell, abolitionist, Episcopal minister, and missionary,
circa 1890s (Photographs and Prints Division, Schomburg Center
for Research in Black Culture, The New York Public Library)

the early settlers of the Empire State." In freedom, Boston took up the
trade of oysterman and became a highly respected member of the black
community. Yet he never forgot his place of birth. Etched in Alexander's
mind were Boston's "burning love of home, his vivid remembrances of
scenes and travels with his [own] father into the interior, and his wide
acquaintance with divers tribes and customs." In later years, Boston
hoped to return to Africa and establish a farm in Liberia, but died be-

fore doing so. It was left to his son to make that journey with his wife
and children in the 1850s.[6]

George DeGrasse's background could not have been more different. Neither African nor European, he was a Hindu, born in Calcutta, and reputed to be the foster son of Admiral Count de Grasse, the
commander of the French fleet that had helped George Washington
triumph over the British at Yorktown in 1781. Before that, Count de
Grasse had served in the French navy in the Mediterranean and India
where he likely adopted George. He died in France in 1788, leaving his
son in the United States.

In 1802, Vice President Aaron Burr, who had undoubtedly become acquainted with the older De Grasse during the revolutionary
war, wrote a letter to his daughter Theodosia in which he referred to "my
man George (late Azar Le Guen, now George d'Grasse)." Two years
later, George DeGrasse petitioned the Court of Common Pleas to become a U.S. citizen. The court agreed that he had resided in the United
States for a period of five years and in New York state for one. So upon
showing proof of good moral character, swearing to uphold the Constitution of the United States, and promising to renounce allegiance to all
foreign states, "the said George DeGrasse was thereupon, pursuant to
the laws of the United States in such case made and provided, admitted
by the said Court to be, and he is accordingly to be, considered a citizen of the United States." Had George DeGrasse been a black born in
Africa, he undoubtedly would not have received U.S. citizenship.[7]

A naturalized Hindu American, DeGrasse chose to cast his lot
with New York's black community when he married Maria Van Surlay.
Maria's racial background was even more complicated than that of her
husband. It's believed that sometime in the early seventeenth century a
Dutchman by the name of Jan Jansen Van Haarlem entered the service
of the sultan of Morocco and married a local woman. One of their sons,
Abram Jansen Van Salee, settled in Brooklyn, where the phrase "alias
the mulatto" or "alias the Turk" was regularly appended to his name.
Maria was born some eight generations later. One of her and George
DeGrasse's children, John, became a doctor and moved to Boston; another, Isaiah, was a Mulberry Street School classmate of Peter Guignon
and Alexander Crummell. According to his contemporaries, Isaiah was

so light skinned it was impossible to distinguish any trace of African ancestry in him.[8]

But I had no luck finding Joseph and Elizabeth Marshall in any published history books. My single source of information about my great-great-great-grandparents has been Maritcha Lyons's memoir. Her comments about her grandparents are fascinating and tantalizing, but ultimately frustrating. Maritcha duly recorded that Joseph was a house painter who had been able to scrape enough money together to build a house for his family on Collect Street, and that "after his decease grandmother erected a rear house and converted the basement of the front dwelling into a store in which she opened a bakery." This fact is preceded, however, with an explanation of her grandparents' background that raises more questions than it answers:

> My maternal grandmother, Elizabeth (Hewlett) Marshall, was distinctly a poor white of English descent. Her mother's name was King and that of her mother's mother, was Bartlett, good old English appellations. She had one brother, James Hewlett, a "play actor" as stage performers were derisively styled in bygone days. She and her sister Mary, in common with girls of their station, were apprenticed. . . . [She united] her fortunes with those of my grandfather, Joseph Marshall, a native of Maracaibo, Venezuela. His family, after the continental fashion, had planned for him to enter the Roman priesthood. This was so contrary to his desire that he hastily and secretly left home.[9]

What did Maritcha mean when she referred to Grandmother Marshall as a "poor white of English descent"? When she used the term "white," was she speaking of skin tone? Surely she was not suggesting that Elizabeth was racially white. The reference to Elizabeth's kinship with James Hewlett lets us know that, however light skinned, she was not white. A member of the African Grove Theater Company as well as a solo performer in the 1820s, and a fairly disreputable character with a criminal record in the 1830s, James Hewlett was much in the public eye. His place of birth was a subject of open debate. James McCune

Smith suggested that he came from the West Indies, trying perhaps to protect the family's reputation. Yet it was a pretty well known fact that Hewlett was "a native of our own dear Island of Nassau [Long Island], and Rockaway is said to have been the place of his birth." And there was certainly no question about his race. He was regularly referred to in the press as "African," "colored," "black," and even "darky."[10]

In her account, Maritcha proudly emphasized her grandmother's English ancestry by noting the maternal surnames of King and Bartlett, but made no reference to Elizabeth's father. So was it Elizabeth's mother who was "a poor white," and did she marry a black man? I don't know. But if Rockaway was indeed their place of birth, I'm surmising that, just as Charity Crummell was related to the Quaker Hickses, Elizabeth and James Hewlett were members of the Hewlett family whose ancestor George had emigrated from England to America in the mid-seventeenth century. By 1658, George Hewlett had become a prominent landowner, and eventually the family gave its name to a town on Long Island.

And what about Elizabeth's husband, Joseph Marshall, a native of the port city of Maracaibo, Venezuela? In 1801 Maracaibo had a population of approximately twenty-two thousand, divided among Spanish nobility, white planters, slaves, and freedmen, mixed bloods referred to as people of color. I'm guessing that Marshall was of Spanish and African ancestry and came from this latter class, anglicizing his name upon his arrival in the United States. In the Venezuelan Spanish colony, missionary activity was as important as military conquest, administrative control, and economic exploration. Free people of color were disbarred from holding public office and restricted in the trades and professions they could practice, but they were welcomed into the priesthood. Perhaps it was that fact rather than any "continental fashion" that led to Joseph's family's plan to have him enter the clergy.[11]

These brief sketches suggest just how complicated the racial and ethnic origins of the men and women on Collect Street were. They claimed diverse national backgrounds, were of different racial mixtures, and had complexions ranging from ebony to ivory. I'm left wondering what made them, in the language of the day, "African."

Their histories differed dramatically. Some were born in the United

States, others in Africa, India, or South America; their ancestors came from places as diverse as England, the Netherlands, Spain, Morocco, and Sierra Leone. Only Boston Crummell was pure African. The rest were Creoles, mixtures of different races. Most seemed to possess visible racial characteristics of skin color, hair, and facial features, although Elizabeth Marshall appeared white. Such complications were less of a problem in the colonial era when racial mixing was more tolerated and race itself not clearly defined. But by the late eighteenth century, racial classification schemes were rapidly spreading throughout Europe and America. The Swedish natural historian Carl Linnaeus, for example, created a hierarchy of *homo sapiens,* placing the African on the last rung below the European and the Asiatic and just above *homo monstrosus.* Linnaeus defined the African's external traits as *black skin, frizzled hair, flat nose,* and *tumid lips.* Mixed-raced persons were increasingly deemed African if they exhibited any of these features, even if attenuated, or if it could be proved that they had African ancestry. To the external characteristics of the African corresponded the internal, devalued traits of *crafty, indolent, negligent,* and *governed by caprice* that rendered him unfit for citizenship.[12]

Ethnically and racially diverse as they were and well aware of the degraded status that accompanied the term "African," the men and women of Collect Street nevertheless chose to band together, create a tight-knit community, and forge an identity and place for themselves as Africans in America. Yet they remained alive to the "elsewhere," the many places across the globe from which their forebears originally hailed. Long before my father and my aunt, they acquired a cosmopolitan sensibility that shaped their outlook in at least two important ways. Engrained in them was a profound appreciation of and respect for cultural difference. They understood that although cultures might vary, this did not mean that one was necessarily superior to the other. They also intuited that individuals like themselves could forge deep affiliations with more than one culture and hold overlapping allegiances that did not contradict one another. These understandings led them to the unswerving conviction that beyond cultural difference lay the universal, ethical value of *character* that all human beings needed to cultivate.

So what was Africa to them? For most of these men and women, the continent was an unknown or at best distant past. Yet on a gut emotional level, its history resonated deeply. It became a metaphor for the experiences of displacement, exile, alienation, suffering, and perhaps future redemption that they and their ancestors had suffered across time and place. More pragmatically, Africa functioned as a strategy. It became a rallying cry through which to gain strength in numbers and engage in effective political and social activism. As a result, they embraced the label "African" as a common heritage and identity. In speeches idealizing the motherland, celebratory street parades, burial practices, and the like, this early "African" community made the continent a source of imagined memories and laid the groundwork for collective action.

St. Philip's Episcopal Church

In his Collect Street land transactions, George Lorillard offered a sixty-year lease on a plot of land to the African Episcopal Society, one of New York's first black community institutions and my family's place of worship. The DeGrasses and Crummells were among its first parishioners and might well have been responsible for its location close to their homes on Collect Street. In the Marshall family, Elizabeth was a Baptist and Joseph a member of the African Methodist Episcopal Zion Church. But their children shifted their religious affiliation to the Episcopal denomination, and by 1840, if not earlier, both the Guignon and Lyons families were members of St. Philip's. The church's history is the uplifting story of black New Yorkers' quest to fulfill their religious needs. But it is also the more hardscrabble story of the tremendous material hardships they faced.

Many black New Yorkers chose to become Episcopalians because Anglicanism, represented by Trinity Church, dominated the city's early religious life and was the first denomination to reach out to them. Under the auspices of the Society for the Propagation of the Gospel, Frenchman Elias Neau began instructing slaves in Christianity around 1705. After his death in 1722, a succession of assistant ministers at Trinity continued his work.

The upstanding members of Trinity Church wanted their black

St. Philip's Church, Centre Street, circa 1819 (New-York Historical Society)

slaves and servants to be good Christians. But they did not want them praying next to them, receiving religious instruction with them, or buried alongside them. So Trinity's black parishioners set their sights on establishing a church of their own with three specific goals in mind: establishing a place dedicated to worship, to the religious instruction of their community, and to the burial of their dead.[13]

The Trinity Church vestry minutes provide a detailed chronological narrative. As early as 1792, black parishioners petitioned Trinity for a lot of land on which to build a schoolhouse. After the destruction of the city's black cemetery, the Negroes Burial Ground, in 1795, a group of black men requested financial aid "to purchase a piece of ground as a burial place to bury black persons of every denomination and description whatever in this city whether bond or free." The city set aside two lots of land on Chrystie Street for this purpose. Trinity contributed toward the expense and also agreed to the formation of an African Catechetical Institution for religious instruction. But the institution had no fixed location and over the years was forced to move from room to room in different buildings.

Black parishioners repeatedly begged Trinity for a permanent home. By 1817 the African Catechetical Institution's Board of Managers became so exasperated with Trinity's foot-dragging that they fired off an angry letter. Signed by Peter Williams, who would later become St. Philip's first pastor, it threatened a mass exodus from the denomination. Black Episcopalians, Williams wrote, held out hope of

> providing a convenient place, of securing to the Church the attachment of a large number of coloured persons. On the other hand, it is most evident that if some such arrangement is not soon made there will be a great falling off in that class of Episcopalians. Your petitioners have to lament that, within the compass of their knowledge, some hundreds have already left the church, whom they have reason to believe would not have done so had some such provision been made for their accommodation. And as heads of families they feel the more anxious for it to be made, lest their children should also be led to depart from that form of worship, and those doctrines which they believe to be most scriptural and most conducive to the interests of true religion.

In May 1818 Trinity Church finally recommended an appropriation of three thousand dollars for a building that would serve as both schoolhouse and place of worship. Perhaps church leaders were motivated to act because of the threat of hundreds of blacks leaving the denomination. Or perhaps they saw a way out of their dilemma when George Lorillard offered the black parishioners "three lots of ground with a sixty year lease" on Collect Street, after which it was "to be held in fee simple, as a gift."[14]

Lorillards, Knickerbockers, and the Making of Gotham

So who was this George Lorillard whose business activities affected so many black New Yorkers in the early nineteenth century? He and his two brothers, Peter and Jacob, were members of what was then called Knickerbocker society. We owe this unwieldy name to Washing-

ton Irving, the prolific fiction writer and essayist whose literary imagination was fueled by New York City and its environs. His fictional Diedrich Knickerbocker was the reputed author of a lengthy history of New
York (1809), a satire of early Dutch settlers that mocked them for their
foolish behavior caused by their addiction to strong drink and strong
tobacco. The name came to apply to the actual descendants of these
Dutch families; as their numbers shrank, the designation was extended
to include English and also French Huguenot families like the Lorillards. A midcentury observer referred to the Knickerbockers as an "old
aristocracy" and noted that "there is no strata of society so difficult to
approach and apprehend." Indeed, these families constituted a closed
circle, marrying and socializing among themselves. They belonged to
the same organizations. Many worshiped at Trinity Church, where they
filled the ranks of the vestry.[15]

The Knickerbockers were citizens of Gotham, another one of
Irving's inventions. Some two years earlier, Irving had published an essay
introducing his readers to the city he named Gotham. The name first
appeared in early English folklore, referring to a town in rural England
named Goat's Town. It was said that its inhabitants were wise men who
deliberately acted like fools during the reign of King John (1199–1216).
According to one account, they did so to avoid paying taxes; in another
version, they hoped their crazy behavior would dissuade the king from
a visit that would prove costly to them. From this came the observation
that "more fools pass through Gotham than remain in it." Like their
medieval forerunners, Irving suggested, modern-day Gothamites might
be fools in appearance only.[16]

Some hundred years later, Gotham was reincarnated in a new
form. In 1941, DC Comics adopted the term Gotham City for the home
of Batman and his heroic exploits. It quickly came to be associated in
the popular imagination with New York City. In contrast to Irving's
Gotham, Batman's Gotham City is a dark and forbidding place. Its
gigantic Gothic architecture dwarfs its human inhabitants. Its streets
are grimy. It is vulnerable to epidemics and earthquakes, rife with crime
and gang violence left unchecked by police corruption. Yet, despite this,
it is a hub of commercial, financial, and cultural activity, containing a
port and shipyards, banks, museums, and a variety of industries.

This Gotham, just like Irving's, is pure fantasy, yet it describes with uncanny accuracy the city that men like the Lorillards were building. Manhattan was fast becoming a thriving commercial center, controlled by a powerful elite whose entrepreneurial zeal enabled them to make great fortunes.

The Lorillard brothers, George, Peter, and Jacob, were the sons of Pierre Lorillard, a French Huguenot who settled in New York in the mid-eighteenth century and quickly made a name and fortune for himself as an importer, manufacturer, and seller of tobacco and related products. A fervent patriot, Pierre was executed by Hessian soldiers during the revolutionary war. His wife carried on the business until their first two sons, George and Peter, were old enough to take over its management, which they did with considerable success. The third son, Jacob, entered the leather tanning industry. The family quickly became part of New York's ruling Knickerbocker class.[17]

In contrast to Irving's depictions, these real-life Knickerbockers went to great pains to portray themselves as an aristocracy noted for its dignity, sobriety, work ethic, church attendance, and philanthropy. Beneath this facade, however, lay a ferocious determination to turn New York into the hub of the nation's commercial, industrial, and financial activities and make a lot of money in the process. They did so in a variety of ways. Some owned large plantations along the Hudson River, others congregated in the city where they engaged in manufacture; many, like Boston Crummell's former master Peter Schermerhorn, were slaveholders. But it was shipping, in all its forms, that dominated. Abiel Low, father of the future Brooklyn and New York mayor Seth Low, increased his wealth by opening up markets in China and founding the prestigious firm of A. A. Low and Brothers. Industries related to shipping grew at a fast pace; Schermerhorn was a ship's chandler, supplying vessels with marine equipment and provisions. Auction houses sold imported goods. Private banks extended credit to merchants, while insurance companies gave them the confidence to trade.

To an astonishing extent, New York's merchants benefited from slavery, mostly by trading in goods produced by slave labor. In these earlier decades, the major imports were sugar, molasses, rum, coffee, and cocoa brought in from the West Indies, which in turn gave rise to a host of industries—distilleries, sugar refineries, and so on—run by men with solid Knickerbocker credentials. In the 1720s, for example, one Nicholas Bayard built the city's most successful sugar manufactory. At century's end, his son sold it to a merchant who converted it into a tobacco and snuff factory.[18]

Also a slave crop, tobacco was another important commodity. Some of America's most prominent men were involved in its trade. George Washington and Thomas Jefferson were tobacco farmers, and a majority of the signers of the Declaration of Independence had tobacco interests. It was, in fact, the British taxation of tobacco that the founding fathers objected to most strenuously. Pierre Lorillard and his friends imported their tobacco from Virginia, South Carolina, Kentucky, and other southern states and then resold it at auction. Lorillard eventually gave up trade to go into snuff manufacture, and set up a shop on the High Road to Boston. It was this business that his sons, Peter and George, took over after their father's death. They moved the store to Chatham Street and added cigars to their list of products for sale; Peter even patented a machine for cutting tobacco.[19]

As successful as his two brothers, Jacob Lorillard went into the leather tanning business, which was concentrated in an area of Lower Manhattan known throughout the nineteenth century as the Swamp; originally called Greppel Bosch (meaning a "swamp or marsh covered with wood"), the area lay slightly southeast of Collect Street. Later on, members of my family moved into that neighborhood. In the late 1840s Albro Lyons operated a boardinghouse for black sailors on Pearl Street, and he eventually consolidated the boardinghouse and his family's home in a residence on Vandewater Street. By the 1850s, Philip White lived down the block from him and established his drugstore at the corner of Frankfort and Gold Streets. Although he did not invent a machine as had his brother Peter, Jacob understood the importance of technology. Ahead of his competitors, he was the first to introduce into the Swamp a new rolling machine that improved the drying of hides.[20]

Knickerbocker families soon realized that they could increase their wealth not only through trade and manufacturing, but also through monopolization of landownership, control of the real estate market, and speculation on the city's increasingly valuable property. At the end of the eighteenth century, Manhattan was undergoing a period of unprecedented growth. Its population doubled from 31,131 in 1790 to 60,529 in 1800. Economic activity boomed. The city rapidly expanded north. Most of Lower Manhattan from Broadway to the East River was owned by Trinity Church and six Knickerbocker families, Bayards, Stuyvesants, and others whose farms ranged between one hundred and three hundred acres. They had built their original homes, manufactures, and stores on this land, but they now began laying out and paving new streets, on which they constructed new and grander residences. They also divided their land into lots to sell, lease, or build rental properties—all at great profit. So began Manhattan's first real estate bubble, which lasted until the Panic of 1837.[21]

By the beginning of the nineteenth century, all three of Pierre Lorillard's sons were active participants in this real estate frenzy. They acquired property in the areas where their manufactures were located, Jacob in the Swamp on Ferry and Gold Streets, Peter and George on Chatham Street near their tobacco manufacture. But they also bought land on just about every street in Lower Manhattan, including Collect Street.

The Destruction of the Negroes Burial Ground

George Lorillard had sold or leased land on Collect Street to black New Yorkers. But he and his brothers had also taken from them. When black parishioners petitioned Trinity Church in April 1795 for help in buying a "burial place to bury black persons of every denomination and description whatever in this city whether bond or free," it was because the Negroes Burial Ground was being sold from under them. As speculators in real estate, George Lorillard and his brother, Peter, were indirect participants in this destruction, buying a portion of the land that had once been part of it.

A court case, *Smith, ex dem. Teller, v. G. & P. Lorillard*, tells the following story. In January 1795, a group of men of solid Knickerbocker stock—Henry, John, and Samuel Kip, Abraham and Isaac Van Vleeck, Daniel Denniston, and the estate of the deceased Samuel Bayard (from the prominent sugar and tobacco family) obtained a deed of partition from the city of New York granting them permission to divide the Negroes Burial Ground into several lots. On today's map, the property extended from Broadway to Centre Street, and from Chamber Street north to Duane Street. Originally, the land had been part of the city's Commons, but in the mid-seventeenth century the government gave it to one Sara Roeleff for services rendered in negotiations with Native Americans upstate. At her death in 1693, Roeleff bequeathed the property to her several children; disputes among her heirs, executors of her will, and later descendants left the property largely unused. Most New Yorkers simply continued to think of it as part of the Commons, that is, as public land. But for New York's black population, this was the place allotted to them to bury their dead. In the 1790s, the Roeleff heirs recognized the enhanced value of the ground, took control of it, and agreed to its partition. One year later, Peter and George Lorillard bought a piece of this land from Bayard's estate for 560 pounds (although they were later obliged to return it to a Bayard heir in 1811).[22]

As an early black institution, the Negroes Burial Ground antedated the founding of St. Philip's by a century. For New York's eighteenth-century black population, it was a hallowed place where they gathered to bury their dead and honor their memory. It was in use as far back as 1712, or perhaps even as early as 1697, when Trinity Church decided that blacks, whether free or enslaved, could no longer be buried in its cemetery. For much of the eighteenth century, the burial ground barely lay within the city limits. It was located between the palisade, which protected the city from attacks by French and Indians, and the Collect (Kalkhook) or Fresh Water Pond. Covering some seventy acres, Collect Pond was fringed by marshland created by its many outlets, and surrounded by wooded hills. A later account of the burial ground published in *Valentine's Manual* in 1847 described its location as a "desolate, unappropriated spot, descending with a gentle declivity toward a ravine which led to the Kalkhook pond. . . . Though within convenient distance from the city, the locality was unattractive and desolate, so that by permission the slave population were allowed to inter their dead there."[23]

Destroyed and built over, the burial ground was rediscovered in

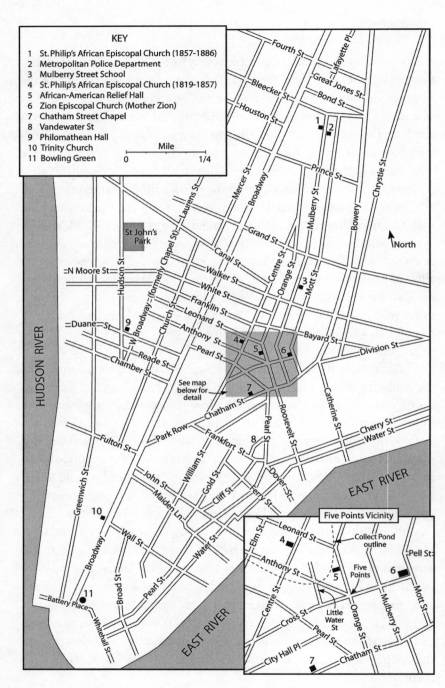

KEY

1 St. Philip's African Episcopal Church (1857-1886)
2 Metropolitan Police Department
3 Mulberry Street School
4 St. Philip's African Episcopal Church (1819-1857)
5 African-American Relief Hall
6 Zion Episcopal Church (Mother Zion)
7 Chatham Street Chapel
8 Vandewater St
9 Philomathean Hall
10 Trinity Church
11 Bowling Green

Mile
0   1/4

Lower Manhattan, 1836–1850 (Courtesy John Norton)

1991; a mere fraction of the skeletal remains buried there have been re-trieved. To date, there is a dearth of information concerning it. Black families who used the Negroes Burial Ground throughout the eigh-teenth century have left us no written documents. Whites have provided a few accounts, although none are contemporaneous. The cemetery's ar-chive resides in the bones themselves and the occasional artifacts found with them. They need to be unearthed, read, and interpreted.

Here's some of what we do know. The *Valentine's Manual* account briefly notes that many early black inhabitants "were native Africans, imported hither in slave ships, and retaining their native superstitions and burial customs, among which was that of burying by night, with various mummeries and outcries." Official documents of the time record that the city prohibited night burials and limited the number of mourn-ers to twelve out of fear of insurrection. Anthropologists currently studying the site have produced additional information. During excava-tion, they discovered more than two hundred cowrie shells, thought to symbolize the sea and thus the return of the dead across the Atlantic to Africa or the afterlife. Other evidence suggests that the deceased were wrapped in shrouds held together by straight brass pins and buried in plain wood coffins. On the lid of one of the coffins ninety-two nails were found hammered in a heart-shaped design, perhaps a Sankofa symbol representing a turning of the "head toward the past in order to build the future." Finally, all the bodies were placed with their heads toward the east, suggesting that when the dead awoke, they would face the rising sun and their African motherland. What the bones and artifacts do not, cannot, yield, however, is any information about the "mummeries and outcries" that accompanied the nighttime burials.[24]

But the cemetery also memorialized the violence repeatedly meted out to New York's black population. In both the Maiden Lane insur-rection of 1712 and the Negro Plot of 1741, blacks accused of con-spiracy were publicly executed on the Commons adjacent to the burial ground—hanged or burned at the stake. In 1741, two of the dead bodies were chained to posts on a hill overlooking the ground. The conspira-tors were then buried in the cemetery. Thus, the burial ground served as a cautionary reminder of the punishment awaiting blacks who ran afoul of those who so rigidly controlled their lives. Writing at the end of the

nineteenth century, white historian Frank Moss understood with amazing sensitivity just how this spot embodied the city's collective memories of racial violence (although he erroneously insisted that such violence was a thing of the past): "The imagination need not be excessively
vivid, when, in going through this district, amid its present scenes of
wretchedness and misery, we almost hear the death cries of the culprits
and the horrible imprecations of the spectators, who gathered in large
numbers to witness the tortures of the condemned wretches."[25]

Later incidents of violence further undermined the sacred nature
of the Negroes Burial Ground. In 1788, black families were obliged to
petition city authorities to stop medical students from stealing corpses
from the graves of loved ones and carrying away bodies "without respect
to age or sex, mangle their flesh out of a wanton curiosity and then expose it to beasts and birds." Predictably, their pleas went ignored until
the student "resurrectionists" began digging up bodies in the Trinity
Church cemetery. White New Yorkers then took to the streets in what
became known as the Doctors Riot. This time, the authorities listened.
The state legislature passed an act banning "the Odious Practice of Digging up and Removing, for the Purpose of Dissection, Dead Bodies In-
terred in Cemeteries or Burial Places."[26]

The demise of the Negroes Burial Ground in 1795 could only have
been devastating to the city's black community. But the men who re-
claimed the land as personal property were undoubtedly indifferent to
the fact that the bones of a people's ancestors lay buried there. They were
interested only in making money—lots of it. In this, all three Lorillard
brothers were spectacularly successful. The first to die, George, left an
estate valued at over two million dollars. At his death, Peter was worth
many millions more; it was said that he was the first man to whom
the term "millionaire" was applied. The brothers' wealth—and their
means of obtaining it—occasioned vitriolic comments. When Peter
died, former New York mayor Philip Hone wrote in his diary: "He was
the last of the three brothers of that name, himself the eldest—Peter,
George, and Jacob—all rich men; he the richest. . . . He led people by
the nose for the best part of a century, and made his enormous fortune
by giving them that to chew which they could not swallow." Even more
caustically, one of New York's leading society figures, George Temple-

ton Strong, observed: "How many cubic miles of smoke and gallons of colored saliva are embodied in the immense fortune that was his last week."[27]

Filth

The lots that George Lorillard sold or rented to black New Yorkers on Collect Street were hardly choice property. Quite the contrary. Not only was the land poor: in the process of enriching themselves, the Lorillards and their ilk had created a host of environmental problems that affected all New Yorkers—black and white, rich and poor, but most especially those of little means.

Much of Manhattan's land was low lying. Drainage was inadequate when rains were heavy, so lots situated below street level became "deep sunk holes, the receptacles of water in the rainy seasons, and the source of many unwholesome and noxious stenches." Human action further degraded the environment. Sewers were open and became easily clogged. Privies overflowed, emitting nauseating odors. Garbage, consisting of shells, ashes, offal, manure, human excrement, and spoiled food such as putrid meat and dead fish, piled up in the streets and went uncollected for days. In the warm weather these garbage mounds attracted swarms of flies and the odor could be smelled blocks away. The city hired cartmen to remove the garbage, but their work was spotty. They often took the manure, which they could sell at profit, and left the rest. Consequently, many New Yorkers kept up the old practice of allowing hogs to roam the streets to scavenge for garbage. But hogs added to the already foul street odors, rooted up pavements, knocked over carriages, and tried to eat children. Even deaths could not solve matters. Dead animals were simply left on the streets alongside the garbage. One citizen sarcastically wrote about how he had come across "dead horses, dogs, cats, and other dead animals lying about in such abundance as if the inhabitants accounted the stench arising from putrid carcasses a delicious perfume."[28]

The activities of merchants and tradesmen compounded these wretched conditions. Those working in the so-called obnoxious trades were responsible for the many "nuisances" that plagued the city. Among these were the offal and entrails discarded by butchers and fishmongers into the streets as well as the industrial waste created by brewers, distillers, dyers, and soap makers. Most obnoxious of all were the tanneries that, like Jacob Lorillard's, were located in the Swamp. A contemporary described the area encompassing Vandewater, Rose, and Jacob Streets as "one vast tan-yard." The vats of standing water attracted mosquitoes, the mounds of uncured skins emitted "noisome smells," and the tanning pits risked contaminating water from wells.[29]

The situation of Collect Street, built on what had once been Collect Pond, was particularly appalling. In earlier days many New Yorkers had claimed that "there was no more beautiful spot on the lower island." But carelessness quickly led to its pollution. One disgusted citizen wrote an open letter to the *New York Journal* in which he complained: "It's like a fair every day with whites, and blacks, washing their cloths blankets and things too nauseous to mention; all their sudds and filth are emptied into this pond, besides dead dogs, cats, etc. thrown in daily, and no doubt, many buckets [of bodily waste] from that quarter of town." Some even went so far as to claim that the bodies of murder victims were dumped in it.[30]

The city finally decided to take action and recommended that the Collect be filled in. Yet in 1812, a grand jury still found "much to complain of; besides great quantities of stagnant water it seems to be made the common place of deposit of dead animals & filth of all kinds, where they are left to corrupt the air and endanger the health of the City." Despite these warnings, the city proceeded to sell off lots in and around the Collect on which buildings soon arose. Many years later, a newspaper commentator assessed the social evil created by this "made ground":

> This will for ever remain of a very porous nature, and the exhalations arising from putrid matter collected in such places, must consequently be a continual annoyance to the inhabitants, and a prolific source of disease. All these things show how extremely improper, nay, how utterly unjustifiable, was the policy which allowed the entire ground to be covered

with buildings, without the least regard to future consequences, without taking into consideration the health and
comfort of a numerous population thus huddled together.

In conclusion, he placed full blame on the "avarice" of a "certain class of
people."[31] It's little wonder that in the mid-1820s George Lorillard successfully petitioned to have the street renamed Centre Street, hoping to
erase the sad history of Collect Pond.

Disease

As the newspaper commentator noted, New York was fertile breeding
ground for disease. In addition to the constant presence of tuberculosis
and venereal disease, epidemics of yellow fever plagued the city in the
decades after the revolutionary war; later years would bring cholera. The
worst outbreaks of yellow fever occurred during the summer months of
1795, 1798, 1805, 1819, 1820, and 1822. In 1798, 714 people were reported
dead; in 1805 the number declined to 270, and then to 166 in 1822. Those
who took sick came down with a fever and suffered from related symptoms such as nausea, clamminess, headache, weak pulse, and a yellowish
cast that covered their skin. They often died within the day, sometimes
within hours, of the onset of the disease.[32]

Although it seems obvious to us that environment and lack of
sanitation were at the root of epidemics like yellow fever, the debate
over their causes raged among New York's doctors, health officials, and
citizens. In the colonial period, most New Yorkers saw disease as a form
of divine intervention over which they had no control. By the following
century, they had come to associate disease with human behavior, moral
or immoral, and believed that individuals were responsible for their own
personal health. Such attitudes worked against New York's most vulnerable population, namely the poor, both black and white. They inhabited the lowest lying land, including the newly made ground. They
lived crowded together in narrow streets filled with standing water, contaminated by uncollected garbage and open sewers, and lacking free cir-

culation of air. They huddled together in ramshackle dwellings, several families often occupying a single structure. The more fortunate lived on the upper floors, the less fortunate in cellars. Both areas, but especially the cellars, suffered from dampness and poor ventilation.[33]

New York health officials began speculating that perhaps disease was caused by negative environmental conditions, infecting individuals who then passed it on to others. They determined to pass laws regulating the sanitary conditions of the city. Quarantine had long been a favored method of control, but now increased attention was devoted to sanitation. The Common Council passed ordinance after ordinance to take care of "nuisances," problems posed among others by "deep damp cellars and filthy sunken yards; unfinished water lots; public slips; sinks and privies; burial grounds; narrow streets; sailors boarding houses and tippling houses; the digging up of made ground; putrid substances, whether animal or vegetable; water."[34]

Health officials acknowledged that commerce and speculation were the life blood of the city. So they tried to find ways to prevent disease "without interfering with the privileges of the citizen, the disposition of private property, and with the domestic economy." Despite these concessions, New York's citizens, especially its merchant class, protested the efforts to place their public affairs—commerce, housing, public health, and so on—under increased regulation. They complained about much of the new legislation, arguing that quarantine was economically too costly and that preventive sanitation methods interfered with their property rights.[35]

True to their class interests, the Lorillard brothers resisted the new public health regulations, despite the fact that they were among those responsible for implementing them and setting an example to the rest of the citizenry. Although they were not prominent municipal leaders, they did participate in city governance, Peter as a fireman and assessor, Jacob as assistant alderman and then as member of the Common Council. It was there that he found himself in the rather uncomfortable position of having to consider legislation that went against his interests, those of his brothers, and those of New York's business community.

The brothers did not always get what they wanted. With steady regularity, the Common Council demanded that all three Lorillards correct "sundry nuisances" on the properties they leased or owned. These ranged from letting a privy overflow to allowing garbage to pile up to storing leather hides during the summer months.

But the brothers often got just what they wanted. All three actively pushed to build up Lower Manhattan in order to increase the value of their property and businesses. More often than not, they used their considerable muscle to cajole the Common Council into making improvements that would benefit them—getting sewers installed, water granted, lots filled in, crosswalks built, streets paved.[36]

Men like the Lorillards were clearly not sufficiently concerned about the fate of less fortunate New Yorkers to change their business practices. Blacks especially were vulnerable to disease, dying in numbers disproportionate to their presence in the city. In 1821 they represented 15.5 percent of total deaths, although they accounted for only about 8 percent of the city's population. By 1825 their death rate was three times as high as that of whites. It was commonly believed that blacks suffered to a greater extent from respiratory illnesses but were more resistant to yellow fever and malaria. A report on the 1820 yellow fever epidemic suggests otherwise. It noted that in one single street 14 out of 48 blacks, all of whom lived in cellars, died, whereas not one of the 120 whites living in the apartments above contracted the disease.[37] It's hardly surprising that so many men of New York's black elite—Peter Guignon and Philip White among them—would choose professions that would enable them to alleviate their community's suffering.

Yet as a large and highly visible segment of the city's poor, blacks were held most responsible for the presence of disease in the city. White New Yorkers accused blacks of spreading contagion and compromising the health of all by indulging in risky behavior such as drunkenness and sexual promiscuity. But they readily overlooked the fact that it was blacks who, attracted by the high wages, did much of the street sanitation. In 1800, blacks took on the task of cleaning out all privy pits and sinks on the East Side. Exposing themselves "to the effluvia of human ordure," they came down with such symptoms as "catarrhs and redness of eyes, nausea, vomiting, pains in the belly, bloody stools, and fevers."[38]

Distance and Proximity

Dominance in commerce, manufacturing, land monopoly, and city affairs put men like the Lorillards in a social and economic class far above that of most other New Yorkers. Nevertheless, geographic segregation between rich and poor, white and black, was difficult to maintain. In the city's early years, merchants' and tradesmen's residential and work places often occupied the same premises, and employees lived with them or close by. Neighborhoods were not separated into residential and industrial areas, nor were they segregated according to class, race, or ethnicity. At the beginning of the nineteenth century, New York's elite families began moving their homes away from the downtown commercial area to more pleasant surroundings, first to Bowling Green, then west to Greenwich Street and St. Johns Park, and up Broadway past Trinity Church. For their part, black New Yorkers lived in homes around Collect Street in the Sixth Ward. From there, they extended toward the East River in the Fourth Ward, and west to the Hudson River in the Fifth Ward. Yet, although blacks were concentrated in certain areas, they still lived among or close to white households. The Fifth Ward, for example, was home both to whites of varying social classes and to blacks. Moreover, even when white merchants and tradesmen moved to residential neighborhoods, they remained within short walking distance of commercial centers and their mixed populations.[39]

Some, like the Lorillards, decided not to move. In 1760, Pierre had located both his home and tobacco shop business on the High Road to Boston near the Commons. When his son Peter took over the business late in the century, he too kept shop and home together at what had become Chatham Street. He remained there well into the 1830s before moving to Chamber Street. In the 1790s, Jacob apprenticed at a tannery on the corner of Pearl and Cross Streets, which he later bought. He subsequently established his store on Ferry Street and lived right next door. Like Peter, it was many years before he moved west to Hudson Street. By staying put, the Lorillards remained in close physical proximity to blacks. Cliff, Cross, and Little Water Streets, where many black families lived, were close to Jacob's home and tannery; Collect Street was a short distance from Peter's home on Chatham Street.[40]

Such proximity to the poor meant that not even the wealthiest could entirely escape the consequences of poverty. Neither was disease ever far from their doorstep. During the summer months when yellow fever was most likely to strike, those who could fled town. Those who remained stared the epidemic directly in the face and sometimes took sick themselves. In 1799 Elizabeth Bleecker, who lived with her parents on Lower Broadway, wrote in her diary about how "a black man came up our alley and laid himself down on the ground" to die. Merchant Grant Thorburn reported visiting the home of a journeyman friend near the East River, and watching over the death of both his friend and an old colored woman who had refused to leave the house.[41]

Yet physical proximity also led on occasion to greater familiarity between blacks and whites, and to more fruitful contacts. Trade was an area of such interactions, and tobacco manufacturing offers some telling examples. In the 1790s, Peter Williams Sr., the father of St. Philip's first pastor, entered the tobacco business. He had been the slave of tobacconist James Aymar, a British sympathizer who returned to England after the revolutionary war. After receiving his freedom, Williams opened a tobacco shop on Liberty Street in Lower Manhattan. Looking back at this early period, a mid-nineteenth-century commentator observed that "the old Negro was then striving to sustain a rival opposition in the tobacco line, with the famous house of Lorillards." While this claim might have been something of an exaggeration, it's likely that Williams was sufficiently important in the business to come into contact with white counterparts like Peter and George Lorillard.[42]

Even more significant, the Lorillard brothers hired blacks to work in their own factory. This decision had a direct impact on my family. When I went back to Crummell's obituary of my great-great-grandfather, I decided to investigate the background of his second wife, Cornelia Ray. The obituary told me that her father was one "P. A. Ray." I found out that his full name was Peter Ray and, armed with that information, I went hunting for his obituary. To my astonishment, I discovered that he had had a long and honorable association with the Lorillards. Born in 1800, Ray became an errand boy in the Lorillard tobacco company at age eleven. It's quite possible that Peter Williams Sr. recommended the youngster to the Lorillard brothers. By the mid-1820s, Ray had become the foreman of the Lorillard factory on Wooster Street and lived on the premises. At his death in 1882 he was a general superintendent of their Jersey City factory.[43] The Lorillards never hesitated to hire or promote Ray according to his abilities.

Beyond helping individuals, the Lorillards extended their benevolence throughout the city to institutions of all kinds. Cutthroat competitors as they were, they also fashioned themselves generous philanthropists and wanted to be remembered as such. The first to die in 1838, Jacob was eulogized by whites and blacks alike. Trinity's Reverend Berrian offered lavish praise of Jacob's good works: "The sagacity, foresight, and diligence with which he managed his affairs, and the fair and honorable means by which he acquired his riches, would have been less worthy of admiration, had they not also been accompanied by liberal views and benevolent designs. His wealth, his influence, and talents were all directed in an eminent degree to the good of men and the glory of God." Black New Yorkers offered similar testimonials. In the newspaper of the period, the *Colored American,* they published a moving tribute proclaiming that "the death of Mr. Lorillard will be most sensibly felt by the poor, and by the benevolent institutions generally, in the city of New York. On all occasions of charity, in which we were concerned, we called on Mr. Lorillard, and never failed to obtain his aid and his counsel."[44]

Did black New Yorkers see a contradiction in the Lorillards' behavior? Were they aware that the brothers had profited from the destruction of the Negroes Burial Ground? Did they take note that the money the Lorillards gave their institutions came from slave labor, which maintained blacks in perpetual bondage, and shady practices that consigned the poor to lasting misery? If so, they never mentioned it. Perhaps they found nothing unusual about city merchants making lots of money by honest and not-so-honest means, and then giving a little of it away to good causes. But one thing that black New Yorkers did come to debate was the double-edged nature of white benevolence. They knew that charity was never simply a gift but carried expectations in return, expectations under which they would increasingly chafe.

CHAPTER TWO

The Mulberry Street School
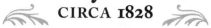
CIRCA 1828

The Five Points

THE WHITE PHILANTHROPISTS who founded the Mulberry Street School placed it in the heart of the Five Points, an area that encompassed an intersection of three streets—Orange, Cross, and Anthony—as well as several adjacent streets—Centre, Pearl, Leonard, Mulberry, and others. It was home to many black families and institutions.

I haven't come across any contemporaneous accounts of the Five Points written by its black inhabitants. Instead, it's Charles Dickens who penned the most memorable portrayal of the area after his tour of the United States in the early 1840s:

> Poverty, wretchedness, and vice are rife enough where we go now. This is the place, these narrow ways, diverging to the right and left, and reeking everywhere with dirt and filth. . . . Debauchery has made the very houses prematurely old. See how the rotten beams are tumbling down, and how the patched and broken windows seem to scowl dimly, like eyes that have been hurt in drunken frays. . . . Here, too, are lanes and alleys, paved with mud knee deep; underground chambers, where they dance and game, . . . hideous tenements which take their name from robbery and murder; all that is loathsome, drooping, and decayed is here.[1]

Five Points 1827, Intersection of Cross, Anthony, and Orange Streets, from *Valentine's Manual,* 1885 (New-York Historical Society)

Such was the perspective of an outside observer. But certainly those who lived there would never have thought to portray their streets or homes in such contemptuous and abject language. To the black denizens of the Five Points, the families of Centre Street, of William Hamilton, Henry Sipkins, Thomas Downing, Peter Williams, and others, held the same status as did the Knickerbockers in their community. Some had Knickerbocker surnames and undoubtedly shared a common ancestor with their white counterparts; it was rumored that William Hamilton was a natural-born son of Alexander. At the end of the nineteenth century, many descendants would refer to themselves as black Knickerbockers.

What qualities did these men and women possess that made them part of an emerging elite class?

Just as savvy as white New Yorkers in understanding the value of real estate, they aspired to property ownership and, whenever possible, bought lots on which to build homes, even if it was limited to the made ground of Centre Street.

They had steady employment primarily in skilled trades. Boston Crummell was an oysterman as was Thomas Downing, who also owned a restaurant. George DeGrasse ran a provisioning business while William Hamilton worked as a carpenter and Henry Sipkins as a porter. Peter Williams and Samuel Cornish entered the ministry. According to Maritcha's memoir, my great-great-great-grandfather Joseph Marshall had steady work as a house painter until he died in 1828, probably as a result of painter's colic, brought on by lead poisoning. Once widowed, Elizabeth Marshall opened a bakery in the cellar of her home and was able to make ends meet. When she was too old to live alone, she sold her property and moved in with her daughter and son-in-law, Mary Joseph and Albro Lyons.[2]

These jobs were never very remunerative, of course, and this early black elite could not count on wealth as a criterion for membership. If they did promote acquisition, it was not merely of money, but also of those qualities that natural historians like Linnaeus claimed African-descended people could never possess. The elite needed to be proactive: members proclaimed to the world at large that they could accomplish just as much as whites; they admonished blacks to be self-reliant in bettering their own circumstances and those of their community. Like their white counterparts, they preached a Protestant gospel of hard work. They promised that education and dedication to work would eventually lead to success, respect, and, in due course, political and civil equality. They encouraged the cultivation of character, the development of the inner values of morality, piety, temperance, and intellectuality. In turn, character would lead to respectability, outward conduct marked by sobriety, modesty, industriousness, economy.

As undisputed leaders of the black community, members of this early elite founded and nurtured a number of institutions. First and foremost were the churches. In the late eighteenth century, Peter Williams Sr. helped found the African Methodist Episcopal Zion Church. Some twenty years later, his son, Peter Williams Jr., spearheaded the effort to establish St. Philip's, and Samuel Cornish formed the First Colored Presbyterian Church. Although these black men affiliated with different religious denominations, they were all welcome to join the New

York African Society for Mutual Relief, founded by William Hamilton and others in 1808. Only recently unearthed, the society's records offer compelling testimony of the founders' racial pride and aspirations to autonomy. According to the certificate of incorporation, members promised to raise funds among themselves to care for those who were sick or infirm and could no longer work, as well as help widows and orphans of deceased members. They reiterated these promises in hymns composed especially for anniversary celebrations: "Bound by strong friendship's closest ties / In social union, we / Mutual relief and aid to give / Each other do agree." By 1820 they had accumulated sufficient funds to buy a building at 42 Orange (later Baxter) Street, in the heart of the Five Points, for eighteen hundred dollars.[3]

When it came to the education of New York's black youth, however, independence from white benevolence was simply not possible.

The African Free Schools

Rereading Alexander Crummell's obituary of Peter Guignon, I was struck by how the opening paragraph so lovingly commemorated not only my great-great-grandfather but also many of their former classmates from "the old Mulberry Street School for colored children." Referring to them as "celebrated students," Crummell diligently listed their names and noted that Peter remained "the friend and intimate companion of every one of these eminent boys not only in their boyhood, but afterwards in their manhood and maturity."

I remembered that some years earlier I had read a published document about the Mulberry Street School that also paid homage to its young students: James McCune Smith's "Sketch of the Life and Labors of Rev. Henry Highland Garnet" from 1865. Born into poverty, Smith was, in his own words, "the son of a self-emancipated bond-woman" and owed his "liberty to the Emancipation Act of the State of New York."[4] Rumor had it that his father was a white New York merchant named Samuel Smith. The young boy was enormously talented in every subject and excelled at the Mulberry Street School. In later years, he

achieved eminence as one of the nation's first black doctors and pharmacists and as a leading black activist as well. Initially Peter's friend, in
later years Smith became a mentor to the younger Philip White. If Peter
was Philip's father-in-law, Smith was in a sense his "godfather."

Smith's sketch of Garnet's life included a list of classmates that
overlapped almost exactly with Crummell's. But each account contained omissions. To my chagrin, Smith left out Peter's name altogether.
Late in his obituary, Crummell referred in passing to Peter's first wife,
Rebecca, but used only her last name, Miss Marshall. Both writers
failed to mention Rebecca's brother, Edward, and Albro Lyons, Mary
Joseph Marshall's future husband, both of whom had been their classmate. Rebecca's and Edward's early deaths cannot fully explain these
omissions since Smith and Crummell recalled others who died young.
Perhaps one reason for their silence was their decision to pay exclusive homage to those classmates who *they* deemed "eminent" and "celebrated," whose impact on the public history of black New Yorkers *they*
assessed to be noteworthy. They were deciding whose memory was
worth preserving and whose was not. They were helping to shape the
archive of New York's black community and, most significantly for me,
determine the presence of my great-great-grandparents in them.

Both men relegated my great-great-grandmother Rebecca to
obscurity, but Crummell at least refused to forget my great-great-
grandfather. He knew that Peter had not been historically important
in the way that he and many others had. But, to Crummell, Peter was
worthy of commemoration because of his "character," most notably his
gift of friendship that enabled him to remain close friends with his
former schoolmates until the day of his death.

I began searching for information about the school that had left
such a profound mark on Peter and his friends. One of the earliest educational institutions for colored children, the Mulberry Street School
was part of the African Free School system, established by the New
York Society for Promoting the Manumission of Slaves, and Protecting
Such of Them as Have Been or May Be Liberated. As hard as I tried, I
was never able to find a comprehensive black archive of the schools. All I
found were some twenty brief articles published in *Freedom's Journal,* the

country's first black newspaper whose short-lived existence ran from
1827 to 1829. Shortly after the paper was founded, its two editors, John
Russwurm and Samuel Cornish, began sending copies to the school's
library.[5] They wanted to provide good reading material for the students,
but they might also have sensed that the library, housed in a white-run
institution, would be better able to preserve the school's history than
their peripatetic newspaper offices. In contrast, the white philanthropists who established the African Free School system maintained a substantial written record of its activities, and Charles Andrews, the British
head teacher of the Mulberry Street School for many years, published a
quasi-official document, *The History of the New-York African Free Schools*.
In turn, John Pintard and his friends preserved these documents in the
archives of the New-York Historical Society.

The Manumission Society's members were no radicals. Most endorsed the Gradual Emancipation Act of 1799, which rejected the call
for the immediate end of slavery. They were committed to improving
the lot of slaves through benevolent acts while delaying their freedom
to a distant future. Indeed, many of them were themselves slave owners,
unable to shake off Linnaean stereotypes about black primitiveness and
inferiority, and fully aware of the degree to which the wealth of the
city depended on southern and West Indian slave economies. They were
quite comfortable with the existing social arrangement where they controlled the labor conditions—"ameliorated" of course—of those who
worked for them.

Putting the concept of amelioration into practice, the Manumission Society established its first African Free School in 1785, limiting
admission to the children of free blacks. Some four years later they
agreed to admit slave children provided their masters gave permission.
After the addition of a separate institute for girls, the schools were incorporated in 1794. Since public education was considered a matter of
charity, these African Free Schools received limited financial aid from
both the city corporation and the state legislature.

Initially, the Manumission Society hired only white teachers, and
student enrollment languished. In 1797, the society changed tactics and
appointed John Teasman, who would later help found the African So-

ciety for Mutual Relief, assistant teacher, elevating him to principal two years later. As enrollment increased, the Manumission Society decided to build a schoolhouse on William Street big enough to hold about two hundred male and female students. In 1820, the boys were transferred to a new building farther north on Mulberry Street able to accommodate up to five hundred students, while the girls stayed in the William Street building.[6]

White Benevolence/Black Identity

On the first anniversary of the African Society for Mutual Relief's founding, John Teasman delivered an address in which he extravagantly praised the work of the Manumission Society. "We must not forget the ingenious and heroic exploits of the standing committee of the Manumission Society in the diminution of slavery and oppression, and in the establishment of freedom and prosperity," he intoned. "Especially we must not, we cannot forget the happy success of the trustees of the African school, in the illumination of our minds."[7] Teasman's praise of the officers of the Manumission Society and African Free School seems strangely at odds with the rhetoric of black pride and autonomy emanating from the African Mutual Relief Society. In fact, Teasman and his colleagues were struggling with broader questions underlying black emancipation and education. How should black New Yorkers define themselves as a community in the early decades of the nineteenth century? How should they position themselves in relation to white benefactors who expressed so much ambivalence over slavery, freedom, and the very nature of African-descended people?

JANUARY 1, 1808

On January 1, 1808, Peter Williams delivered an oration in Zion Church to celebrate the abolition of the slave trade. Henry Sipkins, William Hamilton, and other black community leaders were with him on the

Peter Williams Jr., engraving by Patrick Reason (Moorland-Spingarn
Research Center, Howard University, Washington, D.C.)

podium. Families like the Marshalls, DeGrasses, and Crummells undoubtedly filled the church's pews. Many members of New York's white
elite were present as well. Williams must have realized that his sermon
required a careful negotiation between his community's desire for autonomy on the one hand and white benefactors' expectation of gratitude
on the other. He deliberately began and ended with thankful praise of
all those Europeans and Americans who had labored to abolish the slave
trade.

In the main part of his speech, however, Williams directly addressed the black community, retelling Africa's recent history by casting it in the biblical language of Genesis: the African homeland had
been "the garden of the world, the seat of almost paradisaical joys." All
too soon European traders arrived, however, and insinuating themselves
among such innocence began practicing "all the bewitching and allur-

ing wiles of the seducer." Williams then demanded that his audience
bear witness to the horrors of the Middle Passage and enslavement:
"Behold their dejected countenances; their streaming eyes; their fet-
tered limbs; hear them, with piercing cries and pitiful moans deploring
their wretched fates. . . . See them separated without regard to the ties
of blood or friendship."[8]

This version of history was not based on personal memories or on
ones passed down to Williams by forefathers. Rather they were invented
memories that idealized the African homeland. Not everyone present
had lived through such events. Yet that hardly mattered. Williams's
imagined memories resonated with all those in the audience who had
suffered displacement, alienation, and oppression, uniting them into a
single community. Transported into his own past, Joseph Marshall undoubtedly remembered the family and community he had left behind
in Maracaibo, just as George DeGrasse struggled to remember his boyhood in Calcutta.

Beyond its nostalgia for the homeland and searing descriptions of
the Middle Passage, however, Williams's sermon offered his black audi-
tors little to build upon. Where could New York's black community go
from here? Would African-descended people remain victims forever?
Were they not capable of self-assertive action? Must they always rely on
the benevolence of white philanthropists? As inhabitants of the New
World, they needed useful tools for present and future action. Williams
concluded by exhorting his community in the following terms. "Let us,
therefore," he proclaimed, "by a steady and upright deportment, by a
strict obedience and respect to the laws of the land, form an invulner-
able bulwark against the shafts of malice."[9] Was that enough?

JULY 4, JULY 5, 1827

Some twenty years later, New York State abolished slavery and declared
July 4, 1827, Emancipation Day. To commemorate the event, William
Hamilton delivered an oration held once again in Zion Church. Con-
tinuing in the tradition of Teasman and Williams, he praised the Manumission Society, asserting that "it has stood, a phalanx, firm and un-

daunted, amid the flames of prejudice, and the shafts of calumny." [10]
Hamilton's rhetoric seemingly confirmed that black New Yorkers remained locked in the position of humble supplicant, bowing in gratitude before their white benefactors.

In fact, times had changed.

Black leaders had argued bitterly about how best to celebrate
Emancipation Day. Many wanted orations and a parade on July 4 to
emphasize the connection between black freedom and national citizenship. The Manumission Society opposed this plan, however, insisting
that public demonstrations were unseemly and likely to cause violent
reactions from white spectators; indeed, years earlier, it had dismissed
Teasman as principal of the African Free School after he helped organize
the African Society for Mutual Relief's first anniversary parade. Most
of New York's black leadership proved willing to defer to the Manumission Society's request. Hamilton delivered his address on July 4, but the
very next day black men took to the streets, celebrating in a parade the
likes of which New Yorkers had never seen. [11]

Let's follow the parade through the eyes of the mature James
McCune Smith as he recalled the long-ago event in his 1865 sketch of
Garnet's life. A mere lad of fourteen, Smith stood in the crowd that
day with his close friend Henry Highland Garnet, who had fled slavery
in Maryland with his family and arrived in New York in 1825. Other
schoolmates were there as well. I'd like to think that Peter Guignon was
among them.

> That was a celebration! A real, full-souled, full-voiced shout-
> ing for joy, and marching through the crowded streets, with
> feet jubilant to songs of freedom!
>
> First of all, Grand Marshal of the day was SAMUEL
> HARDENBURGH, A splendid-looking black man, in cocked
> hat and drawn sword, mounted on a milk-white steed; then
> his aids on horseback, dashing up and down the line; then
> the orator of the day, also mounted, with a handsome scroll,
> appearing like a *baton* in his right hand; then in due order,
> splendidly dressed in scarfs of silk with gold-edgings, and
> with colored bands of music, and their banners appropri-

ately lettered and painted, followed, "The NEW YORK AFRI-
CAN SOCIETY FOR MUTUAL RELIEF," "The WILBERFORCE
BENEVOLENT SOCIETY," and "The CLARKSON BENEVOLENT
SOCIETY"; then the people five or six abreast, from grown
men to small boys. The side-walks were crowded with the
wives, daughters, sisters, and mothers of the celebrants, representing every State in the Union, and not a few with gay
bandanna handkerchiefs, betraying their West Indian birth:
neither was Africa itself unrepresented, hundreds who had
survived the middle passage, and a youth in slavery joined in
the joyful procession.

As he remembered that momentous day, Smith reverted to his
youthful self to relive the thrill of the occasion. Yet even in the midst
of his exuberance, Smith took pains to underscore its political significance: the military prowess of the uniformed marchers, the efficacy of
black community organization, and the importance of black solidarity,
in essence an early version of "black power and black pride." To reinforce
his message, Smith reminded his readers that commemorations of the
past like the Emancipation Day could and should be an inspiration to
black youth to look to the future and "march on":

> It was a proud day, never to be forgotten by young lads, who,
> like Henry Garnet, first felt themselves impelled along that
> grand procession of liberty, which through perils oft, and
> dangers oft, through the gloom of midnight, dark and seem-
> ingly hopeless, dark and seemingly rayless, but now, through
> God's blessing, opening up to the joyful light of day, is still
> "*marching on*."[12]

It was not only black youths who felt restless. Let's return to Hamilton's speech and follow it beyond his lavish praise of the Manumission
Society. As Hamilton reached the end, his rhetoric turned fiery and he
threw all caution to the winds. His voice dripping with sarcasm, he attacked the hypocrisy of the founding fathers, and Thomas Jefferson in
particular, whom the nation had paused to commemorate that very day:

I know that I ought to speak with caution; but an ambi-
dexter philosopher, who can reason contrarywise, first tells
you "that all men are created equal, and that they are endowed with the unalienable rights of life, liberty, and the
pursuit of happiness," next proves that one class of men are
not equal to another, which by the bye, does not agree with
axioms in geometry, that deny that things can be equal, and
at the same time unequal to one another.

On the spot Hamilton resolved the question that had stumped Peter
Williams some twenty years earlier: How can blacks become Americans? His ready answer was education. "White men," he angrily intoned, "say you are not capable of the study of what may be called abstruse literature, and that you are deficient in moral character." But, he
asserted, "I feel, I know, that these assertions are as false as hell."[13]

Education: The Philosopher's Stone

On the surface, the African Free Schools' white trustees seemed to be in
full agreement with the black community over the importance of education. As one trustee proclaimed:

If we were asked, What is the first and most important requisite in paving the way for the abolition of slavery? we should
answer, *education*. What is the second? and the third?—our
answer would still be as before—*education*. It is the philosopher's stone, which will turn the baser metals into gold.

Even after the abolition of slavery, however, education remained necessary, since physical freedom without mental freedom would be incomplete: "The laws of the land might declare, that they should no longer
be slaves, but it [is] only by the cultivation of the mind, that they [can]
become truly emancipated and free."[14]

In their educational efforts, white trustees, black leaders, and on occasion black women worked cooperatively. They joined forces to inform families about the African Free Schools, enroll children, and keep up student attendance. A group of black men that included Peter Williams, William Hamilton, and Thomas Sipkins embraced the Manumission Society's plan to divide black neighborhoods into districts and send agents into homes to encourage parents to send their children to school. When black men and women came together to establish the African Dorcas Association, they invited whites on the advisory board and asked Charles Andrews to write its constitution. Known as a "fragment society," the association collected clothes, hats, and shoes to distribute to poor children who otherwise would be unable to attend school. Although men were the first officers of the association, black women soon took control. Isaiah DeGrasse's mother, Maria, was an active member as was Peter Williams's sister, Mary.[15]

Despite such collaboration, however, neither the black community nor the white trustees ever really agreed on what the students' education should consist of. As it turned out, each held widely divergent views, and eventually found themselves at odds with one another. What lay at the heart of their differences was the "proper" place of free blacks in the nation. Were black men destined to remain common laborers or would they be allowed into the liberal professions? Were black women forever to remain domestic servants, or could they be mistresses of their own homes, or teachers if they so chose?

The school trustees often resorted to lofty sentiments about the education of African youth. Yet they were mostly interested in maintaining law and order among New York's black population, in instilling habits of mind and behavior that would prevent any outbreak of social disorder. Simply put, they wanted to keep black youngsters off the streets and prevent them from becoming like "those idle ones who are suffered to grow up uncultivated, unpolished, and heathenish in our streets; and who, for the want of care and instruction, are daily plunging in scenes of sloth, idleness, dissipation and crime." The trustees' concern over proper behavior extended even into black homes. While Peter Williams's agents visited the homes of prospective students to recruit them for school, the trustees went to satisfy themselves that black parents were maintaining proper family values that would make their children obedient charges. Worried over parents' ability to do so, they printed a handbook of school regulations instructing them on how to raise their children. Their advice included regular attendance at church, reading of the scriptures, enforcing discipline at home, teaching cleanliness, warning against dishonesty, and prohibiting bad language.[16]

Black leaders were not at all opposed to family values, good habits, and strict discipline. They too believed that self-regulation and proper behavior in public were of paramount importance. Peter Williams, we may remember, had ended his 1808 oration by encouraging black New Yorkers to maintain "a steady and upright deportment and strict obedience and respect to the laws of the land." But there were two issues on which they would not compromise: a decent education that would give their children opportunities not available to the older generation, and the right of free blacks to control their own destiny.

It would be unfair to attribute the trustees' actions to racism alone. Their attitudes were typical of white philanthropists who founded and supervised the city's charitable institutions. Convinced that the lower classes—Africans, but also immigrant Irish and Germans, Catholics, and even the native born—had little sense of morality and self-discipline, they firmly believed that such impoverished groups needed to be governed by their betters. They devised an education that would limit social mobility and maintain the existing social structure just as it was.

There's theory and then there's practice. There's a plan of action and then there's what actually happened. Whether intended or not, the education that many African Free School students received ended up encouraging them to rise above their impoverished origins and in turn become community leaders.

Charles Andrews, Schoolteacher

Charles Andrews was principal of the Mulberry Street School for many years. His tenure was marked by controversy. British by birth, he arrived at the school in 1809 and remained until his dismissal in 1832. Andrews seems to have been deeply committed to the education of black youth.

When school attendance dropped precipitously in 1827, he made a presentation to the trustees to express his dismay. "Every one present felt grieved," the trustees reported, "that one so devoted to the cause of *African* education should meet with so much to discourage him in his career of usefulness."[17] It was Andrews's discouragement that resulted in the trustees' plan to create neighborhood districts and send agents to visit black families. It's quite possible that Peter and his friends were among their recruits.

In his 1865 comments about his school experiences, James McCune Smith remembered Andrews as a teacher who went out of his way to help his students. He was, Smith asserted,

> of versatile talents; himself not deeply learned, but thorough so far as he went, a good disciplinarian, and in true sympathy with his scholars in their desire to advance. One special habit of his was to find out the bent of his boys, and then, by encouragement, instruction, and if need were, employing at his own expense additional teachers to develope [*sic*] such talent as far as possible.
>
> In spelling, penmanship, grammar, geography, and astronomy, he rightly boasted that his boys were equal, if not superior, to any like number of scholars in the city, and freely challenged competition at his Annual Examinations. In Natural Philosophy and Navigation, which were then new studies in a free school, he carried on classes as far as he was able, and then hired more competent teachers at his own expense. . . .
>
> Without being, in the modern sense, an abolitionist, Mr. Andrews held that his pupils had as much capacity to acquire knowledge as any other children, they were the object of his constant labors, and it was thought by some, that he even regarded his black boys as a little smarter than whites. He taught his boys and girls to look upward; to believe themselves capable of accomplishing as much as any others could, and to regard the higher walks of life as within their reach.

And yet, in stark contrast to Smith, Alexander Crummell recalled with considerable bitterness that during his years at the school their class-mate Thomas Sidney had been the object "of marked dislike of an un-principled school master."[18]

Much of the controversy surrounding Andrews grew from accu-sations of violence in his use of physical punishment to discipline his charges. In the 1820s, whipping students was still an accepted practice, especially for infractions like truancy. In Smith's view, Andrews was simply a "good disciplinarian," willing now and again to resort to physi-cal punishment. In an open letter to *Frederick Douglass' Paper* written in the early 1850s, Smith remembered with some amusement the whipping of student Philip Bell that, he claimed, had ended in laughter. Bell had decided to "play hookey." Fully expecting a whipping when he returned to school, he protected himself with an extra pair of pantaloons and a layer of paper. But "the paper betrayed an unusual sound to Charley Andrew's quick ear" and Bell's ruse was quickly discovered. The whip-ping proceeded until the boy's pleas of "dear Mr. Andrews! my dear Mr. Andrews! brought down the house; even Charley Andrews could cut no more, neither can I."[19] Smith's teasing language here suggests that he believed the whipping to have been justified, even harmless, cer-tainly not malicious or racially motivated.

But my great-great-granduncle, Albro Lyons, gave his grandson, Harry Albro Williamson, a dramatically different account of Andrews's physical disciplining that pits white against black in an ugly racist sce-nario. According to Lyons, the main reason for Andrews's dismissal was his whipping of a young student named Sanders. A black man had come to the school asking to see Andrews, and Sanders had called out to him saying there was a gentleman at the door looking for him. Angered by Sanders's reference to a black man as a gentleman, Andrews apparently gave the student a severe beating. When black parents found out what had happened, an uproar ensued and Andrews was forced to resign.[20]

Did either event happen the way Smith and Lyons remembered? If so, what were Andrews's true feelings and motivations? The one fact that seems certain is that black-white relations all too often circle back to the question of violence, whether real, imagined, suspected, or inti-mated.

School Days

As embodiments of black New Yorkers' quest for learning, the very buildings that housed the schools were revered monuments. Students commemorated their schoolhouses in drawings preserved in the African Free School papers at the New-York Historical Society. John Burns has left us a simple sketch of the William Street School. Then there's Patrick Reason's drawing, technically far superior. A classmate and good friend of Peter's, and later mentor to Philip White, Patrick developed a career as a well-known engraver. His sketch of the Mulberry Street School depicts an imposing brick federal style building, two stories high, and surrounded by a fence. This was the place where Peter and his friends studied under the careful guidance of Charles Andrews, played together, and formed friendships that would last a lifetime.

School days did not always begin auspiciously. Threats of white violence lurked at every street corner as students were insulted, and even beaten or stoned. Parents often felt it necessary to accompany their children to and from school. But some, like Peter's friend George Downing, were fearless. "He was no 'mamby pamby,' no 'soft crabbed boy,'" activist T. McCants Stewart wrote in an article on Downing specially prepared for the *New York Freeman* in 1885. "Single handed and alone, he often fought his way through gangs of insulting white children, and leading other colored boys he sometimes drove the white fellows from the street."[21]

If Peter was still living in Bayard Street, where the *Brooklyn Eagle* obituary claimed he was born, his home would have been close to the Mulberry Street School. I imagine him walking into the school building surrounded by his schoolmates, laughing and joking. It was probably evident even then that Peter did not have the intellectual stature of his friends. But I like to think that he was popular because of the depth of his character. "He never was a boy," wrote Crummell; "not that he was grave; for neither was he at any period of his life staid or serious in his demeanor. On the contrary he was always cheerful, yea, even hilarious in character. But withal he was always manly." Peter's manliness, Crummell went on, "was marked by the moral qualities of boldness, bravery and generosity, exceeding, I think, most of the companions of

African Free School No. 2, engraving by Patrick Reason
(Photographs and Prints Division, Schomburg Center for Research
in Black Culture, The New York Public Library)

his school days." To illustrate Peter's courage, Crummell recalled that a
schoolmate "was suddenly taken with a fit in the rear of the old school
house. All the boys were frightened and stood off appalled. As soon as
Guignon saw the poor fellow he rushed to his rescue; took him under
his arms, dragged him, alone up a high flight of stairs and attended him
until his recovery."[22]

After entering the classroom, each boy proceeded to his designated place. Like many other urban public schools of the period, the
African Free Schools followed the Lancasterian system, created by
British educator Joseph Lancaster in the late eighteenth century and
quickly adopted in U.S. schools. Because Lancaster attended to all as-

pects of schooling, recording them in minute detail in his *Manual of the Lancasterian System,* we have a pretty good idea of what the inside of the Mulberry Street School must have looked like. A two-story building, it would have contained one large room on each floor, the length of which would have been double the width, each one capable of accommodating up to 250 children. The teacher, Charles Andrews or any instructor working under him, sat at a desk in the front of the room, facing the students seated in rows or "forms" behind their desks, probably around twenty-five forms of approximately ten students each. The floor inclined up toward the back so that Andrews could have a full view of all his charges. The forms were organized according to the students' ability, the least advanced in front, the more advanced in the back. The front row made up the "sand class," composed of children learning the alphabet. Sand covered the right side of the desk; with their left arm resting on the desk, students traced letters in the sand with their right hand.

In the late 1820s, Peter and his friends would have occupied the benches in the more advanced forms toward the back of the room. But they would not necessarily have all sat together. Monitors were placed at special desks at the right end of a row and slightly elevated for better observation. These were the more capable students who, following Lancasterian principles, were called upon to teach the younger and less knowledgeable. Although proponents of the system praised it as a highly efficient method of public school teaching, it was above all a cost-saving device. We know from the school's archives that in 1827 George Moore was a monitor and James McCune Smith monitor general for order; Charles Reason occupied the more advanced position of proctor in 1830. The monitors' tasks included getting to school early; taking attendance; making sure all students were properly supplied with slates, copybooks, and pencils; supervising reading, writing, and arithmetic. Monitors also oversaw the "draught stations," in which groups of students stood in front of a board hanging from a wall and covered with words or numbers. Using a pointer, the monitors would call upon students one by one to read or do arithmetic.[23]

A long four-page poem of the period conveys these and other details about the Lancasterian system in a more playful tone. The first lines run as follows:

Before we take a pen in hand,
We learn to write upon the sand:
And when the Alphabet we know,
We write on slates—six in a row.
An easy lesson is prepar'd,
As AB, ab—ARD, ard.
And those who spell, or read, the best,
Have some reward above the rest.
When we in spelling, well succeed
We do appointed lessons read.
The Holy Bible is the source
Of each gradationary course.
A semicircle draught of six,
Whose eyes must on the lesson fix;
With hands behind, attentive stand,
Read—till they hear a fresh command:
Our places, then, at desks we take,
(For standing long, our legs would ache).

The rest of the poem goes on to describe how a monitor might teach penmanship, arithmetic, and grammar, and concludes with a stern lesson on the importance of honesty, cleanliness, and good grooming.[24]

James McCune Smith

In the minds of both Andrews and the school trustees, James McCune Smith stood head and shoulders above all the other students, and they heaped reward after reward upon him. When the Marquis de Lafayette visited the school in 1824, Smith, who was only about eleven years old, was chosen to deliver a public address, which he did in the following words (undoubtedly written for him by one of the trustees).

General La Fayette,
        In behalf of myself and my fellow school mates, may I
be permitted to express our sincere and respectful gratitude

to you for the condescension you have manifested this day, in visiting this Institution, which is one of the noblest specimens of New-York philanthropy. Here, Sir, you behold hundreds of the poor children of Africa, sharing with those of a lighter hue, in the blessings of education; and, while it will be our pleasure to remember the great deeds you have done for America, it will be our delight also to cherish the memory of General La Fayette as a friend to African Emancipation, and as a member of this Institution.[25]

Dr. James McCune Smith, physician and abolitionist, from Week's (Photographs and Prints Division, Schomburg Center for Research in Black Culture, The New York Public Library)

During the school term, Andrews repeatedly singled out Smith for his precocious intelligence. When he created a Class of Merit, "composed of such boys, as are the best behaved, and most advanced in their learning," he placed Smith in it. When it came time to choose a chair for one of the class's monthly meetings, he made sure that Smith would be elected. And since it was the principal's task to appoint the monitor general for order, the highest position a boy could achieve in a Lancasterian school, it was undoubtedly Andrews who conferred this honor on the young man.

At times, Smith was given even greater responsibilities. When Andrews became ill and was frequently absent, the trustees placed Smith in charge of the entire school. In the minutes of their February 1827 meetings, they pronounced themselves highly satisfied with Smith's management, referring to him as a "lad of promise."[26] We're back to the vexed question of motivation. Did the school trustees truly recognize Smith's talents and seek to develop them? Or was Smith's de facto leadership of the school simply a money-saving device? Could they rest assured that Smith would function as their mouthpiece and carry out their orders?

Boys

Given the poor quality of early-nineteenth-century free schools, the many hundreds of children who passed through the Mulberry Street School undoubtedly left with inadequate literacy and math skills. But a small group of students who congregated around Smith pushed themselves—and were pushed by Charles Andrews—to excel. By the late 1820s, Peter and his friends surely possessed basic skills in the three Rs, and didn't need to spend much time on penmanship, spelling, or taking dictation. In fact, by then the students chosen as monitors would have been teaching these rudimentary subjects to their younger charges. Until he became ill, Andrews would have continued to teach the senior boys. In addition to taking more advanced classes in arithmetic and reading, they would have studied specialized subjects such as science, astronomy, and navigation. Andrews's curriculum might well have served as a model for Peter's future brother-in-law, Edward Marshall, and other students who later opened their own schools in the black community.

In arithmetic, drills in the elementary classes proceeded from simple addition through subtraction and multiplication to division. In the more advanced classes, the same drills were performed with compound sums. By all accounts, the mathematical genius was George Allen, who Smith described as "a little boy, perfectly black, so fragile that you might crush him between thumb and finger." It was Allen who in a few minutes solved some "puzzling arithmetical questions" for a visitor to the school. Maybe these were the word problems often given the students that dealt with questions raised in counting houses. They were asked to calculate interest, figuring out, for example, how much a merchant owed if he borrowed X amount on the dollar for a note of Y amount.[27]

The Bible, as the poem suggested, was the source material for reading classes. Every morning, Andrews opened the school by reading a passage from the Scriptures. Given the deeply religious values held by black families, the boys must have paid scrupulous attention to these lessons. It was perhaps during one of these moments that several of them felt called to the ministry. In adulthood, Alexander Crummell and Isaiah DeGrasse were ordained in the Episcopal Church; Henry Highland Garnet became a Presbyterian pastor; Samuel Ringgold Ward, who like Garnet had been born into slavery in Maryland and escaped north with his family, served as a licensed minister in the Congregational Church.

In the afternoons Andrews shifted to readings from instructional texts that offered the senior boys information on a wide variety of topics. He had a broad array of books from which to choose. Donations from trustees and other benefactors had swelled the number of volumes in the school's library to a sizable 450. If Smith's assessment of Andrews as a teacher who endeavored to develop the interests of each of his students was correct, I'd like to think that he selected texts accordingly. He certainly encouraged students to take books out from the library and continue reading on their own.

The texts that Andrews listed by title in his history of the school were *A Father's Legacy to His Children, The Scientific Class Book, Polite*

Learning, Scientific Dialogues, Travels at Home, and *Cook's Travels.* Most of these were British-authored, adapted for use in American schools. Given Crummell's comments that Peter was even in his youth "prematurely mature" and "marked by the moral qualities of boldness, bravery and generosity," perhaps my great-great-grandfather was most taken with *A Father's Legacy to His Children.* This pamphlet consisted of a long letter written by a father, one Russell Freeman imprisoned for debt, to his children. Anticipating his impending death, Freeman put together a set of moral guidelines for his children to live by. He counseled them to abide by the golden rule of "whatsoever things ye would that men should do unto you, do ye the same unto them"; reminded them that worldly pleasures were fleeting; and advised them to have faith in God and to follow His guidance especially in times of adversity and death.[28]

The other books on Andrews's list covered topics in language arts, social studies, and natural philosophy—that is, science. James McCune Smith must have been thrilled with the Reverend Joyce's *Scientific Dialogues.* In this multivolume work, Joyce explained in detail the fields of mechanics, hydrostatics, pneumatics, optics, magnetism, electricity, and galvanism. It was around this time that young Smith sketched a portrait of Benjamin Franklin for a school assignment, so even in these early years he might have been dreaming of becoming the nation's black Franklin.

Charles Reason, Patrick's younger brother, would have been drawn to literary topics. In adulthood, he became an influential black educator and sometime poet. Reading chapters on rhetoric and poetry in *A Short System of Polite Learning,* Charles would have studied prosody and read the works of Shakespeare, Young, Cowper, and Milton. But he would also have become familiar with the burgeoning tradition of African American literature through the pages of *Freedom's Journal;* holding fast to the belief that blacks could achieve racial equality through demonstrated excellence in the literary arts, the editors Cornish and Russwurm regularly featured Afro-British writers Olaudah Equiano, Ignatius Sancho, Ottobah Cuagono, and the African American poet Phillis Wheatley.[29]

As Smith noted, Andrews introduced more specialized courses into the curriculum, notably astronomy and navigation, which often overlapped with geography and geology instruction. The students who excelled in these subjects were George Allen, who Smith described as "little less than a prodigy of calculation and original thought on the abstruse problems of gravity, cohesion, and the laws of planetary motion," and George Moore, about whom nothing is known. In poring over *Cook's Travels,* the two Georges would have discovered how Cook's navigational skills enabled him to travel the world, rounding both Cape Horn and the Cape of Good Hope. As a result of their studies, the two boys could solve problems of all kinds with the greatest of ease: measuring the distance from Washington to London or Calcutta; finding the declination of the sun at 5:30 p.m. on any given day; calculating the distance of Venus and Mars from the sun.[30]

The school trustees expended considerable effort to introduce students to the geography of Africa and countries of the diaspora. They established a Cabinet of Minerals and Natural Curiosities, and sent out an appeal to "captains of vessels and other gentlemen traveling in our own, or in foreign countries" to add to their collection of "minerals, shells, reptiles, curious works of art, etc." The editors of *Freedom's Journal* further specified that they hoped to hear from "gentlemen trading to Africa, or who may have an African production." Students also studied Haitian geography through a pamphlet written in a question-and-answer format that provided factual information, covering the location of the island, its towns, rivers, products, and more.[31]

Chapters in geography books were another matter. Written from a British perspective, *Travels at Home* depicted African and Asian countries as backward and primitive. Africa, the book maintained, was a place of utter wretchedness: its nations were run by despotic governments that engaged in perpetual warfare and encouraged slavery; its people were ignorant and morally degenerate. The young students knew that such depictions of their motherland were distorted and incomplete. They had listened carefully to the lessons imparted by their elders: yes, they were now Americans and should see themselves as such; but no, although Africa was now troubled, they should remember that it had once been great and would one day recover its glory. They needed to remember their African heritage and take pride in it.

In contrast, the young men must have enjoyed sections of the first

volume of *Travels at Home*, which took them on a virtual grand tour
of Europe much like the real journeys that the great Romantic poets
Samuel Taylor Coleridge and William Wordsworth went on as part
of their worldly education. The opening chapters introduced them to
England, extravagantly praising it as a nation where freedom reigned
supreme while marginalizing its participation in the slave trade and slave
system. One of the results of English liberty was to make "Englishmen
better manufacturers and merchants, better cultivators of the ground,
and better philosophers and scholars." The school trustees surely did not
anticipate that such statements might later provide the motivation for
James McCune Smith and Alexander Crummell to set their sights on
university training in Britain when they found the doors of American
institutions of higher education closed to them because of their race.[32]

Andrews's list of books did not include volumes on government or
law. But as they read through *The Literary and Scientific Class Book*, three
students in particular would have been drawn to its few political chapters: Henry Highland Garnet, recently escaped from slavery; George
Downing, who later became a political activist firmly committed to
racial integration; and Thomas Sidney, who until his early death in 1840
led the campaign for black male suffrage in New York state. They would
have agreed with the book's chapter that praised republicanism as the
best form of government and the U.S. constitution as giving "a new dignity and a higher duty to *law*," while remaining fully aware of its failure to protect all members of society. But they must have greeted with
a great deal of skepticism, if not outright laughter, the book's tortured
argument that the *unequal* distribution of property was in fact beneficial
because otherwise everybody would be equally poor (not rich) and no
industries would exist to lift people out of their wretched condition.[33]

Girls

William Hamilton's call to study "abstruse literature" did not extend
to girls. Like most men of his time, Hamilton believed that the goal of
female education was to develop the feminine virtues of modesty and
gentility. To the extent that women were to improve their own minds, it

was to help form the manners of their menfolk. The girls who attended the African Free Schools initially occupied the old William Street building. But in the summer of 1828, the Mulberry Street School opened a female department catering to families living uptown. Maybe this is when Peter's classmate Edward Marshall introduced him to his sister Rebecca, leading to a courtship that eventually culminated in marriage. As in the boys' department, Rebecca's teachers were white; one, Julia Andrews, was Charles's daughter. The girls' education was basic— the three Rs and geography. And in lieu of navigation and astronomy, Rebecca and her friends were taught sewing and knitting.[34]

School Fairs and Examinations

The schools' trustees and teachers also devised educational activities outside the classroom for their young charges. Some were pleasurable, others less so.

One activity that was both instructional and fun was the tradition of school fairs, instituted by Andrews, in which students displayed artifacts they had made during the year. Boys exhibited carts, wheelbarrows, tables, chairs, hammers, crowbars, carpenter's tools, and the like, while girls showed off their sewing, dresses, hats, shirts, pillows, and curtains. It was perhaps at one of these fairs that Peter got to know Rebecca better and began to dream of marriage. Prizes for the best handiwork were handed out in the form of tickets redeemable for money or "those creature comforts which schoolboys and girls so well know how to estimate."[35]

More burdensome and vexing were those public events—one could almost call them exhibitions—in which the efforts of school trustees and teachers to control their students' thinking were barely disguised. It's here that we can best sense the latent violence between white benefactors and black recipients—violence that Andrews's alleged whipping of Sanders brought out in the open for all to see.

At these events students were required to speak in front of audiences composed of well-intentioned whites. School trustees insisted that their compositions were "genuine, unaided productions," but in his history of the school Andrews acknowledged that the majority were written by either a teacher or a trustee. Certainly the repetition of the same ideas and phrases over and over again, echoing Smith's earlier address to Lafayette, makes it difficult to accept that the students wrote the speeches by themselves. Their content made explicit the terms of the benevolent contract. Students thanked their white benefactors for condescending to help black youth acquire an education. Then turning to the audience they begged them to sympathize with their plight as "poor little descendants of Africa" and give generously to the school. In return, they promised unconditional gratitude and full obedience to the school's principles.

The young students were on display. White audience members opined that they were witness to "the interesting spectacle of the sable children of Africa, evincing an endowment of intellect." Assessing the students' learning and scrutinizing their behavior, they reached their own conclusions. In a letter to his daughter, John Pintard complained that the black youngsters reciting a chapter of Hebrews from memory had no understanding of what they were saying.[36] In contrast, others commended the students for their orderliness and the seriousness with which they undertook their studies. Whether they were praising or critiquing, however, whites talked about the students as if they were curiosities on exhibit.

The trustees maintained that they wanted their charges to "become men of distinction." Yet they insisted on controlling the students' thought processes and, as time went on, increasingly emphasized vocational over intellectual training. They established an employment service to place students in trades through a system of indenture; boys were trained in crafts and mechanical arts, girls were taught needlework. Perhaps the exhibition of such items at the school fairs was designed to orient students toward this kind of work. In any event, the trustees noted with satisfaction that some of the boys had entered trades where they worked as "Sail Makers, Shoe Makers, Tin Workers, Tailors, Carpenters, Blacksmiths, etc." They suggested that others could find jobs as waiters, coachmen, barbers, servants, and laborers, while still others could go to sea as stewards, cooks, or sailors. George Allen, that young prodigy in navigation and astronomy, became a sailor. With his strong navigational skills, he saved the ship he was on when both the captain and the mate died; but on the very next voyage the entire crew was lost.[37] Had he been a white boy from a good family, would he have entered the business side of shipping, prospered, and lived to a ripe old age?

In encouraging black youth to stick to manual labor, the trustees were in part responding to the realities of the marketplace. White employers in New York City did not want to employ blacks, and white employees did not want to work next to them. But the trustees were also revealing their prejudices against black achievement, following the adage of to each his proper place. "There is no disgrace incurred," they maintained, "in the pursuit of any calling, however humble. It is the duty of every one to do all the good in his sphere in which Providence has placed him."[38]

Where did Charles Andrews stand in this debate? It's undeniable that he taught James McCune Smith and maybe other students as well "to look upward; to believe themselves capable of accomplishing as much as any others could, and to regard the higher walks of life within their reach." Yet Andrews also promoted trades and crafts in the school fairs and made the navigation class an important part of the curriculum. Most egregiously, he endorsed the conservative American Colonization Society's plan to send free blacks to Liberia. In all these instances, was Andrews merely being realistic about the degree of racism that permeated the American work force? Or was he revealing something about the nature of his own racial prejudices?

In 1832 Andrews was summarily dismissed from his job, raising still other questions. Was it his colonization views, his frequent absences from the school, or his alleged caning of Sanders that brought about his firing? The reasons remain unclear, but what is clear is that "the leading colored men" of the city played an important role. According to Smith:

> This was a sore trial for the "old scholars," whose attachment
> to their teacher was firm and ardent; it led to something of a
> struggle, in which the old heads of the people ultimately tri-

umphed. The principal leaders in this movement were Henry
Sipkins, an uncle to Thos. S. Sydney, William Hamilton, and
that distinguished son of Virginia, Thomas Downing.[39]

James McCune Smith might not have liked the decision of the
"old heads" in forcing Andrews's dismissal. But it taught him an important lesson: that black men were not going to remain humble, grateful, and obedient to the wishes of their white benefactors when they
believed their community had been wronged. Smith must have known
even then that one day he would be called upon to replace these old
heads and that he needed to be ready. And he must have recognized
that despite all its failings, and perhaps somewhat paradoxically, the
Mulberry Street School had well prepared him and his classmates to
confront the future. The curriculum gave them academic knowledge not
readily available to most public school students. The Lancasterian system prepared student monitors to be leaders; even though it might have
been a cost-saving device for the school, it taught them how to assert
authority and command respect.

The Mulberry Street School also gave its young students something that was less tangible and harder to define. It taught them to love
book reading. And book reading developed their imaginations. I'm convinced that the books Charles Andrews made available to them lifted
them, however briefly, out of their neighborhoods, their community,
their city, and invited them to explore a vaster world. I think of this
world as cosmopolitan. In their books, students discovered the many
different cultures that existed in all corners of the globe. Without a
doubt, the authors presented these from a western perspective, emphasizing that cultures were not all equal but that some (white, Christian,
Anglo-Saxon) were superior to others. But book reading offered the students other gifts. It gave them the capacity to be amazed. It allowed free
rein to their imaginations. It invited them to experience different kinds
of aesthetic pleasures. It opened them up to beauty. It convinced them
that they too could be citizens of the world.

CHAPTER THREE

The Young Graduates
CIRCA 1834

IN HIS DIARY ENTRY OF December 17, 1835, eminent Knickerbocker and former New York mayor Philip Hone described with an-
guish "the most awful calamity which has ever visited these United
States." He was referring to the Great Fire of 1835, which destroyed
nineteen blocks and 674 buildings in Lower Manhattan, costing more
than $15 million and resulting in enormous economic repercussions. Yet,
if Hone could have forecast the future, he might have reserved the distinction of "most awful" for the Panic of 1837 in which bust followed
boom. Freed from federal restrictions, banks issued notes in excess of
what they owned. Money was abundant and cheap, credit easy to obtain, and banks eager to lend. Inflation set in. The final blow came when
the price of southern cotton suddenly dropped, an unpleasant reminder
of the city's overdependence on the southern slave economy. Gotham
fell into a deep depression.[1]

Terrible as these events were for Knickerbocker merchants, neither
the Great Fire of 1835 nor the Panic of 1837 were the most awful calamities ever visited upon black New Yorkers. Epidemics and racial violence
trumped both.

Cholera

After the yellow fever outbreaks of the 1820s, it was only a matter of time before another epidemic struck the city. This time it came in the form of Asiatic cholera. In his diary, Hone tracked its progress from the major cities of Europe across the Atlantic to Quebec, where it then spread to Montreal on a cargo ship filled with infected Irish immigrants. He watched helplessly as "this awful messenger of death" invaded New York in the summer of 1832.[2]

Bigger, dirtier, and busier than ever, Gotham remained as vulnerable to disease as it had during the yellow fever epidemics. It was a perfect breeding ground for cholera, which infected human populations through contact with contaminated water. Much of the downtown area near the Hudson and East Rivers was still marshy lowland. Garbage and manure still piled up in the streets. Privies and sewers still overflowed. Animals still roamed the neighborhoods. Nuisance laws still went ignored. The poor still crowded in unventilated apartments and cellars.

Indifferent to racial distinctions, cholera attacked whites and blacks alike as it raced throughout the city. New York's population was slowly segregating itself according to class, race, and ethnicity, but no strict boundaries as yet existed. White elite families like those of Philip Hone and Peter Lorillard lived to the west in the Third and Fifth Wards—the length of Broadway, along Greenwich Street, and around St. John's Park. Others moved northward to streets like Bond, Bleecker, and Great Jones in the Fifteenth Ward. In contrast, some merchants chose to remain close to their manufactures; Jacob Lorillard still resided near his tannery on the Lower East Side. White working-class families, whose homes and shops were similarly close to one another, could be found in Greenwich Village as well as to the east around Corlear's Hook and the Bowery.[3]

Black New Yorkers were sprinkled throughout the city. A number resided to the west in the Fifth Ward as well as in the Eighth, lodged between the elite neighborhoods of the Fifth and Fifteenth Wards. But their greatest concentration remained in the Five Points, which by now had become home to many Irish immigrants. The Marshalls still lived on Centre Street, and the Crummells had moved just a short distance away to Leonard Street, right next to the Garnets and close to Peter Williams Jr. James McCune Smith resided on Walker Street. Within short walking distance of these homes were two black institutions, the African Society for Mutual Relief on Baxter Street and St. Philip's Church on Centre Street.

A New York doctor listed the neighborhoods most devastated by cholera: "The locations most severely affected were on the borders of the rivers, where the ground is low and marshy, as Roosevelt, Cherry, and Water-street; at the foot of Reed-street, Duane-street and vicinity; the neighbourhood of the Five Points; the house in Broad-street, with an old common sewer under it, in which ten fatal cases occurred; Laurens-street, Corlaer's Hook, Yorkville, Harlem, Bellevue, and Greenwich Village." Not only was the city's black population threatened but so were white working-class households in Greenwich Village, and even elite whites needed to be on guard. Jacob Lorillard must have worried about the proximity of his home and business to the Roosevelt, Cherry, and Water Street area, just as his brother Peter might have been concerned that the disease could spread one block from Reade Street to Chamber Street. Yet the doctor also noted that the epidemic didn't attack all areas within these neighborhoods equally; rather it targeted those households most affected by poverty and its attendant evils—overcrowding, poor ventilation, and even poorer sanitation.[4]

Public health officials ordered a quarantine of the city, increased street cleaning, and set about disinfecting outdoor areas with quicklime. Contaminated items were burned, leaving heavy acrid smoke in the air. Those stricken with the disease experienced diarrhea, spasmodic vomiting, and painful cramps that led to dehydration and cyanosis (turning blue from lack of oxygen). Remedies were few and ineffective. Some doctors prescribed calomel, laudanum, or bleeding, or a combination of all three. Others suggested more radical treatments such as tobacco smoke enemas, electric shocks, injecting saline solutions into the veins, plugging the rectum with beeswax or oilcloth to stem the diarrhea. The best remedy, available only to wealthy families like the Hones, was to leave the city altogether. From their country places, they waited, in Philip Hone's words, "until the destroying angel has sheathed his sword and our citizens have returned to their homes." By the end of August, the epidemic finally ran its course, killing 3,513 people out of a total population of approximately 212,600.[5]

To most New Yorkers, the Five Points area had become virtually synonymous with the most extreme forms of destitution. Even so, the Marshalls and their friends were spared from the cholera epidemic. Spared in body, but not in the white imagination since many New Yorkers still blamed blacks for outbreaks of epidemics. Racists held them responsible for the virulence with which cholera ravaged the city. It was blacks' "moral deformity and gross stupidity," their filthy habits and ignorance of proper hygiene that had made the disease so difficult to control. Reformers and public health officials were somewhat more sophisticated in their thinking. They were slowly coming to the conclusion that personal behavior was perhaps not the direct cause of the epidemic. Rather, they speculated that social conditions—namely the poverty that plagued neighborhoods like the Five Points—led to demoralization, which in turn gave rise to poor habits, which in turn opened the door to disease. Predictably, however, the city's response was not to work to improve public health policy and thereby eradicate poverty and its attendant ills. Instead, it encouraged the private construction of housing in open spaces equipped with water, plumbing, and gas lighting—that is, housing for the rich.[6]

Blackbirding

Other awful calamities were visited upon New York's black population, events that came not from the anonymous hand of disease but from acts of human hatred. One was a calamity unimaginable to Hone: seizure of escaped slaves by slave catchers, or "black-birders," as they were called. With the end of slavery in the state, New York had become a destination for fleeing slaves. In his retrospective sketch of Henry Highland Garnet's life from 1865, James McCune Smith noted that although slave hunts were not frequent, escaped slaves still lived in "constant apprehension and jeopardy [that] at any moment they might be forced to fly."[7]

This fear became a reality for the Garnet family one summer eve-

Henry Highland Garnet, abolitionist and editor
(Photographs and Prints Division, Schomburg Center for Research
in Black Culture, The New York Public Library)

ning in 1829. Years earlier, George Garnet had devised a ruse to bring
his wife and children out of slavery in Maryland by asking his master's
permission to attend a funeral, then hiding them in a covered wagon
and heading north. Reaching New York, the family rented rooms in a
building right next to the Crummells on Leonard Street. At the time
of the attempted seizure, Henry had left school and shipped out to sea
as a cabin boy to help with his family's finances. But young Alexander
Crummell was an eyewitness to the event. Years later, in his *Eulogium*
commemorating Henry's life, Crummell recalled: "I saw the occurrence
with my own eyes, playing, after sunset before my father's door. One
evening in the month of July or August, a white man, a kinsman of the
late Colonel Spencer, the old master, walked up to Mr. Garnet's hired
rooms, on the second floor of the dwelling." Immediately recognizing

the danger he was in, George Garnet calmly proceeded into the side bedroom and went straight to the window. As he continued his account, Crummell underscored how desperation can make the impossible possible.

> Between the two houses was an alley at least four feet wide; the only way of escape was to leap from the side window of the bed-room into my father's yard. How Mr. Garnet made this fearful leap, how he escaped breaking both neck and legs, is a mystery to me to this day; but he made the leap and escaped. In my father's yard was a large ill-tempered dog, the terror of the neighborhood. The dog, by a wondrous providence, remained quiet in his early evening slumbers. After jumping several fences Mr. Garnet escaped through Orange Street, and the slave-hunter's game was thus effectually spoiled.

The family was safe, but the blackbirder made sure to destroy everything they owned. They were forced to start over from scratch.

The story doesn't end there; it continues after young Henry returned from his sea voyage. His Mulberry Street School friends tried to console him, but according to James McCune Smith:

> The news fell like a clap of thunder upon the young seafarer; the first shock over, he was roused almost to madness. With the little money he had he purchased a large claspknife, openly carried it in his hand and sturdily marched up Broadway, waiting and hoping for the assault of the menhunters. . . . This raid upon his peaceful family made a powerful impression on Henry. It seared his soul with an undying hatred of slavery, and touched his lips with that anti-slavery fervor and eloquence which has never gone out.[8]

Garnet did not use his clasp-knife. But he was later one of the first black abolitionists to use force—both verbal and physical—in his fight against prejudice and slavery.

Riot

Racism was not just a southern import. It was also a homegrown product that erupted with astonishing venom in the race riot of 1834. At the start, the riot pitted an unruly white mob against the city's white abolitionist leaders; by the end, it was black New Yorkers who bore the brunt of the violence.

Unlike his lengthy descriptions of the other calamities of the decade, Philip Hone devoted far less space to the riot in his diary. His comments appear to blame both sides, as he heaped equal scorn on "fanatical" abolitionists and a "diabolical" mob. Without a functioning press at the time, there's virtually no public commentary from the black community. Nor have individual accounts surfaced as yet in the archives. So it's to white newspaper reports and personal anecdotes compiled by "fanatical" white abolitionists that we owe most of our accounts of the riot.[9]

From the early 1830s on, white mob violence in northern cities rose in direct proportion to the spread of radical abolitionist activity. In New York wealthy merchants like Arthur Tappan and his brother Lewis, John Rankin, and Joshua Leavitt were the vanguard of abolitionism. In 1833, the Tappan brothers established the New York Anti-Slavery Society, followed by the American Anti-Slavery Society, of which William Lloyd Garrison in Boston soon emerged as the undisputed leader. Fueled by religious evangelical fervor, members adopted a program far more radical than that of the earlier Manumission Society. They were fervent anti-colonizationists, favored immediate over gradual emancipation, and promoted black educational efforts as well as black male suffrage. Their methods were equally radical. Interracial collaboration was the bedrock of the movement. Blacks joined the societies, attending meetings alongside their white counterparts. Leaders made effective use of mass mobilization, submitting thousands of petitions to Congress, and employing the U.S. mail to disseminate antislavery newspapers and pamphlets as well as medals, emblems, and kerchiefs.[10]

The Tappan brothers were the instigators of New York's antislavery activity. In the early 1830s, they took over a church building, the Chatham Street Chapel, and turned it into an abolitionist meeting place. It was this free mixing of whites and blacks, this congregation of people who looked like "the keys of a piano forte," that so infuriated working-class white New Yorkers. In the summer of 1834, a mob marched on the chapel and stormed it twice.

The first attack occurred on July 4, when white and black abolitionists gathered together for an Emancipation Day celebration. Peter Williams had helped the Tappans organize the event, and the Marshall, Crummell, and DeGrasse families might well have been in the audience. There's a considerable irony here, because Williams had agreed with his white abolitionist friends that an indoor ceremony would be far more dignified—and thus more acceptable to the city's white population—than a rowdier street parade like the one James McCune Smith had so enjoyed in 1827. The second attack came a few days later when white and black church choirs, including St. Philip's, found themselves competing for the right to rehearse in the chapel. Both times, whites hurled racial epithets at blacks and threw prayer books and benches at them.[11]

The activities in the Chatham Street Chapel brought to the surface the deepest anxieties of New York's white working class, namely fears of racial equality and race mixing, or "amalgamation." They were determined to prevent anything of the kind from happening and to break the backbone of the black community. Bent on destruction, the mob refused to disperse. They first turned against white abolitionists, attacking Lewis Tappan's home and his brother's store, and threatening Joshua Leavitt's residence. Any place that was rumored to have condoned interracial activity—especially sexual—was also threatened. Rioters launched an assault against the Spring Street Church, where they believed an interracial marriage had been performed, and targeted cellars on Nassau Street and Peck Slip known to be inhabited by interracial couples.

Above all, the mob vented its rage against blacks, targeting the Five Points area and working with uncanny precision. Even though they lived on Leonard and Centre Streets, the Marshalls, Crummells, DeGrasses, and Garnets appear to have escaped direct attack. Yet they must have felt helplessly vulnerable as they watched the horrendous events unfold before their eyes. According to Lewis Tappan, "a dozen or more [houses] in Orange, Mulberry, Elm and Centre streets, occupied by colored people, were more or less injured, the roofs torn from several, and the furniture they contained was either burned or broken to pieces." Black businesses, notably a barbershop on Orange Street as well as porterhouses on Leonard and Anthony Streets, were also assaulted. Fearing the worst for Thomas Downing's oyster house, an anonymous writer penned a note to the mayor stating that "he had been inform'd that an attack will be made on his [Downing's] house and requests the authority to interfere if it should be necessary." Finally, the mob turned its fury against black institutions. Rioters pelted the African Baptist church on Orange Street with rocks and inflicted damage on the African Society for Mutual Relief Hall as well as a nearby schoolhouse.[12]

Located on Centre Street, St. Philip's stood in the heart of the Five Points. For its minister and parishioners, the riot was disastrous. As the violence unfolded, Benjamin Onderdonk, bishop of New York's Episcopal Diocese, pleaded with the mayor for help, citing his "knowledge of the respectable and uniformly decent and orderly character of the congregation of that Church."[13] It was yet another indignity for this young parish that had confronted hardship after hardship. First, New York's black Episcopalians had had to badger Trinity into letting them establish a separate church; then they were forced to beg for a space of their own until George Lorillard gave them the sixty-year lease on the Collect Street lots and Trinity parishioners raised funds for the church building; even so, they still depended on Trinity for an annual stipend of $330.

St. Philip's was home to its parishioners in the fullest sense of the word, as both physical and spiritual abode. Like worshipers from all denominations, they revered the physical structure of their church as sacred space in which the here-and-now of historical time and material place represented God, the divine, and the eternal. When St. Philip's first structure, made of wood, burned down in 1819 shortly after being erected, they immediately set about rebuilding it, this time in brick. Now they had to watch as what they had so painstakingly built up over years was destroyed in minutes. Rioters entered the sanctuary, smashed the stained-glass windows with the Eucharistic candlesticks, broke the altar table into pieces and ripped up its hangings, tore the carpets, demolished the organ, and dragged the hand-carved walnut pews into the street and set fire to them.[14]

In a final vindictive gesture the mob turned on Peter Williams's home. Their assault had repercussions well beyond physical destruction. Williams's personal journey of striving against the odds paralleled that of his church. After receiving permission to establish St. Philip's, Williams had to battle the Episcopal Diocese to become the church's pastor. Since he was already a lay reader, ordination into the priesthood seemed the next logical step. But the diocese could not countenance admitting a black man into the ministry and rejected his application. In 1820, the newly appointed Bishop John Henry Hobart finally ordained Williams deacon, and in 1826, priest. Although he had begged for protection for St. Philip's Church, in the aftermath of the riot Bishop Benjamin Onderdonk condemned what he saw as Williams's pernicious radical abolitionist activity and demanded that he resign as an officer of the American Anti-Slavery Society. Williams complied, noting that upon ordination he had promised "reverently to obey my Bishop, to follow with a glad mind his godly admonitions, and to submit myself to his godly judgment." Williams, however, maintained his membership in the society. Some in the black community sympathized with him; others judged him harshly. "Brother Williams was a timid man," Crummell wrote years later; "he had felt all his lifetime the extreme pressure of Episcopal power and had exaggerated opinions concerning it. He became intimidated—nay frightened."[15]

The Mulberry Street School Graduates

Against this backdrop of racial prejudice and violence, I wondered how Peter Guignon and his schoolmates from the Mulberry Street School fared as they entered maturity.

Unfortunately, I know nothing about my great-great-grandfather's life during the early and mid-1830s. His name does not appear in the city directories until the 1840s. If he was in the city, it's likely that he did not have steady work. Or it's possible that, as his obituary suggested, these were the years he spent in California.

But what about the other boys? They were determined to achieve. On the whole, they did better than previous generations, but still their fortunes were mixed. Some went into trade while others tried to further their education. Some remained in the city; a number left but eventually returned or at least maintained close ties to Gotham, thus establishing a pattern of dispersal and return that continued throughout the century.

TRADE

There were those who struggled. Much like his future brother-in-law, Albro Lyons seemed to be floundering, first going into the cigar-making business and then opening up an ice cream parlor. George Allen, whom James McCune Smith had referred to as a "prodigy of calculation," became a sailor and was lost at sea.[16]

Others were more fortunate, helped by the patronage of the more prosperous within the black community and, occasionally, by white benefactors. George Downing followed in his father's footsteps, first working in Thomas's oyster house and then opening his own catering business. In his 1885 character portrait of George Downing, T. McCants Stewart described him as heir to much more than Thomas Downing's catering skills: "He inherited his father's aggressive temperament and manly character. He was reared under Christian influences and taught benevolence; but he was also trained to stand up for his own rights and those of the weak and to repel all invasions with force, if necessary." Like his father, George was constantly on the go: "To him there is no such word as 'rest.' His idea of heaven is ceaseless progressive activity. He could not be quiet if he would; and I am sure that with his views of the needs of the race, he would not be in repose if he could. . . . How could he have done otherwise than fill up his life with thought and work and noble deeds."[17]

In his 1819 valedictorian address at the Mulberry Street School, student James Fields had complained about his future prospects. "Shall I be a mechanic?" he asked rhetorically. "No one will employ me; the white boys won't work with me." Yet Patrick Reason caught the eye of a British-born engraver, Stephen Henry Gimber, who had immigrated

George Thomas Downing, businessman and civil rights leader, circa 1880s, by an anonymous artist (Photographs and Prints Division, Schomburg Center for Research in Black Culture, The New York Public Library)

Studio portrait of Patrick Reason, circa 1890s, photograph by Pifer and Becker (Photographs and Prints Division, Schomburg Center for Research in Black Culture, The New York Public Library)

to the United States around 1829, settling in New York before moving to Philadelphia in 1842. Sympathetic to the abolitionist cause, Gimber did a mezzotint engraving commemorating West Indian emancipation in 1834. It was perhaps these sympathies that led him to train Patrick, who was already showing extraordinary talent. In 1833, Gimber brought the young man into his shop for a four-year apprenticeship, "to learn the art, trade and mystery of an engraver," paying his mother three dollars a week for her son's labor. It was during this period that Patrick did a portrait of Peter Williams for St. Philip's. He also designed a stipple engraving of a kneeling female slave with chains hanging from her wrists accompanied by the inscription "Am I Not a Woman and a Sister?" the counterpart of the famous Wedgwood seal of a kneeling male slave produced in Britain in the late 1780s. By 1838, Patrick was doing well enough to advertise himself in the *Colored American* as a "Portrait and Landscape Engraver, Draughtsman and Lithographer."[18]

EDUCATION: NORTH

There were those in the black community, however, who resisted the idea that all their boys were good for was trade, and held out hope that they would receive a classical education. Community leaders established the Canal Street High School and hired instructors to teach Latin, Greek, and other classical subjects. Alexander Crummell, Henry Highland Garnet, George Downing, and Thomas Sidney were all enrolled. "This school only whet our youthful appetite for larger facilities of training and culture," Crummell later recalled. To satisfy them, "our parents looked one way and another; but not a ray of hope was discoverable on the intellectual horizon of the country."

Hope soon came from outside the city in the form of the Noyes Academy in Canaan, New Hampshire. A group of white abolitionists had decided to open a school for the express purpose of preparing black youth "for admission into any of the Colleges and Universities of the United States [or] to commence the study of the learned professions," and hired a teacher from the Andover Theological Institution to instruct

them. In 1835, three of the Mulberry Street School boys, Henry Highland Garnet, Alexander Crummell, and Thomas Sidney, set off for the
school. Once again, Crummell's *Eulogium* offers an intimate eyewitness
account: "The sight of three black youths, in gentlemanly garb, traveling through New England was, *in those days, a most unusual sight;* started
not only surprise, but brought out universal sneers and ridicule. We met
a most cordial reception at Canaan from two score white students, and
began, with the highest hopes, our studies."

But matters did not remain cordial for long once the good citizens
of New Hampshire determined quite literally to break up the school:
"Fourteen black boys with books in their hands set the entire Granite
State crazy! On the 4th of July, with wonderful taste and felicity, the
farmers, from a wide region around, assembled at Canaan and resolved
to remove the academy as a public nuisance! On the 10th of August
they gathered together from the neighboring towns, seized the building, and with ninety yoke of oxen carried it off into a swamp about half
a mile from its site. They were two days in accomplishing their miserable
work."

Remembering perhaps how blackbirders had almost captured his
family some years earlier, Garnet refused to be cowed.

> Under Garnet, as our leader, the boys in our boarding-
> house were moulding bullets, expecting an attack upon our
> dwelling. About eleven o'clock at night the tramp of horses
> was heard approaching and as one rapid rider passed the
> house and fired at it, Garnet quickly replied by a discharge
> from a double-barrelled shotgun which blazed away through
> the window. At once the hills, for many a mile around, rever-
> berated with the sound. Lights were seen in scores of houses
> on every side, and the towns and villages far and near were in
> a state of great excitement. But that musket shot by Garnet
> doubtless saved our lives. The cowardly ruffians dared not to
> attack us. Notice, however, was sent to us to quit the State
> within a fortnight. When we left Canaan the mob assembled
> on the outskirts of the village and fired a field piece, charged
> with powder, at our wagon.[19]

Undaunted, Garnet, Crummell, and Sidney persevered. With help from Peter Williams, they were admitted to the interracial Oneida Institute in Troy, New York. Under the presidency of Rev. Beriah Green, the school curriculum combined manual labor—work on its farms and in its shops—and academic study, offering advanced courses in Greek, Latin, Hebrew, and the Old and New Testaments. James McCune Smith, who must have later heard about his friends' experiences, inserted an account—both poignant and witty—into his 1865 sketch of Garnet's life. It was at Oneida, he wrote, that the "young seekers after knowledge" found a measure of peace, "not only in a region comparatively free from caste-hate, but under the repose, the intellectual calm, of one of the ablest thinkers of the century." Even petty incidents of racial prejudice could not dampen the young men's spirits. When a proslavery student threw a pumpkin at Garnet during a colloquy, Garnet watched it smash to the floor and impishly commented: "My good friends, do not be alarmed, it is only a soft pumpkin; some gentleman has thrown away his head, and lo! his brains are dashed out!"[20]

Garnet's courage and perseverance during this period are all the more astonishing given the severe physical disability under which he labored. Shortly after returning from sea, Garnet had contracted a swelling in his right leg. Crippled and in constant excruciating pain, he was eventually forced to have the leg amputated. Travel to Canaan and to Troy had been hard enough for Crummell and Sidney, but it was almost unbearable for the sickly Garnet. "I can never forget his sufferings," Crummell wrote with barely suppressed anger in his *Eulogium*, "sufferings from pain, sufferings from cold and exposure, sufferings from thirst and hunger, sufferings from taunt and insult at every village and town, and ofttimes at every farm-house, as we rode, mounted upon the top of the coach." Yet Garnet's illness, Crummell insisted, led to a greater perfection of both body and mind: "After the amputation of his leg, he developed into a new life of vigor and mightiness. Tall and majestic in stature, over six feet in height, with a large head, its front both broad and expansive, his chest deep and strong, his limbs straight and perfectly moulded, his very presence impressed one with the idea of might and manliness." Mental prowess complemented physical manliness. Endowed from boyhood "with a wonderful memory, with a most vivid imagination, with strong native powers of thought, and great originality of mind," Garnet refused to let his illness overwhelm the workings of his mind, using it instead to hone his analytical and imaginative abilities.[21]

Between 1836 and 1843, three of the Mulberry Street School graduates—Isaiah DeGrasse, Alexander Crummell, and Charles Reason—sought admission to New York's General Theological Seminary, the nation's principal Episcopal institute for candidates to the priesthood established by Bishop Hobart in the late 1820s. The same members of Trinity Church who, like George Lorillard, had been so instrumental in the founding of St. Philip's were generous contributors and active fundraisers. There appeared to be a happy convergence of interest between the Mulberry Street School graduates and St. Philip's. The church saw the need to cultivate a black ministry beyond the single person of Peter Williams, and the three young men born and bred in the church wanted to dedicate their lives to serving the Episcopal denomination. Yet their path would not be an easy one.

Opposition came in the form of Bishop Onderdonk. Born in New York City, Onderdonk studied under Bishop Hobart and served as assistant minister at Trinity before assuming the bishopric of New York following his mentor's death in 1830. According to writer James Fenimore Cooper, even Onderdonk's friends admitted that he was "a little Dutch," by which they meant stubborn, plodding, nitpicky, and pretty much devoid of charm. But he was ambitious and determined to increase the number of Episcopal churches, clergy, and congregants throughout the state. Perhaps Onderdonk feared that the growth of black parishes might prove too controversial and interfere with his plans. In any event, he was convinced that Peter Williams had caused enough trouble and decided to prevent future ordinations by denying the requisite theological training to black candidates to the ministry.[22]

The first to bear the full brunt of Onderdonk's ire was Isaiah De-

Grasse. While his former classmates were attending Noyes Academy and Oneida Institute, DeGrasse had matriculated at Geneva College in 1832, leaving in 1835 without having obtained a degree. With the full support of Peter Williams, Isaiah decided to enter the ministry and in 1836 applied to the General Theological Seminary. Maybe both men thought that Isaiah's light skin and miniscule portion of African ancestry would shield him from racist objections, but evidently they had not counted on their bishop. The ensuing conflict involved three antagonists—Isaiah, Onderdonk, and John Jay II. Young Jay was the grandson of the eminent John Jay, first chief justice of the United States, former governor of New York, and a founder of the Manumission Society who, as governor, had enacted the bill for the gradual elimination of slavery. His father, Judge William Jay, was also an ardent abolitionist and what we would call today an activist judge. John Jay II was determined to follow in his forebears' footsteps, and became a fervent ally of black New Yorkers and in particular of St. Philip's parishioners.[23]

We need to thank John Jay II for leaving us a full account of the ugly events that ensued. In 1843, Jay published a pamphlet, *Caste and Slavery in the American Church,* in which he gleefully aired dirty Episcopal laundry in public. Jay's information came directly from Isaiah De-Grasse, who painstakingly detailed all that happened in a diary now lost to us. I marvel at Jay's compositional strategy: he filled the main body of his text with his own interpretation of actions and motivations, while placing excerpts from Isaiah's diary in footnotes. But I guess it's better to be relegated to footnotes than altogether erased.

I focused on the footnotes. Isaiah passed the seminary's entrance exam and was accepted as a student. Onderdonk, however, strenuously objected to the young man's admission. "He seems," Isaiah wrote in his October 11 diary entry, "to apprehend difficulty from my joining the Commons, and thinks that the South, from whence they receive much support, will object to my entering." Yet, Isaiah insisted that "thus far I have met with no difficulty from the students, but have been kindly treated." Sensing trouble ahead, Isaiah decided it would be "judicious" to leave the seminary's dormitory. He then went on to detail his future course of action:

As far as in me lies I will in my trouble let all my actions be consistent with my christian profession, and, instead of giving loose to mortified feelings, will acquiesce in all things, but this acquiescence shall not in the least degree partake of the dogged submissiveness which is the characteristic of an inferior.

My course shall be independent, and then, if a cruel prejudice will drive me from the holy threshold of the school of piety, I, the weaker, must submit and yield to the superior power. Into thy hands ever, O God, I commit my cause.

Isaiah's fears were well grounded, for the very next day he wrote:

At 9 am, I called on our spiritual father again, and sought advice in relation to my present embarrassing circumstance. He gave me plainly to understand that it would be advisable, in his opinion, for me not to apply for a regular admission into the Seminary, although I had taken a room, and even settled, yet to vacate the room and silently withdraw myself from the Seminary. He further said that I might recite with the classes and avail myself of the privileges of the institution, but not consider myself in the light of a regular member. Never, never will I do so!

According to Isaiah, Onderdonk had given in not so much to southern sentiment but to his fear of it, arguing

that the Seminary receives much support and many students from the South, and consequently if they admit coloured men to equal privileges with the whites in the Institution, the South will refuse to aid it and use their influence to keep all from the Seminary south of the Potomac. As head of the Seminary, and knowing the feelings and prejudices of the South, he could not hazard my fuller admission at such expense.

From the extreme excitability of public feeling on this delicate subject, and from my known and intimate connection with the people of colour, there would be a high probability not only of bringing the Institution into disrepute, but of exciting opposing sentiment among the students, and thus causing many to abandon the School of the Prophets.

Without hesitation, Isaiah rejected Onderdonk's compromise solution, scornfully noting that "being a 'hanger-on' in the Seminary, is something so utterly repugnant to my feelings as a man, that I cannot consent to adopt it."[24]

In his quiet leave taking, Isaiah chose to emulate the example set by Peter Williams when Onderdonk demanded that he resign from his position in the Anti-Slavery Society after the 1834 riots. Not so Alexander Crummell, the next to apply for admission in 1839. Onderdonk rejected him with a "violence and grossness" that reduced the young man to tears. Going on the offensive, Crummell openly attacked Onderdonk by publishing their exchange of letters in the *Colored American*, the successor to *Freedom's Journal*. Reading through them, it appears that Crummell had in fact been admitted for orders until Onderdonk intervened to object, providing two somewhat contradictory reasons: the first a seemingly altruistic one, claiming "that great prudence was necessary in order to avoid the doing of serious injury to colored persons," the second more defensive, insisting "that the subject [Crummell] should not be allowed to agitate our ecclesiastical body." To Onderdonk's explicit request that he follow Williams's and DeGrasse's course of action, Crummell responded that he could not submit to the "unreasonableness" of the racial distinction that had dictated their behavior. Appeals to the seminary's board of trustees led nowhere, and after much back and forth Crummell finally withdrew his candidacy. According to John Jay II, this was but another instance of Episcopal actions taken "from dread of popular prejudice, and from fear the southern patronage of the Seminary might be withdrawn."[25]

Onderdonk's contemptuous attitude toward Crummell appears to have left a lasting wound. In *The Souls of Black Folk,* Du Bois noted that after his experience at Noyes Academy, Crummell had struggled with the temptation of hate. "It did not wholly fade away," Du Bois wrote, "but diffused itself and lingered thick at the edges." In his interactions with Onderdonk, according to Du Bois, Crummell faced the temptation of despair: "Like some grave shadow he flitted by those halls, pleading, arguing, half angrily demanding admittance, until there came the final *No;* until men hustled the disturber away, marked him as foolish, unreasonable, and injudicious, a vain rebel against God's law."[26] These became the character traits Crummell was known by for the rest of his life: unreasonable, injudicious, vain.

Charles Reason's case was somewhat different from DeGrasse's and Crummell's. By 1843, St. Philip's vestry had taken responsibility for pushing for the ordination of black priests. Initially, they gave full support to Reason's application. Unsurprisingly, Onderdonk objected. More surprisingly, when Reason threatened to confront the bishop, the vestry hastily put together a subcommittee—which included James McCune Smith—to go and warn Onderdonk of Reason's impending visit. It's hard to tell what their motivations were. They were undoubtedly exhausted by all the melodrama occasioned by the two hotheads, Alexander Crummell and John Jay II. Pragmatic men, they might have realized how useless and maybe even counterproductive such belligerence was. And it's quite possible that they were anticipating bigger battles ahead and adjusted their tactics accordingly. In any event, the matter came to a close when the vestry discovered that Reason had been lax in his private studies and he subsequently withdrew his candidacy.[27]

Crummell had rightly complained that Onderdonk and the seminary's trustees had treated him not as "a man, made in the image of God . . . but as a colored man, not as a candidate, but as a colored candidate."[28] So why did these proud black New Yorkers remain affiliated with a denomination that was so inhospitable, if not downright hostile to them? It's not easy to understand such devotion.

First, they were pragmatists. If they left the Episcopal Church, would any other white denomination be less racist than the one to which they were affiliated by birth? Or, given their community's lack of resources, would any new black denomination they established be able to sustain itself over time? They decided to stick with what they had.

Second, above and beyond denominational politics, St. Philip's was a spiritual refuge. The DeGrasse, Crummell, and Reason families, joined later by members of my own—Albro and Mary Joseph Lyons, Peter and Rebecca Guignon, Philip White—cared so intensely about St. Philip's not despite, but *because,* it was part of the Episcopal denomination. As they arrived for Sunday services, they crossed the threshold into a sacred space deeply rooted in Anglican tradition. This simple act held tremendous significance: it placed New York's black Episcopalians within an ancient, cosmopolitan history and offered them a set of collective memories to place alongside their more recent history of enslavement, degradation, and Americanization.

In the church of her childhood, Maritcha Lyons recalled in her memoir, "doctrines were zealously taught and guarded; forms and ceremonies were rigidly adhered to," a direct reference to St. Philip's unabashed commitment to High Church values. Under Bishops Hobart and Onderdonk, New York's Episcopal congregations had revived the old traditions and rituals discarded by the liberal wing of the Anglican Communion, and endorsed Hobart's ideal of "evangelical truth and apostolic order." Grounded in a deep sense of history, they aspired to return to a pre-Constantinian model of a pure, ancient, and universal Church, insisting that their bishops led back in an unbroken chain of succession to the early Christian church and hence to the Apostles themselves. In religious doctrine, they embraced the tenets of religious evangelicalism that placed faith in the redemptive power and atoning grace of Christ; but, unlike evangelicals, they insisted that only the church and its ministry could grant salvation to believers.

The High Church "forms and ceremonies" Maritcha referred to offered St. Philip's parishioners a religious aesthetic that combined both pageantry and order. They took great pleasure in Sunday services that incorporated the use of incense, the ringing of bells, genuflection, the sign of the cross, and changes of vestments for the clergy, all carried out with the utmost decorum. They delighted in the revised Book of Common Prayer that now included a more elaborate language inflected with an old-world flavor.[29] For old and young alike, High Church doctrines and forms invited black Episcopalians to put aside their daily cares, forget the disordered world of Gotham, merge with ancient religious tradition, and reach closer to their God.

Let's return to the black pastor and the three candidates for orders whom Bishop Onderdonk had treated with such contempt. Despite their humiliation, they managed to surmount adversity. Peter Williams bowed to Onderdonk's demands in order to keep St. Philip's in good standing with the diocese. But he maintained his affiliation with the Anti-Slavery Society, continued to work on behalf of black education, and retained his political interests; it was said that had he lived he planned to vote the antislavery ticket. In time, Isaiah DeGrasse was ordained deacon, then left to serve as a missionary in Jamaica. After many difficulties, Crummell was finally accepted into the ministry and became the most eminent black Episcopal theologian of the nineteenth century. If Reason was forced to abandon his plans to enter the clergy, it was perhaps for the best. He went on to become a prominent black educator in New York City, a teacher to both Philip White and Maritcha Lyons.

JAMES McCUNE SMITH: EUROPE BOUND

James McCune Smith was not with his former classmates because he was pursuing his education across the Atlantic in Great Britain. He was ambitious. While still attending the Mulberry Street School, he was apprenticed to a blacksmith, and after class he could be found "at a forge with the bellows handle in one hand and a Latin grammar in the other."[30] Smith had aspirations to become a doctor, but there were obstacles to overcome: U.S. medical schools proved to be just as inhospitable to young black men as were seminaries. Medicine was still struggling to establish itself as a respectable profession. All too often, the public confused regular doctors with the "irregulars," and derided them as humbugs. So physicians policed their profession with care, determined not to admit anyone who might smell of quackery. Evidently, that automatically included blacks. Smith was rejected by the Geneva College medical school (although the college would later admit Isaiah

DeGrasse) and then by Columbia's College of Physicians and Surgeons. Peter Williams eventually prevailed on a group of white abolitionists to help send the young man to the University of Glasgow in Scotland.

I'm not sure what made Smith so determined to become a doctor. Maybe it was the terrible ravages of the cholera epidemic of 1832 on New York's black community. When he left on a steamship for Europe in mid-August of that year, Smith must have been haunted by images of the sick and dying. Yet in a matter of days he was forced to face the disease once again when one of the sailors on board the ship came down with symptoms of cholera. Writing about his experiences for the *Colored American*, Smith recalled how he watched helplessly as the other sailors dosed the sick man with brandy and pepper and rubbed his limbs.[31] Fortunately, the sailor recovered. Ever persistent, cholera would be waiting for Smith upon his arrival a month later in Glasgow, where it was still raging although with less intensity than the year before. The epidemic, which had caused so much death and destruction on both sides of the Atlantic, must have hardened Smith's resolve to alleviate suffering whenever and wherever he could.

Smith stayed in Glasgow for five years, obtaining his B.A., M.A., and M.D. degrees, and graduating first in his class. In his early years of study he followed a general curriculum that reflected the influence of Scottish Enlightenment thought: Latin, moral philosophy, natural history, and the like. These courses affirmed principles that Charles Andrews had already taught him—the importance of inductive reasoning, of literature and the arts, of moral sensibility. But they also introduced Smith to new forms of knowledge, notably statistics. Medical courses included anatomy, chemistry, materia medica, midwifery, surgery, and botany. Smith was given practical training as well. In anatomy classes, he dissected cadavers. At Lock Hospital, he learned about treatments for venereal disease. During his yearlong infirmary clerkship at the Glasgow Royal Infirmary, he might well have worked with Robert Perry, who was studying the difference between typhus and typhoid fever.[32]

In Britain, Smith found the atmosphere of freedom, the lack of "spirit of caste," intoxicating. As he recalled in his *Colored American* articles, he was embraced by the Glasgow Emancipation Society, spent time in the company of eminent men of science, worshiped alongside white parishioners in the Anglican Church, enjoyed London's cultural scene. In a word, he became a cosmopolitan. Yet he felt like an exile and was happy to return to his native city. The black community welcomed him home in a series of elaborate celebrations, proudly referring to him as our "public property."[33]

CHAPTER FOUR

Community Building
❧ CIRCA 1840 ❧

BY THE LATE 1830S, Peter and most of the other Mulberry Street School graduates had regrouped in the city. For them, it was an invigorating period of maturation and emergence into adulthood. On any given night, passersby could observe the young men streaming into Philomathean Hall at 161 Duane Street. The physical structure of the hall has disappeared from historical memory, yet the significance the place held for black New Yorkers remains alive in the archives. The building was a mecca of civic activism for black youth and "old heads" alike, beckoning them to take part in the community's many flourishing institutions. Fortunately for us, the *Colored American* extensively covered the many meetings held there, since the newspaper's various editors — Philip Bell, another Mulberry Street School graduate, James McCune Smith, Samuel Cornish, Charles Ray, a recent newcomer from Massachusetts — overlapped with the organizations' leadership.[1]

Peter Guignon

Peter was newly wed. "Rebecca was married to Peter Guignon in 1840," Williamson noted tersely in his genealogical records; "she was his first wife." It's clear that Peter married up.[2] Rebecca's parents, Joseph and Elizabeth Marshall, were freeholders; they owned a home on Centre Street and several lots of land north of the city. I'm guessing that Peter lived alone with his mother, probably as tenants in a multifamily dwelling. By the time of his marriage, it's possible that she was no longer alive. I know nothing about my great-great-grandparents' marriage. How did they meet? It's possible that Rebecca's brother Edward, a classmate of Peter's, introduced them during one of the many activities that brought together the African Free School girls and boys, perhaps at the school fairs that Charles Andrews had instituted. Was theirs a love match? Did Joseph and Elizabeth Marshall approve or disapprove of the relationship?

Maritcha's memoir explained at least one gap. Without mentioning any names, she referred to her mother, Mary Joseph, and Rebecca as "two daughters who both joined St. Philip's and in that communion they were married by the beloved rector." In an interesting aside, she added that in "those days things moved leisurely; the rector died before he had given any marriage certificates. There were no public records and the brides of 1840 could do no better than the renowned Cornelia— point to their children and say 'these are my evidences' of marriage."[3] Peter Williams's sloppy record keeping and sudden death—these were the mundane facts that explain the lack of the most basic documentation about Rebecca and Peter's marriage.

My hopes were briefly raised when I came across an 1890 newspaper clipping in Williamson's papers describing Mary Joseph and Albro Lyons's fiftieth wedding anniversary celebration, which was attended among others by the now elderly Philip White and his wife, Elizabeth Guignon White. Glancing back to the golden couple's beginnings, the article noted: "In 1840 the young couple . . . were married in the old frame church on Centre street, a picture of which now hangs upon the wall of their Brooklyn parlor. A portrait of the bridegroom's best man, a celebrated physician of that day, Dr. James McCune Smith who . . . has long since been dead was given a conspicuous place."[4] But Rebecca and Peter's wedding held the same year was not remembered, maybe not even talked about at this celebration.

Despite being newly married, Peter was deeply immersed in community work in the years surrounding 1840. Wherever he had been and whatever he had been doing in the early and mid-1830s, he was now ready to join his former schoolmates, who were slowly trickling back into the city to further the cause of institution building. Peter never exercised sustained leadership, but fulfilled more of a supporting role, leaving leadership to his friends of more forceful character, in particular James McCune Smith. Yet he was involved.

Institution Building

An editorial in the September 9, 1837, issue of the *Colored American* welcomed James McCune Smith back home from Europe, praising him as a sterling example of individual black achievement. "As it is," the writer asserted, "all things are becoming new. The people who long sat in darkness, now have the Heavenly light, and intend to give ocular demonstration of the fact, in patronizing Dr. Smith."[5] Although there were others, Smith was already emerging as an undisputed leader of New York's black community. He could be found everywhere, and his voice could be heard at all times, proposing, arguing, counterattacking.

After paying homage to Smith's accomplishments, the *Colored American* editorial proceeded to consider what black New Yorkers could achieve as a group. "We can, and we intend," the editorial insisted, "(so far as we think it good policy to have separate institutions) to support our moral, literary, and domestic establishments." In other words, we must set about founding and nurturing our own community organizations—whether newspapers, literary societies, political associations, and the like.

Although a seemingly simple promise, the editorial was loaded with ambiguities. Who were the "we"? What was meant by "all things becoming new"? Why insist on "separate institutions"? What made "good policy"?

The "we" were the "old heads" of the community—tradesmen like Boston Crummell and Thomas Downing, and educators like John Peterson and Ransom Wake. But they were now joined by Mulberry Street School graduates, James McCune Smith, Peter and his two new brothers-in-law, and others. Following the conventions of the period, the organizations were closed to women. They were venues where New York's black men met to discuss how best to gain and exercise what they called their "manhood rights": the right to vote and serve in the military; the duty to agitate for these rights; economic opportunity; protection of family and community; improved education of the young. Women were relegated to the background, sometimes invited to attend, rarely to speak, and never permitted to become officers. They struggled to create organizations of their own.

In creating separate institutions, men of the black elite decisively rejected the paternalistic benevolence of white philanthropists like the Mulberry Street School trustees who demanded gratitude, obedience, and worst of all humility as a reward for their largesse. Separate institutions, elite men affirmed, would encourage black New Yorkers to become autonomous and self-reliant, to control their own agenda and course of action. "We," these black men insisted, are quite capable of fighting slavery, eradicating racial discrimination, obtaining an education, and achieving citizenship without the intervention of whites, however well intentioned.

The wording of the *Colored American* editorial — "so far as we think it good policy" — suggested choice, implying that community leaders could decide whether they wanted separate institutions or not. This was not always the case, however. With so few material resources, autonomy was often a mere abstraction, and black institutions were frequently obliged to accept funds from white philanthropists, the Lorillards, the Tappans, and others. The phrase also intimated that black leaders were not so sure separate institutions made good policy. From a pragmatic point of view, they could argue that since theirs was an impoverished community they could ill afford to sever ties with white benefactors. But they might also caution that if they could not always count on help from whites, or if help came with too many strings attached, separate institutions were, insofar as possible, good policy. But then again, it might not be: separation might reinforce the idea that a deep, fixed, and unbridgeable gulf existed between the two races.

Finally, the *Colored American* editorial boldly proclaimed that "all things are becoming new." What were these things, and were they truly new? At pains to distinguish itself from the "old heads" and to establish the legitimacy of its leadership, the younger generation of Mulberry Street School graduates was perhaps overstating its case. But just as the years leading up to emancipation in 1827 had been crucial for debates about black identity, so were the years surrounding 1840 when black New Yorkers reexamined and crystallized their ideas about what it meant to be black Americans.

New York blacks gave themselves a new name. Asserting the Americanness of their people, they eschewed the term "African" in favor of "colored American." Only a few among them, Boston Crummell for example, could claim Africa as a birthplace. For most, the African past was several generations removed and their African identity increasingly attenuated. To sort out their allegiances, they turned to the doctrine of Ethiopianism, a cyclical view of African history that derived its name from Psalm 68, line 31: "Princes shall come out of Egypt, and Ethiopia shall soon stretch out her hands unto God." According to this theory, the continent's early history had been one of great kingdoms and civilizations, yet its present was one of degradation caused by European invasion, African enslavement, and the deleterious effects of the slave trade—depopulation, internal conflict—and yes, heathenism. In time, however, economic development and the civilizing influence of Christianity would restore Africa to its former greatness. So for the present black New Yorkers identified with the country of their birth, while recognizing—always with pride—their special heritage.

The New York Association for the Political Elevation and Improvement of the People of Color: Peter Guignon

Born and raised in the United States, Peter and his friends laid claim to black Americans' right to participate in the national body politic and enjoy all the privileges and obligations of citizenship. For them, this meant the right to vote.

New York state's earlier constitution had placed no racial restrictions on voting. But, worried about the impending emancipation of slaves and the increased number of free blacks that would ensue, the legislature began debating the necessity of instituting voting qualifications with the goal of restricting black men's right to suffrage. Relying on racist theories of black intellectual inferiority, white statesmen argued that black men were too easily swayed by stronger parties or too willingly sold their vote. To prove their worthiness, they would have to show that they had the intelligence and ability to acquire property. In 1821, the legislature instituted a voting property qualification for black men of $250.

Many men of the black elite suddenly found themselves denied a right that had once been theirs. They were not about to take it lying down. In August 1837, a group led by the *Colored American* editors Samuel Cornish and Philip Bell, educator Ransom Wake, and Thomas Downing called for a public meeting to organize a petition drive throughout the state for the restitution of black male suffrage.

It's hard to tell who among New York's black male population could vote in 1840. In 1835, approximately 15,000 blacks lived in the city, 84 of whom were taxed, and 68 of whom met the voting requirements of the 1821 constitution. In 1845, the number of black New Yorkers dropped by about 2,000; yet although the number of taxed had risen to 255, only a mere 91 were entitled to vote.[6] We know from comments in the *Colored American* that Peter Williams voted. My guess is that, as the proprietor of a prosperous restaurant, Thomas Downing did too. And surely the land and homes of the black freeholders on Collect Street met the necessary property qualifications. Peter's brother-in-law Albro Lyons was possibly a voter, since he had established his home uptown on land that I'm guessing had originally belonged to his in-laws, the Marshalls.

In demanding the restitution of the vote, black leaders harkened back to the ideals of liberty, equality, and citizenship enshrined in the U.S. Constitution. But they were also emboldened by the example of Haiti, the former French colony that had achieved independence in 1804 after a long and bloody revolution. Black Americans were intensely proud of the New World's first black republic. They got most of their information about Haiti through reading. The African Free School curriculum supplied basic facts; *Freedom's Journal* and the *Colored American* supplemented with a plethora of articles. Some visited the island. In 1818, a group of disillusioned black New Yorkers that included Peter Williams Jr., Boston Crummell, and Samuel Cornish had formed the Haytian Emigration Society of Coloured People. They carefully distinguished between colonization—conservative whites' attempt to repatriate free blacks to Liberia—and emigration, black Americans' voluntary exile to countries in the diaspora. Williams traveled to Haiti in 1824 to assess conditions for settlement. His report resulted in the emigration of some six thousand people, although he himself remained in the city.[7]

Still others, like Peter and the Reason brothers, were of Haitian origins. Several years before the August 1837 call, they had established the Société des Amis Réuni and named Peter secretary; it lasted from 1833 until at least 1841. I haven't been able to find any written record of the society's goals, but its very name echoes that of the Société des Amis des Noirs, an organization created by liberal French politicians in 1788 to lobby for the abolition of slavery in Saint-Domingue and for the voting rights of the colony's *gens de couleur,* its elite mulatto class. By invoking the name of the famed abolitionist society, these men were both commemorating it and using it as a call to action.[8]

This younger generation quickly added its voice to the elders'. In August 1831, Peter, Albro Lyons, George Downing, Henry Highland Garnet, and others published a call in the *Colored American* for all "Colored Young Men" to attend an important meeting at Philomathean Hall. A Standing Corresponding Committee of ten was formed to draw up petitions, and committees of three persons were established in each ward to circulate them for signatures. Peter was one of the ten men appointed to the Standing Corresponding Committee and was also placed on the Fifth Ward committee. It took another ten months of hard work, but by July 1838 the New York Association for the Political Elevation and Improvement of the People of Color was finally formed and began meeting regularly.

In helping to create the New York Association, this new generation stepped into the foreground. They were working not under the direction of the "old heads" but as equal collaborators. In fact, they trumpeted the advantages of youth. "Young men," they proclaimed, "are important and efficient agents." To justify their newfound activism, they insisted that they were merely obeying the orders of now deceased leaders like William Hamilton, who spoke to them "(as it were) from the Tomb. Youth of my people, I look to you. With you rests the high responsibility of redeeming the character of our people. . . . Oh, Heavens! that I could rouse you. Oh! That I could inflame you with proper ambition!"[9] To the extent that they were asserting aggressive leadership, they seemed to be saying, it was because Hamilton demanded it of them.

Conventions of Colored Men:
Peter Guignon and James McCune Smith

Peter and his friends were experimenting with black political organization. They adopted the interracial abolitionist mantra of "Agitation, agitation, agitation," while working within the black community. Moving beyond the confines of the city, they called for the statewide creation of organizations similar to the New York Association, charging them with drafting and circulating petitions for signatures. Their goal was to deluge the state legislature with the petitions, but before doing so they called on representatives of all the associations to meet at a convention to decide how best to act in concert.[10]

It was not all smooth sailing. Political movements, even those of subordinated groups fighting to overcome oppression, all too often succumb to dissension and divisiveness. This early drive for the restitution of black male suffrage was no exception. Community leaders—young and old alike—all agreed on the wrongs committed against them and the need for redress. But they did not necessarily agree on the political arguments to be made or strategies to be pursued.

James McCune Smith was the focus, and often the instigator, of the turmoil that ensued. Not yet thirty years old, Smith was already emerging as the intellectual force within New York's black community. As one of his staunchest supporters, Peter stood by his side, serving as his mouthpiece and facilitator. Smith was no mere gadfly, but earnestly struggled to come up with the strongest arguments in the fight for black equality. He crafted two arguments. The first was that of universality, the assertion that black Americans deserved as Americans to be granted the universal rights of citizenship; the second, that of particularity, the claim that, given their history of racial oppression, black Americans had a special destiny of suffering and redemption. These intellectual dilemmas would preoccupy Smith and other black leaders in the decades leading up to the Civil War.

Dissension burst out into the open in the summer of 1840 when the state's political associations decided to hold an all-black convention in Albany to devise a general strategy for the restitution of black male suffrage. The *Colored American* repeatedly published a call to attend. There were too many signatories to the call to name here, but they included Peter, his two brothers-in-law, John Peterson, a well-respected educator and St. Philip's lay reader, and both Reason brothers. Smith's name was not on the list.

In early August, a large crowd attended an organizational meeting at Philomathean Hall. That's when the bombshell went off. Its cause was the thorny issue of separate institutions. White abolitionists had already voiced their opposition to the Albany convention, but now objections came from within, most notably from John Peterson. He based his arguments on expediency: since the majority of New York state's population was white and hostile to black political rights, blacks as a minority and a "distinct people" had no hope of "influencing the said white majority, neither by interest, fear, nor by superior intellectual power." Hence, an all-black convention would be counterproductive. Working in tandem, Peter and Smith then asked to speak. Peter presented a series of resolutions against the planned convention, which Smith then rose to support. I'm pretty sure that Smith put Peter up to this, using his quiet and unassuming friend as a stalking horse. Although coming to the same conclusion as Peterson, Peter and Smith's reasoning differed substantially from the older man's. With greater sophistication, they grounded their argument against separate action in principle. Distinguishing people on the basis of skin color was a "virtual acknowledgment that there are rights peculiar to the color of a man's skin, thus fostering prejudice against complexion." Separate action was harmful because it reinforced the idea of separate races. Peter and Smith failed to get their resolutions passed.[11] The Albany convention took place as planned. Because of his status in the community, Smith was nominated as a delegate and reluctantly agreed to attend. But neither he nor Peter appeared.

The Albany convention brought tangible results. By February 1841, its organizers proudly reported that they had collected approximately 2,200 signatures, 1,300 of which came from the city; in addition, about

600 sympathetic whites also signed the petitions.[12] Energized, black New Yorkers held several mass meetings in the city.

Given the heightened excitement, neither Peter nor Smith could stay out of politics for long. Both men attended the New York County convention in October 1841. Throughout the year Smith had been building his case piece by piece. He made himself heard.

Most of the convention delegates argued that black men could not vote because their color precluded them from being able "to perform the duties assigned to other citizens." Hence, the property qualification was unconstitutional because it was based on racial discrimination. Building upon his earlier ideas, Smith was determined to circumvent racial arguments. He maintained that all colored citizens, just like all whites, were subject to taxation, direct and indirect. Therefore, the property qualification was unconstitutional because it violated the principle of no taxation without representation, which had nothing to do with race. Smith (and Peter) presented the case from the perspective of the universal rights of citizens and not of racially discriminatory legislation.[13]

Peter and Smith could devise such sophisticated arguments because of all they had learned at the Mulberry Street School. They, and the rest of New York's black leadership, understood that education was key to political advancement. "The school-master must be aroused," they declared, "and sent abroad to light up the torch of education, and throw light into the minds of the youth of the land." Surely, an educated black population would successfully "overthrow the imputations . . . declaring us to be an illiterate, defenceless, and divided people" and prove its intellectual qualifications to vote.[14]

Black leaders pressed the issue of education from two distinct but related perspectives. They asserted that literacy and literary knowledge would give blacks the rhetorical tools necessary to plead their case convincingly, disseminate it to the public through the press, and thus prove their capacity for civilization and culture. Inverting the argument, however, they insisted simultaneously that political rights were necessary for blacks to fulfill their literary and educational ambitions. It is, they maintained, "the political enfranchisement of our people upon which so much of our religious, literary and local happiness virtually depends."[15]

The Philomathean Society: Peter Guignon

If political and literary happiness depended on each other, it followed that Peter and his friends would work equally hard in establishing literary societies. They were not the first. In 1833, "old heads"—Peter Williams, Boston Crummell, Thomas Downing, and others—had created the Phoenix Society. This organization was not a separate institution, however, but depended on white philanthropy. The ubiquitous Arthur Tappan provided financial assistance and became treasurer; other whites also served as officers. The society's goals were modest, limited to ensuring basic literacy among adults and children throughout the black community.[16]

Peter, however, was a member of another literary society that bore the name of the hall in which it met: the Philomathean Society. This society and its sister organization, the Phoenixonian Society, were autonomous, black-run institutions whose ambitions were loftier than those of the Phoenix Society. Little is known about the Philomathean Society's origins. A notice in the *Colored American* of April 29, 1837, made passing reference to its foundation in 1830. Some years later, Peter and two of his friends, James Fields and Francis Myers, published an "Address of the Young Men of Color in the City of New York" in the May 2, 1840, issue of the paper. It was an open invitation to the young men of the community to "share in the advantages derived from literary pursuits" by helping to revive the Philomathean Society. Explaining the society's original mission, they began by quoting from the preamble of its constitution:

> On what side soever we turn our eyes, in search of the principal pursuits which employ the enterprizing part of mankind, we find a great portion of them engaged in toiling up the rugged ascent of the "Hill of Science," each bearing some mental tribute to the shrine of "Wisdom's Temple," placed on its lofty summit. Yet in this search of the mind's eye, we turn in vain to find among the aspirants of wisdom a proportionate number of our own race, sharing the toils of as-

cension with their more ambitious neighbors, or contributing their mite to the offering of nations. This want of energy
and spirit, (too degrading to be endured by rational beings)
having at length engaged the attention of a few associates,
determined to erase the inglorious record of the past by an
active future, they hereby solemnly engage to support.

Peter and his co-authors then proceeded to invite New York's young
men of color to join the society. The only requirements, they assured
them, were the possession of good character and an agreement to donate
half a dozen volumes to the library. Working collaboratively, they would
fulfill the society's goal of elevating "the colored man to the level of high
moral and mental attainments" through the expansion of the library,
discussion groups, and lecture series.[17]

The Philomathean Society's lectures were reason enough to leave
home on any given evening for Philomathean Hall. Several years earlier,
the society had launched a highly successful series shortly after James
McCune Smith's return from Scotland. Taking advantage of his presence, organizers were able to attract other lecturers who replicated the
best aspects of the Mulberry Street School curriculum. Peter was undoubtedly in the audience, accompanied perhaps by former schoolmates
Edward Marshall, Albro Lyons, Isaiah DeGrasse, and the Reason
brothers. By and large, the lecture topics were not political or racial, but
broadly literary and scientific. The goal was to enhance the audience's
knowledge of western science and culture. Representing Peter's schoolmates were Smith, who spoke on "Organs of the Senses," "Circulation of the Blood," and "Phrenology," and DeGrasse, who addressed the
topic of "Evidences of Christianity." In addition, there were speeches on
such general subjects as chemistry, history, geography, and logic. Ransom Wake gave a lecture on "Oratorical Delivery" in which he argued
that to be effective orators African Americans needed to study not only
literary examples and rhetorical devices but delivery as well.[18]

The series that Peter and his friends organized in 1841 was just as
intellectually stimulating. Subjects ranged from the aesthetic—sacred
music, for example—to topics more concerned with racial uplift and

political organization: the "character and capability of colored men," "power and influence of union," "popular reform." In one of his presentations, Charles Reason combined the literary and the political. Placing himself in the tradition of his favorite poets Milton and Wordsworth, he argued his case in a poem titled "The Spirit Voice, Or, Liberty Call to the Disfranchised" in which he imagined that this voice

'Tis calling you, who now too long have been
Sore victims suffering under legal sin,
To vow, no more to sleep, till raised and freed
From partial bondage, to a life indeed.[19]

Aping or Imitation?

The early black elite has been charged with race betrayal, with selling its birthright, its African heritage, for a mess of pottage—western culture. There are several possible responses to such attacks. The first is that this emerging elite was not engaged in "aping," as black Philadelphia writer Frances Watkins Harper would later put it, but in "imitation." Aping, in Harper's words, was "servile or abject mimicking," while imitation strove for the improvement of self and the larger community.[20] Much like other American groups, members of the elite were merely imitating—adapting to their own purposes—the culture of the nation into which they were born, to which they insisted they belonged, and in which they claimed citizenship. And, as many intuited, imitation could readily lead to competition, to the urge to rival and outdo the originators.

The second response invites us to consider that those in the black elite read and absorbed the works of classical writers and poets, political philosophers, musicians, and artists because doing so brought them sheer aesthetic pleasure, made them delight in the beauty of phrases and images, the musicality of sound, the inspired power of finely crafted arguments, the solace of ritual. In acquiring cosmopolitan culture, elite blacks were able to think of themselves in terms that included, but went beyond, that of "colored American." It allowed them to imagine an ideal world—a world without borders, a global community of voluntary citizens hungry for open cultural and intellectual exchange. In this sense, cosmopolitanism became a tool for negotiating what W. E. B. Du Bois would later call the dilemma of "double consciousness," of being simultaneously Negro and American. If black Americans were cosmopolitans, citizens of the world, they could without contradiction claim to be both African-descended *and* citizens of the United States.

James McCune Smith: Philomathean Society Lecturer

Certainly, nobody could accuse James McCune Smith of aping.

Full of intellectual fervor, Smith struggled to define what he called the "destiny" of his people in three major documents: a lecture, "The Destiny of Our People," delivered as part of the 1841 Philomathean Society lecture series that Peter and his colleagues deemed so significant they insisted on publishing it; some seven speeches on the Haitian Revolution printed in pamphlet form in 1841; and a series of articles that appeared in the *New York Daily Tribune* in 1843 titled "Freedom and Slavery for Afric-Americans," rebutting claims that blacks were worse off in freedom than in slavery. In his political speeches, Smith based his arguments on the universal rights of citizenship. In contrast, in these essays and lectures, he asserted that God had endowed African-descended peoples with a special destiny: the redemption of their race, their nations, and perhaps the world.

Smith began by debunking commonplace myths about the innate inferiority of the African race. First addressing the question of origins, he summarily dismissed polygenesist notions of separate species to affirm the "unity of the human race." He then proceeded to turn racist stereotypes on their head, suggesting that it was black Americans, not whites, who were upholding the democratic ideals on which the Republic was founded. As he proceeded, Smith evinced an amazing ability to manipulate different kinds of discourses, ranging from religious pathos to historical example to statistical analysis. He was in fact speaking out of a double faith, "which holds first to the Bible, and secondly, to American institutions, which have made us free, which will free our brethren in bonds, and which will be triumphant in pulling down the strongholds of tyranny throughout our globe."[21]

"The Destiny of Our People" is shot through with biblical references and religious ideals. Unlike the ancient Jews who never thought of Egypt as home, Smith argued, black Americans were attached through their blood and their tears to the soil of their birthplace; hence, they should not emigrate, but should remain in the United States. Their destiny was to convert the "form" of the current American government into "substance," to "purify" it by replacing slavery and oppression with liberty. They would do so by following the guidelines set by Christ, relying on "right" rather than "might," and "good" rather than "evil." And their weapon would be that of reason: "as physical force is out of the question, the effort must be purely intellectual, and in order to maintain the struggle we must qualify ourselves to reason down the prejudices which bar us from rights."[22]

It might seem paradoxical that Smith chose the Haitian Revolution, whose bloodiness had been widely reported throughout the world, as an example of New World blacks' use of reason to gain their rights. But by means of careful historical investigation, Smith led his readers through the different stages of the rebellion, countering conventional interpretations by arguing that on every occasion black violence had been a legitimate defensive response to assaults by whites. When white Haitians rose up in opposition to granting citizenship to the free colored population, self-defense by the latter was fully justified. It was only when whites reacted to these defensive measures "with a recklessness of purpose truly diabolical," toward both free and enslaved blacks, that slaves "first manifested a disposition to revolt." "Be it remembered," Smith insisted, "that this insurrection was the legitimate fruit of slavery, against which it was a spontaneous rebellion. It was . . . the consequence of withholding from men their liberty." In a final reversal of conventional thinking, Smith argued that Toussaint L'Ouverture's leadership of the rebellion indisputably proved that *he* was the true democrat; it was this educated former slave who, through constitutional means, endeavored to grant the rights of liberty, equality, and fraternity to every Haitian.[23]

The main problem, as Smith saw it, was one of perception. As ignorant as they were prejudiced, whites made assumptions about blacks based on misperceptions. They automatically believed the historical accounts that portrayed Haitian slaves as savages engaged in senseless acts of violence. And they readily accepted the erroneous data of the 1840 U.S. census that indicated that southern slaves were better off than free blacks in the North. In "Freedom and Slavery for Afric-Americans," Smith responded head on. Using sophisticated statistical analysis, he proved that free blacks had greater longevity and lower mortality rates than slaves, and did not suffer from the degree of insanity claimed by the census. To the extent that blacks lived in degraded conditions, it was because racial prejudice had instilled in them the belief that they were naturally inferior, then mocked their ignorance, and caused them to abandon all educational pursuits.

"Urged by a bloodless revolution," however, free blacks *had* established schools, literary societies, newspapers, churches, and benevolent associations, and sent a number of youths to institutions of higher education. Smith concluded by chastising white Americans for their failure to recognize black achievement, and specifically the existence of an elite class—to which he and his friends belonged—similar to their own.

> Men of narrow views and limited information are apt to conceive that society and refinement are confined to the little heaven in which they are privileged to "thunder," regarding all as outcasts—*barbaroi*—who are not embraced within their charmed environ: such men cannot perceive that there is around every intelligent "home," all the elements of refined manners and dignified deportment. There are, thank heaven, a thousand such homes among the free blacks of the free States—homes, in which the sounds of "my wife," "my child," "my mother," "my Father," "*my Bible*," and their thousand clustering joys, weave the sweet harmonies of content and happiness.[24]

Odd Fellows and Freemasons: The Philomathean Lodge

The Philomathean Society did not so much die as transform itself into something else. An 1885 obituary of the recently deceased John Peterson, published in the *New York Freeman,* noted that in his youth the venerable old man had been an early member of the Philomathean Society. Then in 1843, the obituary explained, one Peter Ogden "was delegated to go to England to procure a charter to open a lodge of Odd Fellows in this city which he returned with and the first lodge of colored Odd Fellows, Philomathean 646, was opened March 1, 1843."[25] A second lodge named after William Hamilton followed soon thereafter.

Black secret societies were nothing new. By 1826, four Masonic lodges had been established in the city. Both Odd Fellowship and Freemasonry gripped the imagination of New York's black men. Their membership rolls soon swelled and included many former Philomatheans. James McCune Smith, Thomas and George Downing, and James Fields joined the Odd Fellows, while Peter, Charles Reason, and Samuel Cornish affiliated with Freemasonry. Some — like John Peterson and Patrick Reason — belonged to both orders.[26] Evidently, participation in one did not preclude the other. Like the literary societies that preceded them, these organizations were managed by men of the elite who served as masters and grand masters, but remained open to any man willing to abide by the rules of the orders. They were in effect safe places where all black men were free to assert their manhood in word, behavior, and deed.

It's difficult to talk about either of these organizations because both are shrouded in secrecy, necessary, they maintained, to prevent imposture by hostile outsiders. Their overlapping membership suggests that they were in fact quite similar. Both grew out of conditions of U.S. racism. After being rejected by U.S. Freemasonry, Philadelphian Prince Hall traveled to England to ask the English Grand Lodge to charter the first African Lodge, which it did in 1784. Some sixty years later Peter Ogden was forced to do the same for black Odd Fellowship. Although details remain murky, both orders claimed ancient and universal origins: the Odd Fellows variously dated themselves back to the Goths or to a fifteenth-century order established in London; the Freemasons claimed King Solomon's temple, the Parthenon, Jacob's well, and the Pyramids as early Masonic sites.[27] Much like black Episcopalians' immersion in the Anglican Communion, members of these secret societies were asserting their right to participate in ancient, cosmopolitan traditions broader than those of enslavement and Americanization.

Both Freemasons and Odd Fellows insisted that they were motivated by two beliefs: the Fatherhood of God and the Brotherhood of Man. The first ensured that members of the orders would abide by the "eternal principles" that also guided Christianity: love and truth. The second emphasized "universal fraternity." For blacks, this notion had special resonance. It affirmed not only the brotherhood of lodge members but even more importantly that of men of all races. These abstract principles had practical application. One was mutual relief—the obligation to provide for the sick and pay the burial costs of deceased members and their families. Another was moral self-improvement, the duty to engage in honest industry, avoid intemperance, cultivate an irreproachable character, and exhibit dignified behavior at all times.

So what differentiated the two orders in this early period of their existence? It was a question of emphasis. Odd Fellowship stressed mutual relief, envisioning itself as a vast society that endeavored to extend aid far beyond its own membership. Grounding their identity in their original trade as builders, Freemasons saw themselves as skilled artisans, and referred to their activities as the Craft. To a greater extent than Odd Fellows, they emphasized the importance of individual labor, which, when accompanied by a strong work ethic, would eventually lead to greater opportunities in education, entrepreneurship, and property ownership.[28]

Women

What did black women think? They were not pleased.

In 1853, the anonymous "Charlotte K—" penned several letters to *Frederick Douglass' Paper*, a national newspaper published out of Rochester with a broader subscription base than the earlier New York papers.

In them, she agonizingly relived the havoc Peter Ogden's actions had caused in the black community. Before he brought the Odd Fellows to New York, there had been

> two Literary Societies in active operation, giving public lectures, debates, etc., to which we women folks were admitted. I can assure you those were pleasant times! Our beaux gallanted us to and from the meetings (at one of which I became acquainted with my first husband); and our social circle, especially at tea parties on Sunday evenings, felt the impulse and the culture which flowed from the eloquent and earnest discussions.

But Odd Fellowship ended women's participation in community cultural life and, Charlotte K lamented, destroyed her "domestic happiness" as well. Her husband

> was out every night; on Monday he went to the Philomathean Lodge; on Tuesday to the Hamilton; Wednesday, the Hannibal; Thursday, the Council; Friday, to a Committee meeting on the regalia, or the constitution; Saturday night he had to sit with a sick brother; and Sunday nights, instead of pleasant tea drinkings, he sought male society to discuss "the Order" in some segar or drug shop in the fifth ward. I cannot tell you how much I suffered from this continual neglect, this cruel slight.

The sad irony, she concluded, was that the Odd Fellows actually violated their own principles. They neglected and impoverished their own families by catering to the needs of members and spending too much money on the lodges' balls, suppers, and costly regalia.[29]

A testy George Downing shot back. The literary societies, he suggested, were already dead. If not quite yet, "it would have been an act of mercy to relieve the Philomathean Society in its dying struggles." Neither should Odd Fellowship be held responsible for all the social extravagance of those years; in truth it had held noble aspirations. Interestingly enough, however, at no point in his letter did Downing defend his erstwhile lodge.

In this same letter, Downing suggested that the Philomathean Society's only hope for survival was "the Ladies' Literary Society [which] came to save it, but was carried down. . . . It had been but at best a ghostly existence." The phrase "ghostly existence" aptly describes New York's black female societies of the period, for their traces have all but vanished from the archives. If information about the African Dorcas Society of the late 1820s has been preserved, this is undoubtedly because of its male leadership in its early days. Yet we still know so little about the black women who eventually took it over—Isaiah DeGrasse's mother, Maria, Peter Williams's sister Mary, *Colored American* editor Charles Ray's wife, Henrietta, and her good friend Hester Lane.[30]

And what do we know of the women who founded the Ladies' Literary Society in 1834? Precious little. We need to thank Samuel Cornish for naming Henrietta Ray "one of its brightest stars" in an elaborate eulogy he published at her death. An intimate friend, Cornish chose to emphasize Henrietta's religious character, in particular her forbearance in the face of suffering, but said little about the society.[31]

I wondered what Charles Ray thought of his wife's activities. How much support did he give her? I found no information. Ray, I knew, was struggling over the question of women's participation in male-dominated political organizations. In 1840, he agreed with those in Garrison's American Anti-Slavery Society who believed that women— white and black—should have the right to be officeholders, and had actually put forth the name of his late wife's associate Hester Lane, only to have her rejected. But a mere year later he vociferously (and successfully) opposed the proposal that women be allowed into the Troy Convention as observers, insisting that a man could "do more work abroad without a wife than with her."[32] Maybe he was relieved that Henrietta had confined herself to more modest, feminine endeavors.

Perhaps in continued homage of Henrietta, Cornish reported extensively on the Ladies' Literary Society's third anniversary celebration held a few months after her death. There were readings, addresses, recitation of poems, music. I recognized the names of some of the participants because of their relation to prominent men in the community:

Maria DeGrasse, Miss Crummell, John Peterson's daughter Rebecca. But other names meant nothing to me: Eliza Richards, Fanny Tompkins, Sarah Ennalls. Cornish chose to reprint only one address titled "On the Improvement of the Mind." Its sentiments replicated those of black male leaders in their emphasis on black self-improvement and achievement.

> It is now a momentous time, a time that calls us to exert all our powers, and among the many of them, the mind is the greatest, and great care should be taken to improve it with diligence. . . . Neglect will plunge us into deeper degradation, and keep us groveling in the dust, while our enemies will rejoice and say, we do not believe they (colored people) have any minds; if they have, they are unsusceptible of improvement. . . . Awake and slumber no more—arise, put on your armor, ye daughters of America, and stand forth in the field of improvement.[33]

Other than the Ladies' Literary Society, few black female organizations seem to have existed in New York at this time, and most of them—the Daughters of Wesley, the Female Branch of Zion, the Female Mite Society, the Daughters of Israel—were church related. Their absence from the historical record is especially puzzling given black women's vibrant presence in community affairs in cities like Boston, Philadelphia, Salem, and Rochester. I was faced with a question. Had New York's black women not been activists? Or had they been, but all trace of their endeavors simply disappeared from the archives?[34]

In the late 1870s, Alexander Crummell offered his version of the matter in a testimonial he wrote on behalf of Maria Stewart, a Boston activist and writer who had so antagonized that city's black community with charges of do-nothingism in the early 1830s that she was practically run out of town, whereupon she moved to New York. Crummell remembered returning from Oneida Institute with Garnet and Sidney and being surprised on meeting Stewart to find "a young woman of my own people full of literary aspiration and ambitious authorship. In those days," he continued, "the desire for learning was almost exclusively confined to colored young men. There were a few young women in New York who thought of higher things, and it was a surprise to find another added to their number."[35]

Crummell's comment reeks of condescension; it suggests that New York's black women lacked intellectual ambition, thought only of lower things, and were responsible for their own inaction. But these women were constrained. For one, many cities in the Northeast had active interracial female antislavery societies that were key in launching the public careers of women like Susan Paul in Boston or Henrietta Forten and Sarah Mapps Douglass in Philadelphia; perhaps because of the city's strong ties to the South, such societies did not take hold in New York. For another, to a much greater extent than its counterparts elsewhere, New York's black leadership devoted much of its energy to two causes—the restitution of black male suffrage and entrepreneurship—that relegated women to the sidelines.

Class

In the late 1830s, black porter Peter Paul Simons tried to come to the rescue of the womenfolk in his community. In a speech delivered before the Daughters of Wesley, he decried the damage done to black women by those who looked down on their intellectual abilities. "Those females who considers there grudgement less," he affirmed in bizarre prose, "ought to be outcasts of all popular societies; for there influence might excite the same opinion, of self-incapability in many a promising damsel, and I sincerely contend, that where a female feels the inferiority, she is but a dead member to the intellectual and cultivated society of mankind." Gender issues soon gave way to a debate about class. When Simons asked the *Colored American* editors Samuel Cornish and Philip Bell to publish his speech in their paper, they refused, calling it "worthless trash" that could not be understood "any more than if it had been Greek." Simons counterattacked, accusing the elite of, well, elitism since he was not of "Glasgow College or of DeGrasse's lineage," and challenging the very notion of intellectual elevation.

Here are the two sides of the debate. The elite maintained that literacy, education, knowledge, were *the* keys to success in America and hence virtues to which all black Americans should aspire. Not to do so indicated indifference to self-improvement, to the betterment of the community, and to proving the race's intellectual capacities to white Americans. And so yes, they looked down their noses at men like Simons. For Simons, however, the inverse was true. The elite's virtues were more like vices. Their emphasis on intellectual elevation was a sign of submissiveness to white society, an impediment to black progress, the cause of invidious "classes of distinction" within the community, and a hindrance to "our people from acting collectively for themselves."[36] It's undeniable that the elite's very language of "uplift" and "elevation" connoted inequality and hierarchy: a privileged class, convinced of the rightness of its own values, stooping down to raise the masses to their level. In fact, some could argue that the elite was doing nothing other than replicating the paternalistic agenda of white benefactors like the African Free Schools trustees, elevating the lower orders while simultaneously maintaining the social status quo. To these charges members of the elite responded that, first, uplift extended to *their* own continued self-improvement as well, and second, their efforts in the community proved that they had not, and would never, turn their backs on those less fortunate than they. To them, intellectual elevation was an expression of racial solidarity.

Schoolteachers: Men and Women

Simons was correct when he charged that the elite held education to be the key to black advancement. It was here that New York's black women found their calling, teaching in the city's schools for colored children right alongside black men.

The schools were not doing well. In 1833, the Manumission Society had ceded control of the African Free Schools to the newly established Public School Society (the predecessor of the Board of Education), arguing that this transfer would result in "a more efficient and regular supervision of them, . . . a greater economy of expenditure, more uniformity in the system of instruction and probably a more general interest in the welfare and melioration of the children." A couple of years into the experiment, however, the society acknowledged that the schools were neither efficacious nor useful. None of the rationales had borne fruit. Despite the controversy over Charles Andrews, black parents remained loyal to the Manumission Society, convinced that it had always had the best interests of their children at heart. They were outraged when the Public School Society demoted all the schools except one to the level of primary schools and decided to discontinue the use of spelling books. They were equally furious when they discovered that black teachers were paid less than their white counterparts, and even more so when several were dismissed.

But the Public School Society did do some good. It acceded to the black community's request to change their schools' name from "African" to "Colored," in keeping with black New Yorkers' shift in identity.[37] And it hired an ever increasing number of black teachers. The records kept by the society consist mainly of lists—of schools, of teachers, of pay. Names of male teachers such as John Peterson and Charles Reason are familiar because we know about their other community activities. But the same can't be said of women teachers. Here's a list from 1838:

Public school no. 1:   Caroline Roe, teacher; Elizabeth Roe, assistant
Public school no. 2:   Eliza Richards and Sarah Ennalls, teachers, Maria Stewart, assistant
Primary school no. 3:   Maria DeGrasse, teacher
Primary school no. 4:   Fanny Tompkins, teacher
Primary school no. 5:   Rebecca Peterson, teacher.[38]

Many of the names overlap with those of participants in the Ladies' Literary Society celebration. That suggested to me that in their own way these women *were* community leaders; but in contrast to their male counterparts, and with the exception of the notorious Maria Stewart, their lives were indeed unobtrusive.

By 1837, only one out of four black children attended school. This state of affairs was not acceptable to New York's black leaders. Although they knew the community had few financial resources, their commitment to education as the path to black achievement never wavered. Relying on their own human resources, they set about creating a private school system that ranged from tutoring in specialized subjects to evening schools to academies that offered a comprehensive curriculum.

Mulberry Street School graduates spearheaded many of these efforts. Patrick Reason advertised classes in a "scientific method of drawing" in the *Colored American,* while William Webster appealed to those who wanted to study the science and practice of vocal music using the Pestalozzi system. James McCune Smith opened an evening school in his home in the fall of 1839. Edward Marshall, who had been a teacher at primary school no. 1, was the principal instructor and offered basic courses in the three Rs as well as a smattering of geography.

Women participated in these efforts. Fanny Tompkins advertised the opening of a private seminary for girls in the *Colored American* of September 18, 1841. Not only did she teach sewing, knitting, and the three Rs, but she also offered courses in geography, astronomy, history, and music.[39]

Most ambitious by far was the New York Select Academy, where the first principal was John Brown, formerly head of the boys' department at Colored School no. 1; Philip Bell, Samuel Cornish, Isaiah De-Grasse, and James Fields were trustees. After Brown became ill, Thomas Sidney was appointed principal. Sidney and Alexander Crummell ran the evening school.[40] Remembering Charles Andrews's broad curriculum, these Mulberry Street School graduates offered courses that went well beyond the three Rs: grammar, algebra, geometry, bookkeeping, history, astronomy, natural philosophy, botany, geography, and the use of globes. Even with their few resources, they were trying to pass on to the younger generation some of the cosmopolitan knowledge that Andrews had instilled in them years earlier.

Philip Augustus White

In his eulogy of Philip White printed in the *Brooklyn Citizen* for March 27, 1891, George Downing claimed that Philip began teaching adult classes in the late 1830s even while a student at Colored School no. 2.[41] Although only sixteen years old, it's evident that Philip was mature enough to understand the value of education. Downing never mentioned the name of the school. It could have been the evening school that James McCune Smith opened in his home, where Philip might have served as Edward Marshall's aide. Or maybe it was the New York Select Academy's evening school managed by Thomas Sidney and Alexander Crummell.

Downing described in considerable detail how teaching improved the minds of not only students but the instructor as well. Philip, he wrote,

> was enabled to fasten in his mind the principles he endeavored to explain. To make what he knew available he had to mentally classify and arrange miscellaneous collections of facts, and the conscious power exerted in so doing stimulated him to increase the variety, extent and value of his literary acquisitions. These accumulated facts furnish material for thought, and in the effort of trying to think the mind began to expand, and with growth that is natural and normal, there is always proportion, harmony and strength.

How to account for Philip's maturity?

Born in 1823, at the time of his death in 1891 Philip was a prominent man, respected by blacks and whites alike. He was widely commemorated. The dozen obituaries and eulogies I've found of him all repeat the same basic factual information. To my mind, the most compelling eulogy—because the most detailed, closely observed, and sensitive—was George Downing's.

Downing seems to have been on intimate terms with the White family. Philip's father, Thomas White, came from northern England. A "stern old English gentleman," in Downing's words, "he exacted instant, unquestioning obedience, and supervised manners and morals after the good old fashion of that era." About the origins of Philip's mother, Elizabeth Steele, Downing maintained absolute silence. I know from Philip's death certificate that she came from Jamaica, so that it was her racial heritage that led to the designation of her son as "colored."

But I don't know whether she was born a slave or free, where she and Thomas White met, whether they married, or how they ended up in the United States.

The 1830 census lists the White family as living in Hoboken, New Jersey. There were six children, four daughters and two sons. By 1832 the family had moved to Manhattan where, according to the city directory, Thomas ran a grocery store at 102 Gold Street, on the corner of Frankfort, the very same location of Philip's drugstore some fifteen years later.

Theirs was a close-knit family. Thomas soon became an invalid and was house bound. "His confinement," Downing suggested, "brought him into close and more frequent contact with his children than is customary. They busied themselves in giving him the countless little attentions so essential to the comfort of an invalid, and at his knee, spelled the first reading, recited the catechism and childish hymns and prayers." For her part, Philip's mother "gave him a sense of family pride, virtuous habits and inspired him with an aim to be great and good." Thomas died in 1835, but, "until the loss of their head, this family, obscure but happy, grew and throve in a little world of their own." In his eulogy, Downing wrote of children, but I've found virtually no information about Philip's siblings. The 1850 census indicates that in addition to his mother, a sister, Sarah M., lived with him; her name appears in conjunction with various community organizations in newspapers of the 1860s. So does that of another sister, Mary, who married Richard Thompson. In her memoir, Maritcha wrote that the Thompsons' daughter Elizabeth, known as Bessie, was a favorite niece of Philip's, and that he was devastated by her early death. In passing, Maritcha also noted the death in the 1880s of a third sister, Emma. That's virtually all I know about Philip's siblings.[42]

Reading into this scant written record, I believe the presence of both parents was fundamental to Philip's development and later sense of identity. Unlike Peter and James McCune Smith, Philip knew his white father, who, I'm sure, instilled in him the firm conviction that he was as good as any white man. But like the two older men, Philip was nurtured by a black mother. Downing maintained in no uncertain terms that she lavished her love on her son and that he repaid her in kind: "To her close devotion and judicious training the success of her youngest son was mainly due. For this devoted self-sacrificing mother

Mr. White always expressed the deepest filial affection." The one photograph I have of Philip suggests that he was very light-skinned and could have probably passed for white; yet if his mother was darker skinned I don't think he would ever have contemplated leaving her behind. Even without concrete evidence, we have a sense of how instrumental black mothers were in the rearing of their mixed-race sons.

Thomas's death had a significant impact on the family. Thereafter, it was up to Elizabeth to raise her children on her own and keep the household together. She persevered, beginning with their education. Philip undoubtedly attended one of the low-ranked primary schools before entering Colored School no. 2 in 1836. Located in a brand-new two-story building on Laurens Street, the school was run by black teachers. Ransom Wake was head of the male department and Eliza Richards of the female; the boys' principal teacher was Charles Reason. Much like the advanced senior boys at the Mulberry Street School, Philip was offered supplementary courses in Latin and history, both ancient and modern. "What the course of study provided and the text books furnished, that [Philip] learned," Downing insisted. "He has said of his school work that his lessons were never a task. He memorized all that was required, and always felt that had twice as much been demanded he could have accomplished the same with equal readiness and ease."

The family was impoverished. Quite by accident, I discovered that the Public School Society helped out by hiring Philip and his mother for occasional low-skilled jobs. While poring through the handwritten records of the Public School Society at the New-York Historical Society, I came across the following records of payment: on January 25 and April 28, 1840, three dollars to Philip A. White for making fires in African Public School no. 2 during three months; on June 11, 1841, fifteen dollars to Elizabeth White for cleaning and whitewashing primary school no. 7.[43] These must have been trying times for Philip and his mother; and it must have been Elizabeth's fortitude, sense of family pride, and aspirations for a better life that enabled them to face an uncertain future with dignity.

As the boys' principal teacher, Charles Reason taught Philip. Some twenty-five years later, Maritcha Lyons was one of his students.

Charles Reason, photograph by Denison's Photographic Parlors
(Photographs and Prints Division, Schomburg Center for Research
in Black Culture, The New York Public Library)

In her memoir she portrayed him as a demanding but rewarding task-
master:

Professor Reason, cultured, refined, inclined to be a little
supercilious was quite intolerant of mediocrity; he instinc-
tively shunned the ordinary and the common place, and kept
himself aloof from all that was awkward and unseemly. He
could and would teach, but only if allowed his right of choice
in the selection of his pupils. Those willing and able to submit to his processes, found compensation far in excess of ex-
action. He taught how to study, developed a love of study

for study's sake; to those mentally alert, aspiring, and dili-
gent he disclosed vistas of interest. Satisfaction and wonder,
whoever could be trained to enjoy what he enjoyed in the
way it pleased him had measureless content as complete as
exceptional.[44]

Charles Reason had learned from Charles Andrews, and was now
taking his place as a black instructor of black youth. I'd like to think he
chose to mentor Philip, and that it was he who taught the young man
the supplementary courses in Latin and history.

By the late 1830s, Elizabeth knew that she didn't have to worry
about what would happen to her beloved younger son. The now grown
boys of the Mulberry Street School were watching out for him, developing his talents and preparing him for his future profession and leadership role.

Philip needed to learn a trade. Elizabeth first placed him as an
apprentice to Patrick Reason to learn engraving; once again, a black
mentor replaced a white one. This must have been quite an honor for
young Philip, since Patrick was quickly making a name for himself. Was
Elizabeth disappointed when Philip failed to live up to expectations?
"A three months' probation," Downing confessed, "satisfied parent and
master that the apprentice had not the slightest aptitude for the work."

Philip had ideas of his own, and they centered on James McCune
Smith. If he had indeed taught in Edward Marshall's evening school,
Philip would have become acquainted with Smith at that time and come
to admire the older man. Conversely, it's possible that Philip's rapid
intellectual growth so impressed Smith that he turned to the younger
man when he decided he needed an apprentice in his drugstore. In any
event, things worked out to everybody's satisfaction: "Then the youth's
own plan was discussed," Downing explained. "At the expiration of a
year it was arranged that he should study pharmacy under the famous
Dr. James McCune Smith. Then his life work began in earnest."

CHAPTER FIVE

A Black Aristocracy

CIRCA 1847

AT MIDCENTURY, BLACK New Yorkers found that life, if anything, had grown harsher and more unforgiving. Facing stiff competition from immigrant labor, particularly the Irish, and increased racism from all quarters, black workers found themselves forced out of jobs they had traditionally held as porters, dockhands, waiters, barbers, and cooks, and reduced to the most unskilled and menial forms of labor. Housing conditions were poor. The school situation remained lamentable. Gone were the Philomathean, Phoenix, and Phoenixonian Societies, the New York Political Association, and the *Colored American*. Until Frederick Douglass founded the *North Star* in Rochester in 1847, black New Yorkers were forced to rely on two white abolitionist newspapers, William Lloyd Garrison's *Liberator* and the American Anti-Slavery Society's *National Anti-Slavery Standard,* for news of special interest to them. Horace Greeley's *New York Daily Tribune* served as their local paper; they followed its reporting closely, often contributing articles and placing advertisements.

Gone too were some of the brightest of New York's black elite. Already in poor health, Thomas Sidney died suddenly in the summer of 1840. Isaiah DeGrasse followed shortly thereafter; unable to overcome the racism of the U.S. Episcopal Church, he moved to Jamaica in 1841, only to die a few months later. Above all, in October 1840 there was the devastating loss of Peter Williams. His funeral, carefully recorded by the still-functioning *Colored American*, was truly impres-

sive. In attendance were the city's most prominent Episcopal clergymen, among them the rectors of Trinity Church, Christ Church, St.
George's Chapel, and St. John's Church. Amazingly, the funeral sermon
was delivered by Bishop Onderdonk, the very same man who had forced
Williams to retreat from his antislavery activism and prevented Isaiah
DeGrasse and Alexander Crummell from attending the General Theological Seminary. Amazingly too, students from the seminary, who only
a few years earlier had objected to DeGrasse's presence, formed part
of the funeral procession. The black community turned out en masse.
Marching in the procession were Williams's family, St. Philip's vestry,
members of literary societies, students from the colored schools, and the
general public.[1]

Yet for a fraction of New York's black community, the late 1840s
and 1850s were years of phenomenal success. Self-consciously identifying as an aristocracy, determined to find an economic niche for themselves despite the city's rigorous competitiveness, and eager to prove to
the world that they too could achieve, this new generation of the black
elite thrived. Peter Guignon was still struggling, but Philip was rapidly
coming into his own.

Peter Ray and the Lorillard Tobacco Company

The 1840s proved to be difficult years for Peter. Rebecca died after a
few short years of marriage. I haven't been able to find out anything
about her death. It haunts me. When and how did my great-great-
grandmother die? Where is she buried? Why didn't Williamson say
more about her in his genealogy? Why did Maritcha never mention her?

Sometime around 1847, Peter married Cornelia Ray. Their wedding date had to be after Elizabeth's birth in 1842 but before that of
their son Peter in 1849. By marrying into the prominent Ray family,
Peter made an even greater leap up the social ladder than he had with
the Marshalls. But although this marriage gave him status, it didn't
bring economic stability. While his former classmates pursued a higher
education and became doctors, teachers, ministers, and small businessmen, it's difficult to figure out exactly what Peter was doing.

Peter is listed in the city directory for the first time in 1845 as a porter, and then in 1846–47 as being in "segars." Why cigars? I have two tentative explanations. James Guignon is listed in the city directories as a tobacconist on Chatham Street from 1804 until the 1820s. If he was indeed Peter's father, it's possible that someone in the family still had contacts in the tobacco business and decided to help Peter out. Maybe that contact was a Lorillard, since Peter Lorillard's first shop was located close by on Chatham Street. Or maybe it was Peter's new father-in-law, Peter Ray.

Peter Ray was one of the black community's most respected members. He had been active at St. Philip's since its inception, serving as the vestry's senior warden for all but two years between 1843 and 1862. He worked tirelessly on behalf of black education, cajoling the public school system into hiring black teachers. Above all, Ray had steady employment and a steady income. He spent his entire life working in Peter and George Lorillard's tobacco company, beginning as an errand boy in 1811 and ending as a general superintendent in the company's new factory in Jersey City until his death in 1882. Ray profited from white patronage in a relationship that was as equitable as he could have hoped for, undoubtedly because he brought a special skill to his employers, which they recognized and rewarded accordingly.[2]

Sometimes it pays to be distracted while doing research. After reading about Ray's connection with the Lorillards in his obituary, I went to the Arents Collection at the New York Public Library to find out more about New York's tobacco industry. There I found a small notebook written for the Lorillards, titled "Receipts, chiefly for curing tobacco and preparing snuff," and began poring through its many handwritten receipts. When I got to blank pages midway through the notebook, I assumed there was nothing else in it. Returning the notebook, I mistakenly picked it up upside down, and it fell open to a new front page. It read in its entirety:

Peter Wray or Ray
    Is the name of the mulatto man who sorts out the tobacco for Lorillard, and who is so great a judge of Leaf Tobacco, and which will do best for snuff and which for cutting

for smoking and chewing tobacco. To find him look in the
New York Directory or ask one of Lorillards men. 27 december 1842, he was working for Lorillard in his factory in Laurens St. New York.[3]

I can only call this a case of dumb luck. The note confirmed my suspicion
that Ray was indeed indispensable to the Lorillards' business.

Peter and George Lorillard got their leaf tobacco from the South,
mostly from Virginia and Kentucky. Once picked, stemmed, and cured,
tobacco leaves were pressed into hogsheads measuring approximately
thirty-eight by fifty-four inches. They were then either rolled down the
road hitched to a wagon or swung onto ships to be transported to tobacco manufacturing centers. The principal destinations were southern
states—Virginia, Kentucky, Tennessee, North Carolina, Missouri—but
also New York City. Once unloaded, the hogsheads were taken to a
warehouse for auction. Complaining of insufficient space to conduct
public sales of tobacco, George Lorillard and other dealers petitioned
the Common Council in 1824 to allow auctions at the foot of Fly Market Street, close to the spot that had once been New Amsterdam's principal slave market.[4]

It was said that the Lorillards bought their tobacco in person. But
if Peter Ray was such a great judge of leaf tobacco, I'm sure they took
him with them. They would begin by opening the hogsheads. Ray would
carefully inspect the leaves for quality, and decide which to buy. He had
to select with great care, for the Lorillards put their tobacco to many
different uses, either reselling the leaves in their Chatham Street store
or manufacturing various products in their factory. The Lorillards followed fashion, making whatever pleased their customers. Initially, they
manufactured tobacco for pipe smoking, but by the early decades of the
nineteenth century they were producing snuff. By the 1840s, they had
turned to cigars as well as chewing tobacco. And of course much later
there were cigarettes.

The Lorillard company was renowned for its snuff. Taking snuff
had come from France and Britain to the United States, where it was
first fashionable among the upper classes before filtering down to com-

Peter A. Lorillard, lithograph by Auguste Edouart, 1840 (National Portrait
Gallery, Smithsonian Institution; gift of Robert L. McNeil, Jr.)

moners. Both men and women used it. The snuff user placed a small
amount of tobacco between forefinger and thumb, held it against one
nostril and then the other, inhaled, and then expelled the tobacco into
a handkerchief. The goal was to provoke a sneeze that simulated sexual
pleasure.[5]

The Lorillards had a secret recipe for making Maccoby Snuff, and
many believed that Ray was in on the secret. I found the recipe spelled
out in great detail in the Lorillard notebook, so I'll share it with you.
Condensing its sixty-odd pages, it goes something like this:

> Buy a mixture of tobacco leaf from Kentucky and Virginia,
> preferably around two years old, and make sure it's not too
> ripe but is as sweet as possible. Cut off the butts, or heads,

and pile the leaves in a dry place for three to four months. Then put the leaves in bins for casing or curing, wetting it with liquor (rum, gin, or brandy) and salt water. To make the dry composition, add one tablespoonful refined gum camphor ("get best kind"), coarse salt ("roast it a good deal like coffee"), one tablespoonful gum Arabic ("you had better get the best gum and pound it yourself"), one tablespoon Gum Guiac ("avoid the black, tarry flavored kind, pay the druggist a little extra"). Be sure not to omit any ingredients: camphor gives life and power, and burnt salt flavor, while gum Arabic imparts a sweet taste and Gum Guiac sneezing power. To finish, add all the ingredients to a quart of high-proof alcohol and mix in the tobacco leaves.

The snuff user then bought whatever quantity of the mixture he or she desired and stored it in a covered jar. To sell wholesale, the Lorillards devised the method of packing the snuff into dried and tanned animal bladders, which they probably got from their brother Jacob.

In addition to their manufacturing skills, the Lorillards were innovative advertisers. Like other manufacturers, their father Pierre first advertised through word of mouth, newspapers, and window displays. But, ever in search of competitive advantage, the next generation took to direct mail campaigning. They printed broadsides itemizing their products and sent them to postmasters throughout the United States, who promptly spread the word. When unethical competitors started using these broadsides to push their own inferior products, the Lorillards created private labels and branded theirs according to quality. The labels themselves soon became commodities and were collected as trading cards. Some were pretty racy. For example, Magdalen Smoking Tobacco featured a buxom young woman with flowing hair lying down on cushions. Others had racist overtones. Century Fine Cut depicted Nature, represented by an angelic white woman, delivering tobacco to a seated, passive Native American surrounded by chattering monkeys. The Lorillards came up with still one more invention when dealers in chewing tobacco tried to pass off their "plugs" as a Lorillard brand. They made discs out of tin, stamped them with a brand name, and clamped one on each plug. Some of these "tin tags" carried anodyne labels like Good Smoke, but others bore more dubious names like Climax.[6]

His income was decent and his job assured, but did Peter Ray ever wonder whether he was compromising his deeply held abolitionist principles by relying on the patronage of white manufacturers who traded in a slave crop? It was slaves who produced the tobacco, first picking it in fields, then slinging hogsheads onto boats and hauling them up and down the river.[7] It was his employers who bought the crop from slave owners, and then cultivated them as customers when they came north for the summer by advertising directly to them in *DeBow's Review*.

Did Ray find the Lorillard advertisements, with their suggestive racist and sexual overtones, offensive to his moral sensibilities? Did he worry that he was betraying his temperance beliefs? Worldly Knickerbockers like Grant Thorburn defended the pleasures of smoking, freely confessing to "enjoying the cheap and sober luxury of a pipe." But many African Americans and abolitionists were temperance men and women, who decried the use of stimulants as yet another form of enslavement. They railed against alcohol and tobacco alike. "Tobacco and Rum!" the white abolitionist Gerrit Smith fumed in a letter to the *Liberator*. "What terrible twin brothers! What mighty agents of Satan! What a large share of the American people they are destroying!"[8]

I don't know the answer to these questions, and I certainly don't judge Ray. He had a family to feed, and a community to take care of. He put his money to good use, giving liberally to St. Philip's and supporting black education.

And the Lorillards were good employers. They hired black workers. They provided housing for Peter Ray in a framed dwelling above their Wooster Street store, as well as homes for those who worked at the snuff mill in Westchester County. When they moved their factory to Jersey City, they set up an evening school for the young and opened a library, today's Jersey City Public Library. The working conditions of their employees stood in stark contrast to cigar shops of the period in which tobacco, food, and bedding were all jumbled in one room where men, women, and child laborers all worked, ate, and slept.[9]

Pierre Toussaint, Hairdresser

Evidently, Peter Guignon did not have Ray's success in the "segar" business, because he soon switched trades. He's listed in the city directory as a hairdresser from 1847 to 1854. The 1850 census records him as living and working at 250 Greenwich Street. His household included Cornelia, his daughter Elizabeth, and the newest addition to his family, Peter Jr., as well as three young men who were also barbers.

Again, I can't explain the motives behind Peter's choice of trade except to say that maybe the Guignons intervened a second time, turning to their friends, the former *grand blanc* slaveholding Bérard family who, like them, had left Saint-Domingue at the time of the revolution and settled in New York. They brought with them several slaves, one of whom was young Pierre Toussaint. Emancipated in 1807, Toussaint became a hairdresser, built a thriving business, and bought property. He first rented space from the well-known tanning merchant Abraham Bloodgood on Reade Street before buying his own homes on Church Street and then Canal Street. Toussaint invested his profits in several of the city's fire insurance companies and, when the Great Fire struck in 1835, he lost 95 percent of his net worth, as much as $900,000 in today's money. Ever patient and long-suffering, he slowly rebuilt.

Toussaint succeeded because he was a beneficiary of white largesse, though in ways quite different from Ray. Despite the fact that he had been their slave, Toussaint remained loyal to the Bérards and their circle of friends, even paying off their debts when they lost everything in the revolution. It might be hard for us to understand such behavior but, like Ray, Toussaint had few options. He wasn't about to return to his homeland, which had already disintegrated into chaos. His French friends discouraged him from moving to Paris, where hairdressing was done largely within the household and business opportunities were limited. So he stayed put, shrewdly turning his friendship with the city's white elite families into a veritable money-making machine.

Toussaint was highly skilled in his trade. He worked out of the salon he kept in his home, but the most lucrative part of his work came from his visits to elite households, where he cut and styled the hair of men, women, and children. As contract clients, they paid him a fixed annual sum for weekly visits. Toussaint was especially talented at dressing hair for society events like weddings and balls. He kept up with the current fashion of curling women's hair, but also set new trends, for example weaving flowers into an evening hairdo.[10] It's possible that at the Bérards' and Guignons' instigation, Toussaint agreed to help young Peter Guignon.

Peter Ray and Pierre Toussaint depended on white employers and patrons to make a living. Because they were skilled in their work—unique really—they commanded loyalty, a feat Peter Guignon was never able to achieve. Peter's hairdressing shop was in the heart of the West Side's black community. He undoubtedly drew most of his customers from the neighborhood, offering a variety of services such as cutting hair, shaving men, and curling women's tresses. But here too Peter seems to have failed.

Peter and Cornelia

Peter's name does not appear in any directories for the years 1854 to 1858. I realized that he had fallen on hard times when I found a short, formal letter written by Cornelia to Albro Lyons in December 1854 in the Williamson papers. The constrained tone of her missive is heart wrenching.

> Mr Lyons
>   Sir
>   It is a matter of great embarrassment to me to keep you out of your money so long. But Peter has been rather unfortunate in having so much sickness and this is the reason that you have not had your money, as for myself I have none at present but as soon as my husband sends it, you shall have it without fail.
>   With respects,
>   C. A. Guignon

It sounds like Peter was too sick to work, and maybe even unable to provide for his family. Williamson recalled that in his youth he "often listened to the story of how Elizabeth came to visit my grandparents . . . for two weeks, and, that visit lasted for 12 years; she was a very small child at the time."[11] Maybe the money Peter owed the Lyonses was for Elizabeth's care.

Eventually, a solution was found. In 1858, Peter moved to Brooklyn and began working in the pharmacy that one of Cornelia's brothers, Samuel, had opened in Williamsburgh (now spelled Williamsburg), but left vacant when he emigrated to Liberia. That's where my great-great-grandfather could be found from 1858 until his death in 1885.

James McCune Smith: Pharmacist, Doctor, Mentor

Purely by coincidence, Peter Guignon and Philip White ended up in the same career—pharmacy—but they came to it at different moments of their lives and through different paths. Peter was a man of forty-five, and got his job through marriage ties. In contrast, Philip was only seventeen years old when he began his apprenticeship in James McCune Smith's pharmacy in 1840.

In the late 1830s Smith didn't have a moment's rest. From then until the moment of his death, he threw his energies into helping the black poor and working class. He opened a drugstore and medical practice on West Broadway, advertising in the *Colored American* services that included "Bleeding, Tooth-drawing, Cupping, and Leeching." In addition to black patients, he also treated poor whites who could not afford to be finicky about the color of their doctor's skin. Smith also took on more complicated cases, one of which he wrote up in a brief report titled "Case of Ptyalism with Fatal Termination." In collaboration with a white doctor, Smith had undertaken the care of a young woman who had a chronic hacking cough, salivated profusely, and complained of severe lower abdominal pain. The cough and pain pointed to tuberculosis, appendicitis, or a problem with the ovaries. The swollen tongue and salivation suggested a reaction to pills containing mercury. Following the treatment of the time, Smith and his colleague attempted to reduce the swelling by blistering the back of her neck, applying leeches to it as well as her throat, and cutting her tongue to let it bleed. Despite their efforts, the result was "fatal termination."[12]

Smith was also kept busy as doctor of the Colored Orphan Asylum. Convinced that the city was not doing enough to care for impoverished black children, two Quaker women, Anna Shotwell and Mary Murray, founded the asylum in 1834. Both had inherited their sense of benevolence from older male relatives active in the Manumission Society. Despite their family connections, however, Shotwell and Murray faced an uphill battle. They created an all-female Board of Managers and were immediately criticized for overstepping the bounds of feminine propriety. Citing city policy, the municipal government refused to give them any funds. But success finally came in the early 1840s when the city donated a piece of land on Fifth Avenue between Forty-third and Forty-fourth Streets to erect a new building; thereafter, the city and state governments as well as the Manumission Society began offering financial support. Until its destruction during the Draft Riots in 1863, the asylum sheltered a total of 1,257 orphans and half-orphans as well as neglected and abused children.[13]

As with the African Free Schools, the asylum's relations with the black community were ambiguous. Although it had supported separate institutions when deemed necessary, the *Colored American* railed against the asylum's segregated admissions policy as "contrary to the principles of the Bible, and at war with the best interests of our colored population. . . . They cast boundaries that are difficult to permeate." Black leaders felt left out of its operations. They complained that the asylum had wrongly taken monies from a legacy that should have gone to their own Phoenix Society. They were suspicious of its continued association with the American Colonization Society. They were dismayed when the managers dismissed matron Rachel Johnson, one of the few blacks on staff, and wondered why a white woman was chosen to replace her. They were aggrieved that the asylum, like so many other white benevolent institutions before it, seemed only interested in teaching black children basic skills and then placing them in indentures as domestics or farm hands.[14]

Nevertheless, the white women who ran the asylum were genuinely dismayed by the poor physical health of their black wards, particularly their susceptibility to infectious diseases like influenza, whooping cough, measles, tuberculosis, and smallpox. To set the black community's mind at rest, in 1843 they hired Smith to be the children's doctor. He worked tirelessly on their behalf, making frequent visits to the asylum and also taking them on country outings.

Philip White, Apprentice

Because Smith was so overextended, he took George Downing's advice and brought my great-grandfather into his pharmacy as an apprentice. Philip's tasks, as Downing noted in his eulogy, were so varied that the young man ended up learning far more than he ever would have in a larger establishment.

> The duties of a clerk under such circumstances were numerous, exacting and varying; his reading became limited to the "Dispensatory" and similar technical books; his practice included the various forms of work nowadays distributed among a set of employees, from porter at one end to first clerk at the other. This was, however, of no little advantage to the ambitious young clerk; he had to face emergencies, to assume responsibilities, and to take risks without instruction; the stock had to be kept up, prescriptions compounded, while the trade over the counter was incessant in its transactions. Many preparations that to-day may be purchased were at that time home made, and the treatment of minor ailments came legitimately within the sphere of the duties of a druggist.[15]

Philip entered the field of pharmacy at just the right moment when exciting new developments in the properties and use of drugs were taking place. Up through much of the 1830s, U.S. physicians had based their treatment of disease on drastic "depletive" remedies. During the early epidemics of yellow fever and the 1832 outbreak of cholera, they ministered to the ill by means of bleeding, sweating, vomiting, blistering, and purging. To dispense the cathartics and emetics that physicians demanded, pharmacists chose from among those drugs that were thought to be most efficacious. Rhubarb made a good strong laxative; ipecacunha was a popular emetic; opium served as an analgesic and sedative; and calomel, a mercury compound, was a great favorite because, depending on dosage and length of treatment, it could be used as a laxative, stimulant, sedative, or tonic.

The 1840s marked a critical turning point in medical treatment. Advances in chemistry were creating a more sophisticated understanding of drugs and their effects on the body. Until this point, scientists simply knew that certain plants had medicinal properties from which one could derive drugs. Now alkaloidal chemistry allowed them to identify the active agent in plants and extract it: narcotine could be obtained from opium, iodine from marine algae, emetine from ipecac, and so forth. As a result, the development of alkaloids and other chemical entities allowed physicians and pharmacists to forgo the use of crude drugs. They also began shifting toward more "supportive" treatments, letting go of drastic measures in favor of restoring the body's natural balance. While they continued to prescribe many of the same drugs, they did so in much smaller doses.[16]

Determined to keep up with these advances, Philip assiduously studied the Dispensatory. Along with the United States Pharmacopoeia, it was the pharmacist's bible. Philip probably used the 1833 Dispensatory compiled by two eminent Philadelphia physicians, which incorporated all the latest pharmaceutical findings. It introduced the new drugs, described how they operated on the body on a scientific, rather than a trial-and-error, basis, and underscored the importance of variables such as temperature and solubility. Since Smith advertised Shaker herbs, Philip also needed to study Shaker catalogs that listed as many as 170 plants—whiteroot, bugle weed, Indian hemp, thimble weed, belladonna, poppies, valerian, and the like—many of which were not recognized in the Dispensatory.[17]

Philip worked long hours fulfilling tasks that, as Downing noted,

ranged across a wide spectrum of pharmaceutical duties. As the renowned Philadelphia pharmacist Edward Parrish later remembered, in
this era "in many instances the hands that received and opened the
case of rhubarb, opium or assafoetida fresh from off the ship, in turn
dispensed these remedies in pill-box or vial to the suffering invalid."
The apprentice, he noted wryly, "enjoyed a wholesome development of
muscle through wielding the ponderous pestle, handling the sieves and
working the screw press." To make up pills with a cathartic action, for
example, clerks had to powder drugs like sodium bicarbonate, tartaric
acid, Rochelle salt, and aloes in large mortars. If an enema was called
for, they were obliged to prepare the enema apparatus themselves. They
needed to find a supply of bladders, then tie a pipe securely into the neck
of each, and finally send it out with the irrigation solution.[18]

Downing insisted that Philip's apprenticeship in Smith's pharmacy made him "more self-reliant than he could have possibly become
in the same time in a larger store, with more clerks and an apparent increase in facilities. Here he formed his habits of application, of industry,
and his perseverance and steadiness were developed and strengthened."
In these early days of trade and entrepreneurship, clerks—regardless of
their race or ethnicity—were encouraged not only to learn technical
knowledge and business savvy but also to abide by the virtues of hard
work and honesty. There existed what could be called a clerk's culture
that promoted moral and righteous living or, in the parlance of the day,
the cultivation of character. These same values were the bedrock of the
black community. Indeed, Philip might well have accompanied George
Downing, one of the Reason brothers, or even his future father-in-law
several years earlier to Philomathean Hall to listen to James Fields's lecture, "Decision of Character."

> To one at all versed in reading prominent traits of character,
> nothing is more interesting, than the discovery of the germ
> of a prompt and decided character in a young man or woman
> just starting in life, honestly determined by industry, integ-
> rity and perseverance, to earn a position among their fellow
> men, at once honorable and useful.—Self-reliant, yet diffi-
> dent of their real abilities, they early win the respect and con-

fidence of every good and true benefactor of the world, and find on all sides, friends to cheer and comfort them.[19]

Fields's language here eerily foreshadows Downing's a half century later.

Without question, Philip possessed a "decided character," because his next move was a bold one. In 1842 he applied and was accepted to the College of Pharmacy of the City of New York, from which he graduated in 1844, being, as his obituary in the *New York Age* proudly proclaimed, "the first man of our race to receive a diploma from that institution."[20] Like Ray and Toussaint, Philip took advantage of white patronage, albeit in the form of an institution rather than an individual. I believe his motivations were many: the sheer pleasure of studying pharmacy; his aspiration to excel as both a healer and a entrepreneur and thus earn a position "at once honorable and useful"; his determination to build up contacts among white businessmen whose acquaintance might stand him in good stead in later years. Maybe memories of his father, that "stern old English gentleman," as Downing called him, convinced Philip that with hard work and discipline he could achieve any goal he set for himself.

The College of Pharmacy of the City of New York

In the summer of 1829, the city's most reputable pharmacists gathered together at the Shakespeare Tavern. The purpose: to establish a College of Pharmacy modeled after the one in Philadelphia. The reason: to create a better educated class of pharmacists than presently existed in the city. For much of the nineteenth century, pharmacy occupied a fluid status midway between trade and profession. No special training was required to become a druggist and no restrictive legislation existed to regulate the compounding and selling of drugs. The Pharmacopoeia and Dispensatory were merely tools that the pharmacist could choose to use—or not. Pharmacy was seen as an entrepreneurial field in which an ambitious young man—of any class, ethnicity, and, it would seem, race—could readily make a name for himself.[21]

Many aspects of the current state of pharmacy disturbed the college's founders. One was the vast numbers of nostrums, or quack drugs, that flooded the market. Another was the poor quality of legitimate drugs, a number of which were imported from abroad. In the mid-1840s, members of the college conducted a vigorous campaign against the "Blue Pill" brought from England and containing so little mercury as to render it useless. Additionally, despite the availability of the Pharmacopoeia and Dispensatory, drug formularies varied widely, and too many pharmacists remained ignorant of advances in pharmaceutical chemistry. Most troubling of all was the high incidence of deaths due to accidental drug poisoning. The college's founders were convinced that the study and practice of pharmacy should and could be modernized. They set up a course of study for aspiring students who, after graduation, would be eligible to become members of the college, which now served as a professional association for New York's pharmacists.[22]

To be admitted to the college as a student, Philip needed to fulfill a two-year apprenticeship and take one full course of study. Once accepted, he followed a two-year curriculum consisting of three subjects. Philip was fortunate because his two professors were men of great distinction newly appointed to the college. Laurence Reid from the University of Edinburgh taught chemistry; he served on the college's Committee of Inspection and helped expose the fraudulent "Blue Pill." Benjamin McCready was professor of both pharmacy and materia medica. Whereas pharmacy dealt with the preparation and dispensing of drugs, materia medica covered much the same terrain as the U.S. Dispensatory, listing all the names of plants and describing their origins, parts, and properties.[23] Students typically found the course dry and didactic, but with all his prior reading of the Dispensatory, Philip probably thought it quite easy.

The requirements for graduation were straightforward: students needed to show proof of an additional two years of apprenticeship (four in all) and satisfactory performance in all courses. In addition, they were required to present an "original thesis on some article of the Materia Medica, or a chemical analysis of some substance conducted by himself," and take an oral examination administered by the professors. A two-thirds vote by the trustees present was necessary to pass.[24] Out of

Philip Augustus White

an entering class of twenty-eight, Philip was one of four graduating students.

I wondered about the college's racial politics and hoped I would come across some mention of Philip in its archives. The problem was that I couldn't find any records, and historians of American pharmacy told me they had probably long since disappeared. I refused to give up, however, and when I was informed that the Wisconsin Historical Society held the most comprehensive pharmacy archives in the nation, I decided to take a trip to Madison. My stubbornness paid off. The college's papers were indeed there, and Philip's name was indeed listed for both admission and graduation. There was no reference to Philip's race. It appeared that the trustees were as progressive in matters of race as they were in their profession. I attributed such racial tolerance to pharmacy's entrepreneurial nature, its emphasis on ambition and industriousness over social background, and its internationalism. Several trustees were of European parentage or had themselves immigrated to the United States; if American born, they had traveled abroad to train in French and German schools and may well have assimilated Europeans' more tolerant racial attitudes.

But when I went back over the trustees' minutes pertaining to graduation, I found myself reading between the lines. Who was Secretary John Meakim referring to when he wrote in the March 14, 1844, minutes that "the secretary presented the name of an additional candidate for the diploma," and then listed the four students? Was the addition Philip or one of the other young men? And was there any particular reason why the members' meeting for conferring the degrees was postponed from March 21 to March 28 for lack of a quorum? Finally, should any particular significance be attached to the fact that Meakim did not leave enough space to write the names of all four candidates on one line, but had to make an insertion above it?[25] I can only speculate. Meakim's note might have been totally innocent, or it could have referred to any one of the other candidates. Yet it's also possible that the trustees had not fully thought through the implications of Philip's admission. The college's graduation rates were low because there were no real incentives—financial or professional—to obtain a pharmacy diploma. Unaware of Philip's decided character, the trustees may have assumed that he would be one of the many students who would drop out, and were caught up short when he fulfilled all the requirements. Maybe, after considerable deliberation, they concluded that their only ethical choice was to grant him the degree. If so, they were determined to handle the consequences more carefully. By May of that year, two of Philip's fellow graduates were accepted as members of the college; it would take my great-grandfather thirty years.

By 1847, Philip had opened his own drugstore and placed a simple advertisement in the very first issue of Frederick Douglass's *North Star*, right below that of James McCune Smith: "Philip A. White, Druggist, corner of Frankfort and Gold Street."[26] That was the very same spot where his father had kept his grocery for one brief year in the 1830s. The landlord might have remembered the White family and been happy to rent to Thomas's son, viewing the serious, hard-working young man as a model tenant. Philip kept that corner location until his death in 1891.

I don't think that Philip counted on financial aid from others. Some five years later at an interracial antislavery convention, James McCune Smith angrily charged white abolitionists with having consistently failed to help blacks in need. He cited "the case of a smart young man who had been an apprentice in his drug store, and he got his diploma in colleges. He asked $500 from John Rankin to assist him. It was refused."[27] John Rankin was the same man who had joined forces with the Tappan brothers at the Chatham Street Chapel when their activism touched off the 1834 riots. That young man might well have been Philip White.

Enterprising Blacks

In the February 11, 1848, issue of the *North Star*, Bostonian William C. Nell recorded his impressions of a visit to New York, noting with great pride that he had "visited the Apothecary's Hall of Dr. James McCune Smith, in West Broadway, as also the establishment of Mr. Philip White in Frankfort Street, both of whom are practical men and conduct their business, preparing medicines, etc., etc., etc. with as much readiness and skill as any other disciple of Galen and Hippocrates. . . . [They] are proving their capacity, as I believe, to their pecuniary benefit, and at the same time thus elevating the character of those with whom they are identified by complexion." Some four years later, writing to *Frederick Douglass' Paper* (the successor to the *North Star*) under the pen name Ethiop, Brooklyn schoolteacher William J. Wilson reiterated much the same sentiments: "Quite a combination of enterprising blacks are beginning to appear. They begin to take their places in every pursuit about town and country; and as their thoughts and sympathies partake of their varied and independent occupations, they naturally form an active and efficient business class." Ethiop then added one new word. "I call it," he pronounced, "an ARISTOCRACY."[28]

As he built up his pharmaceutical practice, Philip joined other enterprising blacks to help form this black aristocracy. In many respects, their origins, methods, and values were similar to those of early Knickerbockers. Despite stark differences in race, educational level, and socioeconomic status, both groups constituted what George Foster, the city's greatest observer of the day, termed a "shopkeeping aristocracy."[29]

This new aristocracy was by and large better educated, more professional, and more entrepreneurial than that of William Hamilton's generation. I was astonished by the number of men of science it contained, drawn perhaps to pharmacy and medicine not only because of the money that could be made but also because of the skills demanded, the prestige accrued, and most importantly the power to heal. Besides Smith, Peter Guignon, and Philip, there were also two doctors, Peter's new brother-in-law, Peter Williams Ray, and the youngest DeGrasse son, John, both determined to defy the unwritten rules through which the medical profession policed its borders.

Beyond science, the elite included other professions: teachers like Charles Reason, Ransom Wake, and John Peterson; ministers like Charles Ray and Alexander Crummell; businessmen like engraver Patrick Reason, Peter Vogelsang, manager of steamers on the Albany line, jewelry dealer Edward Clarke, pickle maker Henry Scott, and restaurateur Thomas van Rensselaer. But the elite was broad enough to encompass tradesmen who, Maritcha wrote in her memoir, held jobs as "carpenters, undertakers, printers, shoemakers, tinsmiths, crockery and china ware dealers." To make ends meet, women often worked outside the home. Maritcha's mother was a hairdresser before her marriage. After she was widowed, Grandmother Marshall converted the basement of her home into a bakery, and later decided "to work abroad to support herself and family." "She always said her employers were of the 'quality,'" Maritcha continued. "Five days a week she toiled outside of her home, Saturdays she reserved for domestic duties; on Sunday, she kept the 'sabbath'; this meant a scrupulous avoidance of all but the most necessary secular labor."[30]

Although wealthier than the earlier generation, this new black aristocracy obviously never made as much money or achieved similar status in trade or profession as their white counterparts. Moses Beach's

1855 compilation of New York's wealthiest citizens listed Peter Lorillard Jr. as worth $2 million. Reliable accounts of black wealth are harder
to come by. Like the Knickerbockers, the black aristocracy understood
that, just as much as personal income, investment in real estate was a
path to wealth. Boyd's Tax Book for 1856 and 1857 valued Philip White's
real estate at $9,300, Henry Scott's at $9,125, James McCune Smith's
at $7,734, and Charles Ray's at $3,000. A report from the late 1850s
claimed that the total value of the real estate on which the thousand
most prominent black citizens paid taxes was $1.4 million, while the
total of their deposits in savings banks was estimated at $1.12 million.
Added together, the amount was barely more than that of Peter Lorillard alone.[31] Many of course had much less, and all remained conscious
of the fragility of their financial status. Peter and Cornelia Guignon, we
may remember, were unable to repay Albro Lyons's loan.

This new elite was determined to prove to whites that they were
just as capable of succeeding in what New York valued the most—entrepreneurship. So, to a greater extent than William Hamilton's generation, but much like their Knickerbocker counterparts, they preached a
Protestant gospel of hard work, asserting that business was *the* path to
success, and that trade and profit were *the* most efficacious means of garnering respect and, in due course, political and civil equality.

Wealth, however, was not the most important criterion for admission to the elite. Its members still cherished the traditional values of
"character" and "respectability." Character meant not only cultivating
what James Fields had called "decision," but also promoting piety, temperance, moral development. Respectability was the outward manifes-
tation of character, conduct marked by sobriety, modesty, industriousness. And, despite what historians like to say, skin color had little to do
with respectability. True, Philip was so light-skinned he could pass for
white, but Crummell, Garnet, and Wilson were very dark, and Smith
was somewhere in the middle.

Elite men bonded in all-male venues such as the African Society for
Mutual Relief as well as Freemasonry and Odd Fellowship, which Philip
had just joined. They further cemented these bonds through matrimo-
nial ties, marrying within their class. Many unions resulted from con-

nections made at the African Free School; Peter and Albro married the Marshall daughters, sisters of their former classmate Edward. George Downing and Peter Vogelsang were also married to sisters, Downing to Serena DeGrasse and Vogelsang to Theodocia (named after Aaron Burr's daughter). Their families worshiped at particular churches and formed their own social circles.

St. Philip's, Church of the Black Elite

Looking back on her childhood, Maritcha explained how the elite's social life depended on "a main general distinction—persons attending the same church usually confined their intimate intercourse with members of that congregation." For most, that church was St. Philip's. Peter Guignon and Philip White worshiped there, as did many of the Mulberry Street School graduates—James McCune Smith, Alexander Crummell, Isaiah DeGrasse, Albro Lyons, George Downing, the Reason brothers, to name but a few. It was at St. Philip's that Peter married Rebecca (and Albro married Mary Joseph) in 1840. And it was there that after the tragic death of his son in 1865 "the natural ardor of the man," according to Crummell's obituary, "quickened into a religious zeal," making Peter one of its most valued members. It was at St. Philip's that Philip White became a communicant in 1844. He remained, in Maritcha's words, "an assiduous and devoted son of the church until his decease. For more than forty years, his time, thoughts, energies and resources were at the service of his spiritual mother. No event occurred without having the stamp of his individuality."[32]

The city's second largest black congregation, St. Philip's was located in the middle of Centre Street. An 1840 report on colored churches noted that it was well placed for just about all black New Yorkers. The building itself was not the original one. The first structure, made of wood, burned to the ground shortly after being completed, and was replaced by a solid brick building. Badly damaged during the 1834 riot, by 1840 it was fully restored. The renovated church in the Federal style was approximately three thousand square feet, its exterior plain, without a steeple or cross. The sanctuary could hold up to 2,000 people even though the congregation numbered only 350 members. The interior still lacked "all the modern improvements," yet, the report insisted, it was "exceedingly neat and comfortable" and "characterized by simplicity, good taste and economy."[33]

Many motives attracted the black elite to the Episcopal faith. Some were religious: the beauty of High Church rituals, the purity of its doctrines, the sense of belonging to an ancient and universal tradition that reached back to the first apostles. Others were more secular. St. Philip's mother church, Trinity, was the place of worship for members of the white elite, George Lorillard and Philip Hone among them. Many of St. Philip's early congregants had close ties to Trinity. In guarded language, Maritcha observed that the "quality" families at Trinity "employed exclusively colored servants. To these they were not merely masters and mistresses in the conventional sense, but guardians and censors of manners if not morals. In more than one case even a closer connection obtained."[34] Blacks who had such relationships might well have chosen to remain with the denomination of white family members. They might have hoped that continued religious association with the city's governing elite might garner them political or social advantages.

In contrast to the Anglican Communion, the Episcopal Church was a fairly democratic institution. Laity voted with clergy on matters of importance. Parishioners were not taxed. Moreover, St. Philip's itself was a big tent. If it was home to the black elite, it was also home to the black poor, welcoming the families of unskilled workers—laborers, porters, washers, bootcleaners, sailors, cartmen. Each individual, each family contributed according to their own abilities. Bricklayers and painters rebuilt the church. Cleaners and laundresses took responsibility for the condition of the carpets and the clergy's vestments.

Still, it was the elite that governed St. Philip's through election to the vestry. In 1840, "old heads" like Thomas Downing, Peter Ray, and Ransom Wake were vestrymen. But the younger generation was not far behind. James McCune Smith was elected to the vestry in 1843 and Philip White in 1850. Using the skills they had acquired in business, vestrymen oversaw church finances—buying and selling property, improving the church building, maintaining the cemetery, renting out pews, supporting the sick, needy, and destitute. They did so well that, as Maritcha proudly declared, they "demonstrate[d] the governing capacity of a so-called under race; it show[ed] successful government of the people, by and for the people."[35]

Social Circles: Salons, Friendship Albums

Maritcha's memoir offers a rare and fascinating glimpse into the social lives of the black elite. It tells of the pleasures they enjoyed despite the harsh conditions under which they labored. And it emphasizes the special role of elite women in defining the boundaries, norms, and behavior of their class. "Among the friends of our family," Maritcha wrote, "were two circles founded on personal preference; these were led respectively by Mrs. Clorice Esteve Reason [Charles Reason's wife] and Mrs. Elizabeth West Bowers. The former gathered about her the studious and conservative and kept open house for all visitors of note; the latter was surrounded by the mirth of loving folks, young and old. In this coterie, not to have a good time was impossible. . . . To Mrs. Reason belonged the honor of being able to 'hold a salon'; her strain of French blood made her a queen of entertainers and covered her with a taste in social functions that was irreproachable."

Many pages later, Maritcha added a third woman, her mother, to her list: "Mother was the life of a minor group of young single and married folks who found in her a social woman whose company was as agreeable as when she was a maiden; with her it was possible to have a good time without 'fuss and feathers.' Her guests were frequent, they danced played or sung, played games or sewed for charity and all alike found many an opportunity to pass many delightful hours with her in the home where courtesy, sociability and friendliness reigned supreme." It was permissible, Maritcha observed, for families to move from one circle to another: "No hard and fast lines were drawn, however, the same persons could be met, now in one circle, now in the other." But outsiders were not welcome.[36]

Maybe one of Mary Joseph Lyons's guests brought a friendship album on one of her visits. Like the salon, friendship albums were the special province of elite women through which they created other, more diffuse social circles. The private possessions of a single person, these albums were nevertheless quasi-public documents, circulating from friend to friend, home to home, neighborhood to neighborhood, and even city to city. They functioned as yet another meeting place for members of the elite to display and promote the values they so cherished: respectability, character, modesty, literary knowledge. Owned exclusively by women, men were occasional contributors. Similar to scrapbooks, the albums were made up of various items—poems, essays, letters, watercolors—which dealt with the female themes of friendship, marriage, motherhood, domesticity, piety.

The few albums that have survived were kept by Philadelphia women in the late 1830s and early 1840s, a fact that once again underscores the greater absence of New York women from the archives. Black New Yorkers do appear in the albums, but only as contributors, not owners. One album belonged to Martina Dickerson and contains several poems submitted by Rebecca Peterson. Peter Williams Jr.'s daughter, Amy Matilda Cassey, who had moved from New York to Philadelphia after her marriage to the prominent merchant Joseph Cassey in 1828, owned a second album; its pages are graced by entries from four Mulberry Street School graduates, James McCune Smith, Isaiah De-Grasse, and the two Reason brothers.[37]

The very term friendship album connotes intimacy. If that's true, these albums offer intimacy at a distance, once again refusing to shed light on the private, inner lives of nineteenth-century black New Yorkers. Whether contributed by women or men, the majority of the pieces were not original but copied from works of favorite writers. They tell us less about the personal emotions of the contributors and more about what they valued: literary knowledge of eighteenth- and nineteenth-century authors, the aesthetic sensibility their works reflected, and the moral values they embodied. Study Rebecca Peterson's entries, for example. Whether original or not, her poem to Martina Dickerson on friendship is highly stylized, revealing little of her true feelings for her friend. The copied poem "On My Lady's Writing" by Anna Barbauld is a commentary on proper feminine values. The poetic speaker praises the lady's penmanship, connecting its evenness to both her subject's inner self—her steady temper and strong judgment—and her outer appearance of neat dress and graceful manners.[38]

The Reason brothers copied male authors. Charles excerpted lines from Wordsworth's "Excursion" as well as from the lesser known Scottish poet Robert Pollock's "The Course of Time," which asserted that "true happiness had no localities; no tones provincial; no peculiar garb"; it resides instead wherever charity and sympathy are to be found. Patrick's entry consisted of a paragraph from Washington Irving's short story "The Wife." In it, he deftly married originality to copying by reproducing Irving's words in artistically fanciful characters. Yet his choice of story was itself impersonal, unless taken as a cautionary tale. It's about a wealthy man's fear of confessing to his young wife that he has lost all his money, and her loving acceptance when he finally does. This was not the Casseys' fate, but perhaps Patrick was preparing Amy Matilda for that eventuality.

James McCune Smith and Isaiah DeGrasse submitted original pieces, but neither entry betrayed any personal feelings. Smith wrote a poem about Scotland's river Clyde and its environs as a place of freedom. In a short essay, DeGrasse argued that far from being a religion of gloominess and despondency, Christianity was "nought but affability, cheerfulness, benevolence" visiting "alike palaces of grandeur and cottages of poverty." His most intimate comment, if that's what it can be called, came in his concluding paragraph: "Such is religion, and, Mrs. Cassey, may all its golden pleasures, and choicest blessings ever hover around, and breathe her hallowed influences within your delightful and hospitable dwelling."[39]

Black Broadway

Respectability invited simple pleasures, but extravagance was frowned upon. In one of his "Ethiop" columns in *Frederick Douglass' Paper*, William J. Wilson described with a strange mixture of pride and repulsion the cultural excesses of the black community's entertainment district, Church Street, "alias (black) Broadway":

St Charles, St. Dennis, and Eldorado [hotels] are here. Talk
not of your Astor, and your Irving House. In one respect,
they are but the mere shadows; the substance is here. Pleasure here is neither mockery, nor is she mocked. Enter one
of these resorts, and behold, for yourself, my dear sir. Rose-
wood and marble tables, spring sofas, and wilton covers, are
scattered around in confused order; fashionable books, peri-
odicals, and papers of the day, theatre bills and opera cards,
are strewed about like autumn leaves. Easy chairs that yield
to your touch, ere you are fairly seated in them; Billiard-
tables, Pianos, Sporting-Rings, and Debating-Galleries; in
fine, all the requisites for fancy gentlemen are here. Wealth
may be found at your Astor, and your Irving, but easy negligence, careless abandonment and refined freedom may be
studied here. . . . If you would know the height of fashion,
you can as well learn it there, as in upper tendom. Patent
leather boots and claret coats, tight pants and pointed col-
lars, French wrappers, and Scotch shawls, diamond rings and
studded breast-pins, gold watches and California chains, all
are exhibited here, from finer forms, and with more taste,
than above Bleecker Street. Better Wines and Claret, better
Champaign, and Havannas are to be had here too. No smug-
gling in of second quality; all are good judges. Most of the
whites of your Astor, Irving, Howard and like resorts, are
fresh from the country. Money they have, but good judges
of these luxuries, never.

Ethiop judged black Broadway and its "fancy gentlemen" superior in
taste and refinement to white Broadway and the "upper tendom" (the
elite of the elite) living above Bleecker Street. But he also looked askance
at the confusion and carelessness that such high living engendered.

An appetite for luxury too easily resulted in the frittering away of
energies needed for more serious endeavors. "Oh, sir," Ethiop lamented,
"if the inclination of these young men could be changed, if the congregated motive power could be made available, what might not be done
in a very short space of time, for the improvement of our people! Here

are the requisites for a mighty people. Here are bone and muscle and intellect; and above all, life and vivacity; great power of endurance, notwithstanding this pernicious hot-house and pot-house culture."[40]

Just as damaging was the possibility that white observers might deem such manifestations of black leisure proof of the racial stereotypes they held. In 1852, southern visitor William Bobo published a damning account of the goings-on of Church Street. "Suppose we go in," he suggested, beckoning his readers into the St. Charles hotel. "Passing through a long dark passage we enter a drinking saloon. Here seated around a large table, sit a party of negroes, playing cards and drinking rum after the most approved style. The barkeeper is the proprietor. The others are gentlemen 'ob town,' who spend their leisure hours and dollars at the St. Charles Exchange. Some of these gents are moneyed men, and board at this hotel . . . probably with their 'wife,' upon the European manner of living." Black New Yorkers, Bobo suggested, were totally devoid of respectability. To counter men like him, the black elite counseled a course of action similar to that of an 1837 resolution demanding that "it behooves us to place the most careful watch over our own demeanor, living down, by consistent and virtuous conduct, every charge which may be brought against us."[41]

James Hewlett, Play Actor

Nobody, absolutely nobody, was exempt from adhering to these social norms. The phrase "careful watch over our own demeanor" could be interpreted as the black elite's desire to regulate the behavior of the masses. But it also referred to their belief that respectability was a means of social advancement for all. By behaving respectably, they would prove to racists like Bobo, who maintained that blacks were permanently fixed by nature in an underdeveloped, primitive state, just how wrong they were. Through education, hard work, and perseverance they would show that blacks were capable of the same achievements as whites.

Infractions incurred harsh penalties and could lead to ostracism, even from one's own family. In combing through Williamson's genealogical charts, I came across a reference to Elizabeth Hewlett's

James Hewlett as Richard III in imitation of Edmund Kean,
engraving by I. Scoles (Portrait Prints, Harvard Theatre Collection,
Houghton Library, Harvard University)

brother, James, my great-great-great-granduncle. Williamson's nota-
tion is tentative, handwritten rather than typed, and it claimed a failure of memory, almost as if the genealogist didn't want to acknowledge
the man on paper: "which of the above James Hewlett was related I do
not now recall, but it was the custom to place, in the early days, a 'play
actor' in the circle of very undesirable folks and in accordance with that
sentiment, Hewlett was practically disowned by his family."[42]

The details of James Hewlett's acting career are fascinating but
incomplete. Here too, it seems that it was racial politics—not natural
primitiveness—that hampered Hewlett's career. He was a member of
the African Grove Theater formed by William Brown in 1821. Initially,
the African Grove was simply a "tea garden" in Brown's backyard where
black New Yorkers congregated for musical events and social activities.
Once the theater company was formed, it played in different rented
downtown locations until Brown opened his own space on Mercer
Street in 1822. From then until the early 1830s, Hewlett performed with
Brown's company, and also in many other venues—close to home at the
Military Garden in Brooklyn, somewhat farther afield in Philadelphia,
Saratoga, and Alexandria, Virginia, and even across the seas in London and South America. Hewlett aspired to be a pure Shakespearean
actor; he played the lead role in *Richard III* and also gave solo performances of scenes from *Othello*. Much like other budding actors of the
day, he honed his craft by imitating famous Shakespearean performers
like Edmund Kean. Some of Hewlett's other roles were more explicitly
subversive, however, indirectly hinting at the subordination and resistance of minority groups: the Native American warrior chief in the bal-
let *Pantomine Asama,* the insurrectionist leader of *King Shotaway; or the
Insurrection of the Caribs,* the anticolonial lyrics of nationalist Scottish
ballads.[43]

Black New Yorkers flocked to performances at the African Grove
Theater. So it might not have been Hewlett's acting or even his politics that his family found so offensive; Grandmother Marshall might
have enjoyed watching her brother in the roles of Richard III or King
Shotaway. But racism made theatergoing a dangerous activity. From the
start, white New Yorkers were hostile to Brown's enterprise. They complained about noise from the tea garden. They objected to the theater's

staging of Shakespeare's most popular play of the day, and they resented Brown's aggressive recruitment of white customers. In 1822, conflict burst out into the open. The police raided the theater during a January performance and arrested the actors. A group of rowdy whites followed suit in August, storming the theater and causing a riot. Hewlett seems to have escaped bodily harm, although Brown was severely beaten.[44]

It's also true that Hewlett could single-handedly stir up plenty of bad publicity that must have made his family cringe. First, there were uncomplimentary reports (possibly true, possibly not) about his performances that smacked of the stereotype of the childlike, primitive black. Pamphleteer Simon Snipes insisted that when Hewlett sang ballads, he translated the lyrics into black dialect, reciting lines like "is dare a hart dat nebber lu'd," for example. British actor Charles Mathews, who had befriended Hewlett while touring the United States, also satirized him in public. Returning to London, Mathews created a show based on his American trip in which he mocked Hewlett's "strange" and "ludicrous" alterations to *Hamlet,* which included his singing of "a real Negro melody" at the end of the performance. Hewlett responded by publishing a rebuttal in a local newspaper, defending his own acting abilities as well as the right of blacks to perform Shakespeare. Although a laudable act of self-defense, the letter also opened Hewlett up to more bad publicity.[45]

Then there were Hewlett's repeated problems with the law. In some cases he was a victim or mere bystander. When he decided to open a scouring shop (drycleaners) in 1823 to make ends meet, a competitor named Cox beat him up. In 1825, Hewlett took a position as a ship steward, and was obliged to testify in court after a passenger was accused of repeatedly assaulting the only other passenger on board. But in later years, Hewlett turned perpetrator. In 1835, he again signed up as a ship steward. While still in port, he was arrested and convicted of stealing various articles from the ship—including several bottles of wine and porter—and served a six-month sentence. In 1837, he was accused of seducing and abandoning a white woman, and was sentenced to one month's hard labor. Later that same year, he was caught stealing a watch from the house of a man who had just died, and was returned to prison. Despite his pleas, "Gentlemen, don't put me in the newspapers; it will hurt my character," his misdeeds were widely reported in the press.[46] After this episode, Hewlett disappeared from public view. I searched in vain for mention of him in the newspapers and then, in desperation, turned to death records. In the coroner's report for 1840, I came across a reference to one "Hewlett, colored," who died by drowning on May 25. I have no way of knowing whether this was my great-great-great-granduncle. If so, how did he drown? Was this a final act of disgrace?

Philip White

To recover the daily life of an "enterprising black" from lost memory, I want to imagine my great-grandfather going about his work, errands, and visits in Lower Manhattan one day in the early 1850s. In his walk, he traverses territories that are variously strange and familiar; at times he's an alien, at others right at home. Yet in thought, action, and purpose, he's deeply bound to the many communities to which he's connected through familial, social, and professional ties.

Not quite thirty, Philip was the very embodiment of respectability. His recent change of residence portended upward mobility. Without explanation, I handed three Manhattan home addresses to a young librarian in the Map Room at the New York Public Library. He tracked them on his map, looked at me and commented: "This is a story of social ascent!" and then added, "a map tells more than a thousand words." What the librarian had just identified were Philip's home addresses: 23 Grand Street, where he lived from 1847 to 1849; his residence in 1850, which was at 81 White Street; and his final Manhattan address at 40 Vandewater Street, where he moved in 1856, remaining there until migrating to Brooklyn in 1870.

Knowing that he had a busy day ahead of him, Philip rose early.

As he was getting ready, he reflected on his good fortune. The 1850 census had valued his drugstore at four hundred dollars, and he had just moved with his mother and younger sister Sarah Maria into a new home on White Street. True, he had exchanged one simple wooden frame dwelling for another, but there were several upscale brick and stone houses in surrounding streets. Like much of New York, Philip mused, this was an area of contrasts. Broadway was close by with its many public buildings, the International Hotel, Palace Hall, a Lutheran Church, the Apollo Rooms, and others. But just a few blocks to the east lay black Broadway, Church Street, and its many offshoots, that Bobo had so derisively portrayed. His next move, Philip promised himself, would be to a brick house, and, if lucky, closer to his store.

Philip decided to walk through the Five Points to get downtown. The neighborhood was just as squalid as when Charles Dickens had visited it in 1841, probably even more so. Poverty was still endemic and crime still rampant. The area was now largely Irish, but Philip noted the increased number of Jews on Orange Street who ran "fences," shops from which they bought and sold stolen goods—clothes, hardware items, jewelry, watches, and the like. Philip was well aware that if he peered into the rear of these shanties he would see living quarters where entire families, huddled together, cooked, ate, and slept. At night, a different kind of selling would be going on. The saloons would open, drunks and prostitutes would flood streets and alleys, and the sale of liquor and sex would continue until morning.[47]

Philip remembered that the Five Points had once been the center of black life where families lived in close proximity to community institutions. But now both people and institutions were dispersed throughout the city. Only the African Society for Mutual Relief remained on Orange Street and St. Philip's on Centre Street. In just a few years his beloved church would follow the movement of its parishioners and relocate uptown. Black homes now stood in most of the city's wards, but they congregated mostly in the West Side's Eighth Ward, and also to the south in the Fifth, and to the north in the Ninth, Sixteenth, and Twentieth.

As he hastened his steps toward his drugstore, Philip wondered whether he should not follow James McCune Smith's example and take on an apprentice. On the spot, he decided to advertise for one. The offices of the *Daily Tribune,* which the black community used as a local paper ever since the demise of the *Colored American,* were on Park Row, only a few blocks from his store, so he could easily stop there first. The street housed all the city's major newspapers, Greeley's *Tribune,* Bennett's *Herald,* Webb's *Courier and Enquirer,* and the new upstart, the *Times.* With the technological developments in printing, these presses had been forced to expand upward in structures as high as five stories and outward by taking over adjacent buildings. The area was crammed with people; typesetters, press operators, bookkeepers, and reporters scurried back and forth while the ever ubiquitous newspaper boys hawked their wares. Treading carefully, Philip finally arrived at his destination. His ad was brief and direct: "Colored Boy—Wanted, an intelligent, well educated Colored Boy, 14 or 15 years of age to learn the Drug business. Apply to PHILIP A. WHITE, cor. Gold and Frankfort sts. N.Y." Philip smiled in satisfaction as he realized that *he* would now be mentoring a younger man just as Smith had mentored him ten years earlier.[48]

Turning east into the Fourth Ward, Philip reached his drugstore. On the corner of Gold and Frankfort Streets, the store was located in an area known as the Swamp, which lay south of the Five Points and extended all the way to the East River. Under the Dutch, the Swamp had been a marshland called the Greppel Bosch. Now it was even more congested than the Five Points. By 1861 the Fourth Ward was considered the most densely populated place on earth, containing 290,000 inhabitants per square mile.[49]

Many of New York's old merchant class had gotten their start in the Swamp. Most especially, it had been home to the leather industry where merchants tanned hides in yards and stored them in immense warehouses. The now deceased Jacob Lorillard had built his tannery on Ferry Street close to William Kumbell, who was still in business. Another deceased leather merchant, Abraham Bloodgood, who had been Pierre Toussaint's landlord in the early days, had lived on Frankfort Street, close to where Philip's drugstore was now located.[50]

But plenty of poor people—mostly Irish—also inhabited the Swamp. Living in appallingly overcrowded conditions, they were chronically ill, suffering from malnutrition, lack of ventilation, poor sanitation, and lung problems like tuberculosis made worse by the fumes emanating from the tanning yards.

In the four years that Philip had been part of the Swamp community, he'd gotten to know the residents and felt that they were slowly learning to trust one another. Although he craved economic security,

Philip remained strongly committed to his role as a healer, and he gave away medicine to those too poor to pay. Such charity had been absolutely necessary during the 1849 cholera epidemic, when suffering and death were literally at his doorstep. And, for now, their simple expression of thanks was payment enough. In turn, Philip was grateful to the many businessmen in the Swamp who appreciated his industriousness and charitable disposition and went out of their way to bring him trade.[51]

Philip entered his store and surveyed it with satisfaction. Like most drugstores of the day, it was well stocked with toilet articles and perfumery, to which he was slowly adding hardware items such as window glass, paints, oils, and mirrors. He also sold liquor, fully aware that although many of his customers claimed that they were buying it for medicinal purposes, they would undoubtedly drink it instead.

Philip's main task, however, was dispensing drugs to the sick. Just as in his apprenticeship days, he spent long hours at his prescription counter, since, like most pharmacists, he prepared almost half of his prescriptions right on the premises. Philip's cabinet was made of cut glass, and it held everything needed to fill a prescription. He stored his Shaker herbs in tin canisters neatly stacked one on top of the other, and poured various extracts, tinctures, waters, acids, and syrups into bottles lined up in neat rows. All the containers were carefully labeled. Tools such as scales, spatulas, labels, and corks lay close at hand next to the ever indispensable Dispensatory. Complete with a coal stove and gas or alcohol lamp for heat, a mortar and pestle or drug mill for grinding, Philip's prescription counter was a true laboratory where he could compound almost any drug on the spot.[52]

Philip set to work filling a prescription for his good friends Albro Lyons and William Powell, who were joint owners of the Colored Sailors' Home at 330 Pearl Street near the East River. They had sent word that several of their sailors were suffering from diarrhea and vomiting, and were worried that these symptoms portended a new outbreak of cholera. Philip thought it unlikely since there had been no recent reports of the disease. He thought back in horror to the 1849 epidemic, which had started in an immigrant boardinghouse on Orange Street and then spread rapidly through the Five Points to the rest of the city. The epidemic had been short-lived but intense: 5,017 dead in four months. Thankfully, health officials were now pretty much convinced that the disease was not a moral failing but a result of social and environmental conditions. And to their credit, health practitioners were now devising less drastic treatments. They no longer indulged in excessive bleeding and purging. And although they still recommended calomel taken in combination with either laudanum or opium pills to stem the diarrhea, and camphor to relieve cramping, they now prescribed them in lower doses.[53] Philip prepared his prescription with great care.

Having finished, Philip headed downtown toward Pearl Street to deliver the prescription, wending his way through one of the city's most commercial districts. Shipbuilding industries dominated the East River waterfront area. This was where shipping magnates like John Jacob Astor, Archibald Gracie, William Aspinwall, Robert Minturn, and others had made their fortunes, trading in goods of all kinds, including slave products, across the world. Longshoremen swarmed the port. Most of them were Irish, and Philip knew how determined they were to keep black workers off the docks. The area also housed trades associated with shipping, reputable ones like boardinghouses and outfitting stores for sailors, and less reputable ones like grog shops and brothels.[54] William Powell had fared well, opening his Sailors' Home in the late 1830s. But he was now thinking of moving his family to England and had arranged for Albro Lyons, who owned two Seamen's General Outfitting Stores on nearby Baxter and Roosevelt Streets, to take over the business.

The Colored Sailors' Home was a landmark in the black community. In the very same newspaper article in which he had mentioned Philip's newly opened drugstore, William Nell had heaped praise on Powell's home. "An Oasis in the desert," he called it, where "the Banner of Reform floats conspicuous." The home enforced temperance and encouraged reading; at mealtime the conversation dwelled "on the various questions incidental to the elevation of man."[55] Philip fully agreed with Powell's philosophy that it was the responsibility of the more fortunate in the community to elevate the less fortunate. After having determined that the ill sailors were only suffering from a mild case of dysentery,

THOMAS DOWNING

Thomas Downing, one of the pioneers of New York city. He at one time owned the property at No. 3 Broad street, now occupied by the Morgan-Drexler building, a structure valued at $3,000,000. Born in 1791, he knew intimately every New Yorker of prominence up to the days of the Civil war. It was he who saved James Gordon Bennett's New York Herald from going under by advancing a loan of $10,000 to Bennett.

Thomas Downing, New York City, pioneer and restaurant owner, circa 1860s (Photographs and Prints Division, Schomburg Center for Research in Black Culture, The New York Public Library)

Philip left, promising to return with books for the home's already substantial library.

Now hungry, Philip decided to splurge by dropping in at Thomas Downing's oyster house on Broad Street. Philip always entered Downing's establishment with a sense of amazement that the son of freed Virginia slaves had done so well in the competitive world of New York's eating houses. Downing knew his oysters as well as Ray did his tobacco. When the oyster trade was still new, Downing would get up at two in the morning to row over to the Jersey Flats and gather the oysters himself. Now he left that work to others. But with competition as stiff as it was, he still went out at midnight to wait for the oyster boats, or even to sail out to them, so he could beat the competition and get the best catch.[56]

Downing's restaurant was simply furnished and lacked the adornment of other oyster houses, but that hardly mattered. Because of its proximity to the Customs House, the port, the merchant exchange, banks, and other important businesses, Downing counted some of New York's most powerful men among his customers: Samuel Swartwort, collector of the port; William Price, district attorney; Jonathan Coddington, postmaster; Abraham Lawrence, president of the Harlem Railroad, to name just a few. Philip had often watched as Downing passed messages back and forth from customers at one table to another. Because of all this message carrying, people assumed that Downing wielded influence at the highest level of city government; as a result, scores of office seekers flocked to his establishment.[57] Whether the rumor was true or not, it had the effect of bringing in more customers.

But Philip also knew the difficulties Downing, like so many other black men in the city, faced on a daily basis. Dickens had dined in his restaurant; he had sent Queen Victoria some of his choicest oysters and she had thanked him by having a gold chronometer watch delivered to him. Yet racism dogged Downing at every turn. Mobs had assaulted his establishment on more than one occasion. A jealous competitor had tried to destroy his business by writing a letter to the *New York Post* in which he proposed that city newspapers issue a public denunciation of Downing's abolitionist sentiments and call for a public meeting "to proscribe all negroes who sell oysters, and all white people who eat oysters sold by them." Only then, the competitor concluded, "I might get my stale stock off my hands, and soon afford to supply a fresh article on moderate terms, and, at the same time, receive a just reward for my devotion to the constitution."[58]

Philip was also aware that Downing fretted over the fact that racism forced him to discourage blacks from patronizing his restaurant. His own light skin would not attract notice, but this was not an option for darker-skinned blacks. Philip remembered the uproar that Charles

Reason and Alexander Crummell had caused years earlier when they had written several angry letters to the *Colored American* publicly excoriating their friend Thomas van Rensselaer for refusing to seat blacks in his restaurant or for trying to "colonize" them by placing them behind a screen or relegating them to the kitchen.[59] Putting these troubling thoughts aside, Philip enjoyed his plate of oysters, then left, promising Downing that he would deliver some papers to his son.

Heading north, Philip decided to visit his old mentor, James McCune Smith, who was confined to his home on North Moore Street suffering from symptoms of congestive heart failure. As he proceeded up Broadway, Philip thought of how well George Foster had captured the contrasts of the avenue in his most recent book. In the morning, Foster noted, Broadway was "hushed and solitary"; the few who were about could amuse themselves watching "the awakened swine gallop furiously downward to have the first cut of the new garbage." Later in the day, however, a mass of people would surge through the street, "a human river in a freshet, roaring and foaming toward the sea." Then there were the contrasts of buildings. Among some truly fine structures others had sprung up haphazardly—a brick schoolhouse or a clapboard barn here, a penitentiary or pound there. Finally, what caught your eye depended on where you looked: down, a rotten cellar door; straight ahead, "a plate-glass window stuffed with gaudy cashmeres and mildewed muslims"; above, "an interminable line of crooked well-posts, armed with glass bottles, and held together by wire clothes lines."[60]

Philip paused only to admire Alexander Stewart's new department store on the corner of Chamber Street. Five stories high and designed in the Italianate style, it resembled a Renaissance palace: white marble exterior, Corinthian columns on the ground floor, cornice work above the windows, all topped by a dome eighty feet high. Inside, the store stocked a profusion of goods marketed specifically to female customers. But Philip knew one woman who out of loyalty would resist Stewart's enticements. Grandmother Marshall loved to tell the story of how the English immigrant Samuel Lord teamed up with George Washington Taylor in 1826 and opened a store on Catherine Street to sell "plaid silks for misses' wear, hosiery, and elegant Cashmere long shawls." On opening day "she hurried over to make an early purchase, of a yard of white ribbon, to give the 'boys' good luck, for she knew them both well."[61] She was not about to desert them now.

Turning west off Broadway to get to Smith's home in the Fifth Ward around St. John's Park, Philip was once again reminded of the city's contrasts, in this instance of changes wrought over time. In his childhood, this neighborhood had been highly fashionable and home to some of New York's best families. The park was among the finest in the city, ringed by mature trees and handsome Federal style rowhouses, and graced on its east side by the elegant St. John's Chapel. But the pressure of commercialization from both downtown and the Hudson River waterfront had precipitated the flight of the "upper tendom" farther north, above Bleecker Street. Smith had been fortunate enough to buy a good brick house on North Moore Street, one block south of the park.[62] Since Smith was tired, Philip made his visit brief.

Philip's final destination was George Downing's catering establishment on Bond Street above Bleecker in the Fifteenth Ward. He traced his steps back to Broadway and proceeded north across Canal, thinking of how this section of the avenue offered a set of contrasts different still than those mentioned by Foster. He knew that come nightfall the entire area up to Houston Street would be overrun with people, customers in search of good food, good drink, good entertainment, and yes, good sex. The area had become a center of the city's sex trade. Prostitutes were everywhere: in hotels, in private supper rooms of restaurants, in upstairs drinking rooms of saloons, in brothels that lined the side streets, on the streets where they handed out calling cards. Walt Whitman was certain that in no other place could vice show itself so "impudently."[63] Except for the amount of money that traded hands, how different, Philip wondered wryly, was this sex trade from that found in the Five Points?

Crossing Bleecker, Philip reached the Bond Street/LaFayette Place area where the white elite—the Wards, Lows, Minturns, Schermerhorns, and others—had settled. The neighborhood was quiet and secluded; large trees shaded the houses from the inquisitive gaze of passers-by. Philip was intensely proud that some in the black community had managed to set up shop amid such exclusivity. George Downing's store was at 690 Broadway; his ads in the *Tribune,* which boasted such specialties as pickled oysters and boned turkey, were directed at both black and white customers.[64] Patrick Reason's engraving shop was on Bond Street itself, at number 56; the street's residents were patrons of the arts, and Patrick undoubtedly owed much of his commercial success to them.

Philip knew that the white elite willingly patronized the best black businesses. So maybe, he thought, as he entered Downing's store, Frederick Douglass was right when he opined in a *North Star* editorial that black New Yorkers were now seeing "the accursed load of popular contempt and scorn by which we have been weighed down for centuries, gradually diminishing. They see the violent waves of malignant prejudice slowly but surely subsiding; the long despised race to whom they belong, steadily rising in position, and rapidly gaining respect and consideration."[65]

CHAPTER SIX

Whimsy and Resistance

CIRCA 1853

FREDERICK DOUGLASS WAS dead wrong. Instead of bearing witness to the waning of racial prejudice, the 1850s gave birth to what we commonly call "scientific racism." At first, its proponents simply referred to it as "the nigger business." Then, when they began to fancy themselves men of science and sought to endow their work with gravitas, they coined the term "niggerology." Consider some of the scientific arguments made by proslavery southerners.

John M. Daniel: "Negroes are not *men,* in the sense in which the term is used by the Declaration of Independence."

E. N. Elliott: "The Negro is . . . a variety of the human race. . . . By himself he was never emerged from barbarism, and even when partly civilized under the control of the white man, he speedily returns to the same state if emancipated."

Josiah Nott: "In the broad field and long duration of Negro life, not a single civilization, spontaneous or borrowed, has existed, to adorn its gloomy past. . . . The superior races ought to be kept free from all adulterations, otherwise the world will retrograde, instead of advancing, in civilization."[1]

Some niggerologists were even homegrown. In 1853 a New York doctor, John Van Evrie, proclaimed: "The Negro is not a black white man, or a man merely with a black skin, but a different and inferior species of man."

Building upon earlier racial thinking, scientific racists were determined to prove that Negroes were a species separate in origin from whites, mentally and morally inferior, incapable of advancement and improvement. Given these racial disparities, they opined, any attempts at social mingling—or worse, at miscegenation—would be disastrous to western civilization.

Scientific racism reflected the deep-seated beliefs of many Americans, but it also actively shaped them. Its very language breathed new and ferocious vigor into racial stereotypes; hateful caricatures poisoned the lives of black Americans on a daily basis. Even more devastating were the material consequences of discriminatory legislation and practices, and the ever thriving system of southern slavery that increasingly imperiled their survival.

Black New Yorkers were not immune to this new strain of racism. They were protected neither by their free status nor by their northern residence. After all, it was the New Yorker John Van Evrie who argued that even freedom and education could not transform the Negro any more than "it would be to change a cow into a horse, or to raise the dead."[2] In the years leading up to the Civil War, black leaders devised a variety of counterattacks on a variety of fronts—local, national, and even cosmopolitan.

Once again, black leaders organized around James McCune Smith. In a notice published in *Frederick Douglass' Paper* in May 1855, Rev. J. W. C. Pennington informed visiting "colored ladies and gentlemen" that they were entitled to use the city's public transportation on equal terms with whites. If they encountered trouble, Pennington continued, they should "call upon Dr. Smith, 55 West Broadway, Mr. T. L. Jennings, 167 Church St., or myself 29 Sixth Ave., and we will enter your complaint at the Mayor's office."[3]

Smith, Pennington, and the rest of the black community never knew quite what to expect. It seemed that the rise of scientific racism would have been accompanied by a stricter regulation of race relations. But that's not exactly what happened. When black New Yorkers assumed acceptance, the door might just slam in their face. Conversely, when they expected hostility, they might just get kindness. Sometimes they made the strangest of allies. Or they were left with the unpredictable. The rule of whimsy reigned.

Street Culture

Walking around the city, Van Evrie and his friends must have despaired at witnessing the many public spaces—streets, marketplaces, saloons, dance halls, hotels, and the like—where whites and blacks of New York's lower classes freely associated with one another. In his *Glimpses of New York City,* southerner William Bobo noted with horror the inter-racial character of Church Street. It was not so much a Negro street, he wrote, as one "where Dutch and negroes stand on the same platform," drinking and gambling at places like the St. Charles Exchange. "Did you ever see," he asked with disgust, "such a mixture of negroes and whites all on an equality"?[4]

It was in places like these that blackface minstrelsy flourished from the 1820s on. Although not its birthplace, New York was a fertile breeding ground. Minstrelsy first emerged as an expression of alien-ation on the part of the city's underclass—*both* black newcomers fleeing the South and disaffected white youths who donned blackface as a ges-ture of solidarity against civic authority. This mixed population invented strange, new, rhythmic movements, dancing for eels at Catherine Mar-ket and wheeling Jim Crow by the docks. Over time, however, min-strelsy grew in popularity, moved into theaters, and became a business. Van Evrie and his friends got their way as black performers were banned from the stage, audiences segregated, and what was once free rebellious expression hardened into nasty racial stereotypes.

Amazingly, one of minstrelsy's most prominent stages was the Chatham Theater, the very same place where the Tappan brothers had conducted their interracial abolitionist meeting that led to the 1834 riot. A theater before the Tappans turned it into a chapel, by 1839 the build-ing had reconverted to its original purpose. It was there that T. D. Rice, best known for his Jump Jim Crow performances, appeared, as did Dan Emmett and his famed Virginia minstrels. It's there that you could fol-low the travails of Jim, hero of "de New York Nigga":

> When de Nigger's done at night washing up de china,
> Den he sally out to go and see Miss Dinah,
> Wid his Sunday go-to-meetins segar in his mouth.

So many stereotypes make their way into the song. The narrator happily invokes the N-word; he sings in a dialect that gets more pronounced with each verse; Jim is hardly a man, since he must wash china; whites mock his dandified appearance; it's obvious that he can't keep a woman since he later finds Dinah on the street with none other that "Arfy Tappan" (raising the specter of amalgamation); and at the Bowery he finds Rice acting "de brack man" and bringing "de money in." But, never mind, you won't get to see the performance anyway, " 'Cause de neber hab rom to let in de nigga."[5]

The black elite avoided places like Church Street and the Chatham Theater. In both their political activism and their social lives, they put their trust in appearing respectable, keeping company with respectable people, and patronizing respectable venues. Nevertheless, they faced the unpredictable. Would they be accepted on the same terms as other Gothamites? Relegated to a segregated section? Suffer the humiliation of being turned away? The rule of whimsy reigned.

Public Transportation

Travel on city conveyances was a necessity, but a trip on a railroad car could be perilous. Public transportation, as we know from history, has so often been a battleground of race relations where the close proximity of blacks and whites produces unwanted (for some) physical intimacy and raises the dangerous specter of racial equality.

In the 1850s, New York's rail companies were privately owned. There were no laws on the books regulating who could and couldn't board a streetcar. As Maritcha dryly noted in her memoir, "riding, for colored folks, depended upon the whims of respective stage drivers." Experiences varied. Ignored or jeered at by drivers as she tried to get to and from school, the teenage Maritcha was often forced to walk several miles on her own. When the elderly Thomas Downing accompanied a woman friend uptown, the conductor made several attempts to throw them off his car. Downing steadfastly refused, claiming he was not in violation of any law; his fame alone saved him from mistreatment. As the doctor of the Colored Orphan Asylum, James McCune Smith needed to ride uptown every day during an outbreak of the measles. When the asylum's managers discovered that the conductors refused to accept him on their cars, they encouraged him to hire a private conveyance at their expense.[6]

But if it so chose, the law could intervene on the side of blacks. Elizabeth Jennings, the daughter of the same Thomas Jennings listed as a contact person in Pennington's newspaper announcement, put it to the test in 1854. For years, she had ridden the Third Avenue railroad car to church without incident. One Sunday, however, a conductor refused to allow her and a friend to board, telling them to wait for the next car specifically designated for blacks. An angry Jennings remonstrated, maintaining that she was "a respectable person, born and raised in New York" and that he was "a good for nothing impudent fellow for insulting decent persons while on their way to church." The conductor and a police officer dragged her from the car and, in her words, "drove me away like a dog." Jennings sued and, amazingly, was awarded approximately $225 plus court costs. Yet this was about half of what she had asked for.

In his opinion in the Jennings case, the judge stated that streetcars should be available to "colored persons, if sober, well-behaved, and free from disease." Although welcome, the comment also made plain whites' continued stereotyping of blacks, and hinted that simply being black could be enough to place a traveler outside the category of respectable, sober, well-behaved. In 1855, Pennington was forcibly ejected from a Sixth Avenue car, propelling him to place his notice in *Frederick Douglass' Paper*. In 1856, the same happened to Peter Porter and his wife. Both sued; Pennington lost his case, but in 1858 Porter won on appeal, leading him to proclaim that now "the five cents of a colored man were as good as those of a white man."[7] Not quite true, since conductors continued to remove blacks from their cars.

High Culture

The black elite felt most secure at cultural events that brought them together with their white counterparts. It was here, they believed, that class would trump race. In a series of newspaper columns published in

Frederick Douglass' Paper, Philip Bell insisted that "color-phobia is fast abating in our Island City," and as proof cited the many instances where he and his friends happily mixed with members of the white elite. When he attended a lecture at the Mercantile Library, the audience was "an equal admixture of black and white. Side by side sat they, no shrinking of the aristocratic white lady from companionship with the black one. The white philanthropist Peter Cooper sought an introduction to the black savan, Dr. J. W. C Pennington." Similarly, Bell noted that at the newly opened Academy of Music, "Democracy prevails: no 'Negro pew,' no place for 'respectable persons of color'; the black amateur of music takes his seat beside the white professor of la belle science." Finally, he mused that at Goupil's art gallery, spectators found themselves in the presence of an "inimitable and inspired work of art [such that] no prejudice can enter. Caste is forgotten, and colorphobia is rebuked into silence."[8]

Yet the elite could never be sure. When New York's Crystal Palace, built after the London original, opened in 1853, it became a popular tourist destination. Nevertheless, a contributor to *Frederick Douglass' Paper* wrote, black New Yorkers "have been casting the 'Horoscope,' as to whether colored people would be admitted." In her memoir, Maritcha recalled that "about 1856, mother took her flock to visit Crystal Palace, located somewhat above where the Grand Central depot now stands." She then added somewhat cryptically: "For this outing the preparations were very extensive."[9] Was Maritcha merely referring to the burdens of a long trip with children? Or does her comment betray the family's anxiety over possible rejection and the need to prepare for whatever might happen: be respectable, dress well, behave with impeccable manners, and don't break down if admission is denied.

Even in more select settings, whimsy prevailed. James McCune Smith freely visited Niblo's, one of the fanciest spots in town for fine dining and sophisticated entertainment, while Pennington was denied entrance to attend a lecture there. In perhaps the most bizarre twist of irony, blacks were prohibited from attending the concert of one of their own, Philadelphia singer Elizabeth Taylor Greenfield, known as the "black swan." A contributor to *Frederick Douglass' Paper* informed readers that a placard outside Metropolitan Hall announcing her upcoming performance advised that "no colored person can be admitted, as there is no part of the house appropriated for them." "Prejudice against color" like this, he fulminated, was "the most brainless, brutal, and inconsistent thing," especially given that whites had no problem accepting the intimate presence of black cooks, butlers, coachmen, or barbers. Blacks protested and were finally allowed entrance; the chief of police was on hand for fear of a disturbance.[10]

Black Abolitionists: The James Hamlet Case

There was little to be hopeful about in the nation's legislative and judicial decisions that were fast chipping away at the few rights black Americans still possessed. The decade began with the Fugitive Slave Law of 1850, mandating the return of escaped slaves captured in free states to their owners in the South. Hard on its heels came congressional passage of the Kansas-Nebraska Act of 1854, allowing settlers to decide the slavery issue through the vote and thus effectively repealing the Missouri Compromise of 1820, which had prohibited slavery in the territories. The final blow occurred in 1857 with the Supreme Court's Dred Scott decision, opening federal territory to slavery and denying African Americans the right to citizenship.

James McCune Smith's office was the place where black leaders planned their responses to these events. Until his death in 1865, he was the heart and soul of New York's black community. His medical and pharmaceutical practice was located in a brick building on West Broadway between Thomas and Anthony Streets. Behind his office was a backroom, which, Maritcha wrote, functioned as a "rallying centre." It was "visited daily by men, young and old [who] held discussions and debates on all the topics of the day." They constituted, she continued, a "constructive force that molded public sentiment which had much to do in bringing about a more favorable state of things affecting the colored people of the State."[11]

In the early 1850s, Peter would have been part of these debates. He was among those who responded to the first test case of the Fugitive Slave Law when James Hamlet, an escaped slave living as a free man in

Williamsburgh, was captured in September 1850, remanded into slavery, and sent to Maryland to be sold.

The black community's swift response to Hamlet's plight was not new, but the culmination of a long tradition of rescue. In 1835, David Ruggles, a free black man originally from Connecticut, had founded the New York Vigilance Committee for the purpose of protecting fugitive slaves (as well as free blacks accused of being slaves) from being kidnapped. The committee's task was to identify slave hunters, keep a lookout for endangered blacks, and hide them in stations on the Underground Railroad until they could get safe passage out of the city; Frederick Douglass was among those rescued. Unlike many other organizations of the period, the Vigilance Committee extended deep into the black community. In addition to its leadership, which at various times included Albro Lyons and Charles Ray, the Vigilance Committee set up an Effective Committee composed of a hundred persons whose job it was to collect dues from ten to twelve other community members. Women were active participants, serving on the Effective Committee and raising money under the auspices of the Ladies' Literary Society.[12]

So black New Yorkers were prepared when James Hamlet was captured. Peter and his friends circulated the following handbill:

THE FUGITIVE BILL!
THE PANTING SLAVE!
FREEMEN TO BE MADE SLAVES!
Let every colored man and woman attend the GREAT
MASS MEETING to be held in
ZION CHURCH,
Church street, corner of Leonard on TUESDAY EVE-
NING, OCTOBER 1, 1850, for your Liberty, your Fire-
side is in danger of being invaded! Devote this night upon
the question of YOUR DUTY in the CRISIS.
Shall we resist oppression? Shall we defend our Liberties?
Shall we be FREEMEN OR SLAVES?

Fifteen hundred people turned out for the meeting to denounce slavery and raise money for Hamlet's freedom. William Powell presided. Several vice presidents were named: first James McCune Smith, followed by Peter, Albro Lyons, and Charles Reason. Powell, Smith, George Downing, and others delivered long, impassioned speeches. They described the horrors of escaped slaves being seized and sent back into slavery; they disputed the constitutionality of the Fugitive Slave Law, claiming that it violated habeas corpus; they complained that the mayor had turned a deaf ear on their pleas for protection; they called for petitions to the state legislature; they threatened armed resistance. At the end, Charles Ray rose to announce that eight hundred dollars had been raised, enough to secure Hamlet's freedom.[13] In early October, Hamlet returned to the city a free man and was greeted by several thousand supporters at City Hall Park.

Hamlet's case underscored the very insecurity of free blacks in the North. The Zion Church meeting handbill warned that under the terms of the Fugitive Slave Law no one was safe. The law struck at the very heart of the black community. It forced many of its members to recall the condition of their birth. Smith had been born a slave of a slave mother in New York City. Garnet's family had escaped from slavery to New York only to have their home invaded by slave hunters and themselves pursued through the streets. Like the Garnets, Samuel Ward and his parents had been runaway slaves from Maryland; in 1851, Ward became so apprehensive about his family's safety that he moved to Canada. Since Hamlet might well have hidden his slave status from his neighbors, black New Yorkers must have wondered whether there were others like him in the vicinity. And, as the handbill suggested, the rule of whimsy was in full force; at any moment, any of them could be snatched from their homes or off the streets, charged with being a runaway slave, and sold South without having the chance of proving their free status. Federal officials, they knew, would not bother themselves much about the legal niceties of their civil status. Members of the black elite understood that everything they had worked so hard for—their businesses, property, education of their children—was now threatened.

Black and White Abolitionists

THE AMERICAN ANTI-SLAVERY SOCIETY

Newspaper reports of the Zion Church meeting observed that it was attended mostly by "colored people, with a slight and visible sprinkling of white Abolitionists." Since the early 1830s, the presence of northern white sympathizers at rallies such as these was common. The activities of the American Anti-Slavery Society brought together white abolitionists like Garrison and the Tappan brothers, and blacks from across the North. Priding themselves on interracial cooperation and impelled by intense evangelical fervor, the society's members initially shared the same values and goals. They called for immediate emancipation, rejected colonization schemes, and strove for moral perfection.

Such intermingling was not without danger. The presence of Peter Williams and the Tappans on the same platform in 1834 had inflamed the passions of white New Yorkers and resulted in a race riot. The same scenario repeated itself, albeit on a lesser scale, in May 1850 at the anniversary meeting of the American Anti-Slavery Society at the Broadway Tabernacle. The convention brought together what one New York newspaper mockingly referred to as Garrison's "nigger minstrels"— Samuel Ward and Frederick Douglass—as well as white abolitionists like Lewis Tappan and Henry Ward Beecher, the younger brother of Harriet Beecher Stowe, whose novel *Uncle Tom's Cabin* would soon rock the nation. They were interrupted by one Captain Rynders, a notorious proslavery rabblerouser, and his Empire Club gang of prizefighters and sporting men, who rushed the platform, hurling obscenities and claiming that Douglass was not a human being but descended from the ourang-outang. Alerted ahead of time, the chief of police was there, but he stood by passively before eventually clearing the premises. Attendees repaired to Powell and Lyons's Sailors' Home to conclude the meeting.[14]

If there were dangers from without, there was also dissension from within. Even though Lewis Tappan and Garrison shared the same platform at the Tabernacle meeting, they had long since gone their separate ways. Garrison was committed to the idea that human beings could free themselves from sin and achieve moral perfection. He believed God had made women the equal of men, and wanted to give them a greater voice in the abolitionist movement. At the same time he was convinced that all institutions were corrupt because human, so he counseled antislavery activists not to place any faith in church, government, or party politics, and to regard the Constitution as a suspect, proslavery document. Against mounting calls for armed resistance, he clung to his belief in the power of moral suasion. On most of these points, the Tappans disagreed. They had little interest in women's rights but wanted to stay focused on abolition. They embraced political activism as an effective tool in the antislavery struggle, and they backed those political parties sympathetic to their cause.[15] By 1840, a split was inevitable; many black New Yorkers abandoned Garrison to follow the Tappans into their newly created American and Foreign Antislavery Society.

GERRIT SMITH AND TIMBUCTO

In the mid-1840s, the white abolitionist Gerrit Smith approached James McCune Smith, Charles Ray, and a few others with a novel plan. A wealthy landowner, he proposed to set aside 120,000 acres that he owned in the Adirondacks, then carve it up into forty- to sixty-acre lots that he would give away to impoverished blacks. Gerrit Smith's goal was to adapt the Jeffersonian ideal of the independent yeoman farmer to mid-nineteenth-century black Americans. He was undoubtedly also influenced by the recent founding of utopian societies, such as John Humphrey Noyes's perfectionist community and George Ripley's transcendentalist Brook Farm. Removed from the competitive harshness, racial tension, and seductive dangers of city life, Gerrit Smith argued, blacks would form a peaceful and productive self-sustaining community.

Smith and Ray responded enthusiastically to Gerrit Smith's plan, envisioning the settlement, named Timbucto after the mythical city in West Africa, as a place where blacks could live and work free of the whimsy of white racism, yet remain within the borders of the United States to continue their antislavery agitation and acquire enough property to qualify for the vote. Selecting the land-grant beneficiaries, they relocated approximately twenty to thirty families. But this Timbucto turned out quite differently. The families were unprepared. Many who attempted to claim their land were swindled out of their lots or charged a service fee. Once settled, they were baffled by the obligations of land ownership. They knew nothing about taxes; they lacked agricultural skills; the soil was too poor for cultivation, or the harvesting of wood too expensive. By the mid-1850s, Timbucto was pretty much defunct.[16]

Maybe the settlement would have thrived if it had had greater socioeconomic diversity. But, to the black elite, Timbucto represented primarily a solution to the economic plight of New York's black underclass. There were few economic incentives for men like James McCune Smith, who despite the odds were succeeding in the city, to pull up stakes and move. In a letter to Gerrit Smith, Smith confessed that he "would gladly exchange this bustling anxious life for the repose of that majestic country," but worried that "the country is yet too sparse to give support to a physician. Until I can make enough to secure an income of $400 per annum," he concluded, "I must defer settling in the country."[17] In essence, Smith and his friends were underwriting a community segregated not only by race but also by class.

POLITICAL ACTIVISM:
WHIG AND LIBERTY PARTIES

Asserting their right to citizenship, in the 1840s black Americans became increasingly involved in party politics. They had few palatable choices. In New York, Peter Guignon, Thomas Downing, and other "old heads" threw their support to the Whig Party. Probably the best that could be said about the Whigs was that they were not proslavery Democrats. They were descendants of the earlier Federalists, the party of the American aristocracy, who had filled the ranks of the New York Manumission Society and the pews of Trinity Church, and in the 1830s fiercely opposed Jacksonian Democrats. Whether indentured or enslaved, many black New Yorkers had been attached to Federalist families and followed their lead in religious and political matters. Federalist values were attractive to New York's black entrepreneurial class: old-fashioned qualities like austerity and virtue, but also more recent liberal ideas promoting individualism, education, the chance to realize one's potential to the fullest, and a capitalist system that embraced property ownership, active markets, and the profit motive. Moreover, Federalists trumpeted doctrines like equal rights of all (whatever that might mean) and the leveling up not down of all citizens (however that might be accomplished).[18]

Peter's former classmate Henry Highland Garnet, who was becoming increasingly radicalized, was not impressed. He created an uproar at the 1843 Buffalo National Convention of Colored Citizens where he delivered a fiery speech advocating slave resistance and warning "that there is not much hope of redemption without the shedding of blood." Bringing almost as much passion to party politics, some six years later he openly accused Peter and other "colored Whigs" of being willing to "sell yourselves for nothing to the pro-slavery Taylor Whigs." Garnet continued with a series of rhetorical questions to which the first answer was a resounding "no," and the second an equally impassioned "yes": "Is it respectful to yourselves to be found giving your political support to men who despise, and buy, and sell you? Do they not shut you out of their schools, churches,—their stages and hotels, and equal political privileges?" The stumbling blocks for Garnet were the two men who had been the Whigs' presidential candidates, Henry Clay, the former slaveholder and colonizationist, and Zachary Taylor, a Louisiana-born general who had led U.S. troops during the Mexican-American War.

Blacks who wanted to become politically involved, Garnet advised, should throw their support to the Liberty Party, which, though "few in number, have stood by our rights in all the storms that have assailed us—and even to this day, they are arrayed around the shattered pillar of truth, while the majority have forsaken us." Formed the same year as the American and Foreign Antislavery Society to encourage antislavery activists to enter party politics, the Liberty Party championed abolition and equal rights. It was dominated by men like Frederick Douglass, Samuel Ward, the Tappans, Gerrit Smith, and Beriah Green, former president of the Oneida Institute, who had welcomed young Garnet,

Crummell, and Thomas Sidney to his school after they had been driven out of Noyes Academy.[19]

Political Theories: Defining Nationality

Just as black New Yorkers split over their support for political parties, so they differed in their political theories. As the 1850s advanced, black leaders took considerable pains to define what constituted "nationality." First were those I'll call the interracial constitutionalists, who sought to adapt the nation's founding documents to the politics of the 1850s. They were made up of white and black abolitionists who split off from the Liberty Party to form the Radical Abolition Party. Their radicalism lay in their vision of an inclusive American nation; at their 1856 convention they nominated Gerrit Smith as their presidential candidate and James McCune Smith as his running mate.[20] Building on arguments of earlier intellectuals and buttressed by recent historical events, they challenged the common interpretations of such terms as "man" and "equality." "Man," they insisted, was a universal concept, as was his thirst for liberty; Negroes were men in exactly the way the term was used in the Declaration of Independence. Both the Declaration and the Constitution were inclusive documents, and the phrases "all men are created equal" and "inalienable rights" fully applied to black Americans.

Independent of their white colleagues, black leaders adopted not only the substance but also the form of American representative democracy as embodied in the U.S. federal system. In the mid-1850s, they founded the National Council of Colored People, which in its structure and operations shadowed the U.S. government. The council itself functioned as the elected executive branch, and it set up committees that operated much like the federal departments; complementing the council was a legislative body of elected members representing each state.[21]

In striking contrast to those affiliated with the Radical Abolition Party, men like Garnet and Crummell began formulating a different concept of Negro nationality. In the late 1840s, both had spent time in England, Garnet as an antislavery lecturer, Crummell as a student at Cambridge University, where he obtained a doctorate in divinity. But neither ever forgot the self-imposed obligation to help elevate their people, both spiritually and materially. By the early 1850s they were ready to expand their definition of who their people were to include all African-descended populations.

They traveled. Garnet spent three years in Jamaica as a Presbyterian missionary. After receiving his degree, Crummell went to Africa and settled in Liberia, where he worked as a missionary and educator for the next twenty years. With something of the prophet in him, Crummell imagined himself a latter-day Abraham whom God had commanded, as he wrote in a letter, to "get thee out of thy country and from thy kindred, and come into the land which I shall shew thee."[22]

They began thinking diasporically. Crummell, like other black intellectuals of his time, subscribed to the concept of Ethiopianism, a cyclical view of African history that decreed that Africa had once been great and though now fallen would one day rise to its former greatness. Translating this philosophy into practical terms, in 1858 Garnet founded the African Civilization Society with the goal of establishing "a grand center of Negro nationality, from which shall flow streams of commercial, intellectual, and political power which shall make colored people respected everywhere." The society was to help develop cotton production in Africa, which would eventually outstrip that of the United States and thereby undermine the U.S. slave system.[23]

Their views were controversial. Black leaders accused both Crummell and Garnet of espousing ideas and agendas that were too much like those of the American Colonization Society. In addition, Garnet was charged with hypocrisy for not having followed the path of permanent emigration himself. "Our friend Garnett [sic]," George Downing snidely noted, "left his country for Europe, afterward left Europe with his family for the West Indies, which was to have been his future home; afterward returned to his native home and settled himself down; and now we find him engaged in what I call a wild goose chase in Africa."[24]

Ironically, Garnet's and Crummell's attitudes remained peculiarly American. Yes, they wanted blacks in Africa and the diaspora to achieve through their own efforts without any interference from whites, but neither man could shake off the idea that these efforts would come primarily, maybe even exclusively, from blacks living in the United States. Given Africa's current degraded state—its heathenism, lack of education, lax morals, and poor work ethic—the continent could not redeem itself, but needed to rely on civilizing forces from the West: first Christianity, whose churches would convert heathen Africa, and second, Yankee entrepreneurship, consisting of business skills acquired in the harsh competitive climate of the United States.[25] Baldly put, Garnet and Crummell both subscribed to what could be called U.S. black exceptionalism: the notion that all blacks are equal except those from the United States who are superior. Despite their enslavement, or maybe even because of it, U.S. blacks had achieved in ways that other African-descended peoples had not, acquiring Christianity, education, and entrepreneurial know-how. As a result, Garnet and Crummell envisioned Africa and the diaspora more as a field of endeavor for U.S. black men to prove their superiority rather than an opportunity for worldwide collaboration among black peoples.

Philip White: The New York Society for the Promotion of Education Among Colored Children

Peter was not present in any of these organizations or debates. His move to Williamsburgh, his poor health, the demands of a new family, and his financial struggles undoubtedly curtailed his activism. But Philip was absent as well, apparently limiting his participation in black public affairs to one single organization: the New York Society for the Promotion of Education Among Colored Children.

Black New Yorkers had not forgotten their community's earlier admonition that at times "we think it good policy to have separate institutions." Discovering that even among white friends the rule of whimsy often obtained, they were prepared to heed the warning.

Take the *Tribune* editor, Horace Greeley. In contrast to the arch-conservative James Gordon Bennett who ran the *Herald*, Greeley was considered a liberal reformer. Black New Yorkers, however, came to question many of his political stances. He hated the abolitionist agitation of the Tappans. He equivocated on the Fugitive Slave Law. He dragged his heels on the issue of slavery, clinging to the belief that, under pressure from free labor and markets, slavery would eventually disappear. Worst of all were Greeley's choices for president, all conservative Whigs: Henry Clay, Zachary Taylor, and Winfield Scott. When Greeley announced for Scott during the 1852 elections, James McCune Smith printed a vitriolic ad hominem attack in *Frederick Douglass' Paper*, charging him with being nothing more than a "flagrant prostitute."[26]

Even more painful were betrayals by white abolitionists. These friends, black New Yorkers complained, sat next to them year after year at antislavery meetings but slammed the door in the face of black youth seeking employment. If he was indeed the young man to whom John Rankin had refused to lend five hundred dollars to start his business, Philip would have experienced such betrayals firsthand. White abolitionists had no good answers to such accusations. When Arthur Tappan was charged with not hiring colored men in his store, his feeble reply was that the one person he had offered the job to was "not qualified." When his brother was asked why he had not given the captaincy of a ship sailing to Africa to a black, his hollow excuse was that he did not own the ship but had merely chartered it. White abolitionists still did not realize that blacks were no longer satisfied with mere expressions of support. "Since 1826 down to now," one black leader noted cynically, "those who professed to be the strongest abolitionists have refused to render the colored people anything else but sympathy."[27]

So black New Yorkers understood that "separate institutions," like the New York Society for the Promotion of Education Among Colored Children, remained a necessity.

Dismayed by the degree to which the Public School Society had allowed the city's colored schools to deteriorate, in 1847 a number of graduates from the Mulberry Street School—Peter, his two brothers-in-law Edward Marshall and Albro Lyons, James McCune Smith, and others—along with community elders like William Powell and John Peterson, had come together to form the Society for the Promotion of Education Among Colored Children. Encouraged perhaps by his mentor, Smith, or his future brother-in-law, Peter, Philip joined them shortly thereafter. At twenty-five, he was already fully committed to a cause to which he would devote his entire life.

At the annual meeting of officers in 1851, Philip was elected secretary, a position he would hold well into the mid-1860s, if not later. He served with some of the community's most prominent leaders: William Powell was the society's president and James McCune Smith its treasurer; the board of trustees included Henry Scott, Samuel Cornish, Albro Lyons, Patrick Reason, and Charles Ray, who soon replaced Powell as president.

Whereas white trustees were able to preserve a written record of the early African Free Schools in the archives of the New-York Historical Society, New York's black community lacked such resources. Evidence about the Society for the Promotion of Education Among Colored Children is scant. According to its acts of incorporation, its initial mission was to create separate schools for black children. Soon a second was added: the establishment of normal schools for the training of black teachers. "Education," exclaimed one member, "is one of the most important and laudable attainments which the human mind can be possessed of; and why not make public teachers professors? . . . It is now high time that we show [whites] that we can think for ourselves as well as they can do."[28]

Although Smith groused that Horace Greeley was nothing but a "flagrant prostitute," we need to thank the *Tribune* editor for his assiduous coverage of black education throughout the 1850s. It appears that the Society for the Promotion of Education Among Colored Children never established a normal school. In 1850 it ran two schools, one located in the basement of St. Philip's Church and a second on Thomas Street. The roster of teachers replicated that of the public schools: John Peterson, his daughter Rebecca, and the rest of their male and female colleagues. The curriculum consisted of reading, arithmetic, grammar, drawing, and needlework—a far cry from the cosmopolitan education offered at the Mulberry Street School. Attendance remained low.[29]

The situation of public colored schools was still dire when the Public School Society was absorbed into the newly formed New York Board of Education in 1853. Attendance dropped from a high of sixteen hundred students in 1834 to a mere nine hundred. "It is evident," a New York State Assembly document concluded in 1859, "that the colored children are painfully neglected and positively degraded. Pent up in filthy neighborhoods, in old and dilapidated buildings, they are held down to low associations and gloomy surroundings." Some months later, as officers of the Society for the Promotion of Education Among Colored Children, Philip and Charles Ray wrote a report of their own to the commissioners of education. Agreeing with the state assembly's assessment, they argued that the poor condition of black schools was all the more unjust since black New Yorkers paid their fair share of school taxes, and a greater percentage of their children went to school that did white children. The request that followed was a carefully calculated political and rhetorical maneuver reflecting Philip's cautious and temperate nature. Although he and Charles Ray undoubtedly knew the idea was far-fetched, they began by suggesting that New York look to Boston's recent decision to integrate its public schools. Then they backtracked. Turning pragmatic, they requested that "if in the judgment of your honorable body common schools are not thus common to all," the commissioners might see fit to erect two new buildings where "the children will be taught with far less expense in two such school-houses than in the half dozen hovels into which they are now driven."[30]

Despite the dominance of the all-powerful Board of Education, the Society for the Promotion of Education Among Colored Children refused to disband. Instead, it devised a means to continue overseeing and encouraging the education of black children. In 1855, it instituted an annual Ridgeway Prize, named after Englishman Charles Ridgeway, a hairdresser at the Irving House who bequeathed $650 to the society at his death. Philip and James McCune Smith were two of the three-member Prize Committee. They must have observed the annual ceremonies with pride as students sang and recited, administrators gave speeches, ministers delivered sermons, and prizes were distributed: a gold medal for mathematics; silver for general scholarship; books for the best reader and writer, as well as for best declamation, painting, and drawing. Some of the awardees, with names like Vogelsang, Zuille, Peterson, Hamilton, Williams, were clearly children of the elite. But there were other names I didn't recognize—Wilkins, Stanley, Stokely, Remson.[31] Who were these children? What happened to them in later life?

St. Philip's

PHILIP WHITE, VESTRYMAN

In 1886 the *Brooklyn Daily Eagle* published an article about prominent blacks in Brooklyn that had this to say about "Druggist White": "He is beginning to take greater interest in his race and his friends are stimulated by his progressive spirit."[32] The imputation was clear: in earlier years Philip had been *less* interested in his race and his spirit had *not* been progressive. I was confused. Clearly, in the 1850s Philip had devoted himself to the cause of black education, but it's also true that he had not participated in other political or social reform organizations. The ever-independent Philip, I discovered, was charting his own path, making choices that at first glance might seem inconsistent and contradictory. Indeed, even as he worked within a separate black educational institution, Philip was fighting to gain St. Philip's admission to New York state's Episcopal Diocesan Convention, that is, to have a black parish accepted as an integral part of a white religious institution.

It was Philip's position as vestryman that gave me insight into the *Daily Eagle*'s comment. The vestry minutes tell the story of Philip's rise to prominence at St. Philip's: first elected to the vestry in 1850, Philip held that position until 1854 and, with the exception of a couple of years, from 1865 to 1875. After that, he served intermittently as warden until 1880, and then was elected senior warden every year from 1884 until his death in 1891.

So Philip was a vestryman in 1852 when a fugitive slave named Preston was captured and remanded into slavery. As in the Hamlet case, black New Yorkers sprang into action, requesting that notices for a mass meeting be read aloud in the city's black churches. Smith approached St. Philip's white minister, Reverend William Morris, who, George Downing fumed in a letter to *Frederick Douglass' Paper*, responded that it was "our duty to obey the Fugitive Slave Law":

> The slaveholder came. . . . He disregards all obligations, all ties; he drags him [Preston] from our gates. Would that this was the last of the infamy. But our Reverend and MOST

CHRISTIAN adviser, if called upon to "put asunder" those
that "God hath joined together"—to screw on the thumb
screw—yes, he would feel it to be his "christian duty to obey."
Aye, he even takes his place to entwine with the rope which
shall bind him and keep him from fleeing to some christian
gate.

As if that were not bad enough, Downing continued, St. Philip's vestry
"passed a vote of thanks to said Reverend and approved of his entire
course." He then proceeded to list the names of the vestrymen one by
one, starting with Philip. Only one, Downing claimed, opposed the
resolution, and that was his father.

Unable to let the matter rest, some two years later Downing returned to Morris's admonition, charging in yet another letter that "a
white one of his vestrymen, with a sanctimonious grin, exclaims Amen!
to the Reverend's exclamations."[33] Although Downing called out St.
Philip's vestrymen in the plural, I think his animus was specifically directed against Philip. Downing placed his name first on the list and his
reference to one of the white vestrymen could only have been a play on
words: white as in skin color, racial composition, weak character, and
last name.

This incident explains the *Brooklyn Daily Eagle*'s later comment.
I've thought it over many times, and reached the inevitable conclusion: Philip was indifferent to the plight of the slave. My initial reaction
was one of utter dismay. I wanted my great-grandfather to be a dedicated race man, a hero of the antislavery cause just like Downing and
Smith. But one can't choose one's ancestors, can one? So rather than
condemn, excuse, or apologize for Philip's behavior, I've simply tried
to understand it. It's not easy. Philip was devoted to his mother, Elizabeth; coming from Jamaica, she must have had ties to slavery, either as
a slave herself or the child of a slave mother. Nevertheless, Philip's personal history was different from that of men like Smith and Garnet who
had had direct experiences with slavery. And it was different from those
whose fathers were white but remained distant if not unknown. Philip
was nurtured by his white father for the first ten years of his life. Perhaps
Thomas White impressed upon the boy lessons he would never forget:

that character, not race, was the measure of the man; that the privileges of citizenship were his due; that he should not have to fight for them, and certainly not fight on behalf of others.

In that sense it's fair to say that Philip took little interest in his race. Yes, his commitment to black education indicated that to some degree he did care, yet he wanted to educate young men to believe in themselves just as he did. And no, he did not agree with statements like the one author Frances Harper would make a few years later: "Identified with a people over whom weary ages of degradation had passed," she wrote, "whatever concerns them, as a race, concerns me."[34] Philip did not identify with those degraded by slavery, and their concerns were not his.

In the 1850s, Philip's goal was to help St. Philip's obtain a secure place within the American Episcopal Church. This quest created a wide cast of characters that pitted not only black parishioners against white churchmen, but also parishioner against parishioner, and churchman against churchman. Yet it also gave rise to unexpected alliances, most especially with white churchmen. Most tellingly, however, it revealed the utter whimsy of scientific racism, exposing how the character and behavior of white men (and white men of the cloth at that) were often a lot more suspect than the Negro's.

REVEREND MORRIS

In his letters to *Frederick Douglass' Paper*, Downing charged Philip White with being all too willing to follow the lead of St. Philip's white pastor, Reverend Morris.

Peter Williams's death in 1840 had left an aching void at St. Philip's. Quite naturally, the church wanted another black minister to lead it, but finding one proved to be a difficult task. Bishop Hobart had taken six long years to ordain Williams, and later Bishop Onderdonk had denied Isaiah DeGrasse, Alexander Crummell, and Charles Reason the requisite training for the ministry. By the mid-1840s, DeGrasse was dead, and Reason was a teacher. Only Crummell had persevered; he was finally ordained by Bishop Alfred Lee of Delaware in 1844. Crummell had not yet left for England and Africa and was an obvious candidate for the position at St. Philip's. But his prickly personality stood in the way. Although James McCune Smith, a member of the vestry at the time, lobbied on Crummell's behalf, others were wary. He was not appointed.

With no black candidates in the ministry, St. Philip's turned first to Alexander Frazer and then after his death to William Morris. Ordained by Onderdonk, Morris had been assistant minister of Trinity Church before becoming rector of Trinity School. In 1849, the vestry appointed him officiating minister, a position he held for ten years.

Morris was his pastor, but was that reason enough for Philip to heed his call to obey the laws of the land? Like many committed Christians then and now, my great-grandfather must have concluded that there was no place for politics in the church. He undoubtedly remembered how Onderdonk had chastised Peter Williams for his abolitionist activity and forced him to resign his position in the American Anti-Slavery Society.

Philip had a quite specific reason for wanting to ban politics from St. Philip's: admission to the Diocesan Convention. St. Philip's parishioners were unshakeable in their conviction that acceptance was essential to their religious identity: it would establish their church as a legitimate black parish within a larger white religious order. The Episcopal Church conceived of itself as a national institution structured around the concept of denominational unity. Individual parishes made up the local level; these were then grouped by region to form dioceses, each one headed by a bishop and administered by a convention. Diocesan conventions met annually, and General Conventions comprising all the dioceses triennially. Conventions were not mere bureaucratic meetings but were considered integral components of church structure, a demonstration of its unity. Not to be admitted to the convention meant not to be part of the diocese, not to be in union with the Episcopal denomination.

St. Philip's had a difficult road ahead. The church knew it could count on John Jay II. He came from a distinguished family of Episcopalians and antislavery activists and had taken up Crummell's cause against Onderdonk in the 1830s, airing his denomination's racism publicly in pamphlets and newspaper articles. A majority of white Episcopalians, however, agreed with scientific racists who declared that whites were the superior race, the standard bearers of civilization, while blacks were inferior, forever mired in barbarism. Preeminent among them was George Templeton Strong, a prominent member of New York's elite, lawyer, trustee of Columbia College, vestryman at Trinity Church. Although antislavery, Strong was equally anti-black; he qualified as a "niggerologist" since he used the N-word in his diary like a tic.

There were more men like Strong than Jay in New York's Episcopal Diocese, and they were prepared to fight St. Philip's admission to the Diocesan Convention. They rested their case on the claim that Hobart had only acceded to "the admission of a colored person as a candidate for Holy Orders . . . upon the distinct understanding, that in the event of his being admitted to Orders, he should not 'be entitled to a seat in the Convention, nor should the congregation of which he may have the charge, be represented therein.'"[35]

SEX AND THE BISHOP

Strong operated according to the rule of whimsy. He adhered to a double racial standard according to which blacks were by nature brutes and could not be civilized, but excuses could readily be found for bad white behavior. In 1844, Bishop Onderdonk, a middle-aged, balding, graying, bespectacled, thin-lipped man of the cloth, was brought before an ecclesiastical court and charged with "immorality and impurity." His sins were twofold: excessive drinking and gross indecency toward women. For several years he had been the subject of idle gossip, openly referred to as the "touching bishop" because social drinking led him to touch those with whom he was conversing. But court records suggest more egregious behavior. In one testimony, a witness confirmed that during a thirty-minute carriage ride, Onderdonk had rested his hand on her bosom while talking with a passenger in the front seat! Although tempted to leap from the carriage, she remained silent for fear of being heard by those sitting in front. The court voted to suspend Onderdonk indefinitely, in effect prohibiting him from further fulfilling any church functions.[36]

Writing in his diary, Strong dismissed the charges against Onderdonk as "this most pitiful attack on the Bishop's character . . . [by] amateurs in stink and stercoration." And, he continued with breathtaking misogyny, "all I dread is that some silly slips of sickly virginity, whom the Bishop may have shaken hands with, looked at, or (shocking to relate) actually *kissed* (the ungentlemanly old ruffian!) will be brought forward, with some imperfect recollections, distilled by vanity . . . self-importance and their own impure suggestions, to swear to—heaven knows what—of an attempted rape and a heroic resistance."[37]

The reaction of St. Philip's vestry made it strange bedfellows of the very racist Strong. Adhering to conventions of respectability as closely as they did, they would never have countenanced such behavior from one of their own. But, rather than take advantage of his plight, the vestry wrote Onderdonk a letter of sympathy, hand delivered by Peter Ray and James McCune Smith. Reading back through the minutes, Philip could find the following:

> We feel especially humiliated in your humiliation, because we have reason to believe, that during the course of your ministry, we have been blessed with an unusually large share of your sympathy, support and attention. . . . Be assured that our confidence in you remains unshaken; our love, respect, and veneration unaltered; and we shall greatly rejoice when the time shall come for us again to listen to your counsel and admonitions, and the word preached by you.

To make their position official, the vestry followed up with a resolution stating "that Bishop Onderdonk should not resign the Episcopacy of the Diocese under the present circumstances." Even the usually independent minded Smith voted in favor. Onderdonk's letter of response was effusive in its gratitude.[38]

What was St. Philip's trying to accomplish? George Strong provided one answer. In his diary he made clear that what was at stake in

Onderdonk's trial was the future direction of the Episcopal Church, which in the 1840s was riven by a deep division between High and Low Churchmen. During his episcopacy, Hobart had managed to preserve a delicate balance between evangelical truth and apostolic order. But, dedicated to High Church ideals, Onderdonk went to extremes, obsessing to the point of fussiness over every detail of what he considered proper Episcopal ritual. Onderdonk's high-handed pronouncements infuriated Low Churchmen, and they used his sexual escapades to get rid of him. As one who favored Onderdonk's policies, Strong lamented his downfall and was consoled only by "the very general feeling of sympathy for the Bishop that seems to exist even in quarters where one would least expect it."[39] One of these unexpected quarters was the High Church St. Philip's. Religion trumped morality, and it placed both a racist ideologue and his victims in the same camp.

St. Philip's vestry minutes provided a second answer. In a canny political move, the vestry took swift advantage of Onderdonk's predicament and newfound benevolence toward them to appeal to him for help. They appointed a committee composed of Smith and Henry Scott "to wait on Bishop Onderdonk and state that the vestry is anxious to have the parish represented in the next Diocesan Convention; and to enquire what are the necessary steps for that purpose."[40]

ADMISSION TO THE DIOCESAN CONVENTION

Neither the meeting with Onderdonk nor admission to the 1846 Diocesan Convention happened. I can't imagine the sickened reactions of Philip and his fellow parishioners as they read the language of the convention's rejection, which could have been lifted straight from a Van Evrie's textbook.

> When society is unfortunately divided into classes—when some are intelligent, refined, and elevated, in tone and character, and others are ignorant, coarse and debased, however unjustly, and when such prejudices exist between them, as to prevent social intercourse on equal terms, it would seem in-

expedient to encounter such prejudices, unnecessarily, and
to endeavor to compel the one class to associate on equal
terms in the consultations on the affairs of the Diocese, with
those whom they would not admit to their tables, or into
their family circles — nay, whom they would not admit into
their pews, during public worship. . . . We deeply sympathize
with the colored race in our country, we feel acutely their
wrongs — and not the least among them, their social degradation. But this cannot prevent our seeing the fact, that they
are socially degraded, and are not regarded as proper associates for the class of persons who attend our Convention.[41]

Given such open contempt, it's a wonder that the men of St. Philip's
did not give up. They didn't, but their efforts in the late 1840s seemed
at best dispirited.

Ironically, it was the arrival of William Morris that gave them
new impetus. In the fall of 1852, Morris, Philip, and Peter Ray were
chosen to represent St. Philip's at the Diocesan Convention. By now,
Philip had displaced his former mentor, James McCune Smith, as both
vestryman and convention delegate. He must have felt honored by his
church's trust in selecting him to succeed Smith. The three members of
the 1852 delegation — one white man and two blacks — decided on a plan
of action: avoid racial politics and simply argue that as a parish in good
standing St. Philip's was entitled to admission to the convention.

We can better understand Morris's seemingly contradictory actions — obey the proslavery laws of the land but fight for equal rights for
a black parish — if we view his motives as inspired by purely religious beliefs in which racial thinking played no part. Morris could then simultaneously claim that true Christians (whatever their race) should not
meddle in politics, and that exemplary Episcopalians (whatever their
race) should be in union with their diocese. This was a position Philip
wholeheartedly endorsed. So St. Philip's delegation must have cringed
when John Jay II stood up during the 1852 convention deliberations and
proposed a resolution repudiating admission based on "caste." The outcome was inevitable: the resolution failed and St. Philip's was denied
admission.

Success finally came at the convention of 1853, and Philip was there to savor it. Jay kept silent on the issue of racial discrimination. Apparently exhausted by this drawn-out struggle, the convention by-passed debate. Nineteen parishes were presented, St. Philip's the very last. It was admitted by a vote of 215 to 46.[42]

With quiet satisfaction, St. Philip's vestry minutes merely noted that: "Peter Ray for the Delegates to the Convention reported the ap-plication of St. Philip's Church for admission to the seventieth Diocesan Convention was successful and the church is now in full union with the rest of the Diocese." With considerable venom, Strong wrote in his diary: "Another Revolution. John Jay's annual motion carried at last, and the nigger delegation admitted to the Diocesan Convention."[43]

I wondered what James McCune Smith thought of his former apprentice. Was he exasperated by Philip's refusal to embrace the anti-slavery cause? Dismayed that Philip had replaced him on the vestry de-spite his many years of service? Upset that he had not been part of the very first delegation seated at the Diocesan Convention? A brief let-ter Smith wrote to John Jay would seem to bear that out. In it, Smith complained that the vestry secretary (Philip) was not giving out any information about the upcoming convention. Yet as soon as he heard of St. Philip's admission, Smith fired off a letter to *Frederick Douglass' Paper* highly complimentary of the delegation: "The delegates from St. Philip's are Peter Ray, senior warden, superintendent of Lorillard's im-mense tobacco factory, Philip A. White, chemist and apothecary, and Henry Scott, merchant—all worthy, intelligent and respectable men."[44] By 1858, Philip and Smith were attending the Diocesan Convention together as delegates. If there had been grudges, neither man appeared interested in holding on to them. They were well aware of the impor-tance of collaborative work in the black community.

SEX AND THE REVEREND

Philip and his fellow vestrymen expressed their gratitude to Morris in several ways: verbal thanks and a renewal of his contract for another five years. Over the next several months, it became clear that this white minister was a changed man. "Our excellent pastor of St. Philip's," James McCune Smith commented approvingly, "actually preaches against the Nebraska Bill."[45] Did Morris have a change of heart and now believe that religion and politics could in fact mix? Or was he trying to get right with as many of the church's parishioners as possible?

As Philip and the rest of the congregation were soon to find out, Morris was having problems of his own—termed of a "domestic nature"—even while espousing St. Philip's cause at the Diocesan Convention. In 1856, he informed the vestry that he could no longer continue his ministerial duties because of his impending trial by the Ecclesiastical Court.[46] Once again a white man of the cloth was being charged with the kind of sexual behavior with which scientific racists demonized blacks. The details of the court records are lurid; they make Onderdonk's trial pale by comparison.

It appears that sometime around 1853 Morris tired of his wife and sought to get his marriage annulled. Frustrated in his plan, he turned abusive. He allegedly referred to her as a "drunken whore," accused her of having an affair, and claimed that their son was not his child. Turning violent, on one occasion he supposedly grabbed her and dragged her across the floor; on another he pressed her against the sideboard until she was blue in the face. Mrs. Morris eventually went on the offensive, hiring lawyers and accusing her husband of the very same crimes. Her charges were a lot more specific. A witness testified that Morris had had an affair with one Jane Hayden and had seen him "kissing her, holding her on his lap and spitting into her mouth," and also taking candy out of her mouth and eating it. They had been observed together in bed. They were known to have traveled to Europe as a couple. Another witness maintained that Morris had also committed adultery with one Ann Spread. She had gone into his bedroom and closed the door, later appearing downstairs with "her dress crushed and her face flushed."

Morris's defenders had a lot more clout than George Templeton Strong. The clergy all lined up behind their colleague to give positive character testimony. Morris, they asserted, was "very cheerful, exceedingly benevolent; extravagantly so; and his conduct as far as I ever saw irreproachable." Even better, he was a "man of purity and integrity of character upright in his principles. Ingenious and unsuspicious in his manner, liberal and generous in his disposition." The verdict was minimally damaging. On a split vote Morris was found guilty of depreciation of his wife's character and impropriety with Ann Spread. There was no ecclesiastical censure.[47]

I won't even try to explain the dissonance between Morris's personal and religious behavior, or why St. Philip's kept him on rather than fire him. Surely, if one of their own had engaged in such disreputable behavior, he would have been ousted immediately. I can only surmise that they remained grateful for the way he had fought for them and were determined to stick by him.

In 1858, it appeared that harmony might at last reign at St. Philip's. The vestry still hoped to hire a black minister, but when their efforts failed, the congregation sent a petition requesting that Morris be given yet another five-year contract. I couldn't find Philip's or Peter's name on the list. But for the first time, women were signatories: they included Peter's wife, Cornelia, his daughter Elizabeth, and his former sister-in-law Mary Joseph Marshall. Women, it seemed, were beginning to make their presence felt. Morris declined the invitation, and thereafter slipped into obscurity.[48]

Frederick Douglass' Paper: **Defining Race and Culture**

"I am a plain Dutch negro, with only one head, without horns or tail: I am well known in the Flats, and Harsimus and Bergen, and way up to Hell Gate, and am a lineal descendant from one of the folly fellows whom Washington Irving alludes to in his sketch book, as shining and laughing on our side of Buttermilk Channel."[49] I imagine Philip coming home after a long day of work, picking up his copy of *Frederick Douglass' Paper,* which he subscribed to, and reading those lines in a column signed by "Communipaw" with a broad smile on his face. The article in question was part of a literary exchange carried out in the paper between 1852 and 1855 among three men writing under the pen names of Communipaw, Ethiop, and Cosmopolite. Their identities were not a mystery, but an open secret among the paper's readership. Ethiop was the Brooklyn schoolteacher William J. Wilson, Cosmopolite was Philip

Bell, and Communipaw was none other than James McCune Smith. The pen names were not chosen at random. To the contrary, each established its creator's particular perspective on race.

Under their ironic and playful tone, these three men were conducting a serious debate about the place of blacks in the city, the nation, and the cosmos to figure out what it meant to be "African" or "colored." *Frederick Douglass' Paper* provided an ideal forum for refuting the niggerologists and devising their own definitions and interpretations of race.

Wilson initiated the debate. In naming himself Ethiop, he drew attention to his undiluted black blood and proudly identified himself with Africa. "I am not ashamed to own," he wrote early in January 1852, "that through my veins flow, freely flow, dark Afric's proudest blood." Throughout his columns, Ethiop suggested that certain essential traits— suffering, patience, endurance, submission to the law, Christian turning of the other cheek—inhered in "dark Afric's blood"; put together, they created Negro nationality. In statements like these, Ethiop was simply repeating Smith's earlier contention about the special destiny of the Negro race. He claimed, for example, that only a black would be able to revitalize modern American religion: "Who will be the Luther of this age and country? Under all circumstances, he evidently must come from the Africo-American side."[50]

There was a downside to Ethiop's theory, however. His definition of Negro character differed little from those of white liberals, like Harriet Beecher Stowe, whose concept of "romantic racialism" offered a less malignant, but nonetheless racist, view of blacks than scientific racism. According to this softer version, blacks were permanently fixed in a childlike state; like Stowe's Uncle Tom, they were naive, docile, willing to be guided, spiritual, and all forgiving. Equally troubling was that this line of reasoning—defining race through a series of essentialist traits—came dangerously close to that of the niggerologists. Positive racial traits were simply substituted for negative ones, and racial categories defining black and white remained firmly in place.

In contrast, Philip Bell chose the pen name Cosmopolite, drawing from the worldly sensibility of eighteenth-century British culture. Perhaps remembering Charles Andrews's early schooling, Bell fashioned himself into a citizen of the world who, even as a black man in America, was free to partake of cosmopolitan high culture. It was Cosmopolite who related with delight his participation in the city's high-cultural events: a lecture on the life and character of Toussaint L'Ouverture at the Mercantile Library; a performance of Donizetti's *La Favorita* at the Academy of Music; concerts at the Broadway Tabernacle; browsing through Bailliere's bookstore that specialized in scientific books; visits to Goupil's gallery, a Parisian institution that had expanded its art empire to world capitals, to view the popular religious artist Ary Sheffer's painting of the Temptation.

To Bell, his ability to enjoy these events was proof positive that "color-phobia" was fast disappearing in the city. In fact, he went further, arguing that cosmopolitanism transcended race and led to color blindness. From that, he drew two conclusions. The first was that cosmopolitan experience made its participants forget about racism, uniting them into a single, universal "race" of common humanity. "Thus," he argued, "art knows no distinction of color, science recognizes no prejudice."[51] The second was that "education and wealth" were the weapons through which blacks would make their way into a world of cosmopolites and conquer racism.

In the 1840s, James McCune Smith had trumpeted theories similar to Ethiop's concept of the special destiny of the Negro race and Cosmopolite's notion of raceless universality. But by now he had moved well beyond both positions, turning to New York's favorite literary son to forge a more sophisticated and modern view of race. Since Washington Irving's writings appeared with some regularity in *Frederick Douglass' Paper*, readers like Philip needed no literary gloss to explain what Smith was up to.

According to Irving's fictional historian, Diedrich Knickerbocker, author of *Diedrich Knickerbocker's History of New-York*, the first Dutch settlers to come to North America landed at a village named Communipaw, now Jersey City. They lived in perfect harmony with both Native Americans and "Dutch Negroes," whom Knickerbocker credited with "being infinitely more adventurous and knowing than their masters," until a group of Dutchmen decided to sail "in quest of a new seat of empire" and settled on the island of Manna-hatta.[52] If you accepted Knickerbocker's version of history, Communipaw was the original Dutch settlement antedating Manhattan, a small harmonious interracial community rather than a seat of empire.

Smith never re-created the community of Communipaw in his writings. Instead, his "village" was Lower Manhattan. In ten sketches titled "Heads of the Colored People," Smith drew a series of portraits of its black inhabitants in which he conveyed deep sympathy for common folk and intimate knowledge of city streets. His first subject was a poor crippled black news vendor. On Sundays, the man could be found on West Broadway, between Anthony and Leonard Streets; on weekdays he stationed himself at the corner of Broadway and Duane Street. Born in Virginia, like so many unskilled black men of the period he had been a sailor; but his days at sea ended when his legs were frozen in a shipwreck and had to be amputated. He resorted to selling newspapers but barely made ends meet.[53] Confined to a narrow existence, this poor commoner lived a life seemingly at the other extreme from Cosmopolite's. Yet his experiences as a sailor and news vendor suggested that, like the original inhabitants of Communipaw, he too was connected to a global world.

By reinventing himself as Communipaw, Smith gave himself a new ancestry. Placing himself in the lineage of the village's original inhabitants, he presented himself as a composite of different races and ethnicities, as a man of peace rather than a conqueror. In contrast to Ethiop (and the niggerologists), Communipaw scoffed at the idea of racial purity, insisting that single races no longer existed and hence all racial categories were false. Addressing Ethiop directly, and riffing on Shakespeare, he argued that racial mixing was a historical inevitability: "'Black spirits and white, / Mingle, mingle mingle'; and however dear to you may be your ebon hue, your great-grandchildren will be 'many a whitey brown.'... It is quite too late in the day to get up an association for the propagation of the pure African, or Irish, or any other breed."[54]

In Smith's mind, cultural mingling inevitably followed racial mingling. In a separate column, he turned to another popular author of the day, the British poet Tennyson. Quoting from "The Charge of the Light Brigade," Communipaw playfully unfolded an elaborate argument about poetic imitation and literary theft. Tennyson had committed "flat burglary," Communipaw asserted, by stealing his lines from a Congo chant. "Canga bafio te, / Canga moune de le, / Canga do ki la, / Canga li" was the original version of Tennyson's "Cannon to right of them, / Cannon to left of them, / Cannon in front of them / Volleyed and thundered." Not only had Tennyson stolen from another source, but his source derived from African, not European, culture.[55]

What was Smith up to? By charging that the great Victorian poet stole lines from a Congolese chant, he was elaborating his own version of cosmopolitanism. High culture, he suggested, was not pure but the result of borrowings from different cultures, African as well as European. Cosmopolitanism was not raceless, as Bell would have it, but rather a form of mingling in which elements from different cultures became so intertwined they could hardly be separated out. Communipaw's playful and ironic tone emphasized this point. Please don't take my interpretation of "The Charge of the Light Brigade" too seriously, he seemed to be saying. Maybe it's correct, maybe not. The one lesson readers needed to take away was that they should never make assumptions about what constituted high culture.

Applied to the United States, the implications of Smith's theories were considerable. At the very moment when American intellectuals were striving to define national identity, Smith was arguing that all cultures, that of Britain as well as of the United States, had come into being by means of theft resulting in different forms of "mingling." Americans needed to acknowledge what the early families of Collect Street had long known: that racial, cultural, and hence national purity—of white, black, European, African—was mere myth. In effect, Smith was questioning the very notion of race, of what it meant to be American or Negro, thus challenging niggerologists and elites who determined fitness for citizenship. While complicating his theories of cosmopolitanism of the 1840s, Smith returned to the same central issue: that of double consciousness, of the dilemma of being simultaneously American and Negro. The solution, he suggested, was simple: if the categories of white, black, European, African, are invalid, then the problem of double consciousness no longer exists and the so-called "Negro" should be granted "American" citizenship.

Left unresolved was how Smith could transform his meditations on race into an effective political tool that black New Yorkers could seize upon and a persuasive message that white New Yorkers—both elite and working class—could readily embrace.

CHAPTER SEVEN

The Draft Riots

≈ JULY 1863 ≈

IT WAS A LOTTERY—the simple act of reading names drawn from a barrel—that sparked the riot. Early on the morning of Monday, July 13, 1863, hundreds of white workers from the Ninth Ward took to the streets. The weather was infernally hot. In his diary, George Templeton Strong described the day as a "deadly muggy sort with a muddy sky and lifeless air." It matched the surly mood of the crowd. Rather than proceed to their places of employment, they converged on Central Park where they held a brief meeting. Holding high "No Draft" placards, they then descended on the Provost Marshal's office in the Ninth Ward at Third Avenue and Forty-seventh Street, where the lottery was about to start. At ten-thirty, the Provost Marshal began calling out names as they were taken from the wheel. As he read off the last one, a stone came crashing through the window, and the destruction began. The crowd smashed the wheel, scattering the pieces of paper on which the names had been written. They destroyed all the furnishings and set the building on fire. The New York City draft riots, the largest incident of civil disorder in the nation to that date, had erupted.[1]

Two years earlier, on April 12, 1861, Confederate forces had launched an attack on the Union army at Fort Sumter, South Carolina. On April 15, President Lincoln declared a state of insurrection in the South and called for seventy-five thousand volunteers to put it down.

As the war progressed, the federal government became desperate for more soldiers and decided to enact a draft law. In March 1863, Congress passed a National Conscription Act decreeing that all male citizens (by definition white) between the ages of twenty and thirty-five were to be enrolled in the military, and a lottery then conducted to determine who would actually serve. The act granted federal officials considerable authority to intrude in the daily life of the citizenry—namely, the power to conduct house-to-house visits for enrollment purposes and to arrest those who resisted. Stunningly, it also included a provision exempting from service those who could offer an acceptable substitute or pay three hundred dollars. It was the poor, not the rich, who were to fight Lincoln's war.

Of all the stories in this book, the history of the New York draft riots is by far the best known. It's been told over and over again in print and on screen. Perhaps because of its violence. Perhaps because of the innocence of the victims. Perhaps because of the fiendishness of the mob. And there's a written record.

For the next week, white and black New Yorkers alike could follow the progress of the riot in their newspapers. In addition to government, police, and eyewitness accounts, it's the city papers that have left the most extensive paper trail. Philip and his friends found heartfelt reports of the horrors unfolding in the streets in the *Tribune*, the *Times*, antislavery papers like the *Liberator* and *National Anti-Slavery Standard*, as well as the *Weekly Anglo-African*, the city's new black newspaper founded in the early 1860s by William Hamilton's two sons, Thomas and Robert. Putting aside James McCune Smith's earlier charge that Greeley was nothing but a flagrant prostitute, black New Yorkers were now appreciative of his support for the Union and grateful for his extensive coverage of the riots, especially since the reporting in the *Weekly Anglo-African* relied heavily on articles retrieved from the *Tribune*. Indeed, the degree to which the newspapers tended to reprint one another's reports is striking. One of the unforeseen consequences has been a more limited historical record.

Rioters and Rioting

Over the weekend of July 11, members of New York's white working class grew increasingly angered that they were being asked to risk their lives in an armed conflict in which neither those who had decided on the war—political elites who could buy their way out—nor those who they believed to be the cause of the war—blacks excluded by law from service—were forced to fight. Although many were native born, a large percentage of this working class were new arrivals from Ireland and Germany. These immigrants, the Irish in particular, could barely make ends meet. From the moment they landed in New York, they toiled at the bottom of the labor market, vying with black workers for unskilled and semi-skilled jobs. Economic competition increased their racial animosity and jealous determination to lock blacks out of gainful employment. Yet to better-off whites they were loathsome creatures, derided in the same abusive language typically reserved for blacks.

At first, New York's white workingmen caught the war fever. Military service, they figured, would provide steady employment, allow them to wave the flag of patriotism, and offer a life of adventure. Their fever waned quickly. Thousands died on the battlefield. Others came home sick, maimed, disfigured. In the city, inflation was rampant; prices rose while wages fell.[2]

The rioters came from different parts of the city. Some were journeymen in the older artisan trades, while others—mostly Irish Catholic—were common laborers or workers in newer industrial occupations. Over the four days of rioting, the composition of the mob gradually shifted as both native-born Americans and German immigrants retreated. More likely to be skilled workers and property owners, their animosity toward political elites and blacks was not nearly as great as that of the Irish.

The mob's targets were varied, but put together they covered just about every aspect of city life. Their work of destruction had a perverse logic of its own. They descended on the Provost Marshal's office to disrupt the lottery that was going to send them to a war they didn't want to fight. When they came across Superintendent of Police John Kennedy rushing to defend the building, they beat him to a bloody pulp. They invaded the Armory at Second Avenue and Twenty-first Street, seizing all the weapons they could find. They set about destroying all means of communication — telegraph lines, railroads and streetcar tracks, ferries and bridges — to prevent city officials from calling for reinforcements from both inside and outside the city.

They vented their wrath against anybody or anything that smacked of wealth and privilege — swank mansions on Fifth and Lexington Avenues, banks where the elite made their money, department stores like Brooks Brothers where they spent it. Strong was disgusted. Like a bad habit he could not get rid of, he still referred to blacks as "niggers." But he had equal contempt for lower-class whites. Above all, he wanted the Union preserved. On the third day of the riots, he became seriously frightened, so "by way of precaution," he wrote in his diary, "I had had the bathtubs filled, and also all the pots, kettles and pails in the house." He took to praying for rain, opining that "mobs have no taste for the effusion of cold water."[3]

The mob attacked the building of the *Tribune*, looking for its troublemaking editor while singing a ditty to the tune of "John Brown's Body":

> We'll hang old Greeley to a sour apple tree,
> We'll hang old Greeley to a sour apple tree,
> We'll hang old Greeley to a sour apple tree,
> And send him to straight to hell. . . .[4]

Most especially, they poured their venom upon New York's black population.

Reading through the newspapers, it seemed that the organizing principle of the reporting was to list the mob's horrific acts as random assaults against random individuals of the wrong color caught in the wrong place at the wrong time, proceeding geographically from one ward to another and, within each ward, from one street to another. Geography mattered.

Decades earlier, black New Yorkers and their institutions had concentrated in the Five Points area, housing families like the Marshalls, DeGrasses, Crummells, Garnets, and Williamses; churches like

St. Philip's and Mother Zion; organizations like the Philomathean Society, the offices of *Freedom's Journal* and the African Society for Mutual Relief. By 1860, however, the black community was no longer so geographically delimited; only the African Society remained in its original Baxter Street location.

In addition to their community, however, black New Yorkers lived in city neighborhoods made up of diverse peoples. By now the white elite—the Upper Tendom—had walled itself off in exclusive residential enclaves. But artisans, skilled and unskilled laborers, still tended to live in close proximity to their workplaces. In these neighborhoods, native-born Americans mixed with Irish and German immigrants as well as with blacks. Racial and ethnic differentiation occurred within city blocks, or even buildings, rather than from neighborhood to neighborhood.[5]

So at the time of the draft riots black New Yorkers lived in two places—black community and local neighborhood—that were quite distinct. Given their dispersal and that of their institutions, they could not rely on community collaboration. Could they count on their neighbors? "Love thy neighbor as thyself," Christian ethics demand of us. But is that truly possible? Despite close proximity, my neighbor might remain a stranger. How can I love a stranger? And might physical intimacy breed not love but hostility, even hatred?[6] The rioters must have perceived their black victims as strangers: strangers on a strange street, but also, as accounts intimated, strangers in their own home neighborhoods. And their neighbors did likewise.

Here's a sampling:

Abraham Franklin, a cripple. The mob hanged him in front of his mother near their home on the corner of Twenty-seventh Street and Seventh Avenue. They left when the police interrupted their work, but later returned to hang him once again and mutilate his body.

James Costello. Pursued by a rioter when he left his home at 97 West Thirty-third Street on an errand, he turned and shot the man in self-defense. The mob set upon him, mangled his body, then hanged it; after cutting it down, they dragged it through the gutter, smashing it with stones, and finally burned it.

Jeremiah Robinson. Hoping to escape the mob, he dressed in his wife's clothes, but, betrayed by his beard, was captured and killed on Madison near Catherine Street. His body was then flung in the river.

A seven-year-old child living with his grandmother and widowed mother. They were forced to flee their house on East Twenty-eighth after a mob set fire to it. Separated from his family, the boy was struck with cobblestones and pistols. He died from his injuries.

Samuel Johnson, a resident of Roosevelt Street. His father William was brutally attacked by rioters on Second Avenue near Thirty-sixth Street and left for dead. He dragged himself home only to find his son dying from injuries inflicted by the mob.

Mary Alexander, who lived on West Twenty-eighth Street, chased out of her house by the mob, although her life was spared.[7]

When it was all over at least 150 people, black and white, were dead and millions of dollars in property lost.

How could this have happened in New York City?

White Democrats and White Republicans

For decades, the city had been in a state of ideological war over the issue of slavery. On the eve of the Civil War dissension had reached the point of explosion.

New York politics was dominated by merchants with last names like Astor, Havemeyer, Belmont, and Tilden, all Democrats who lined up solidly behind the South. "What would New York be without slavery?" commerce analyst James De Bow wondered. "The ships would rot at her docks; grass would grow in Wall Street and Broadway, and the glory of New York, like that of Babylon and Rome, would be numbered with the things of the past." Aware of where their economic interests lay, these men took to calling themselves Peace Democrats and preached conciliation with the South. If that was not possible, they would side with their race. They hailed Fernando Wood's election as mayor in 1859. A fellow Peace Democrat, Wood agreed "that the South is our best customer. She pays the best prices, and pays promptly." Once war appeared inevitable, he proposed secession, not of South from North, but of the city from the rest of the country. As a free city, New York could do as it pleased—support slavery, trade with the South, ignore federal tariffs.

City politicians and merchants turned unpeaceful, however, once the Confederacy decided to lower tariffs in its ports, thereby making commerce through New York expensive and undercutting the city's trade with Europe. Feeling betrayed, they were ready to switch sides. For a time, war proved to be an economic blessing as demands grew for increased production in industries of all kinds—shipbuilding, refining, maritime engineering, clothes manufacturing, communications. The stock market went bullish. The Republican merchant-banker George Opdyke captured City Hall.

Undeterred, Peace Democrat politicians cannily played on the fears of the city's immigrant population, who in the wake of emancipation became increasingly worried about the specter of former slave labor flooding the North in the event of a Union victory. Elected to Congress, Fernando Wood and the new Democratic governor Horatio Seymour took to proclaiming that Lincoln's policies had substituted "niggerism for nationality."[8]

In contrast, New York's white Republicans were a varied lot, refugees from now defunct political parties. Some, like Henry Ward Beecher, had been Free Soilers and became early, enthusiastic supporters of Abraham Lincoln. Others, like Horace Greeley, were former Whigs who proceeded cautiously. Greeley's conversion took time. He refused to endorse Lincoln until after the presidential nomination had taken place. He initially thought secession and peaceful disunion preferable to armed conflict. But by the beginning of the Civil War, even Greeley had been transformed into an ardent Unionist ready to fight to the finish.[9]

The Black Elite: Quest for Citizenship

For the black elite, politics was a more complicated matter. Its members were divided over both strategy and goals.

Some were determined to pursue their quest for citizenship. The state's property qualification still denied most black men the right to vote. In the aftermath of the Supreme Court's Dred Scott decision that ruled black Americans unfit for citizenship, men of the elite multiplied their efforts to regain the elective franchise. Much like the *Colored American* in earlier years, the *Weekly Anglo-African* became a forum for debating strategy. In May 1860, it reported on a planning meeting organized by many of the same activists of the 1830s and '40s: James McCune Smith, Charles Reason, Henry Highland Garnet, and others. The result was the formation of the New York City and County Suffrage Committee of Colored Citizens, which planned an all-out campaign in support of a state amendment repealing the property qualification.[10] To facilitate the task of those black men who could vote, ballots on the amendment were distributed to different venues throughout the community. White voters clung to their prejudices, however, and rejected the referendum, 337,984 to 197,503, in the state, and 65,082 to 10,493 in New York County.[11]

In contrast, men like Alexander Crummell believed blacks should abandon the United States altogether. Still living in Liberia, Crummell returned to visit New York in 1861 and embarked on a lecture tour of the Northeast. In speech after speech, he trumpeted the virtues of Liberia, which, he asserted, was the only nation that could redeem this fallen world. Yet, without apparent irony, Crummell simultaneously reiterated his earlier claim that Africans were living in such a degraded and unenlightened state that black Americans needed to emigrate there and assist them. Using his newspaper as a podium, Frederick Douglass accused Crummell of portraying Liberia in an inconsistent light—sometimes glowing, sometimes gloomy—and promoting a brain drain of black Americans who were badly needed at home. Undeterred, Crummell pressed on, even going so far as to approach the American Colonization Society to discuss possible commercial projects in Liberia, and to back Lincoln's obnoxious (but thankfully temporary) scheme to repatriate emancipated slaves to Liberia, Haiti, or even Panama.[12] Black leaders were infuriated.

As war became increasingly inevitable, many in the black elite were perplexed over which party to support: they were skeptical of Democrats and Republicans alike. Democrats, they knew, were unabashed proslavery men. But summing up the opinion of many, Thomas Hamilton argued that Republicans were not much better and in fact might be worse, because they were hypocritical and cowardly. "Where it is clearly in their power to do anything for the oppressed colored man," he asserted in the *Weekly Anglo-African*, "why then they are too nice, too conservative, to do it. They find, too often, a way to slip round it—find a method how not to do it. If too hard pressed or fairly cornered by the opposite party, then it is they [who] go beyond said opposite party in their manifestations of hatred and contempt for the black man and his rights."[13]

Once Lincoln declared war, however, the black elite threw its full support behind his efforts. In William Powell's words, "never was there a greater opportunity for the American nation to put an everlasting end to Negro slavery." When Lincoln issued the Emancipation Proclamation some eighteen months later, on January 1, 1863, they were positively jubilant. Accompanied by white activists, they came by the thousands to a mass meeting in the great hall of the Cooper Institute reminiscent of the one held in 1850 to protest the capture of James Hamlet. Henry Highland Garnet presided over the gathering, and after reading the proclamation aloud he addressed the assembly.

Garnet argued that "with his eyes set on the God of Justice" the president had now fulfilled his promise of emancipation. He then proceeded to recall how at the onset of war New York's black men, eager to serve their country and show proof of their capacity for citizenship, had petitioned the governor for permission to join the military. Tongue in cheek, Garnet noted that "when the offer became public, the people (the white people) were horror-stricken, and some of them turned up their noses till they almost met their foreheads, fearing lest white men and black men should fight shoulder to shoulder to save the country." Facing the opposition of Superintendent of Police Kennedy, the very same man who would soon be attacked by the mob, black leaders were forced to suspend their plans. But Garnet was determined that blacks should serve, and he warned Jefferson Davis: "Jeff must know that the black man, when he joins the army, goes to win." In closing, Garnet asked the audience to rise to its feet and give three cheers, in the following order, for God, Abraham Lincoln, "our native land," the "stars and stripes," the abolitionists, and amazingly enough, the "honored head" of the *Tribune,* Horace Greeley.[14]

The Colored Orphan Asylum

James McCune Smith was safe in his home on North Moore Street, which was not attacked by the mob. But he must have wept upon reading the *Tribune*'s lengthy description of the destruction of the Colored Orphan Asylum. By far the best known of all the draft riots' events, it was recounted over and over in newspapers of the day as well as in more recent histories. It's come to symbolize the utter horror of the riots—the fiendishness of the mob, the helplessness of the victims.

Located far from the impoverished wards that were home to New York's black population, the asylum occupied a large, handsome building on a choice piece of land on Fifth Avenue, near the opulent mansions of the Upper Tendom. The interior was spacious: there were two playrooms in the basement, a kitchen, dining room, bathrooms, and two infirmaries on the first floor, a large schoolroom in each wing. The asylum housed so many of the black community's neediest children that few were sent to New York's almshouses. There were an increasing number of success stories. After completing their indentures, two girls felt confident enough to ask the Board of Managers to help them enter Oberlin College so that they could train as teachers. One young man was able to buy a house and garden. Another moved to Boston and became a hairdresser.[15]

Success came in another form as well. On the eve of the Civil War, the asylum was moving toward greater interracial cooperation. Prominent white abolitionists like John Jay and Henry Ward Beecher had long lent their presence and name to the annual anniversary celebrations. But blacks were now increasingly involved. James McCune Smith was still the doctor in charge. A black woman, Adelaide Butler, also known as Aunt Delia, became matron in 1853. Emerging from the shadows into

Colored Orphan Asylum, Fifth Avenue between Forty-third
and Forty-fourth Streets, exterior yard with uniformed girls, 1861
(New-York Historical Society)

public light, black women began organizing benefit fairs on behalf of
the orphans. Among the 1860 fair's "directresses" were wives, widows,
daughters, and sisters of many community leaders: Mary J. Lyons, Mal-
vina Smith, Ann Ray, Eliza Peterson, Mary Wake, Mrs. C. B. Ray, Mrs.
William J. Wilson, Charlotte Ray, and yes, even Philip's sister, Sarah
Maria White.[16]

The *Tribune*'s account of the attack on the asylum is harrowing in
its detail.

The Orphan Asylum (in Fifth Avenue, near Forty-Sixth Street) was fired about 5 o'clock in the afternoon. The infuriated mob, eager for any outrage were turned that way by the simple suggestion that the building was full of colored children. They clamored around the house like demons, filling the air with yells. A few policemen, who attempted to make a stand, were instantly overpowered—several being severely or fatally injured. While this was going on, a few of the less evil disposed gave notice to the inmates to quit the building.

The sight of the helpless creatures stayed, for a moment, even the insensate mob; but the orphans were no sooner out than the work of demolition commenced. First, the main building was gutted, and then set on fire. While it was burning, the large wing adjoining—used as a dormitory—was stripped, inside and out. Several hundred iron bedsteads were carried off—such an exodus of this article was never witnessed before perhaps. They radiated in every direction for half a mile.

Carpets were dragged away at length; desks, tools, chairs, tables, books of all kinds—everything moveable— was carried off. Even the cape and bonnets of the poor children were stolen. The writer picked up fragments of vestments for a quarter of a mile down Fifth avenue. While the rioters stripped the building of furniture, their wives and children, and hundreds who were too cowardly to assist the work of demolition, carried them off. The wing, while yet unburning, swarmed with rioters, who seemed endowed with a demoniacal energy to rend to pieces, rob and destroy.

Shutters and doors were torn off and tumbled into the streets. These were seized and torn to pieces almost before they touched the ground, and, with everything else, carried off with surprising celerity. Several persons were injured, and it is supposed some killed, by the falling of shutters and furniture from the windows. Even the gutters were hewn off, and the chimneys tumbled down.

The fire-engines were there in great numbers, but were

not permitted to work, except upon the adjacent buildings. What was very marked, as the destruction proceeded, was the absence of excitement. Things were done quietly and coolly by the rioters as if they were saving instead of destroying property. Mingling with the crowd—which amounted, perhaps to 5,000 or 6,000 persons—were many who were evidently not of them; but except in cases of incautious utterance, they were not molested.

One or two persons who attempted a remonstrance were summarily disposed of, being beaten and trampled under foot. There were some who, though they took part in the plunder, seemed to regret the occasion, and one—a drunken Irishman too, with bloated face, a gigantic fellow—whispered in the writer's ear, with evident good will: "Take yer watch out ' yer pocket, honey, or some o' the b'yes will take care of it for yer."[17]

The rioters came from the outside. There was nothing random about their attack. They were looters, shamelessly helping themselves to goods—or, to twist the writer's words, "saving property"—that they could never have bought on their own. Yet that doesn't begin to explain their vindictiveness. In 1834, a mob had attacked the Chatham Street Chapel because of its interracial activities. Similarly, the rioters now vented their rage at whites who they believed were giving so much to undeserving blacks, at their black beneficiaries who, if equipped with education and jobs, would increasingly become economic competitors, and at an institution that portended possibilities of interracial cooperation that would leave them out in the cold. Caught off guard by their ferocity and realizing that they themselves might be targets, the asylum's neighbors did not (could not?) come to the rescue.

According to the *Tribune*, one or two anonymous bystanders did protest. Theirs was the first act of decency I had come across. There would be others. But in each case the kind rescuers remain shadowy, unnamed, unexplained figures. How had their sense of humanity prevailed over their fear of the mob's violence? Why them, and not others? Was it simply another instance of the rule of whimsy at work?

The Black Elite and the Draft Riots

I wondered what happened to individual members of the black elite.
Were they immune from attack or not? Did class trump race? In the
July 24 issue of the *Times* I came across an account of J. W. C. Pennington's fate, which differed little from the others I had read thus far.
Pennington had returned from out of town to find that "the mob had
attacked my residence; my own, with other colored families, had been
expelled and I was at once set upon by a mob with stones, brickbats, etc.,
with the shout, "Kill the d——d black neager, etc." He fled and wandered around the city in search of his loved ones.

But was it not possible that New York neighborhoods might have
functioned like small villages, where daily face-to-face contact with
relatives and friends, but also with customers, tradesmen, co-workers,
landlords, tenants, and the like gave rise to acceptance, camaraderie,
even social intimacy? If so, did blacks still live among strangers who
hated them? Did they not have neighbors who loved them, or at least
tolerated them, and looked out for them when under siege?

HENRY HIGHLAND GARNET

In his sketch of Garnet's life, James McCune Smith offered a short account of his friend's fate during the draft riots:

> The Rev. Mr. Garnet was too prominently known to escape
> the attention of the July rioters; they rushed down Thirti-
> eth Street where he resided, loudly calling him by name. By
> the lucky forethought of his daughter who wrenched off the
> door-plate with an axe, his house escaped sacking, and his
> own life and that of his family were preserved by the kind
> acts of some white neighbors.[18]

The mob came from outside Garnet's neighborhood. Known to
them by reputation, he was not quite a stranger; but neither was he a

neighbor since they couldn't locate his exact address. Yet he had neighbors—nameless, faceless—who cared enough about his family to protect them.

WILLIAM POWELL

For William Powell and Albro Lyons, conflict was inevitable. In the
early 1850s, the two men had dissolved their partnership in the Colored
Sailors' Home on Pearl Street and gone their separate ways. But ten
years later, they were both back living and working in their old Fourth
Ward neighborhood. They must have rued the day they returned. By
the early 1860s, the area had become increasingly working-class and
Irish. Merchants still maintained businesses there but had moved their
households to more distant residential enclaves. Irish longshoremen
patrolled the port, determined to maintain their monopoly on dock
work. Both Powell and Lyons had strong ties to the black community,
but their neighborhood relationships were weak. The combination was
combustible.

In the summer of 1851, Powell had made a bold move, sending
what he deemed a "sensible petition" to the state legislature. He began
by complaining that he and his family were being denied the benefits
of U.S. citizenship, which should have been theirs by right for the following two reasons. The first was that his grandmother Elizabeth Bar-
jona had been a cook for Congress during the revolutionary war and
thus had helped further the cause of American independence. The second was that his father had been a slave, one of the many who had en-
riched the soil of his native land with his sweat and blood. Given their
country's refusal to recognize their rights as citizens, Powell requested
funds to emigrate "to the Kingdom of Great Britain, where character
not color—capacity and not complexion, are the tests of merit."[19] The
petition fell on deaf ears, yet by the end of 1851 Powell and his family
had found a way to move to England on their own.

Ten years later, with news of impending war, and hopes for a
brighter future, Powell returned to New York, opening a new Sailors'

Home on Dover Street. In addition to providing living quarters for black sailors, the home housed a labor union he had founded, the American Seamen's Protective Union Association, designed to improve the condition of black sailors; it soon counted approximately fifty-five members. The home served as a "shaping-up" hall where union members could be hired without having to pay bribes or special fees to land-sharks or land-lords.[20]

Fifty-five black sailors traipsing in and out of 2 Dover Street could not have gone unnoticed for long. Irish sailors and longshoremen couldn't have liked it much. And, when the rioters arrived, Powell's neighbors didn't care enough to come to his aid.

In the July 24, 1863, issue of the *Liberator*, Garrison published a letter from Powell that detailed his family's harrowing escape from the mob. After the demolition of the Colored Orphan Asylum, Powell's is probably the best-known account of the mob's destruction of black property. Rioters arrived at his doorstep the very first day. Not knowing that Superintendent Kennedy was badly injured, Powell appealed to him in vain for protection. Alone and abandoned, he wrote, "myself and family were prisoners in my own house to *king mob* from which there was no way to escape but over the roofs of adjoining houses." At some point,

> the mob commenced throwing stones at the lower windows until they had succeeded in making an opening. I was determined not to leave until driven from the premises. My family, including my invalid daughter, (who is entirely helpless), took refuge on the roof of the next house. I remained till the mob broke in, and then narrowly escaped the same way. This was about 8 1/2 pm. We remained on the roof for an hour; still I hoped relief would come.

While the rioters plundered the house, Powell and his family cowered on the roof, where the rain that Strong had hoped for beat down on them mercilessly. Worried about their own safety, neighbors did not stretch out a helping hand but carried their own belongings to their roofs just in case the mob decided to "fire" Powell's home.

Help finally came in the form of a Jewish neighbor who, Powell seemed to suggest, intuitively sympathized with his family's plight: "The God that succored Hagar in her flight came to my relief in the person of a little deformed, despised Israelite—who, Samaritan-like, took my poor helpless daughter under his protection in his house; there I presume she is now, until friends send her to me." With a rope this Good Samaritan had given him, Powell "took a clove-hitch around the clothes-line which was fastened to the wall by pulleys, and which led from one roof to the other over a space of about one hundred feet." In this manner, he lowered the rest of his family down to the next roof, and then from one roof to another until he came to a friend's house where they waited until police came and took them to the station. They remained there with seventy other bruised and beaten men, women, and children until they could be conveyed to safety.

Powell concluded his letter on a bitter note. He was a loyal Unionist eager to serve his country; for that reason, he had just received a commission in the naval service. Yet his fellow citizens had treated him like an enemy. He had abided by the American work ethic, built up a business, and accumulated some property. Yet the rioters had stripped him of all his possessions and "scattered [them] to the four winds, which 'like the baseless fabric of a vision, leaves not a wreck behind' except our lives."[21]

ALBRO LYONS

Although Albro Lyons had been Powell's partner in the Pearl Street Colored Sailors' Home, he and his family had lived in Seneca Village, a community founded in the mid-1820s when the owner of a vast tract of land between Eighty-first and Eighty-ninth Streets and Seventh and Eighth Avenues began selling plots to interested black families. The motivations for establishing Seneca Village were several. One was to create a neighborhood where black New Yorkers could live together in relative peace and security. Another, equally important goal was to encourage property ownership and thereby enlarge the class of black freeholders who could meet the $250 voting requirement.

Seneca Village is the closest approximation to what we think of as a black community: a segregated enclave of black homes and institutions. According to the 1855 census, the total number of inhabitants was 264, but due to underreporting it might have been much higher. In the early 1850s, German and Irish families began moving in. Amazingly, all three groups managed to get along, suggesting that Seneca Village might have evolved into a viable multiethnic, multiracial community. But the Democratic mayor Fernando Wood and his cronies seized Seneca Village's land to begin construction of Central Park. By 1857, Seneca Village no longer existed.[22]

After Powell left for England, Lyons took over the Colored Sailors' Home on Pearl Street and in the late 1850s moved it and his family to 20 Vandewater Street in the Fourth Ward. In addition, he owned an outfitting store for seamen on nearby Roosevelt Street. James Gordon Bennett's *New York Herald* mentioned the destruction of the Lyons home in the briefest of notes: "In Vandewater street, a negro boarding house, kept by a man named Lyons, who, though black, is a strong Democrat, was pulled to pieces, and is now doubtless, being used as fire wood by many of the residents of the Fourth Ward."[23] Except that Lyons was not a strong Democrat.

I found a much fuller account in Maritcha's memoir. Although her father's home was not a center of black labor organizing, it functioned as a stop on the Underground Railroad. "Under mother's vigilant eye," Maritcha recalled, "refugees were kept long enough to be fed and to have disguises changed and be met by those prepared to speed them on in the journey toward the North Star." Maritcha suggested that since the house was "semi-public," people "could go in and out without attracting special attention." Maybe yes, but maybe no. In a sketch of their father's life, Charles Ray's daughters noted that their house, also a stop on the Underground Railroad, was frequently abuzz with activity. They recalled in particular an incident in which a conductor rapped at the door, and then whistled loudly when it opened to signal fourteen fugitive men to enter, alarming even the family.[24] If similar incidents occurred at the Lyons home, they would have attracted a good deal of attention, undoubtedly to their neighbors' great displeasure.

Maritcha did not witness the destruction of her childhood home. But she must have memorized the account she heard her parents tell over and over again, and come to feel that she had been there herself.

> A rabble attacked our house, breaking window panes, smashing shutters, and partially demolishing the main front door. Had not the mob's attention been suddenly diverted, further damage would certainly have ensued. The stones thrown in were utilized as material to form a barricade for the otherwise unprotected main front doorway. . . .
>
> As the evening drew on, a resolute man and a courageous woman quietly seated themselves in the exposed hall, determined to protect their property, to sell their lives as dearly as may be should the need arise. Lights having been extinguished, a lonely vigil of hours passed in mingled darkness, indignation, uncertainty, and dread. Just after midnight, a yell announced that a second mob was gathering to attempt assault. As one of the foremost of the rioters attempted to ascend the front steps, father advanced into the doorway and fired point blank into the crowd. Not knowing what might be concealed in the darkened interior, the fickle mob more disorganized than reckless, retreated out of sight hastily and no further demonstration was made that night.

At dawn, Officer Kelly from the Oak Street police station finally appeared, calling out his name so that Lyons would not shoot at him. He then sat on the steps and sobbed because he did not have enough men to protect Lyons's home.

Undeterred, the mob came back the following day and launched a third and successful attempt against the house. A German neighbor, as nameless, faceless, and silent as all the other Good Samaritans in these accounts, took Mary Joseph in, while Albro escaped to the police station. When it was all over, Maritcha's parents returned to a ravaged home: "Its interior was dismantled, furniture was missing or broken. From basement to attic evidences of the worst vandalism prevailed. A fire, kindled in one of the upper rooms, was discovered in time to prevent a conflagration." In what appears to have been a final blow, "the dismayed parents had to submit to the indignity of taking refuge in the police station house."[25] Perhaps they at least had the comfort of finding their old friends the Powells.

The destruction of these two homes occurred, I think, because both households fulfilled multiple functions—private and public—inimical to the mob. Powell and Lyons had worked hard to build their homes. To them, they were a haven in which to raise their families, a shelter for black men and women in need, and a well-deserved reward for successful entrepreneurship. That is exactly what the rioters were intent on destroying. They deliberately struck at the heart of the black household. They attacked black property and wealth, which from their point of view could only have been ill gotten and illegitimate. In his letter to Garrison, Powell estimated his personal property at $3,000. Maritcha described the Lyons home, which might well have once belonged to a tanning merchant like Jacob Lorillard, as a "large brick building"; in 1862, it was assessed at $5,500.[26] In addition, the rioters were determined to destroy black enterprises and prevent black sailors from seeking "white" work on the docks. Finally, they set about eliminating black community institutions dedicated to improving the lot of black Americans.

In their accounts, neither Powell nor Maritcha stated whether the rioters were neighbors, strangers, or both. But what is certain is that they were bent on destruction, and the people who lived near these black families—with one exception in each case—found no compelling reason to come to the defense of the victims.

PHILIP WHITE

On Friday, July 17, John W. Rode, a sergeant from the fourth precinct station on Oak Street, sent Albro Lyons two notes, carefully preserved in the Williamson papers. They appear to have been written after Albro and Mary Joseph had salvaged what little they could from their ravaged

home. In the first one, Rode proposed to leave their clothing at the
precinct until "everything will be settled." His P.S. intimated that he
was still not sure order had been fully restored in the city: "I have got
three policemen watching your house to prevent fire, etc." Lyons must
have replied with another suggestion, for Rode's second note reads in
its entirety:

New York July 17th/63

Mr. Lyons
Sir

    I have received yours from the bearer. And I cannot
answer whether I can comply with it. I will see you this afternoon as I mentioned in the other note, as I have been ex-
cused from my Captain for that purpose. I cannot say to day
what will occur to morrow. I will be at said Drug Store at
3 O'Clock P.M. this day with Horse & Wagon.
    yours &

John W. Rode
Sergt. 4th Prect.[27]

What had Lyons requested? And why did he suggest meeting at
"said drugstore" in the middle of the afternoon when trouble was still
possible? Whose drugstore was it? Could it have been Philip's? If so,
how could it have been a safe meeting place for a white police officer and
a black victim gathering up his few remaining earthly possessions?

Strangely enough, during the riots Philip's drugstore remained a
safe place. His story never found its way into newspaper reports of the
day. Maybe it was not deemed newsworthy enough, since it was not the
story of a poor hapless black victim beset by a fiendish Irish mob. Or
maybe it was deemed too newsworthy, because it might have alerted
rioters to the fact that there was still more black property to be destroyed. But I found a full account of what happened in the Williamson
papers. Family members must have told the story innumerable times,
and it was undoubtedly repeated over the years by others. Williamson
diligently recorded it, and he must have been the one who provided the

anecdote to the *New York Times*, which, eager to celebrate the life of "one of the best-known colored men in this city," saw fit to print it in Philip's obituary:

> When the riot was at its height a crowd of men gathered at White's store to defend it from attack. Mr. White was warned by some of the business men that he would be wise if he hid himself. He said: "What have I to fear? Even if these men here could not protect me, there are as many men among the rioters who would fight for me as there are those who would injure me." Not the slightest attempt was made to harm him or his property.[28]

What made Philip so sure that the mob would harm neither his person nor his property? After all, he lived only a few doors down the street from the Lyonses at 40 Vandewater, and his drugstore was within a stone's throw at the corner of Frankfort and Gold Streets. Like Lyons's and Powell's Sailors' Homes, Philip's pharmacy was an important landmark in the black community. First William C. Nell and later Frederick Douglass had praised it in newspaper columns of the 1840s and '50s as proof of successful black entrepreneurship. By now, Philip was even more prosperous. In December 1861 and January 1862 he took out a series of advertisements in the *Weekly Anglo-African,* offering his customers goods of all kinds: "perfumery, fancy soaps, fine hair and tooth brushes, pure wines and brandies for medicinal purposes, family articles, and Havana segars"; "Badeau's strengthening plaster for the lame or weak back, pain or weakness in the side, chest, stomach or limbs"; and "physicians prescriptions carefully prepared." In particular, Philip promoted what appears to have been his own concoction: "White's vegetable extract for the preservation, beauty, growth, and restoration of the hair," which, he promised, would clean dirty and greasy hair, get rid of dandruff, restore circulation so as to prevent grayness or baldness, and ultimately produce "luxuriant brilliancy."[29]

Here's where Philip's strategy of going along and getting along rather than raising a ruckus, of accommodation rather than protest, paid off. In contrast to Lyons and Powell, Philip had made his business inte-

is, that the undersigned duly appointed religious service for the day, and thought that he violated no propriety in striving to raise money to pay a church debt—not being conscious of invading the administration—invested sacredness of the day.

JAMES LYNCH,
Georgetown, D. C.

TAKING AN INVENTORY.—The Charleston Mercury of the 15th ult., says that one of General Drayton's negroes, from Hilton Head, reports that Commander Drayton, of the Federal Fleet, who is a brother to the General, visited the plantation of the latter some days ago and took a complete inventory of the negroes, crops, &c., now on the place.

The Richmond papers suggest possibly he considers it his share of the spoils of the expedition, and had a desire to know how much he was worth.

SAMPLES.—A good story is told of the late W. E. Burton, which we have never seen in print. While traveling on a steamboat down the Hudson, he seated himself at the table and called for some beefsteak. The waiter furnished him with a small strip of the article, such as travellers are usually put off with. Taking it upon his fork, and turning it over and examining it with one of his peculiar serious looks, the comedian coolly remarked, "Yes, that's it; bring me some."—Hartford Press.

MR. CHASE'S OPINION OF REBELS.—At a dinner given at the Union Club to the Hon. S. P. Chase, on the occasion of his last visit to New York city, he said in a speech made in reply to a toast: "The blackest negro in South Carolina, black as midnight, is, in my sight, whiter than the whitest rebel." Among the gentlemen present who vehemently cheered this sentiment was Wm. B. Astor.

MISCELLANEOUS.

THE ZOUAVE AND SLAVE ENVELOPE Price per thousand $5; per hundred 60 cents; packages of 25 each, 20 cents.
Orders should be addressed
THOS. HAMILTON
48 Beekman Street, N. Y

MEDICAL.

PAIN-KILLER.

We can recommend on the best authority,

Advertisement for P. A. White's pharmacy, *Weekly Anglo-African*, December 21, 1861 (Houghton Library, Harvard University)

gral—indeed indispensable—to his local neighborhood. Douglass had noted that Philip's drugstore was patronized mainly by the poor whites in his neighborhood. The *Times* obituary elaborated:

> The Swamp neighborhood was quite thickly peopled when he went there, but he had a struggle for some years to keep afloat. During that time, however, he was never unmindful of the poor, and the services and material of his store were willingly given without pay to any one who needed them. . . .
>
> His acts of kindness and charity were numerous, and scores of poor families were befriended and helped by him not only with medicines, but with food and money. Those whom he helped had a chance to show their gratitude during the draft riots of 1863.

Since his arrival in the Swamp in 1847, Philip had been determined to establish a viable local business. He put down roots. He got to know his neighbors, who were increasingly poor Irish. They knew him to be a hard worker. Even after hiring an apprentice, it's quite likely that, given his methodical nature, Philip stood behind his prescription counter, helping to compound the drugs his customers so badly needed. My great-grandfather might have wanted to make money, but he was also dedicated to the art of healing, to bringing relief to a community ravaged by chronic poverty, malnutrition, and disease. So he was willing to give away medicines free or donate food and money when necessary. Under such circumstances, race, class, and ethnicity hardly mattered.

Philip's neighbors had a stake in the survival of his drugstore. The *New York Times* obituary stated that Philip felt certain of the protection not only of those standing guard at his drugstore but also of "many men among the rioters." The comment suggests that the mob was composed of men Philip knew, his poor Irish neighbors, prepared to destroy the property of other black New Yorkers—perhaps Powell's or Lyons's homes—but determined to "fight" for Philip's.

My great-grandfather had achieved a delicate balance. He did so, I think, through a canny combination of altruism and calculation. I imagine Philip's drugstore as a meeting place in which he successfully brought together potentially antagonistic groups in his neighborhood united by need. And he forged a mutually interdependent relationship between himself and his poor Irish neighbors in which benevolence and self-interest were inextricably intertwined for the benefit of all concerned. By giving away medicines, Philip was helping to maintain the stability of the neighborhood in which he lived and worked, and to safeguard his own position in it. Accepting his benevolence over the years, his poor Irish neighbors were eventually able to repay him by protecting him during the riots. In so doing, they were also ensuring that the drugstore they depended on so heavily would survive the riots and continue to serve them.

Yet Philip's balance was even more delicate than his neighbors imagined. The *New York Times* obituary had this to add about Philip:

> His industry and obliging disposition won for him also the favor of business men in the Swamp, many of whom took pains to put trade in his way until he was firmly established. The opportunities thus opened to him inclined some wholesale orders which led him into that branch of the business. It soon became so profitable that he bought the store property and was rated prosperous.
>
> He clung to the retail branch of his business even after he became a wholesale dealer, few in the neighborhood, indeed, knowing for some years that he had interests beyond the counter.

The methodical Philip had patiently built up strong business relations with white merchants in the Swamp, men whose interests were similar to his and whose property might also have been targets during the draft riots. Philip was much more than the small self-employed local tradesman his neighbors thought him to be. He was now engaged in the lucrative, but far more invisible and impersonal, business of a wholesale dealer. His advertisements in the *Weekly Anglo-African* reflected this change. Listing himself as a "wholesale dealer in drugs, dyes, patent or proprietary medicines, fancy goods, perfumery," Philip urged country dealers to buy from him, promising that his goods could not be undersold if paid for in cash.[30] In time, he was able to buy his store property.

But perception is all. To his poor Irish customers, Philip remained the hardworking shopkeeper whose generosity compelled their loyalty. To the businessmen of the Swamp, he was an entrepreneurial young man whose business prospects they were happy to further. To both groups, his drugstore contributed to the welfare of their neighborhood. They did not want it destroyed.

ST. PHILIP'S

Philip, however, could not protect his beloved church. "Police Headquarters," observed a *Tribune* report on July 23, "looks more like an arsenal than the great rendezvous of our Metropolitan force. United States soldiers and volunteers, regular and special policemen, stand at the corners of the streets that bound the edifice, and the African church in front of it swarms with soldiers." This African church was none other than St. Philip's, which, following the flight of blacks out of the Five Points district and other Lower Manhattan neighborhoods, had purchased a Methodist church building on Mulberry Street in the Fourteenth Ward and moved into it in 1857. Even though they still had few resources, parishioners continued to lavish the same care on their sanctuary as when they were located on Centre Street. They were determined to make the physical structure of their church reflect their sense of the divine, especially as envisioned by the Episcopal denomination. They formed a series of subcommittees, of which Albro Lyons was a member, to secure a chandelier for the new building and also to determine how best to alter the church's chancel "to make it conform to the usage of the Protestant Episcopal Church."[31]

St. Philip's stood across the street from Police Headquarters at 300 Mulberry. Presumably its location made it safe from destruction by the mob, and in fact the church was not ransacked as the earlier building on Centre Street had been during the 1834 riots. But poring through the vestry minutes I discovered a heartrending account of assault from

Metropolitan Police Headquarters, Mulberry Street near Bleecker, lithograph by A. Brown and Company (printed in *Booth's History of New York,* volume 7, Emmet Collection, Miriam and Ira D. Wallach Division of Art, Prints, and Photographs, The New York Public Library, Astor, Lenox, and Tilden Foundations)

St. Philip's Church, Mulberry Street, photograph by G. Stacy, probably 1863 (New-York Historical Society)

unexpected quarters that parishioners experienced as only slightly less distressing. In 1863, Philip was no longer on the vestry, but those who were—Peter Ray, John Peterson, James McCune Smith, and others— were adamant about preserving memory of the violation in writing.

> It may be recollected that it was our pleasure and duty to be permitted to assemble ourselves in our sanctuary on the Sunday of July 12th for our usual devotions and humble praise and thanksgiving. But on the succeeding day July 13th 1863 anarchy and confusion took the place of law and order and for several days pillage, arson, murder reigned supreme in our midst. Men, women, and children having seemingly, suddenly become transformed into the vilest and savagest of fiends. During the reign of this state of affairs, at a late hour Tuesday night July 14th 1863 the police authorities took possession of our parish to quarter military who had been summoned hither to bring order over chaos, restore law and maintain the peace of the city. Thus our parish has been in their possession since the above mentioned date until Friday noon July 31st 1863. In consequence of such occupation our church has been greatly defaced and damaged and left in an untenable condition requiring thorough renovation. . . . [We must] have our parish put in a restored condition in every respect as soon as possible so that we and our fellow parishioners may once again through God's providence be permitted to draw near and assemble in our old, accustomed, beloved, and familiar spots in united prayer, to mingle our voices in praise and thanksgiving to "God our refuge."[32]

The soldiers who had turned St. Philip's into a barracks had been careless, and having defaced the church sanctuary, they never thought to repair the damage before leaving.

Parishioners were devastated. They launched a campaign of private solicitation. Members of Trinity Church donated liberally. The next generation of Lorillard sons gave, as did a son-in-law, the prominent merchant John D. Wolfe. So did John Jay and Philip Hone. St. Philip's vestry also appealed to city and federal authorities. In November General Edward Canby, who had been assigned by the army to deal with the riot, finally agreed to pay for damages. But he attached conditions: He would pay one month's rent only if the amount was ascertained by affidavit of property owners in the vicinity. He would reimburse the church for stolen money, books, and other property provided knowledgeable persons specified their exact value by affidavit. He would cover the cost of repairs in the amount fixed upon by estimates submitted beforehand by disinterested parties. There were to be no complaints after the work was finished. Yet it would be almost three years before the vestry sent my great-grandfather to collect a check for $1,100 from the city comptroller. Even then, St. Philip's continued to wrangle with the War Department over the number of months it was owed restitution for the "military occupation." On July 18, 1871, exactly eight years after the riots, the matter was finally put to rest. In all, St. Philip's was reimbursed approximately $1,500 of the $2,500 it had requested.[33]

General Canby's statement, sent through lawyers to St. Philip's vestry, reeked of condescension and suspicion. I wonder what he said in private. Maybe it was something on the order of the comments made by former volunteer special William Stoddard about the African Methodist Church, which had also been used as an army barracks during the riots. Authorities grudgingly agreed to pay this church for new carpets as well as new books for the Sunday-school library, he wrote sarcastically, "on the ground that the unrighteous police, soldiery, and 'specials' had read up forever all there was left of the old," but drew the line "with a good deal of quiet fun" at reimbursement for the Sunday collections missed when the church was undergoing repairs. "That church and the Orphan Asylum," Stoddard concluded cynically, "both made money by the mob, but in somewhat different ways."[34]

How could any of this have assuaged the sense of desolation felt by St. Philip's parishioners? For families like the Lyonses and the Powells, who had been driven out of their homes only to discover that they could not even turn to their church for solace, the feelings must have been especially intense. They found themselves subjected to still other

forms of violence. There was the physical violation of defacement of
their sanctuary. There was the spiritual violation of defilement of their
sacred space. There was the psychological violation of denial of legitimacy by the authorities. In the wake of the riots, St. Philip's parishioners required reparations, not only economic but spiritual and emotional as well.

Reparations

In fact, all black New Yorkers were in need of reparations. In his annual
report as a city missionary, Charles Ray described the aftermath of the
riots in harrowing terms:

> This was a week which scarcely has a parallel in this or any
> other country, unless it were in the Sepoy massacre in India.
> It was a brief time of the reign of an infatuated mob—the
> Reign of Terror. Seldom has a people been so hunted and
> driven in all sections of the city, and so filled with conster-
> nation and dread as were our people during those scenes.[35]

The most vulnerable among the survivors went mad. The *Tribune*
printed an account of a company of soldiers who discovered a "negro
with his clothes nearly torn from his back" rushing up Seventh Avenue "with the most distressing cries." Deciding that he had become a
"raving maniac, growing out of the intense excitement . . . against which
he was unable to maintain his mental balance," the soldiers brought him
into the arsenal where he wandered around "utterly crazed." Even more
distressing was the fate of one William Henry Yates, who committed
suicide after overhearing the mob talk of killing him and burning his
house. According to the *Tribune,* Yates first attempted to kill himself
by slitting his throat with a razor, but when he found that "death would
not ensue from hemorrhage," he resorted to "hanging himself to the cellar door by means of a small cord," thereby ending "his earthly career by
strangulation."[36]
    Others—some five thousand black men, women, and children

who had managed to keep their wits about them—took flight. Many
sought shelter in the wild briars, bushes, and low woods on the ridges
that bordered the city, on Blackwell's Island, in the swamps and woods
back of Bergen, New Jersey, and in the barns and outhouses of farms
on Long Island and Morrisania. Luckier ones fled to the Elysian Fields
in Hoboken, the scene of picnics and baseball games in happier days,
where they improvised a refugee camp. Luckiest of all were those who
had close friends in other cities. On her own, Mary Joseph Lyons took
her children across Long Island Sound to New London, Connecticut,
and from there to Salem, Massachusetts, where they were taken in by
the Remond family.[37]

The *Weekly Anglo-African* provided an invaluable service by publishing notices to inform readers of the fate of community members. It
printed a long list of the colored sufferers of the late mob; denied the reported deaths of John Zuille and Peter Porter; noted Albro Lyons's temporary change of residence to Peter Guignon's home in Williamsburgh
and subsequent return to Vandewater Street; publicized the reopening
of both Charles Ray's and Henry Highland Garnet's churches.[38]

Some semblance of normalcy seemed to be returning to the lives
of black New Yorkers. Yet their numbers dwindled from a high of 16,350
in 1840 to slightly under 10,000, approximately as many as in 1820.[39]

Who among New York's white population would come forward
to restore property and possessions to those blacks who remained in the
city, to repair their bruised spirits and wounded dignity?

THE POLICE DEPARTMENT

William Powell trusted Superintendent Kennedy enough to call for
his help when his house was being attacked. Officer Kelly came to the
Lyons's home and sobbed like a child because he had not been able
to protect it. In the aftermath of the riots, John Rode promised to
send three policemen to guard Lyons's house from being burned to the
ground and agreed to meet Albro at "said drugstore" with a horse and
wagon. Both the Powells and the Lyonses, and many other black families as well, were given shelter in police stations until it was safe for them

to leave the city. New York's policemen worked valiantly to restore law and order, often at the risk of becoming victims of the mob.

The newspapers went to great lengths to praise the police for bringing terrified blacks into their stations, protecting, clothing, and feeding them. In its July 25 issue, the *National Anti-Slavery Standard* reported that more than two hundred blacks "of both sexes and all ages, from the infant at the breast to the white haired grandfather," were being sheltered at Police Headquarters. Housed in the upper floor of the station, the refugees were provided with trunks and boxes to use as seats; beds were placed on the floor; and they received substantial rations of food. Another account described how "through the kindness of the chief officers of the police," the station's courtroom was set aside for Sabbath school; church services soon became crowded with over a hundred black women and children.[40]

Even from a distance of some sixty-five years, however, a tone of humiliation hovers over Maritcha's description of her "dismayed" parents taking shelter in the police station after the riot. Part of it had to do with their sudden homelessness. But it was also because police protection came with certain assumptions and expectations. Once again, black New Yorkers were reminded of the degree to which benevolence was so often accompanied by ignorance, thoughtlessness, and stereotypes that made dependence difficult to bear. Rank-and-file policemen believed that most black New Yorkers were servants and expected them to behave as such while in their station. "The rooms," one report observed, "are scrubbed and dusted and kept in excellent order by the Negroes, many of whom are employed as servants—making themselves very useful. They work well and cheerfully, and have earned the good opinion of the officers in charge."[41] I don't think that either Albro or Mary Joseph Lyons would have objected to helping keep the station house clean, but I'm sure they didn't like assumptions of their servitude.

Hoping to find more information on the draft riots and their aftermath, I made my way to the municipal archives. To my surprise, I found myself faced with what turned out to be the most egregious example of institutional forgetting that I encountered in the course of my research. None of the staff seemed to know what I was talking about. After much debate, they produced three dusty gray boxes stuffed with uncatalogued claims and counterclaims. I wondered whether these documents had remained buried because of their content.

It appears that the police department's goodwill quickly evaporated when the time came to make good on financial reparations for the victims. I found a litany of rejections by city officials couched in a language of thinly veiled contempt that reminded me of the earlier comments made by General Canby and William Stoddard. Maybe because the violence was over, maybe because money was involved, attitudes had clearly changed. Not only were black petitioners denied compensation, they were repeatedly accused of fraud. Time and again, the police argued that claimants did not live where they said they did, or had not really been attacked, that there was no proof of rioting in the area specified, or no corroborating witnesses. Sticking to legal niceties, city authorities denied claims that they felt were indirect rather than direct consequences of the riots—those of a woman who dropped her bundle of clothes while running from the mob or of a fruit vendor whose raspberries rotted because he was afraid to leave his house. They seemed convinced that blacks were constitutionally incapable of telling the truth. All too often their reports concluded with comments like "it is all a base fabrication," "she is a counterfeit," "it is all a gross imposition," "there is not a word of truth in this statement," "it is a cool and deliberate *lie,* and he knows it."[42]

COMMITTEE OF MERCHANTS FOR THE RELIEF OF COLORED PEOPLE

If there were to be reparations, they would have to come from private parties. The city's leading merchants eagerly took up the challenge. By July 23 they had set up a Committee of Merchants for the Relief of Colored People Suffering from the Late Riots in the City of New York. Maybe their enthusiasm came from a sense of responsibility that they had not done enough to rein in the pro-southern pronouncements of their fellow merchants; or perhaps it stemmed from the guilt they felt for having adopted similar attitudes. Within weeks, the merchants published a report in which they stated their purpose with the utmost clarity: to provide aid to black New Yorkers left destitute by the riots. But they had additional goals, and their motives were mixed. They were determined to reassert the municipal authority they had been forced to relinquish over five terrifying days to an underclass they despised. They also recognized the need to rehabilitate their reputation and that of the city on which they had staked their fortunes, to assure the world that law and order had been restored, and that New York was once again a safe, welcoming place for businessmen and tourists alike.

The merchants clung to the belief that they were part of a tradition of private philanthropy that had long existed among their class. "I have been forty-one years a merchant in my present location," Jonathan Sturges maintained. "During this period I have seen a noble race of merchants pass away. I cannot help calling to mind the many acts of charity which they performed during their lives. . . . I trust we shall be quick to continue these acts of humanity, thus showing that the race of New York Merchants is not deteriorating." Their report consisted primarily of reprinted newspaper items detailing the destruction of black property and naming those attacked or killed by the mob. The authors went to great lengths to describe how they had gone about raising funds to compensate victims, putting their lives at risk for the sake of charity. They concluded by providing a long list of donors: abolitionists like John Jay, Gerrit Smith, and the *Tribune* but also some whose forefathers had made their fortunes in slave products, the Minturn shipping family, the Bayards, operators of sugar manufactories, the de Forest rum distillers, as well as the China trade firm of A. A. Low and Brothers.

They were, these men claimed, dispensing charity with kindness: "There are no harsh or unkind words uttered by the clerks—no impertinent quizzing in regard to irrelevant matters—no partizan or sectarian view advanced. The business is transacted in a straightforward, practical manner, without chilling the charity into an offense by creating the impression that the recipient is humiliated by accepting the gift." But no different from the benevolence of the police and city officials, the merchants' charity was accompanied by assumptions, expectations, humiliations. The merchants assumed claimants to be imposters until proven innocent, or in their words, "worthy objects of charity." They insisted on making personal visits "to ascertain the facts of the case . . . and save us from imposition."[43] Only then were petitioners given a small stipend and jobs sought for them—as servants, of course.

When the merchants argued that their gifts should not be construed as "humiliating," they were in fact underscoring that that was precisely what they were: they suspected claimants of being frauds, took pains to emphasize their dependence, and pigeonholed them as a servile class. The humiliation must have been especially unbearable for men like Albro Lyons who over the years had accumulated considerable personal property. In the Williamson papers, I discovered Albro's neat handwritten list of belongings destroyed or stolen by the mob. A bitter reminder of all that the family had lost, it gives some idea of their wealth and elite status:

1 English rug	$15.00
4 mahogany chairs	$16.00
1 pair French mantel vases	$10.00
1 pair large fancy cut Cologne bottles	$6.00
1 large size pagoda	$6.00
1 looking glass, gilt frame	$20.00

The list goes on for pages. It even records the items that the Lyons children had lost. For Maritcha, it was her poplin, organdie, and French calico dresses, muslin skirts, a pair of kid gloves, and a workbox.[44] Still, Lyons must have considered himself one of the lucky ones. His claims were taken seriously. The Merchants' Relief Committee awarded him $500 and the city $1,502.20.

More than anything else, the merchants wanted to ensure long-lasting social and economic stability in the city that would keep the lower classes—both blacks and whites—in their place. To that end, they recognized the necessity of black labor. They worried that if the city's black population remained unemployed, it might become a permanent "pauper race" that would drain the city's charitable institutions or, just as bad, that white laborers from the country might flood into the city, thereby reducing wages, and becoming equally mired in poverty. At the same time, they expected black laborers, much like the Mulberry Street School students in the 1820s, to discipline themselves and "remember that true liberty is not licentiousness, it is obedience to law, it is cheerful compliance with the obligations imposed by society for the good of the whole."[45]

Following the model of the Mulberry Street School trustees, the merchants enlisted members of the black elite to help them carry out their cause. Just as Peter Williams, William Hamilton, and Thomas Sipkins had earlier visited the homes of black parents, so Garnet, Charles Ray, and John Peterson now visited black claimants to ascertain their needs. Once again, these men balanced humility with self-assertion. A month after the riots, Henry Highland Garnet presented the assembled merchants with an elaborate document engrossed on parchment by Patrick Reason and elegantly framed. In it, Garnet began by thanking the merchants profusely, comparing their charity to that of New Testament figures, the Good Samaritan in Luke and the righteous in Mark:

> When we had fallen among thieves who stripped us of our raiment and wounded us, leaving many of us half dead, you had compassion on us. You bound up our wounds and poured in the oil and wine of Christian kindness and took care of us.
>
> We were hungry and you fed us. We were thirsty and you gave us drink. We were made strangers in our own homes and you kindly took us in. We were naked and you clothed us. We were sick and you visited us. We were in prison and you came unto us.

But Garnet also made demands. In his conclusion he pointedly reminded the merchants that they had not yet fulfilled their obligations toward black New Yorkers. "Protect us in our endeavors to obtain an honest living," he insisted. "Suffer no one to hinder us in any department of well directed industry, give us a fair and open field and let us work out our own destiny, and we ask no more."[46]

THE UNION LEAGUE CLUB: STRONG AND JAY

Another private entity, the newly formed Union League Club, re-sponded to at least one of Garnet's demands. Perhaps more than any other organization, it came closest to offering black New Yorkers mean-ingful reparations.

George Templeton Strong was among the founding members of the club. It would be a gross exaggeration to suggest that he had con-verted to abolitionism as Greeley had a few years earlier. But there was a shift in tone in his diary. Although he still called blacks "niggers," he had at least come to see them as innocent, persecuted victims. "There is the unspeakable infamy of the nigger persecution," he fulminated. "They are the most peaceable, sober, and inoffensive of our poor, and the outrages they have suffered during this last week are less excusable — are founded on worst pretext and less provocation — than St. Bartholomew's or the Jew-hunting of the Middle Ages!" Strong now heaped all his contempt on Paddy, lumping all Irish into one indistinguishable mass of "biped mammalia . . . that crawl and eat dirt and poison every community they infest," and ignoring the actions of individuals like Officer Kelly or Philip's neighbors.[47]

Strong was above all a Unionist, and support for the Union was the motivating impulse behind the Union League Club. The founders' goal was to bring together prominent city men loyal to the federal gov-ernment and dedicated to the preservation of the Union. Its core mem-bers were descendants of the country's first settlers, men of colonial stock. They planned to gather around them an elite cadre of profes-sional men, scientists, writers, artists, and intellectuals. They would also seek out representatives of the younger generation and train them to be the nation's future leaders. The club's membership was eclectic. There was Strong. There was the China trader Abiel Abbott Low. There was Robert Minturn, son of the old shipping magnate and the club's first president; although an antislavery Whig, he had chosen to vote for the Democratic presidential candidate James Buchanan in 1856, and had made noises in favor of conciliation with the South. Yet other members included Superintendent of Police Kennedy and men like John Jay and Peter Cooper who had long supported black New Yorkers.[48]

It seems passing strange that George Templeton Strong and John Jay belonged to the same club. Jay had been a committed abolitionist for as long as anybody could remember. Many of his views must have struck his peers as intemperate. He was convinced that the draft riots were a Confederate plot hatched in Richmond for the purpose of turning New York into a rebel city. Like Henry Highland Garnet, he had been an early proponent of military service for blacks. "To arms!" he called out in the July 10, 1862, issue of the *Weekly Anglo-African*. "Lose not a moment, but be ready promptly to meet the call of our common country—organize yourselves in companies at every convenient point—obtain drill masters—practice the manual exercise and evolutions steadily and with a will—accustom yourselves to the prompt obedience of military discipline . . . that companies . . . may be speedily filled when the order comes for you to march."[49]

In 1864, the Union League Club rushed to make this call a reality.

CHAPTER EIGHT

Union and Disunion

CIRCA 1864

BLACK NEW YORKERS WERE energized. They had found allies—
predictable and unpredictable—within the white community and believed that, as they worked together, freedom, citizenship, and national
reconciliation would soon be more than a promise. Almost immediately,
however, they faced a dizzying cycle of acceptance and rejection, union
and disunion, both in the nation and in their own community.

Raising Black Regiments

After the riots, Union League Club members decided to do the un-
thinkable and recruit a black regiment, ultimately raising three: the
Twentieth, Twenty-sixth, and Thirty-first Regiments of the United
States Colored Troops. Filled with pride, they documented their efforts
in an extensive *Report of the Committee on Volunteering*. New York's black
leadership threw them their full support. Governor Seymour promised
not to interfere. Overcoming its initial reluctance, the War Department
agreed to set up living quarters and a drill ground for black soldiers on
Riker's Island, which was then federal property.

At first, problems abounded. Men were tricked into service with
the promise of lucrative civilian jobs such as coachman, then drugged,
and forced onto Riker's Island. There, they crowded into old, worn tents

where the cold inexorably seeped in. They were overcharged for coffee and water. Disease spread. Although disqualified from official service because of his amputated leg, Garnet was made honorary chaplain. He brought a measure of order to Riker's. Enthusiasm soon ran high. Even Strong got behind the effort. "Rumor of a Corps d'Afrique to be raised here," he wrote in his usual cynical way soon after the proposal was aired. "Why not? Paddy, the asylum-burner, would swear at the dam Naygurs, but we need bayonets in Negro hands if Paddy is unwilling to fight for the country that receives and betters him." Once the regiment was raised, Strong was proud of what his club had done. "Our labors of a year ago have borne fruit. The Union League has done something for the country."[1]

On March 5, 1864, the Twentieth Regiment left Riker's Island for Manhattan. The soldiers marched from the East River to Union Square, where they stopped for a flag presentation ceremony. Unlike the Emancipation Day parade of July 4, 1827, this was not a black affair, but a public event that brought together blacks and whites, men and women. Led by Superintendent Kennedy, one hundred policemen, members of the Union League Club, and their friends, the soldiers paraded down the streets. They made, according to the *Tribune*'s lengthy account, "a fine appearance in their blue uniform, white gloves, and white leggings. They are hearty and athletic fellows, many of them six feet tall, straight, and symmetrical." The crowd, the *Tribune* continued, was truly representative of the entire city, as "citizens of every shade of color, and every phase of social and political life, filled the square, and streets; and every door, window, veranda, tree and house-top that commanded a view of the scene was peopled with spectators." Few, if any, white racists threatened trouble. Cheers replaced jeers.

At the ceremony, Garnet and other black leaders sat on the podium alongside members of the Union League Club and city dignitaries. Charles King, president of Columbia College, made a speech that must have thrilled black New Yorkers' hearts in its extension of the sentiments of the Declaration of Independence to all black Americans: "You are in arms," he intoned, "not for the freedom and law of the white race alone, but for universal law and freedom; for the God implanted right of life, liberty, and the pursuit of happiness to every being whom He has fashioned in his own image." What was this statement if not recognition of shared humanity and a promise of citizenship? On another platform erected in front of the Union League Clubhouse sat the wives, sisters, and daughters of club members. They had painstakingly stitched a flag for the regiment and requested that Charles King present it during the ceremony. He did so, and in his speech he praised them as "loyal women," their purpose as "patriotic," and their commitment to create a "sacred banner" second only to "the religion of the altar."

Black New Yorkers were elated. Their men were finally being given the chance to fight and show proof of their capacity for citizenship. The entire city seemed to be coming together in a show of racial reconciliation, all the more astonishing since, as Charles King reminded his audience, a mere few months earlier "the homes of these soldiers were attacked by rioters, who burned their dwellings stole their property, and made the streets smoke with the blood of their unoffending relatives and friends."[2] Circumstances had indeed changed, but many patterns remained intact. White elite men were still extending benevolence to black men from whom they then expected gratitude as well as to their womenfolk on whose behalf they spoke. Moreover, it's not at all clear what was going through the minds of white working-class men and women observers.

New Activists

If you confined your reading to the *Tribune*, it would not be clear what black women were up to either. If you perused the Union League Club's *Report*, it would appear that they were content simply to express "sincere gratitude for the great and good work" of the club. But black women were far from idle. In the mid-1850s, their efforts on behalf of the Colored Orphan Asylum had thrust them into public life; now they were broadening that work to include those affected by the war. In late 1863, men of the black elite—among them members of my family, Peter Guignon, Peter W. Ray, and Albro Lyons, and their friends James

McCune Smith, Charles Reason, George Downing, and John Peterson — had established the American Freedmen's Friend Society to raise money and collect clothes for black soldiers and emancipated slaves. Women of the older generation, like Cornelia Guignon, as well as of the younger, which now included Elizabeth Guignon and Maritcha Lyons, held fund-raising fairs. They sold articles to benefit the freedmen, set up a wheel of fortune for entertainment, offered ice cream to the hungry, hoping "to move many a dollar in the right direction."[3]

By early 1864, black women were ready to go it alone and establish their own relief organization, the Ladies' Committee for the Aid of Sick Soldiers. Led by Henry Highland Garnet's wife, Julia, the committee requested and received permission from the commander at Riker's Island to establish a kitchen connected to the hospital; in no time, the women were feeding some sixty soldiers. The organization's membership contained names I expected, wives of activists like Garnet and John Peterson, schoolteachers like Sarah Ennalls and Fanny Tompkins. I was heartened to see Philip's sister Sarah Maria White, and his niece Elizabeth Thompson, on the list. But I was astonished to read the name of one of the two men who had agreed to help the committee: in addition to Garnet, who was serving in his capacity as chaplain, the other was "Philip A. White, Auditor."[4] Philip and Garnet were as unlikely allies as John Jay and George Templeton Strong.

Philip was beginning to take a greater interest in his race. Maybe it was the influence of the apparently more progressive women in his family. But I think it was also because he was now convinced that citizenship for all was close at hand. Philip, I believe, saw citizenship as his right and was ready to fight for it for himself and his peers. In 1860, he had joined James McCune Smith's drive for black male suffrage in the state by adding his drugstore to the list of places to pick up ballots. Now he could appreciate to the fullest the broader efforts others had shouldered — civil war and military service — to bring citizenship to all black Americans, free-born and newly freed. That was a goal toward which Philip could work.

Black Soldiers: Brothers-in-Law
Peter Vogelsang and John DeGrasse

I searched in vain for names of members of the black elite on the lists of the Twentieth, Twenty-sixth, and Thirty-first Regiments, but I finally found two New Yorkers serving in other state regiments. They happened to be brothers-in-law. Peter Vogelsang, who married Theodocia De-Grasse, enlisted as a solider in the famed Fifty-fourth Massachusetts regiment. John DeGrasse, brother of Isaiah, Theodocia, and Serena, served as an assistant surgeon with the First North Carolina Volunteers. They began their military careers with different regiments, in different states, holding different positions, but early 1864 found them on the same battlefield in Olustee, Florida. For one, service would bring acceptance and glory, and for the other rejection and humiliation.

Boston's white abolitionist community had worked hard to raise the Fifty-fourth Massachusetts. Governor John A. Andrew had authorized its formation. Prominent antislavery leaders helped in recruitment, including the parents of its first commander, Colonel Robert Gould Shaw. Troops were composed primarily of free blacks, among whom were two of Frederick Douglass's sons. Shaw's father personally recruited the forty-six-year-old Peter Vogelsang. Shaw was dubious that a man that age would be able to pass the required physical exams, but in no time Vogelsang rose to become sergeant of Company H. The Fifty-fourth left Boston in May 1863, and on July 10 and 11—just as the draft riots were erupting in New York City—the regiment launched its assault on Fort Wagner in South Carolina. Shaw was killed along with 116 of his men; another 156 were wounded or captured.[5]

Vogelsang was not among them. Several companies from the Fifty-fourth had been sent to James Island as a diversionary tactic. On July 16, Confederate forces attacked and forced a retreat. Nevertheless, the soldiers of the Fifty-fourth stood their ground long enough to prevent a complete rout. Forty-two men were killed, and Vogelsang was severely wounded. In a letter written to the *Liberator* from his hospital bed, he made light of his own predicament, but sorrowfully recorded the death and destruction around him. His company, Vogelsang reported, had been cut off from the rest of the regiment but continued

Peter Vogelsang (Courtesy of the State Archives of Florida)

fighting. He had "the satisfaction of dropping one little fellow" and taking his gun as a trophy. Then "the rebs came so thick and fast, and on horseback, too, that it was 'Sauve qui Peut.'" A good runner, Vogelsang "did his prettiest and managed to outrun the rest of his party." He swam across a creek, hid in the tall grass, then raised himself to see what was going on, "when 'crack,' 'whiz,' and I could just see a fellow (about the width of 'West Broadway' from me) on horseback, who had just given me 'my dose.'" Badly wounded, Vogelsang lay helpless in the mud, water, and his own blood for hours until rescued. Once in the hospital boat, medical staff cut off his clothes, wet his wounds—"a big hole in my left chest"—covered him with tent-cloth, and told him to drink whiskey every four hours. He knew he was among the lucky when the casualties from Fort Wagner were brought on board. "Such a sight," Vogelsang lamented. "Blood, mud, sand and water, broken legs and arms, some dying and some dead."[6]

Vogelsang recovered by February 1864, in time to march to Olustee, where the Fifty-fourth was ordered to help Union forces cut off supplies to the Confederate army. It was there that his regiment met up with his brother-in-law's. John DeGrasse was an assistant surgeon with the First North Carolina Volunteers (renamed the Thirty-fifth Regiment of the United States Colored Troops). The youngest DeGrasse sibling, he received his medical degree from Bowdoin College in 1849, opened a practice in New York City, but then moved to Boston. In a truly progressive move, the Massachusetts Medical Society admitted him as a member in 1854. In spring 1863, DeGrasse mustered in as an assistant surgeon at New Berne, North Carolina. Unlike the Fifty-fourth, the Thirty-fifth was composed mainly of former slaves, but its commander came from yet another prominent New England abolitionist family: Colonel James Beecher was the younger half brother of Henry Ward Beecher and Harriet Beecher Stowe. When fully staffed, the regiment's medical team consisted of a head surgeon, two assistant surgeons, and a hospital steward. Their duties ranged from ensuring the cleanliness of the soldiers' bedding and clothing and supplying them with enough food and drink to more medical tasks: operating on wounds, changing dressings, treating diseases like smallpox, whose symptoms were high fever, nausea, vomiting, and muscle aches, or scurvy, caused by a deficiency of vitamin C.[7]

I don't know how Vogelsang performed at Olustee, but his brother-in-law John DeGrasse insisted that he had fulfilled his duties, was "untiring in my efforts in caring for the wounded," and stayed on the battlefield until dark. The head surgeon of his regiment, Dr. Henry Marcy, supported by the hospital steward Delos Barber, maintained that he had not. Instead of attending to the wounded, they charged, DeGrasse had become intoxicated, retired to his quarters in a drunken stupor, and could not be roused. A court-martial ensued.

Here too, the black archives failed me. I found no mention of the court-martial in the DeGrasse family papers at the Massachusetts

John Van Surlay DeGrasse
(Museum of African-American History, Boston)

Historical Society or in any histories of blacks in medicine. John suffered a much greater humiliation than his brother Isaiah ever had, and
it was, I believe, a profound sense of shame that led to the suppres-
sion of the event from family and community memory. The military
records at the National Archives contained, however, a full account
of the proceedings.[8] There were fourteen witnesses in all; five testified
against DeGrasse, nine in his favor. Among those opposing him were
James Beecher, the head surgeon Marcy, and the hospital steward Barber. Their testimony carried weight.

    In all, there were five charges. Two were similar to the Olustee
accusation: intoxication and dereliction of duty at Cedar Creek in June
and then at Darby's Station in July. The evidence against DeGrasse in all

three instances was that he was seen drinking, smelled heavily of liquor, sat in an "unsettled position on horseback," became quarrelsome, and that once in camp fell into a deep sleep and could not be roused. In a statement at the conclusion of the trial DeGrasse rebutted the charges one by one. He began by expressing surprise, arguing that until this moment, some seven months after the battle of Olustee, nobody had ever complained to him about his supposed drunkenness. He then pointed to the many witnesses who testified that he was not intoxicated. Responding specifically to the Olustee charge, DeGrasse maintained that after the battle he had sent his horse ahead and stayed behind on the field alone with the stretcher corps until dark. After walking twenty miles to camp and suffering from "excessive fatigue," he had indeed gone to bed. Knowing that the wounded soldiers Dr. Marcy wanted him to care for had been able to walk to camp, he felt their cases could wait until morning. Turning to the Cedar Creek incident, DeGrasse noted that Beecher was hardly in a position to assess his condition since he was at the head of the regiment while he, DeGrasse, was at the rear. If he was unsettled in his saddle, it was due to heat and exhaustion. Finally, when he reached camp, he had had a bath drawn and changed into clean clothes before going to sleep, hardly the behavior of a drunken man. And if Beecher claimed he could not wake him, soldier Freeman Grice had had no problem doing so.

The other two charges against DeGrasse involved "conduct unbecoming an officer and a gentleman." The first concerned taking liquor, specifically whiskey, from the medical supplies for his own personal use. DeGrasse readily admitted that he had done so, not for himself alone but for other officers and enlisted men as well, and not for personal consumption but as medical treatment for exhaustion. This was not a "misapplication," he argued, but entirely within U.S. Government regulations.

The last charge, in some ways the ugliest, involved a civilian. DeGrasse was accused of having insulted a black woman working as a laundress on board a steamer by making unwanted advances toward her. Specifically, he had formed his fingers in the shape of a pistol, placed his hand under his jacket near his penis, and said something to the effect of

"See how you made it stand?" or "How stiff is it?" DeGrasse categorically denied the charge, and pointed out that the only black woman who had been on board the steamer at that time had sworn the event never happened.

DeGrasse was convinced that there were hidden motives behind the charges. Although he admitted he had no hard evidence, he pointed his finger at Henry Marcy, particularly at the "uncommon and untiring assiduity with which surgeon Marcy has worked up this case, his punctual and constant attendance here for the past five days, using every effort and all the means in his power, to procure a conviction—manifesting inside and outside the court as much interest as though it was a personal matter, or a suit where his money interest was at stake."

I have no hard evidence either, but I would like to believe DeGrasse's side of the story. The bulk of the testimony concerning his intoxication and dereliction of duty came from Marcy and the hospital steward. DeGrasse's explanation that his behavior at Olustee and Cedar Creek was due to exhaustion made perfect sense. Moreover, whiskey, as Peter Vogelsang could testify, was a common medical treatment. Finally, his treatment of the black woman seems to befit a troublemaker more like the wayward James Hewlett rather than a prominent doctor, married man, and father of a newborn child.

Certainly, racism flourished among the white officers, and specifically the doctors, of the Thirty-fifth. I found evidence in an earlier incident involving DeGrasse and the other assistant surgeon, Daniel Mann, who served with DeGrasse in fall 1863. In October of that year, Mann wrote a letter complaining that DeGrasse had been placed "in the superior or at least most important position" and was "disposed to dispute my right to rank him." The response from a white officer made clear what was at stake. The presence of "Mann (white) and DeGrasse (a Negro)" made for an "unfortunate combination," he wrote, giving rise to "difficulties of a serious nature," namely the decision to "elevate the Negro doctor over the white one."[9]

But then the waters get muddied. In his letter, Mann insisted that he was not so much troubled about rank as he was about DeGrasse's management of the hospital, and that he, Mann, had an obligation to "take care of medical supplies, especially spirituous liquors and to protect the hospital fund from misuse." Basically, Mann was accusing DeGrasse, just as Marcy did later, of misappropriating liquor. The officer who supported Mann's claim agreed that DeGrasse had "abused his privileges" and "committed misdemeanors," and concluded that charges should be preferred against him.

Interestingly enough, in this episode James Beecher stood up for DeGrasse. He did so, however, not so much because he believed in or cared about the young black surgeon but because he was stung by the accusation of intemperance in his regiment. There was not one instance," he maintained, "brought to my notice of an intoxicated officer and but one, of an intoxicated man, a thing which can probably be said of no other regiment, certainly in the Dept." DeGrasse, he concluded, was "dispensing hospital liquor to nurses and stretcher corps when on extra duty" in accordance with governmental regulations. Beecher was so perturbed that he threatened Mann with court-martial.[10]

Here's one way of connecting the two incidents. Henry Marcy joined the regiment as head surgeon in November 1863, right in the middle of the Mann-Beecher charges and countercharges. He might have worried that Beecher would prefer DeGrasse to him, and concluded that persuasive accusations of misappropriation of liquor and drunkenness were charges that might sway Beecher's opinion. Marcy must have been aware of Beecher's past. In the late 1850s, while serving as a missionary abroad, Beecher discovered that his wife was an alcoholic. The couple returned home, his wife was institutionalized, and Beecher made officer in a New York regiment where one of his brothers served as chaplain. He fell in love with another woman and was guilt ridden. Fearing that he was going mad and would be court-martialed, the Beecher family obtained an honorable discharge for him and placed him in a sanatorium. After his wife died, Beecher reentered the army as commander of the Thirty-fifth, courted the woman he loved throughout 1864, and married her a year later.[11]

Here are the two possibilities I'm left with. A black army surgeon addicted to alcohol and unable to perform his duties. Or an unstable commanding officer with a history of alcoholism in his family and at-o woman not his wife, coupled with a white doctor threatened

tracted to a woman not his wife, coupled with a white doctor threatened by a competent black doctor. If the latter, the trial raises larger questions: When would a black man's authority ever be accepted? When would his word ever be taken over that of a white? When would blacks' capacity for citizenship ever be acknowledged?

DeGrasse concluded his statement with a defense. "My character as a gentleman and my upright deportment," he wrote, "have never been questioned by officers or men until these, I think, unfounded charges were preferred." To this he added a plea: "My honor and my reputation are at stake, not only here in the army, but at home and wherever I am known." He was found guilty of all charges and cashiered. Details of his life thereafter are murky. He died in Boston in November 1868.

Beecher moved his family to upstate New York. Increasingly "queer" in behavior, he eventually went mad and wandered from one insane asylum to another. In 1886, he ended his life by putting a bullet through his mouth.[12]

Henry Highland Garnet

DeGrasse's court-martial pitted black man against white, but within the black community tensions flared among black men. Perhaps James McCune Smith alone could have made his former schoolmates realize the folly of internal dissension at a time when unity against the real enemy—white racism—was essential. But he was slowly dying.

For years, Smith had suffered from an enlarged heart and what he called an "overworked nervous system." In the early 1860s, his health deteriorated rapidly; death came in November 1865. The *Weekly Anglo-African* published an obituary that was long but restrained in tone, as if any expression of sorrow would open an outpouring of uncontrollable grief. It stuck to an enumeration of facts: Smith's illustrious career at the African Free School; early apprenticeship to a blacksmith; later private education; medical school in Glasgow; position as doctor of the Colored Orphan Asylum; participation in the antislavery movement; affiliation with the Episcopal Church. Only when he reached the moment of death did the writer let himself go:

He will be greatly missed, not alone in the line of his profession, and by his immediate family connection, but as a public man; and his death is as well lamented by them as by his family and relatives. A large circle of friends, with weeping hearts, attended his funeral, among whom were ten clergymen of different denominations, and most of whom followed him to his quiet resting place.[13]

Smith had been too ill to attend the National Convention of Colored Citizens held in Syracuse in the fall of 1864. Henry Highland Garnet had called for the convention in order to figure out how best "to promote the freedom, progress, elevation, and perfect enfranchisement, of the entire colored people of the United States." Among those in attendance were old-timers Frederick Douglass, George Downing, J. W. C. Pennington, and Robert Hamilton, joined by men of the younger generation like Peter Guignon's brother-in-law, Peter W. Ray. If Garnet expected unity in a time of crisis, he was sadly disappointed. From the beginning, controversy dogged him inside and outside the convention hall. Aired on the convention podium and in newspaper columns, the disagreements were public and acrimonious.

On the city streets, delegates had to contend with the hostility of the good citizens of Syracuse. Douglass reported that he had been confronted by a group of men who demanded to know "Where are the d—d niggers going?" Worse still, a group of Irish rowdies accosted Garnet and threw him to the ground. They took his wooden leg, stole his silver-plated cane, and forced him to crawl through the mud.[14] Horrified delegates took up a collection and raised forty dollars to replace Garnet's cane.

Amity between Garnet and his co-conventioneers ended there, however. Garnet was unhappy that Douglass had been elected president of the convention even though he, Garnet, had been the one to call for it. Still more humiliating were the suspicions voiced over his involvement with the African Civilization Society. Garnet complained that even "at this late day in his career . . . there had been a strong disposition to throw him on the shelf, on account of his connection with the African Civilization Society." George Downing pressed the attacks. He

angrily denounced the African Civilization Society as a "child of prejudice" and Garnet as a race traitor who had remained silent when the
society's members declared that "it would be well if every colored man
was out of the country."

Garnet won the verbal battle. With his sharp sense of wit intact,
he wondered who was really lame: "Mr. Downing and I have in days
gone by had many hard intellectual battles. He has hurled against me
all the force of his vigorous logic, and I struck him back again with all
my power. If I smarted from his blows, I think I may say he went away
a little lame; and he has never forgotten it."[15] But he lost the ideological war. Black leaders sensed that victory was at hand and threw all
their energy into acquiring the full rights of citizenship in the land of
their birth.

Rejected by his own, Garnet was, however, embraced by the nation and savored one final triumph. Early 1865 found him hopeful. He
was convinced that the wounds that had torn the nation apart could be
healed, North and South, blacks and whites unified. By heeding the
painful lessons of the past, the nation could build a brighter future. In
February, he was honored as the first black American to address the U.S.
House of Representatives. His "Memorial Discourse" memorialized
slavery itself. Recognizing that slavery was a universal system, Garnet
placed his speech within a long tradition of antislavery testimonies delivered by illustrious men—from Plato and Socrates to Moses and Au-
gustine, and finally to Thomas Jefferson, Patrick Henry, and Lafayette.
Turning specifically to America's involvement in the slave trade, he
spoke of how it had deprived Africa of its children and turned men into
brutes. But with the passage of the Thirteenth Amendment a month
earlier, Garnet now proposed to look forward. He urged "reformers of
this and coming ages" to heed the call of the three E's: "*Emancipate, En-
franchise, Educate.*"[16]

A few months later the war ended. The South surrendered at
Appomattox, the Confederacy went down in defeat, the Union was
preserved, and the Thirteenth Amendment dealt slavery its final blow.
Triumph did not last long, however. Lincoln was assassinated and black
New Yorkers were devastated. "Men had learned to trust the future of
the nation to his keeping," Robert Hamilton wrote in the *Weekly Anglo-*

African. "We all regarded him as more than equal to any coming emergencies, and in the joy of our hearts were forgetting past afflictions, in the joyous sunlight of a golden peace in which he figured as the great central peacemaker. No matter what course he had chosen, we would have cheerfully acquiesced in it." It was now up to the people, he concluded, to undertake the enormous task of thinking out "this problem of peace, or rather the principle on which alone peace can safely rest."[17]

Garnet put together a committee, the National Lincoln Monument Association, to erect a Colored People's National Monument in memory of the slain president. Its membership included James McCune Smith, Frederick Douglass, William J. Wilson, Philip Bell, and yes, George Downing. Eager to create a monument that would endure, Garnet did not want to memorialize Lincoln in the evanescent form of the spoken or written word. Nor did he want a mere physical monument that might also fall victim to the passage of time. Instead, Garnet proposed building a school in the District of Columbia for "the education of the Children of Freemen and Freedmen, and their descendants forever."[18] His plan never materialized, but a monument commemorating Lincoln was finally built.

It's not the Lincoln Memorial you're familiar with—the massive sculpture of a seated Lincoln enshrined in a vast neo-Grecian temple-like structure adorned with a peristyle of fluted Doric columns. That monument, located near the Tidal Basin in downtown Washington, D.C., and attracting millions of visitors a year, was constructed much later, between 1914 and 1922.

The Colored People's National Monument stands in the much lonelier site of what is now Lincoln Park in southeast Washington. It depicts Lincoln standing erect beside a whipping post around which swirls a vine. With his right hand, he grasps the Emancipation Proclamation lying atop the post. As if in benediction, his left hand stretches over the body of an unshackled slave kneeling in front of him. The word "emancipation" is carved in large block letters on the base of the pedestal.

The unveiling ceremony took place on the eleventh anniversary of Lincoln's assassination. Congress declared the day a holiday so that all who wanted could attend. President Ulysses S. Grant was seated on the

Abraham Lincoln standing above crouched slave wearing manacles,
sculpture by Thomas Ball, between 1875 and 1910 (Library of Congress)

platform surrounded by members of his cabinet, Supreme Court jus-
tices, senators, and many prominent blacks, including Frederick Douglass and George Downing. Garnet was not with them, and his name was
never mentioned.

Wounds could not be healed. Garnet never regained his former
standing in the black community. He traveled throughout the country,
returning to New York in 1870, poor, unhappy, and after the death of his
beloved wife, very much alone. A second marriage to Sarah Tompkins
proved unsatisfactory, and they separated after a year. For Garnet, there

was only one solution left: emigration. His opportunity came years later when President James A. Garfield appointed him United States minister and counsel general to Liberia. To those who feared for his health, Garnet responded: "Would you have me linger here in old age, in neglect, and in want? . . . I cannot stay amongst these ungrateful people who have completely forgotten me. No, I go gladly to Africa."[19] Garnet left for Liberia in November 1881, only to die in February 1882.

George Downing

George Downing might have gotten the better of his former schoolmate. But it was a hollow victory. An ardent integrationist, Downing was forced to spend the rest of his life fighting to realize the promise of emancipation.

Andrew Johnson succeeded Lincoln in the White House. In February 1866, Downing and a delegation that included Frederick Douglass met with the new president. Downing stated their case in bold and simple terms: "that we are not satisfied with an amendment prohibiting slavery, but that we wish it enforced with appropriate legislation." In other words, the delegation was demanding black male suffrage as a protection against possible injustice. Johnson's response was a portent of darker days ahead. As if giving a history lesson, he proceeded to triangulate racial hatred and expose the race and class fault lines that were still tearing the country apart. Masters degraded slaves, treating them as nonhuman property to be bought and sold at will, he explained. In turn, the slave held in contempt the poor white man who was "struggling hard upon a poor piece of land." And so the poor white man opposed "the slave and his master combined [as they] kept him in slavery by depriving him of a fair participation in the labor and production of the rich lands of the country." With all of this hatred to go around, Johnson refused to contemplate any measure that would, in his words, "commence a war of races."

There was nothing left to be said, and the delegation left. But Downing and his colleagues published a written response that took exception to Johnson's position. "Peace between the races," they argued, "is not to be secured by degrading one race and exalting another, by giving power to one race and withholding it from another, but by maintaining a state of equal justice between all classes, first pure and then peaceable."[20]

Unbowed, Downing continued his fight for equal justice and won several battles. He had moved his family to Newport, Rhode Island, in the 1850s, and established several food businesses there and in Providence. With the opening of his hotel, the Sea-Girt House, he became quite famous. Awed by its utter luxuriousness, *Frederick Douglass' Paper* devoted an entire article to it, referring to it as "a *first* class fashionable hotel" and opining that Downing would "be amply repaid for his enterprise and heavy outlay of capital, his name being familiar with the visitors at Newport, as a popular and successful caterer."[21] When the hotel burned to the ground in 1860, Downing lost approximately forty thousand dollars. Undeterred, he immediately set about building another, equally grand establishment.

Downing had clout in Newport, and he didn't hesitate to use it on behalf of his race. His children attended separate "caste schools," which he deemed inferior to white ones, so he waged a twelve-year campaign to integrate the Rhode Island public school system. When Albro Lyons moved his family to Newport in the wake of the draft riots, the two families joined forces. Young Maritcha and her mother Mary Joseph added their voices to Downing's repeated petitions for school integration. In her memoir, Maritcha recalled that, after being denied entrance to the local high school, she appeared in person before the Rhode Island state legislature: "I, but sixteen years old, made my maiden speech and, in a trembling voice plead for the opening of the door of opportunity." Concluding a letter to the legislature, Mary Joseph Lyons requested a change in the law so that

> it may be said by Rhode Island, "We have not the fertile prairie produce, the prolific Southern Sun, the gold of California, the copper of Michigan, the coal of Pennsylvania and the oil, but this one point of duty we have — to educate every

soul. Every native and every foreign child that is cast on our coast shall be taught at public cost the rudiments of knowledge, and at last the ripest results of art and science."[22]

They succeeded.

Shortly thereafter, Downing moved to Washington, D.C., while still maintaining his home and business in Newport. More strongly committed to integration than ever, he set about knocking down one racial barrier after another. In his 1885 *New York Freeman* article, T. McCants Stewart enumerated Downing's many accomplishments during his Washington years. Consider the following:

Accepting a proposal made by a Rhode Island congressman, Downing took charge of the restaurant in the House of Representatives, where he made contact with politicians of both parties and, emulating the earlier example of his father, took advantage of his situation to deliberate with them on "matters of legislation concerning black Americans." When a perplexed employee one day asked how he should handle a group of blacks who had just entered the restaurant, Downing unhesitatingly replied: "Serve them and send to me any one who may complain." He was part of a group that successfully lobbied for the integration of the Senate gallery. The Downings were also the first black family to occupy a box in a Washington, D.C., theater.[23]

Downing worked closely with Radical Republican Charles Sumner and prevailed on him to ensure the abolition of Jim Crow cars on the Baltimore and Ohio Railroad. Years later, he recalled that as he sat by Sumner's deathbed, the senator clasped his hand and whispered to him, "Do not let my civil rights bill fail."[24] The bill, guaranteeing that every person, regardless of race, color, or previous condition of servitude, was entitled to the same treatment in public accommodations, was signed into law by President Grant in March 1875.

Reconstruction brought other successes as well. The passage of the Thirteenth Amendment abolishing slavery in 1865 was quickly followed in 1868 by the Fourteenth Amendment, granting citizenship to all those born on American soil, and the Fifteenth Amendment in 1870, which at long last granted black men the right to vote. At the same time, the federal government established the Freedmen's Bureau, designed to protect the civil, political, and legal rights of newly emancipated slaves and provide them a public school education.

But black Americans still inhabited an ever shifting racial landscape and were soon called back to political struggle to lobby against the post-Reconstruction repeal of civil rights legislation. Many black New Yorkers faced unexpected shifts in personal and professional fortunes. As a group they were geographically mobile. In *Black Manhattan,* James Weldon Johnson detailed their postwar migration. "In the earliest days," he wrote, "the Negro population of New York, lived, naturally, in and about the city at the tip of Manhattan." Johnson then traced its movement northward, noting that up until the 1880s the majority lived on Sullivan, Bleecker, Thompson, and other nearby streets. By 1890, however, "the centre of the coloured population had shifted to the upper Twenties and lower Thirties west of Sixth Avenue." According to Johnson, a change in activity accompanied these geographic shifts. "In New York the Negro now began to function and express himself on a different plane, in a different sphere," namely in entertainment and professional sports. Those who clung to the old ways moved to Brooklyn. "For some decades," he concluded, "most of the upper class and well-to-do coloured people had lived in Brooklyn. . . . A large number of them owned homes there, and Brooklyn was the centre of social life and respectability."[25] My family was among them.

PART TWO

Brooklyn
1865–1895

CHAPTER NINE
Peter Guignon's Private Wars
CIRCA 1862

THE DRAFT RIOTS HAD inflicted untold hardships on New York's black population, the effects of which would reverberate for years to come. I wondered how those who, like Peter Guignon, had moved to Brooklyn fared in the years leading up to the Civil War. I pretty much lost sight of Peter after his appearance at Albro Lyons's and James McCune Smith's side during the mass meeting for James Hamlet in City Hall Park in 1850. I knew that he married Cornelia Ray sometime in the 1840s and that their first child, Peter Jr., was born in 1849. Although Peter and Cornelia hoped for a larger family, they lost subsequent children in infancy. From 1847 until 1854, Peter was listed in the New York City directories as a hairdresser. He then vanished, only to reappear in the 1858 Brooklyn directory, residing and working as a druggist in Williamsburgh.

I was convinced that Peter's move to Brooklyn augured well. Until the draft riots, his comrades from the Mulberry Street School had been successful, fulfilled in their chosen careers, actively engaged in politics, married with families, and as financially secure as any black New Yorker could be at the time. In contrast, Peter had suffered through the early death of his first wife, Rebecca, and floundered in trade. But the early 1860s turned out to be years of uncertainty and sorrow for him. Against a backdrop of public and as yet unresolved racial conflict, Peter faced personal and familial travails that must have broken his heart and crushed his spirit.

Brooklyn

In increasing numbers, black New Yorkers were deserting the island of Manna-Hata, Washington Irving's fabled land of milk and honey that the ancient inhabitants of Communipaw had made their seat of empire, and that was later renamed Gotham. They were fleeing to the less developed and quieter town of Brooklyn. Peter, his brother-in-law Peter Williams Ray, the Hamilton brothers Thomas and Robert, and James McCune Smith joined William J. Wilson and others who had been Brooklyn residents for years.

Blacks had been in Brooklyn since its inception. Shortly after settling in Manhattan, the Dutch crossed the East River, founding Breuckelen and other towns (Flatlands, Flatbush, New Utrecht, and Bushwick). As in New Amsterdam, they enslaved Africans, who even after gaining their freedom were never given the same rights as white citizens, but were forced among other things to pay higher taxes and duties. Once the British took over Kings County in 1664, they adopted the same methods that they had in Manhattan, increasing the number of slaves and imposing harsh conditions on them. In 1790, approximately 40 percent of white families in Kings County owned at least one slave. Throughout the eighteenth century, the proportion of blacks to whites remained high. In 1801, there were approximately 4,000 whites in Kings County, 1,500 free blacks, and 330 slaves.[1]

The town of Brooklyn grew slowly. In 1820, its population was only slightly more than 7,000 inhabitants, compared with over 130,000 in New York. A tidal wave of Irish immigration soon swelled its numbers, and by 1835 Brooklyn was big enough to obtain a city charter. With approximately 25,000 inhabitants, it was the seventh largest city in the United States. When the towns of Williamsburgh and Bushwick merged with Brooklyn on January 1, 1855, it jumped to third largest, with a population of 205,000. The newly consolidated city was a mix of industry and country life. Shipyards, warehouses, and factories of various kinds—glass works, casting furnaces, tanneries, stone-cutting yards, breweries—lined the East River from Red Hook to Greenpoint. As in Manhattan, Brooklyn's most important commercial and manufacturing enterprises were based in slave commodities. Sugar dominated,

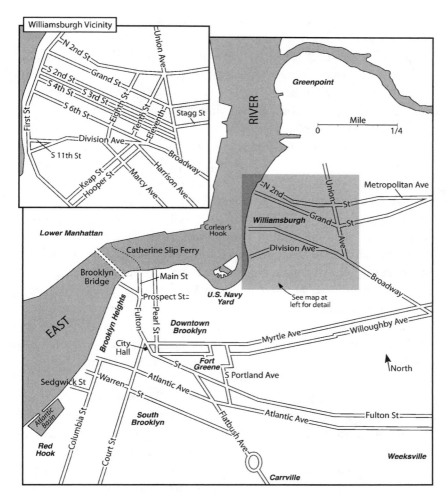

Brooklyn, circa 1874 (Courtesy John Norton)

and families like the Havemeyers made their fortune in refineries, distilleries, and sugar warehousing. The city's residential sections lay away from the shorefront. In Williamsburgh, two-story frame homes were typical. Pigs roamed the streets, and families often kept goats and cows in their yards, selling milk to passersby. Outside the city proper, Flatbush, Flatlands, New Utrecht, and Gravesend remained rural towns surrounded by open spaces and farmland well into the 1870s.

The city teemed with immigrants. By 1860, around the time Peter appeared in the city directory, 37 percent of Brooklyn inhabitants, or 104,000, were foreign born, 54 percent of whom hailed from Ireland and 25 percent from Germany. They dwarfed the city's black population, who now numbered a mere 4,900. Unable to keep pace with European immigration, black Brooklynites dwindled to slightly over 1 percent of the population in 1870.[2]

Although their percentages were in steady decline from the 1830s on, Kings County blacks made their presence felt. After emancipation in 1827, the slaveholding Lefferts family sold off parcels of their extensive land to their newly freed slaves. From this former farmland two black communities, Weeksville and Carrville, emerged in the 1830s in what was then Brooklyn's Ninth Ward, now Bedford-Stuyvesant. Named after their founders, these communities were all-black enclaves much like Seneca Village in Upper Manhattan. The men of the approximately one hundred families living in Weeksville and Carrville were primarily tradesmen—barbers, tailors, carpenters, painters, butchers, shoemakers, coopers, and ropemakers. Just as blacks had done decades earlier in Lower Manhattan, they established their own institutions—a school, churches, a burial society, mutual relief organizations, an orphanage, and a home for the aged.

In subsequent years blacks who came to Brooklyn moved into the Fort Greene area, which was known as part of the city's "Black Belt." Although an integrated neighborhood where whites vastly outnumbered blacks, in 1860 Fort Greene contained more than half of the city's black population. Many, like William J. Wilson and his family, were part of the black elite. Entrepreneurs rather than artisans and tradesmen, Fort Greene residents counted real estate agents, restaurateurs, and undertakers among their ranks. They too established their own churches and schools. To a greater extent than blacks in Weeksville and Carrville they formed social clubs and literary societies similar to those across the East River.[3]

Peter Williams Ray

Peter and Cornelia didn't relocate to any of these areas, however, but moved instead to Williamsburgh, where they shared a home with Cornelia's brother, Peter Williams Ray. Peter Guignon's association with the Rays can only be called serendipitous. Through his marriage to Cornelia, my great-great-grandfather not only started a new family and acquired a new set of relatives, but also began a new profession. Peter Williams Ray had followed in James McCune Smith's footsteps, becoming a doctor and setting up a medical practice. Another brother, Samuel, had opened a drugstore nearby, but left it vacant when he decided to emigrate to Liberia. The Ray family evidently thought well enough of their new relative to allow this untrained, almost fifty-year-old man to take over the drugstore and set himself up as a pharmacist. (It's possible that they did have a few reservations, since Cornelia is listed as co-owner in all the city directories.) Living together, working collaboratively, and sharing common interests, the two Peters must have forged close bonds, in ways, as events soon revealed, that they could scarcely have imagined.

In the late 1850s, Peter Williams Ray had already distinguished himself. Just about the same age as Philip White, he too had apprenticed in James McCune Smith's pharmacy. In a sign of how much times had changed since the 1830s, Ray was admitted to a U.S. medical school. He matriculated first at Bowdoin College Medical School, probably around the same time as John DeGrasse, then transferred to Castleton Medical College in Vermont, where he received his degree in 1850. During his three years of training, Ray took courses in anatomy, physiology, chemistry, materia medica, surgery, obstetrics, and pathology. When he opened his medical practice, he specialized in obstetrics, perhaps because Castleton's training in this field was especially good. "In surgery and obstetrics," its catalogue boasted, "the means of instruction are ample, in the instruments, apparatus and appliances . . . which are necessary to aid the teaching of these branches of medicine."[4]

Settling in Williamsburgh, Ray prospered. He married Cordelia Scottron, the sister of one of Brooklyn's most prominent young black men. An ambitious businessman brimming with new ideas, Samuel

Scottron had made his fortune by obtaining a patent for an adjustable mirror for barbers, in which two mirrors were placed opposite each other to allow a barber to view both sides of a customer's head at the same time. He also manufactured looking glasses, mantel mirrors, wood moldings, extension cornices, and imitation onyx used by lamp and candle makers. Eager to help other blacks succeed in business, Scottron was an active participant in the Committee for Improving the Industrial Condition of Negroes in New York.[5]

Ray was not to be outdone by this brother-in-law. In late 1861, the *Liberator* printed a short article pointing to the presence of "many men of wealth, intelligence and refinement" in the black community, much as the *North Star* had done in the 1840s and *Frederick Douglass' Paper* in the 1850s. In listing African American members of the medical profession, the article placed Ray's name right after that of James McCune Smith.[6] Following Smith's lead, Ray not only established a thriving medical practice but also became politically active, attending state and national conventions where he commanded a great deal of respect.

Ray's political activism replicated the earlier efforts of Smith and other Mulberry Street School graduates, namely the struggle for the restitution of black male suffrage in New York state. In the mid-1850s, Ray attended a state convention in Troy held expressly to devise a strategy to repeal the state's property qualification for voters. The convention proceeded to form a permanent lobbying organization, the New York State Suffrage Association; Ray helped write its constitution and was appointed to its board of managers. Increasingly aware of the importance of grassroots activism, Ray and his colleagues refined the organizational efforts of the earlier voting rights movement. They created a tiered system in which the state society broke down into county associations, which in turn were made up of city clubs. Ray was instrumental in the formation of the Colored Political Association of the City of Brooklyn and Kings County as well as the Young Men's Elective Franchise Club of Williamsburgh. In their statement of purpose, the organizations' founders emphasized their status, as *native-born* Americans, as property owners, and their deep investment in civil society. "Many of our petitioners," they declared, "have resided during their entire lives in, and are Freeholders of this State,—their families are permanently located within its boundaries, their social relations are established within its limits, and their entire pecuniary interests are inseparable from its welfare."[7]

In 1860, Peter W. Ray, Peter Guignon, and their colleagues in the Kings County and Williamsburgh associations joined forces with Manhattan counterparts—Philip, James McCune Smith, Charles Reason, Henry Highland Garnet, and others—to lobby for the repeal of property qualifications for New York state voters. Like Philip, Peter Guignon made his drugstore available as a pickup point for amendment ballots. Despite the fact that only 1,250 black votes were at issue, Brooklyn's white Democrats mounted fierce resistance. Their arguments were predictable. Giving northern blacks the vote would risk antagonizing the South and harm economic relations between the two sectors; it would degrade the status of white workingmen to that of blacks, and result in the triumph of black labor over white. Just to make sure that white voters understood what was at stake, the *Brooklyn City News* issued a final warning reminding them that they were being asked to decide "whether ten or fifteen thousand sooty Negroes shall be raised to a political level with yourselves in this State. You are asked to deposit your vote in the ballot box, cheek by jowl with a large 'buck nigger.'" Brooklynites voted down the amendment 23,400 to 5,535.[8]

Beyond political causes and maybe even beyond familial ties, the two Peters were bound together in Freemasonry brotherhood. Decades earlier, the two men had joined Odd Fellows and Masonic lodges in New York along with other Mulberry Street School graduates. Now settled in Brooklyn, they affiliated with the new Stone Square Lodge no. 6 under the jurisdiction of the United Grand Lodge of New York, which combined all of the state's African American lodges. The ardent Masons Patrick Reason and John Peterson were also members.

One of the chief principles of Freemasonry is secrecy. Nevertheless, Peter Guignon's grandnephew Harry Albro Williamson compiled vast quantities of notes, minutes, and commentary on the organization that he left in his collection. There I discovered that at the Grand Lodge's annual meeting in 1862, Peter put forth his lodge's request that a committee be appointed to investigate "the origin of masonry among

colored and white men in the United States." Although his suggestion was adopted enthusiastically, I haven't been able to find any such
document. It was Williamson himself who finally put together a history
some seventy years later, although he never managed to publish it. His
account repeats many other writings on Freemasonry: its ancientness
and universality; its mission as an agent of civilization; its alignment
with traditional Christian doctrine; its ethic of equality, brotherly love,
and mutual helpfulness. In particular, Williamson emphasized black
Freemasons' belief in the ideal of equality, which he interpreted in two
ways: the equality of black men obligated to help one another in time
of need, and the equality of men of all races bound together in universal
brotherhood. Moving beyond the concept of equality, Williamson then
proceeded to suggest the possibility of black superiority. White lodges,
he argued, had violated the principle of universality by keeping blacks
out of their orders. They had become corrupt, and hence it was left to
black lodges to uphold the purity of original Freemasonry.[9]

Williamsburgh's Black Community

When Peter and Cornelia joined the Ray family in Williamsburgh, the
neighborhood, like Brooklyn proper, was a mix of homes, factories, and
commercial establishments lining the East River, major thoroughfares,
and even some side streets. In the late 1850s, approximately 30 percent
of Brooklyn's blacks lived in Williamsburgh. Like Fort Greene, it was a
mostly white neighborhood with black homes clustered in one particular area, bordered by Grand Street to the north, Eighth Street (renamed
Marcy Avenue) to the east, and South Sixth to the south.[10] The Ray/
Guignon residence was initially at 15 Stagg Street, but the two families
later moved to 282 South Fourth Street, while the drugstore stood at the
corner of South Second and Eleventh Street (renamed Hooper). They
were close to James McCune Smith, who fled New York in 1864 after
the draft riots and established his residence at 162 South Third Street,
where he died a year later. When Peter Williams Ray moved to Brooklyn proper in the late 1860s, Peter Guignon relocated just a few doors
away to 383 South Fourth Street, where he acquired a new neighbor, his

father-in-law Peter Ray, who now lived at 117 South Second Street. The 1870 census suggests that Peter Guignon was doing well financially: in addition to Cornelia, his household included one female servant and two clerks; his home was valued at five thousand dollars and personal income at three thousand dollars.

From a study of insurance maps, it's evident that these streets were typical of Williamsburgh in this period: the Ray/Guignon households occupied one of the neighborhood's many frame dwellings, which were only occasionally interspersed with brick structures. Peter's drugstore, where his brother-in-law had an adjoining office, occupied the ground floor of a spacious four-story brick building.

Williamsburgh's black families lived within a stone's throw of one another. I don't think such close proximity had existed since the early days when the Marshall, DeGrasse, and Crummell families lived on Centre Street, with many of their friends nearby in the Five Points district. Settling in a new town and a new neighborhood, these families were desperate to escape the landscape of Lower Manhattan, where just about every street held unwanted reminders of the violence perpetrated against their people. Especially after the draft riots, they were determined never again to live far apart from one another, unable to protect each other in times of trouble, and dependent on the whims of strangers. They created a new community made up of old friends from the same social circle. Living close to one another, they could visit freely back and forth. Their children could walk in safety to Colored School no. 3 at the corner of Union and Keap Streets. And even though the Rays, Guignons, Hamiltons, and Smiths still crossed the East River to Manhattan on Sundays to attend St. Philip's, other families worshiped locally at Zion A.M.E. Church, which had begun in an old white Methodist Chapel on Metropolitan Avenue, St. James Episcopal near Union Street, or Third Baptist on Stagg.[11]

Yet Williamsburgh's black residents also forged ties with white neighbors. In his 1933 autobiography, James Weldon Johnson recalled a childhood visit in 1884 to his granduncle and aunt, William and Sarah Curtis, who lived on South Second Street. "My playmates," he reminisced, "were for the greater part the white boys and girls who lived on our side of the street and those across. The only colored playmates I had were a girl named Edith Mathews, who lived just around the corner, and two brothers by the name of Jackson, who lived on the same street four or five blocks away."[12]

Insurance maps of the period suggest another fact: that many of the area's shop owners and businessmen were Germans, sporting names like Knaup, Schnaderbeck, Dengel, Strubel, and Huschle, who had chosen Williamsburgh as a place to live. As in Manhattan, blacks' relations with Germans were less acrimonious than with the Irish. Their merchant class worked hard to put themselves on a sound economic footing, become homeowners, and provide for their families. They were churchgoers, family oriented, and respectable, striving to become American in much the same way as the black elite. It was said that Peter Williams Ray counted many Germans among his patients. And in his writings on Freemasonry, Williamson noted that in 1867 one of the German American lodges of the *Verein deutsch-americanischer Freimaurer*, working under the jurisdiction of the Grand Lodge of Hamburg, put the principle of universal brotherhood into action and invited Ray into their lodge.[13]

White-black interactions such as these have given rise to the myth that nineteenth-century Brooklyn was kinder to blacks than was Manhattan, that it was a safe haven of sorts. History doesn't bear this out. Racial discrimination and racial violence flourished in Brooklyn as well, coming from expected and unexpected quarters.

The Watson-Lorillard Tobacco Factory Riot

Knowing my interest in the Lorillard family, several historian friends suggested that I look into an attack on the Lorillards' Brooklyn tobacco factory in the summer of 1862. I decided to investigate. Since there were no black newspapers in Brooklyn at this time, I started with the *Brooklyn Daily Eagle,* whose masthead proudly proclaimed that "this paper has the largest circulation of any evening paper published in the United States." I found what I was looking for in the August 5 issue. The article's headlines occupied six lines and ran as follows:

The Irrepressible Conflict in Brooklyn.
SERIOUS RIOT BETWEEN WHITE MEN AND NEGROES
The Former Attack a Tobacco Factory
in which the Negroes are Employed
ATTEMPT TO BURN THE FACTORY DOWN
INTENSE EXCITEMENT
The Arraignment of the Parties — They
are Held to Bail[14]

All the elements that precipitated the New York draft riots some eleven months later were already at work in Brooklyn in the summer of 1862: white workers' antagonism toward blacks who held decent jobs they didn't deserve as well as toward the elites willing to employ these undeserving blacks.

The *Brooklyn Daily Eagle* and the *Brooklyn Daily Times* along with the *New York Tribune* and the *New York Times* gave extensive coverage to these riots. They couldn't all agree on the single event that ignited the violence, but they reported assiduously on the rumors that abounded, all of which raised the usual bugaboos about blacks (and black men in particular): sex, manhood, economic competition, residential integration, and the like. Some claimed that a group of black men had insulted a white woman, others that a black man had bested an Irishman in a fight, "a source of humiliation too grievous to endure"; still others insisted that blacks were willing to do factory work at lower wages than whites or that they were about to move into white neighborhoods; finally, it was noised about that Democratic politicians had incited the Irish to violence.[15]

What is certain is that on Monday, August 4, a mob of Irishmen attacked Thomas Watson's tobacco factory, located at the foot of Sedgwick Street in South Brooklyn and adjacent to another factory owned by one of Peter Lorillard's sons, Jacob, who had followed his father in business. Both factories had been operating for about eight or nine years. Adopting his father's progressive racial employment practices, Jacob Lorillard hired both white and black workers. Still working in the Manhattan factory, Peter Ray was not among them, but as a long-time employee he had perhaps recommended some of the black workers to young Jacob. Watson also hired blacks, and the newspapers specified that he had preempted any potential racial conflict in his factory by placing white employees under a white foreman and blacks under a black man. Neither employer had had any problems. When rumors of a riot spread on Monday morning, Watson, Lorillard, and a third tobacco merchant named Charles Kelsey went to Police Headquarters to ask for protection and were promised it. Lorillard's foreman William Egner, whose name suggests Germanic origins, took precautions. He sent his black employees home, and then bolted the doors and windows to the factory. Watson's black foreman was not so prescient. While white employees who lived nearby went home for lunch, black workers from more distant neighborhoods remained on the premises.

That's when trouble struck. About fifty to seventy-five Irishmen congregated in front of Watson's factory. They threw stones and bricks into the building, attacked their victims with pitchforks, and set fire to the building, screaming, "fire the buildings—burn out the d—d niggers."[16] The defenseless blacks—about five men and twenty women and children—retreated to the second floor loft, where they were eventually rescued. At the end of the day, one black man had been beaten and a few of the officers bruised. Watson was forced to close his factory, leaving his workers unemployed. Lorillard's black employees were too afraid to return to work. If nothing else, blacks paid a heavy economic penalty.

The subsequent court proceedings detailed in Brooklyn newspapers raise many questions. Who were the police helping, the attackers or the attacked? Amazingly, Brooklyn's superintendent of police charged his own officers with negligence, but at the court hearing Lorillard, Watson, and Kelsey all came to their defense and praised their efforts. The charges against them were dismissed.

The men accused of rioting had good Irish names: Keenan, Flood, Toole, Spaulding, Maher, Daly, Sullivan, and the like. Were they rioters or not? The lawyer for one of the ringleaders, Patrick Keenan, requested that his client be tried separately. But the judge refused, noting that by law it takes at least three to riot and thus the charge of rioting would no longer apply to Keenan. Could the rioters be accused of assault and battery? A lawyer maintained that they could not, arguing that these specific charges had not been included in the complaint. He was over-ruled.[17]

The trial was postponed repeatedly. Newspapers gradually lost interest and all coverage stopped around August 19. I haven't been able to locate any court records, so I don't know the outcome of the trial. I wouldn't be surprised if nothing came of it.

By and large the newspapers sided with the black victims, un-doubtedly preferring their helplessness to the power of a mob that could not be controlled. They attributed the riot to the brutish nature of the Irish and their unremitting hostility toward blacks due in large part to fears of economic competition. But scrolling through the newspapers on microfilm, I soon realized there were other issues at stake. Next to an article on the riot in the August 6 issue of the *Brooklyn Daily Times* I found a column titled "The 'Drafting' Panic." Dripping with heavy sar-casm, the author castigated "the weak-kneed gentry" who rushed to the City Clerk's Office to present their affidavits for exemption from military service. "Great, fat, hulking fellows," he mocked, "make affa-davit that they are so weak in the knees that they can't walk. One has the gout, and another rheumatism. This man has a rupture and that one has lumbago. In short everybody who is badly frightened at the idea of 'having to face the music' is affected, if you will believe him, with some grievous malady."[18] Privileged gentry, Irish poor, black victims—these were the three elements that would combine and explode across Man-hattan one year later.

Brooklyn: Hotbed of Abolitionism and Racism

The mob attack on the Watson and Lorillard tobacco factories needs to be placed in the larger political context of the pro- and antislavery agi-tation that soon boiled over into civil war. Like Manhattan, Brooklyn was a hotbed of abolitionist and equal rights agitation. In addition to black activists like Peter Williams Ray, there were white abolitionists like Arthur and Lewis Tappan who had fled across the river to Brooklyn Heights after the New York riots in 1834 to continue their antislavery agitation.

But the greatest rabble-rouser of all was Henry Ward Beecher, who had moved to Brooklyn in 1847 to become minister of the Congregationalist Plymouth Church. Beecher's politics were consistently radical and his church was virtually synonymous with abolition, attracting Brooklyn worshipers but also churchgoers from Manhattan who crossed the East River on "Beecher's ferry" on Sundays. An eloquent speaker, Beecher electrified his audiences with his radical oratory as he condemned "Slave Power," called for immediate emancipation, and backed disunion as a last resort. As a Lincoln man, he prevailed on the presidential candidate to visit his church. He later gave sermons celebrating Lincoln's election, welcoming the advent of civil war, and calling for the admission of black soldiers into the Union army.[19] Of all the events held at Plymouth Church, the most notorious were Beecher's slave auctions. As a stop on the Underground Railroad, the church sheltered many fugitive slaves. In the 1850s, Beecher hit on the device of raising money to buy freedom for slaves by holding mock auctions at the church. In response, white racists threatened to "clean out the damned abolition nest at Plymouth Church."[20]

So racial animosity in Brooklyn was the norm, not the exception, and the tobacco factory riot of 1862 inevitably created a ripple effect. The *Brooklyn Daily Times* reported that a few days after the violence two black women walking on Court Street were accosted by two young and "partially intoxicated" Irishmen who abused them "using violent and indecent language." They were promptly arrested. Rumors also spread that a "large body of Irishmen" were planning an attack on Weeksville to "clean the niggers out." Still "smarting under a suspicion of having been caught napping" during the riot, the police came out in full force to protect Weeksville.[21] Nothing untoward occurred.

A year later, in their coverage of the draft riots the New York newspapers intimated that many black New Yorkers sought safety in Brooklyn. It's certainly true that a number did flee across the East River, but I'm not sure how much of a safe haven Brooklyn proved to be. The river was not exactly an impenetrable border. Trouble-minded Brook-lynites crossed to New York to take part in the rioting while looters from New York fled to Brooklyn with the merchandise they had stolen from Brooks Brothers and other stores. In Brooklyn itself, the absence of the police, who were in New York helping to quell the riot, was an open invitation to violence. An angry crowd of some two hundred people set fire to two grain elevators in the Atlantic Avenue basin. Mobs assaulted black individuals and homes in nearby East Warren Street and a little farther away around Prospect Street. Fearing for their lives, some blacks sought shelter in police precincts. Others took refuge in Weeksville. When rumors spread that the area was about to be attacked, members of the community organized for armed resistance. The mob never material-ized, but when rumors still persisted the next day, frightened Weeksville residents packed up their belongings and left. The safest place of all was undoubtedly Williamsburgh, where members of a German society pro-tected hundreds of blacks in the Turn Verein Hall.[22]

The Abortion Case

At the exact same moment of the tobacco factory riots, Peter Guignon and Peter Ray were being subjected to another form of racial violence, which came, not from the lowly Irish, but from elite whites, and not as a physical assault but, as in John DeGrasse's case, as an attack on their honor as professional men.

When I returned to reread the page of the *Brooklyn Daily Eagle* where I had found the first reference to the tobacco factory riot, my eyes unexpectedly caught the name of Dr. Peter W. Ray. The headline of the article read: "The Alleged Abortion Case in the Eastern District." Peter Guignon's brother-in-law was being charged with the death of a patient as a result of a botched abortion! Finding the article was once again dumb luck. But I wondered whether the presence of the two news items on the same page was just coincidence or whether there was a link between them.

The *Eagle, Brooklyn Daily Times, Brooklyn News,* and to a more limited extent the *New York Tribune* covered the case in all its gory detail. According to their reports, Ray had a patient named Mary Burns who gave the following statement as she lay bleeding to death:

> I do not know my age; my child was born on Monday; Dr. Ray attended me, and some days previous to the birth of the child performed an operation on me with an instrument; I cannot describe the instrument because the Doctor did not let me see it; I paid him four dollars for this operation, and he did it for the purpose of effecting an abortion; he never produced an abortion on me before; I went to him without being directed by any third party; Dr. Ray has called on me since he performed the operation; he furnished me with medicine for the purpose of producing an abortion previous to the operation; I took six bottles at six and sixpence per bottle, but it did not have the desired effect; the operation was performed in Dr. Ray's office; the colored Doctor is the one I mean, and he lives in South 2d street, corner of Eleventh. The child is now in the out-house where I threw it; I know that I am in a dangerous condition, and have no hope of getting well, and knowing this, the statements I now make are correct.[23]

Burns died a few days later. In confirmation of part of her story, an empty bottle was found in her room labeled "Put up by Dr. P. W. Ray for Mary Burns; June 18; to be taken three times a day; price six and sixpence." Night scavengers employed by the city discovered the infant's body in the rear of the South Third Street house where Burns lived as a servant. Coroner Murphy (note the Irish last name) decided to hold an inquest into the death of Mary and her baby. The proceedings were eerily similar to DeGrasse's court-martial.

Ray steadfastly maintained that he could not remember any patient by the name of Mary Burns; reading through the lines, it's evident that she was an unmarried white woman of Irish or maybe Scottish extraction, whom the newspapers guessed to be about forty years old. In an ironic twist on invisibility, it was now the black doctor who could not distinguish between the many white female patients with whom he came into contact. For reasons not stated, Ray was not allowed to testify in his own defense. So what we have is the testimony of six men—four white doctors, Cornelius Schapps, L. M. Palmer, O. H. Smith, and Nelson L. North, and two colored men, Peter Guignon and his clerk, George E. Francis. Their accounts are confusing, not to say contradictory, as were the circumstances surrounding the case.

Cornelius Schapps was the first witness. He testified that he had performed the postmortem exam, and found the body to be that of a healthy woman who had hemorrhaged to death after delivering a child. In his opinion, the woman's excessive flow of blood was a result of premature labor having been provoked by "mechanical means"—not drugs—in a futile attempt to save the mother's life. According to his terminology, this constituted an abortion. The other three doctors offered a different version of events, testifying that they saw no evidence of an abortion having been performed either by mechanical means or by drugs. Hence, they concluded, Mary Burns had bled to death as a result of a miscarriage. Dr. Palmer further stated that he had attended the deceased woman several times for uterine hemorrhage and had prescribed medications, suggesting the possibility of a chronic condition. Dr. Smith gave hearsay testimony that a servant girl employed in the same family had told him Mary Burns had had a miscarriage. But all three doctors acknowledged that they could not tell whether an abortion had been performed or not. "I had no means whatever of knowing the cause," Dr. Smith admitted; "a skilled man could produce an abortion without leaving any scars and a knife might have been introduced several times. . . . I do not know that an abortion produced by drugs could be detected by examining the uterus; indeed, I do not know any drugs in the world that will produce miscarriage with any celerity."[24]

Was Ray just such a skilled man? He specialized in obstetrics and had taken a course at Castleton Medical College where training included the use of "instruments, apparatus, and appliances." It's hard to know whether Dr. Smith's comment was a statement of fact or an insinuation.

But there was more at issue than an abortionist's knife. In her deathbed testimony Mary Burns maintained that Ray had first given her medication to induce an abortion and, only when that failed, resorted to mechanical means. Here's where Peter Guignon's and George Francis's testimonies became relevant.

Taking the stand, Peter began by describing his work habits. As a pharmacist, he himself did not prescribe drugs, leaving that task to medical doctors; his job was simply to compound them. After filling prescriptions, he placed them in a "wire" but did not necessarily copy all of them into his book. Peter then moved on to the case at hand. He did not remember Mary Burns herself but recalled the circumstances. While standing in front of the pharmacy door smoking a cigar, a female patient had come up with a prescription in his brother-in-law's handwriting, saying that "her month was up, she hadn't any money." Peter had called his clerk, George Francis, to fill the prescription and trusted her to pay later. He concluded by saying he had never known Ray to perform an abortion. Francis concurred with Peter on almost every point—that Ray had written the prescription and that he, Francis, had filled it—but then he added: "I have sometimes put up prescriptions containing 'ergot' for Dr. Ray." Ergot, the newspaper columnist informed his readers, was "a medical substance which tends to produce abortions."

The prescription was produced. Written out to Mary Burns, it was indeed in Ray's handwriting and read as follows. "Tinct. Cinchona, comp. 1 oz.; Tinct. Gentian, comp. 1 oz.; Tinct. Cardamum, comp. 1dr; teaspoonful 3 times a day." The doctors agreed that this was simply a tonic, "not harmful in nature."[25]

Matters did not stop there, however. First, Dr. Schapps came forward to declare that he could detect no odor of gentian in the bottle, immediately raising the question of whether the compound it contained had been the same as the one prescribed. Given that there was not enough liquid in the bottle for a chemical analysis, it was impossible to know. The *Tribune* came right out and recklessly asserted that the content of the bottle was different from that of the prescription. Moreover, when the coroner seized Peter Guignon's prescription book as evidence, it turned out that several pages had been torn out. Following the *Tribune*'s lead, the *Eagle* opined that these pages "probably contained the prescription that was really furnished."[26] And Francis's testimony that sometimes Ray compounded abortifacients undoubtedly hung heavily in the air. All these facts cast both Guignon and Ray in a shady light.

Coroner Murphy had already made up his mind. He wasn't interested in going after Peter Guignon, who after all was a mere untrained pharmacist, but sought to throw the full weight of opinion and prejudice against Ray. Here's how the newspapers reported the end of the inquest:

> The coroner decided that the testimony of Dr. Ray was not admissible. Coroner Murphy said that he had no more evidence to be produced. Under the testimony, which they had heard, he thought the Jury would be justified in holding him to await the action of the Grand Jury. The deposition of the woman had been substantiated in two points. She had spoken of medicine, and the empty bottle was found in her room. She had spoken of her child, and its dead body was found in the vault. At the time of the deposition she was perfectly calm and reasonable.[27]

The jury deliberated for twenty minutes and came back with the following verdict: "That the said Mary Burns came to her death by hemorrhage caused by an abortion produced by Dr. P. G. Ray [sic]." When Ray was asked whether he had anything to say, he responded, "I am not guilty of the charges preferred against me. I do not know that I have ever seen the deceased." Whereupon he was taken to jail, after which he posted bail in the amount of six thousand dollars.[28]

Now it's our turn to ask questions. How did the jury reach such a verdict? There was no proof of a mechanical or drug-induced abortion or of what was in the empty bottle. Yet the jury must have taken this testimony as true fact. But much of it—abortion by mechanical means, a compounded prescription containing ergot—was mere insinuation. Nevertheless, there are unresolved questions. Had Peter written the prescription down in his book? If so, was it on one of the torn-out pages? Who had torn them out? Had someone tampered with the prescription bottle? Had the two Peters been framed?

The *Eagle* readily acknowledged that Ray was a "well qualified physician" with an "excellent reputation in his section of the city . . . ranking among the most skillful medical and surgical practitioners."[29] Yet the legal system chose to believe the word of a white servant girl, who admitted that she had never seen the abortion instrument, over that of a well-qualified and respected black doctor whose testimony was deemed inadmissible. Had he done so, Ray would probably have stated that Mary Burns was one of the many unmemorable young women for whom he had prescribed a tonic to ease the pain of miscarriage. Why, then, a guilty verdict in twenty minutes? Why were competent black doctors like Peter Ray and John DeGrasse so suspect?

The Kings County Medical Society

Searching for more clues, I returned to the August 5 issue of the *Brooklyn Eagle*. What I found was yet another article on the tobacco factory riots printed on the front page in the far left-hand column. Titled "The Anti-Negro Riots," it was indeed about that incident, but the second paragraph made a rather strange detour that explicitly linked Peter Williams Ray's professional travails to larger social concerns.

> Making due allowance for the condition of the two classes, there is but little difference in the quarrel between the colored factory laborers of South Brooklyn and the white laborers that they compete with, and that which took place between the doctors of the Kings County Medical Society, and a colored medical practitioner, a few days ago. The Society refused admission to the colored doctor because of his color. They do not want to associate with him. So far as they can they disqualify him from practice. Had the Kings County Medical Society been composed of uneducated laborers, they would have hustled Dr. Ray into the street for venturing to claim fellowship with him. With a clearer sense of the duty of every man to obey the law, they adopt a ridiculous sub-

terfuge, and disqualify the doctor. Their mode of action was
different, and after all, scarcely entitled to more respect; but
the feeling which actuated them is the same.

This would have been strong stuff from any newspaper, but it was particularly so coming from the *Eagle,* which was well known for its anti-
black sentiments.

Indeed, the very next paragraph of the article went on to claim
that "the never-varying edict of God" had set an insurmountable barrier
between blacks and whites, and prophesied that "degradation" and "an-
nihilation" would attend both races if any attempts were made to bridge
it. Yet the *Eagle* opined that racism in the professional classes was no
different, was just as insidious and ugly, as among the rabble. The only
real distinction was the elite's hypocrisy, their pretense of obeying the
law and resorting to "ridiculous subterfuge" to cover it up.[30] Although
the violence involved in this subterfuge was not physical, it was no less
hurtful to both Ray and Guignon (as it was to John DeGrasse). They
were personal attacks on their honor, their integrity, their manhood.
And they also constituted a policing of professional boundaries, a determined refusal to accept black men as professional equals out of fear that
this might lead to other forms of social and intellectual equality.

Brooklyn's medical doctors were not prepared to accept black
physicians as equals any more than white workers were prepared to allow
blacks access to decent jobs in the Watson and Lorillard tobacco factories. Earlier in the summer of 1862, Ray had applied for membership in
the Kings County Medical Society. At the beginning of the nineteenth
century, the New York state legislature had become increasingly worried about the medical profession's inability to regulate itself and get rid
of "quacks, irregulars, and charlatans" practicing without a degree or a
license. It passed legislation mandating the creation of county medical
societies and compelling all practitioners to become members. In turn,
the societies would license each applicant and grant a diploma.[31] Failure
to join meant forfeiture of license. So Ray was only following the law
when he applied to the Kings County Medical Society.

Ray's candidacy, according to the *Brooklyn News,* proceeded smoothly until it was discovered just before the vote that he was "only three-fourths white—the other fourth being the same as the ancient Adam is supposed by many to have been—black." The reaction of the society's members to the news was mixed, but the prevailing tone was definitely one of indignation. Opponents were stymied, however, in their efforts to translate emotion into action. They knew that the law compelled Ray to apply for membership and for the society to accept him. Even after considerable discussion, they still couldn't figure out an elegant way to demand that he withdraw his candidacy. As hard as they tried, they were unable to uncover any irregularities in his application. Shifting from procedural to substantive grounds, one member suggested that Ray could be rejected because it was said that he sold quack medicines in his drugstore (might he have been thinking of my great-great-grandfather as well?). But some honest soul responded that the same could be said of many present. The final argument, if it could be called one, boiled down to this: that they could show "by science that this was a white man's Society. . . . Admitting a colored man would be to a certain extent amalgamation, and amalgamation had a tendency to deteriorate—therefore a colored man could not be admitted." The meeting concluded with the decision to appoint a committee of three to investigate Ray's standing and "find some good reason for rejecting the applicant other than the color of his skin."[32]

The men appointed were Drs. Smith, Norton, and Schapps, three of the four doctors who testified a few weeks later at the abortion inquest. Were they in on, or even responsible for, the ridiculous subterfuge? Without evidence, I can't condemn them. Their testimony at the inquest was cautious and far from damning. Dr. Smith maintained that there was "no means whatever of knowing the causes" of Burns's hemorrhaging to death. Dr. Schapps was the only witness who suggested that a surgical abortion had been performed, yet he speculated that Ray had only been trying to save Burns's life. Were these three white doctors in secret sympathy with Ray? Embarrassed at the role they had been asked to play? Did they sense that, whatever they might say, prejudice alone was evidence enough to bind Ray over to a grand jury? That they could keep their hands clean and let Coroner Murphy do the society's dirty work?

Once again, despite my best efforts the paper trail in both newspapers and court records went cold, leaving me unable to piece together the end of the story. But this much is clear. White elites and professionals were as loath to accept black men as equals as was the rabble. Ray did not go to jail: I found records of his attendance at Stone Square Lodge no. 6 meetings in September and throughout the fall of 1862. That meant that his status as a Grand Master—a mason singled out as a model for his brethren and given the task of instructing them in the Craft—had not been in jeopardy. His fellow masons evidently stood in solidarity with him. Nevertheless, the episode must have been utterly humiliating to both Ray and Guignon.

At the National Library of Medicine, I went through all the issues of the *Proceedings of the Kings County Medical Society* that I could find. Although Ray went on to have a thriving career as a doctor and pharmacist and became a member of the New York state medical association (which probably licensed him), he was never admitted to the Kings County Medical Society.

Peter Guignon Jr.

My great-great-grandfather's travails were not yet over. The years following the abortion inquest brought even greater heartache.

As a youngster, Peter had received the best education available to New York's black children at the Mulberry Street School, and he was determined to give his son the same opportunity. That meant sending Peter Jr., now a lad of sixteen, to Oberlin College. But on July 26, 1865, young Peter died. My first inkling of his premature death came from Crummell's obituary of his old friend. Describing the son as "much like his father, full of manly beauty, spirit and promise," Crummell refused to elaborate on Peter Jr.'s death beyond noting that, "sent to Oberlin College, he lost his life, suddenly, by a most painful accident." Maritcha's memoir was equally cryptic. Explaining her decision not to attend Oberlin, she simply wrote: "A relation of mine had met with an accidental death there."[33]

I went through the New York newspapers to see whether I could track down any more information and finally found two obituaries, a brief notice in the *New York Tribune*, and a longer one in the *Weekly Anglo-African* that offered little more in the way of information:

> GUIGNON—In Oberlin, Ohio, on Wednesday, July 26, Peter Guignon, jr., grandson of Peter Ray and only son of Peter and Cornelia Guignon, aged 16 years, 3 months and 1 day.
>
> The relatives and friends of the family are most respectfully invited to attend his funeral on Sunday, at 3 o'clock p.m., from the residence of his parents, No. 282 South-fourth-st, Williamsburgh, Long Island.

Following that information, the *Anglo-African* quoted some sentimental verse that referred to a tearful mother and father fixing their eyes on God while their boy's face shined down waiting for God to bring them to him.[34] Family tragedy had struck just as my great-great-grandfather had at long last achieved both personal and professional satisfaction and was in a position to help his beloved son do the same. Ironically, healthy ambition—the desire to uplift his family and provide for the next generation—backfired, bringing death instead of fulfillment.

Founded in 1834 as a manual labor school, Oberlin College modeled itself after the Oneida Institute in upstate New York. Its mission was to civilize and evangelize the western part of the country by providing all its students with a "useful education" and preparing the more talented for the ministry or teaching. To do so, Oberlin devised a two-pronged approach that included a Manual Labor Department and an academic curriculum that was eventually divided into three tracks, Preparatory, Collegiate, and Theological. Oberlin, its founders insisted, would cultivate the whole person, developing a sound mind in a sound body.[35] Students were by and large the children of simple and unmonied farmers hailing from Ohio, New York, and New England. But they were neither exclusively male nor white. As evangelical Christians, Oberlin's founders considered abolition part of their mission. Before the Civil War, the college was a hotbed of antislavery activism to which radicals like the Tappan brothers threw their full support, financial and otherwise.

Black students were never very numerous, approximately 5 percent of the student population. As in the larger society, prejudice flourished among some white students. In response to an anxious letter from her family in Massachusetts, a female student wrote back reassuringly that "we don't have to kiss the Niggars nor to speak to them without we are a mind to." But teachers and administrators held fast to their principles of racial egalitarianism. According to one faculty member:

> The white and colored students associate together in this college very much as they choose. Our doctrine is that *mind* and *heart*, not *color*, make the man and the woman too. We hold that neither men or women are much the better or much the worse for their *skin*. Our great business here is to educate mind and heart. . . . We believe in treating men according to their intrinsic merit—not according to distinctions over which they can have no control. If you are a young gentleman of color, you may expect to be treated here according to your real merit; and if white, you need not expect to fare better than this.[36]

As a student in the Preparatory Department, in class Peter Jr. sat next to young men who were all (or almost all) white. His teachers were white as well. He lived in an almost exclusively white world.

Oberlin wanted its students to be high-minded and serious. In the early years, leisure activities were few and consistently highbrow: lectures, dramatic readings, musical performances. As time passed, however, students found increasing ways to amuse themselves, and school officials became more tolerant. They socialized in one another's rooms. Boys played cricket and baseball. Girls indulged in fashion. Mixed events—walks, picnics, sleigh riding, skating, horseback riding—were fast becoming the norm. Yet some prohibitions remained: close contact between the sexes, gaming (playing cards, checkers, chess), smoking, and drinking.

It seemed that Peter Jr.'s life at Oberlin was a pleasurable combination of study and fun in an atmosphere relatively unpoisoned by racial prejudice. So what happened? I finally found answers in the local Oberlin paper, the *Lorain County News*. They satisfied my craving for facts, but also troubled me. I quote in full:

> FATAL ACCIDENT. Scarcely a week elapses but that some community is shocked by the report that one of its members has met with fearful death by the careless use of firearms. But the terrible warning, in the results of such carelessness, seems to be of no avail. We are obliged this week to add another to the fearful list of those who have been hurried to eternity—a life cut off in the prime of youth and summoned unprepared to another world. On Wednesday last, about one o'clock, Mr. Peter Guignon, a young colored man, of New York City, and a student in the Preparatory Department here, when about to start out on a hunting excursion with several associates, was shot through the head by the accidental discharge of a gun in the hands of a Mr. Wilson, his room-mate, and one of his best friends. It appears that the gun had been fired but a few moments before, and had been reloaded by Mr. Guignon without Mr. Wilson's knowledge, and after several ineffectual attempts to discharge it again by some of the party, it was placed beside a door without uncocking it. Mr. W., who in the meantime had been up to his room for a few moments, returned, and making some jesting remarks to young G. about some cigars which he claimed were due to him, took up the gun, still cocked, and in a playful manner, threatened to shoot him if he did not repay the cigars. Scarcely were his words finished, when the gun went off, the charge passing through the left eye of the unfortunate youth, and lodging in the back of his head. He died instantly. A coroner's inquest, under Esquire Bushnell, elicited the above facts and gave a verdict accordingly. The body was forwarded by express to his afflicted parents in New York.[37]

Putting Oberlin's racial idealism into practice, Peter appears to have been part of a tight-knit group of young men, mostly all of whom were white. The camaraderie among them seems genuine enough. Their leisure activities—hunting, smoking, joking around—betoken the kind of intimacy forged in boarding school, where students are thrown together in dormitories and classes for long stretches of time.

I found it ironic that the cause of the joking and subsequent tragedy was over cigars. For better or for worse, Peter Jr. had been brought up in a family where cigars were a part of daily life. His grandfather had worked his entire life in the Lorillard tobacco company. His father was in the cigar business for some years and, as his testimony at his brother-in-law's inquest made clear, Peter Sr. was himself a cigar smoker. Yet at Oberlin College smoking was frowned upon as a stimulant and considered a violation of temperance principles.

Another death, another inquest, but this time with different players and a different outcome. The victim was a young black man, the perpetrator white, and the verdict accidental death. I'm fully prepared to accept the jury's verdict. Nevertheless, the scene of a white boy threatening to shoot a black boy, even in jest, even over unpaid cigars, sends chills down my spine. I can't blame Maritcha for her reticence.

CHAPTER TEN

Philip White in Brooklyn
CIRCA 1875

ACCORDING TO THE CITY directories, Philip White moved his home from Lower Manhattan to Brooklyn in 1870, but maintained his pharmacy in its same location until his death in 1891. The date puzzled me. Why hadn't my great-grandfather left in the aftermath of the draft riots, which had traumatized so many in his community? Did he believe that the protection of his neighbors and the kindness of local businessmen during the riots meant that his safety was assured for years to come and that he could continue building up his drugstore business without worrying?

If Philip hadn't moved in 1863, why not in 1867, the year he married Elizabeth Guignon? Did he not want to provide a new home for his new bride? As with Peter, I know nothing about their courtship. In 1867, Philip was a middle-aged man of forty-four and Elizabeth a young woman of twenty-five. Why did Philip wait so long to marry? Did he delay starting a family out of professional ambition? Why did Elizabeth marry a man almost twenty years her senior? Was theirs a love match? How did it come about?

In one of his reminiscences, Harry Albro Williamson remembered his grandparents' story of how Elizabeth, as a small child, came to visit for two weeks but stayed for twelve years. The census tells us that in 1850 Elizabeth was living with her father, stepmother, and their new baby on Greenwich Avenue. I'm not sure whether that twelve-year period would have been before or after that, or whether it was really that long.

Elizabeth might have gone to live with the Lyons family in Seneca Village right after her mother's death when the still struggling Peter felt unable to care for her. Or Peter and Cornelia might have decided to leave Elizabeth in Manhattan when they moved to Brooklyn in the mid-1850s. If so, she would have been living on Vandewater Street right down the block from her future husband. Whatever the case, Elizabeth had ample opportunity to meet Philip, given the many different interests that brought him together with her father and uncle on a regular basis—St. Philip's, meetings of the Society for the Promotion of Education Among Colored Children, agitation on behalf of black male suffrage.

Hoping that city maps might provide me with clues, I went to consult one and found my answer. It was the building of the Brooklyn Bridge. When we think of the bridge, we tend to focus on the technological skill required for its construction. We stand in awe of the heroic efforts and tragic deaths of its two chief engineers, John Roebling, who died from an infection developed after an accident crushed his foot, and his son Washington, who suffered a crippling attack of "caisson disease" that left him paralyzed and unable to leave his room. We applaud its completion and the grand inaugural ceremony held in 1883.

Yet the process of building the bridge was long and tedious. Although the state legislature first considered a proposal for a bridge over the East River in 1857, it was not until 1866 that a bill was approved. Construction became imperative after the river froze over during the harsh winter of 1867, forcing suspension of ferry services; approximately five thousand people walked over the ice to get to the other side. The first order of business was to build the unsuspended approaches and anchorages leading up to the bridge's span. On the Manhattan side, this required clearing six blocks between Chatham and Water and Frankfort and Duane Streets. According to a contemporary observer, iron and masonry ascended some 1,560 feet "from Chatham Street, over North William and William Streets, over Rose and Vandewater Streets, over Cliff and Pearl to Cherry Street."[1] Philip's drugstore on the corner of Frankfort and Gold was saved, but his home on Vandewater Street was demolished.

So it was urban renewal that forced the newlyweds to move. Perhaps it was just as well, since the Swamp was fast deteriorating. Many of those who saw their property destroyed were local tradesmen like Philip—butchers, grocers, and the like. But some were notable New Yorkers—among them the landlord William Astor, John Jacob's son, and the Smull brothers, who were leather tanners. Some buildings had been important sites, such as George Washington's first executive mansion, at 1 Cherry Street. Nevertheless, like most port areas, Manhattan's anchorage was seedy, housing disreputable hotels and saloons where prostitution and gambling were common activities. Building the bridge offered the opportunity, as one commentator put it, of "ridding the area of its infamous associations."[2]

Unlike the Rays and the Guignons, Philip and Elizabeth did not settle in Williamsburgh but moved into a house at 358 Pearl Street, between Myrtle and Willoughby Streets, in a racially and ethnically diverse neighborhood close to the downtown area. I'm guessing that the ever independent and practical Philip felt no need to live near his relatives but chose this location primarily for business reasons. In the 1870s Brooklyn's industry, manufacture, and commerce continued to expand at a rapid rate. Shipyards lined the East River, as did warehouses that stored anything from ice, flour, and tobacco to coal and lumber. Farther inland there were oil works, flint and glass manufactures, and white lead works. To the east, Brooklyn Heights sat on a bluff overlooking the river; even then it was the city's most prestigious address and home to prosperous merchants like the shipping magnate A. A. Low. Philip's neighborhood was located somewhat to the south in today's Borough Hall area. He was in fact quite close to City Hall, once Brooklyn's architectural jewel but by the time of the Civil War overshadowed by the massive Kings County Court House erected to the rear.[3] Maps and censuses of the period indicate that frame houses lined Philip's block and, to an even greater degree than Peter's Williamsburgh neighborhood, were inhabited by a mixed population of Germans, Irish, Italians, and even Cubans.

Just as important for Philip, Pearl Street was within a short distance of the ferries. Before the bridge was finished, he was one of the 250,000 to 300,000 daily commuters who depended on the city's ferry system. Philip needed only to walk a few blocks west from his home to

Main Street and, paying his fare of two cents, catch the Catherine Slip ferry that would deposit him on the Manhattan side not far from his drugstore. After the bridge was built, the commute became even easier.

Philip was an undisputed leader of New York and Brooklyn's black elite. He was professionally successful and financially secure. He was a pillar of St. Philip's and a founder of many of the community's new institutions. His family stood at the center of elite social life.

Domestic Life

Even if the building of the Brooklyn Bridge had not forced the newly-weds to move, their growing family would have. Philip and Elizabeth had three daughters, born in rapid succession: Ellie Augusta in 1868, my grandmother Cornelia Steele in 1869, and Katherine Maria in 1870 (a fourth daughter died in infancy in 1873). As with Peter, I was told virtually nothing about Philip or his family. My oldest sister recalled that many years ago she asked our aunt Dorothy what her mother was like and whether she had a photograph of her. Dorothy apparently paused, walked into her bedroom, and came out with a photograph that she thrust in my sister's hand. It was a photograph, not of Cornelia, but of her tombstone. Years later, the bitterness the daughter felt toward her mother had not subsided. Cornelia's life story was buried with her in her grave and Dorothy was not about to dig it up.

I remembered the scrapbook page that had started me on my quest: Philip's obituary and an assortment of poems pasted next to it. I pulled the page from my files. One poem in particular caught my eye:

REFERENCES
Suppose the Lord should say to me, when I get over there:
"Your references I want to see, I hope I'll find them fair.
Where have you lived and worked and played? Give me the
names of those you've known.
Who'll tell the record you have made?" I'd mention those I call
my own.
I should not give familiar names nor those of persons great,

Nor offer lordly sires and dames my character to state,
But I should say: "They knew me best—my wife and children
three.
To what I was they can attest, go question them of me.
"Send to the little home I tried to keep with mirth aglow.
Better than all the world outside the man I was they know:
Oh, Lord, I did not rise to fame; high worth Thou cannot find,
But I preserved my home from shame, and there they'll call me
kind."
When at the last the Lord demands my references from me,
Where all men stand with empty hands to face eternity,
This I would have as final proof of how my life was spent:
My own to say "beneath our roof lived laughter and content."

Whatever its source, the poem was obviously placed here in allusion to Philip and his family. Disregarding his business associates, his customers, his fellow vestrymen at St. Philip's, my great-grandfather chose his "wife and children three" as references to testify about what he cared about most: home life.

Parties

Outside their home, Philip and his family reigned supreme over elite society. They socialized with the Guignons, the Rays, who had one daughter, and other families. For each girl, the parents gave an elaborate debutante party recorded in exquisite detail in the society pages of T. Thomas Fortune's *New York Freeman* (earlier named the *Globe,* later the *Age*), the area's most important black newspaper of the period. While the minutiae of entertainment varied slightly, the parties were equally remarkable for their lavishness.

Coming first in March of 1886, Ellie's debutante party was deemed "the most brilliant social event for many years" and served as the model for future occasions. It took place in the Whites' "splendid home," which for the occasion was made "odorous with beautiful natural flowers, while all the arrangements were rich in their appointments." Dancing began at ten in the evening, when the young "buds," as the girls were called, "were introduced into the festivities of social life." A "supper luxuriant in all its details" was served at midnight, after which dancing resumed. The ladies wore "rich and elaborate costumes." Ellie was decked out in "white surah, Oriental lace front, hyacinths, diamonds." Coming from Newport, Mena Downing wore "cream cashmere, lace trimmings, natural flowers," while Georgie Downing was dressed in "blue satin, old gold trimming, diamonds," and Rebecca in "pink satin, natural flowers." The older women wore more conservative attire; Elizabeth was in black surah and natural flowers, and Cornelia Guignon in black silk. Ellie received many "beautiful and valuable presents, among them two silk dresses from her parents and a diamond ring from Mrs. Guignon."[4]

The following year, family friends gave a party in honor of Cornelia. Although it was labeled a "calico ball," the newspaper columnist noted that "calico, pure and simple, was conspicuously absent; but the many beautiful combinations of sateens and other materials formed a scintillation of moving colors that dazzled the beholder." Striving perhaps for novelty, the writer chose to focus on the attire of the men present as well as on the food served.

> Some of the gentlemen also availed themselves of the chance to vary the monotony of evening dress, by displacing the usual expanse of white above the low-cut vests with figured or colored patterns, and wearing the colors of the lady of their choice in a necktie or in a broad ribbon passing diagonally across the breast. The supper consisted of a tempting and toothsome menu, including oysters, salad, terrapin, tongue, creams, charlottes, fruits, sauterne, champagne, etc.[5]

There were many other social occasions as well: the Nemo Club reception, where "dudes" and "buds" danced the night away; the Second Assembly Dance; the Charles Ball, which featured a cakewalk contest; and others. In each report, the newspaper editors pronounced the food more elaborate, the attire more elegant, the company more brilliant than the last. During the summer months, the partying simply moved out of town to Newport or closer to home to Sea Cliff on Long Island.

The "summer birds of passage" stayed with friends who owned vacation homes or settled into black-owned establishments, such as the Foblers' Woodbine Cottage in Sea Cliff, and amused themselves with "fine surf bathing, driving over good roads, boating, sailing, fishing, clambakes, picnics, hops, concerts, *ad infinitum*."[6]

The same names appear over and over again on the guest lists in almost tiresome iteration. They included the remaining members of New York's old social circle—the widowed Charles Reason from Manhattan, the Downings from Newport, Albro and Mary Joseph Lyons who had come to Brooklyn to live out the rest of their years near their children. Joining them was a younger set. Some were native New Yorkers, among them the municipal employee Charles Lansing, and Jerome B. Peterson, Fortune's co-editor at the *Age* (and later my grandfather). Two sisters, the schoolteacher Sarah Garnet (Henry's widow) and Susan McKinney, one of the first African American women doctors, were daughters of prosperous Long Island farmers. Still relatively close to home, caterer James W. Mars hailed from Connecticut and businessman Samuel Scottron from Philadelphia. But others had southern origins: lawyer T. McCants Stewart was born in Charleston, South Carolina, and newspaper editor T. Thomas Fortune in rural Florida. These men and their wives formed a tight-knit, socially exclusive group bound by time-honored friendships, close associations, and mutual interests.

Social Clubs: The Society of Sons of New York, the New York and Newport Ugly Fishing Club

The elite's exclusivity defined more than private guest lists. It also shaped club activities that were mere extensions of home entertainment. Postwar clubs were a new phenomenon, private and by invitation only. Bringing together both black New Yorkers and black Brooklynites, they emphasized class (social standing in the community, professionalism, money, leisure time), patriarchy (the bonding of men of business), and exclusivity (restriction to a privileged few).

Not even Philip could gain admission to the Society of the Sons of New York. His place of birth, Hoboken, automatically disbarred him. The club was organized in 1884 when, according to the *Globe*, "about twenty New Yorkers met together for the purpose of organizing an association to be composed solely of natives of this city and their descendants, for beneficial purposes."[7] It held strictly to its membership requirement of birth in New York, welcoming Charles Reason, Peter Williams Ray, George Downing, Charles Lansing, and Jerome B. Peterson. Others, like T. McCants Stewart or T. Thomas Fortune, were admitted as honorary members, but could not participate in club deliberations. I'm not sure there was much to deliberate, since the Sons of New York never seemed to have fulfilled their beneficial mission. Reading through accounts of the society's activities in the *Globe* and *Freeman*, it appears that its one and only purpose was socializing. The Sons of New York threw receptions—lots of them—similar to the private parties given by families. The one difference was the number of invited guests, which could reach as high as five thousand.

I don't know whether Philip cared that he was not a Son of New York. He had the satisfaction of being a member—indeed a leader—of an even more exclusive group, the New York and Newport Ugly Fishing Club. Founded in 1865 by a group of men "for the object of cultivating a love of piscatorial pleasure," the club eventually abandoned its fishing pursuits in favor of social activities. Its membership included many men who later joined the Society of the Sons of New York. The Ugly Fishing Club differed from the latter in several respects, however: birthplace was not a criterion for membership; events were held in private homes rather than public venues, lending them an even more exclusive air; activities carried a more serious tone.

Let's travel back in time. We're invited as guests to attend the club's nineteenth annual dinner. Decked out in our best finery, we take a carriage to the residence of Mr. George E. Greene at 113 West Twenty-eighth Street. The other guests are gentlemen of high repute, both locally and nationally. We proceed to the dining room where "magnificent tropical plants adorn the table, the sweet perfume lulling the sense while heavy silver candelabra diffuse a soft mellow light upon the surroundings." The dinner itself is "a masterpiece of the caterer's art." I'll reprint the menu for those of you who weren't able to join us:

Oysters on half shell
Soup:
Mock Turtle, Greene's style
Fish:
Bass, with Lobster sauce, cucumbers à la Commodore
Entrée:
Chicken croquette à la Victoria
Roasts:
Bone Turkey, mushroom sauce, petit pies and potatoes,
Sweet Bread Patties à la Reine
Roman Punch
Cigarettes and olives à la P. A. W.
Game:
Canvas Backs and Quail, Dressed celery and Jelly
Sweets:
Ice cream, Fancy cakes
Fruits:
Bananas, Oranges, Grapes
Coffee, Liquors, Cigars

We note with amusement that many of the dishes are named in honor of club members: Greene is our host; the Commodore is the current president of the club, James W. Mars; and P.A.W. are the initials of my great-grandfather.

We're pleased to discover that these erstwhile fishermen are committed to mental feasting as well and that after-dinner speeches are part of the program. J. Q. Allen begins by offering a toast to "Our Invited Guests." Then T. Thomas Fortune delivers a scholarly lecture on the press, emphasizing the importance of independent black newspapers in the "elevation of the race." He's followed by George L. Ruffin speaking on the judiciary. Most intriguing is Ruffin's exposition, reminiscent of Communipaw's earlier concept of racial mingling, of the "coming man" as one "combining the qualities of the Gallic, Teutonic, African, and Latin races." Rev. P. A. Morgan's subsequent remarks on the church seem somewhat out of place, but truly outrageous is James C. Matthews's address, "The Future of the Democracy under Democratic

Rule," in which he has the gall to defend the Democratic Party as the Negro's "natural" political home. Fortunately, spirits are restored with the reading of a letter from George Downing that's "full of good counsel and good cheer."[8]

Class

"My privilege has been to listen to Prof. Reason, George T. Downing, Philip A. White and Dr. Crummell in an intimate exchange of thoughts and opinion," Maritcha wrote in her memoir. "Reason, sarcastic, cynical, witty; Downing, aggressive, with a determination as inflexible as his principles; White, an alert thinker and able debater and Crummell, ready to emphasize salient points, destroy sophistries and expose fallacies. The friendship among these men was of the sort, no lapse of time, no length of distance, no external changes could weaken or attenuate." I wondered what kind of exchanges of opinion had left such an indelible impression on Maritcha's mind. Maybe one of them concerned a recent newspaper article accusing the black elite of being nothing more that "whitewashed" blacks.[9] To pick up on Frances Harper's earlier language, they were being charged with slavishly aping the most unpalatable aspects of white society.

Philip and his friends understood these accusations. They left it to the ever eloquent Crummell, who had returned from Africa in the early 1870s and assumed the rectorship of St. Luke's Episcopal Church in Washington, D.C., to speak for them through his public lectures and writings. Crummell's starting point was to reaffirm the importance of education and what old William Hamilton had called "literary character" to uplift both the elite and the larger black community. Crummell, Maritcha remembered, warned the black elite of their "deeper responsibility and added duty toward the lowlier neglected brethren of your race. If our enlightened men and women," he queried, "do not devote themselves to the noble duty of our race progress and race elevation, of what use is their enlightenment? I would call upon all our public men and women to point out the special losses of the race and to urge the means of reparation."[10]

Crummell was well aware of the difficulties ahead. With forceful logic, he itemized the attacks of scientific racists against black Americans. First, he argued, they tried to deny black intellect. Having failed, they tried to suppress it. Forced to acknowledge the recent advances in black education, they now claimed that blacks were mere imitators—or rather apes—and sneered at the Negro's "flexibility" and "pliancy" as "simulations of a well-known and grotesque animal." To counter these charges, Crummell built on Harper's comments about imitation, placing them in historical perspective. Imitation, he asserted, is *the* means by which civilization progresses. All great civilizations from the Greeks and Romans on have been imitators, and it is their imitative faculties that have enabled their greatness. Picking up on James McCune Smith's earlier argument about cultural theft, Crummell then delivered this bold statement: "These great nations laid the whole world under contribution to gain superiority. They seized upon all the spoils of time. They became cosmopolitan thieves. They stole from every quarter. They pounced, with eagle eye, upon excellence wherever discovered, and seized upon it with rapacity."[11]

The American Negro operated under the same principle. "Give him time and opportunity," Crummell insisted, "and in all imitative art he will rival them both." Not merely a recipient of civilization, he would become one of its agents, taking his place among the "loftiest men . . . producing letters, literature, science, philosophy, poetry, sculpture, architecture, yea, all the arts." Yet Crummell understood the concerns of critics of the black elite. With utter candor, he fretted that under the current circumstances imitation might result not in greatness but in dissipation, in a yielding to an "aesthetical culture" that was as materialistic as it was superficial. In an 1886 speech, he warned that such aesthetical tendencies, "while indeed they give outward adornment, and inward delicate sensibility, tend but little, in the first place, to furnish that hardy muscle and strong fibre which men need in the stern battle of life; nor, next, do they beget that tenacity, that endurance, that positive and unwavering persistence, which is the special need of a new people, running a race which they have never before entered upon; and undertaking civilizing achievements, from which their powers and capacities have been separate for long centuries."[12]

Were Crummell's worries justified? From one perspective, the black elite *could* in fact be charged with frivolous aping. They appeared to be unthinkingly replicating some of the silly pretensions of New York's "Knickerbocracy" and its chief spokesperson, Ward McAllister, who in the early 1870s created the "Patriarchs," a select club of the city's best twenty-five men, and later established a list of New York's "Four Hundred."[13]

Several impulses might have been at work. For one, society life is fun and pleasurable. Who doesn't love to dress up, eat fine food, and dance the night away? For another, it's possible that members of the black elite were convinced that their new lifestyle would serve as an effective counterargument to the scientific racists, serving as proof positive that they were just like white elites, monied, fashionable, socially adept, American citizens just like them. This strategy was fraught with peril, however. It risked mockery from whites of all classes, who could not take seriously the idea that blacks of any class could be their social and intellectual equals. More dangerously, it risked separation from the less fortunate of their race, from those who thought of the elite as whitewashed blacks.

Class distinctions had existed in the black community before the Civil War, but as demographic shifts swept the country at century's end, they became even more sharply defined. Black migrants from the South flooded into the North: 70,000 arrived in the 1870s, followed by 88,000 in the 1880s, and 140,000 in the 1890s. Most of those who came to the New York area settled in Manhattan. Many fewer chose Brooklyn, where the black population only rose from 5,000 in 1870 to 10,300 in 1890, while the total population increased from 396,000 to 1,170,000. Furthermore, the number of blacks in Brooklyn was dwarfed by the influx of Irish- and German-born inhabitants, which stood at approximately 90,000 each, as well as by the rapidly increasing Italian and Russian populations. Stuck at the bottom of the socioeconomic ladder, most blacks still maintained unskilled jobs, the men working as laborers, porters, whitewashers, and seamen, the women as domestics and laundresses. Only a few occupied skilled trades as barbers, tailors, carpenters, or dressmakers. In her memoir, Maritcha noted how much these postwar decades constrained black lives. With considerable bitterness, she

complained that competition with European immigrants, advances in
technology, and the rise of labor unions had combined to create a "tri-
angular" relationship of "cupidity, caste and callousness" that effectively
"disbarred" blacks from economic life.[14]

Concerned for its own social and economic stability, the elite was
anxious about, if not threatened by, the influx of blacks into the area.
As in the years before the Civil War, those who were well off feared
that whites would lump upper- and lower-class blacks together and
treat them all with the same degree of contempt. Some chose to wall
themselves off, retreating into the privacy of their homes and clubs and
attempting to reassure whites that they were no different from them.
They distanced themselves from the newcomers by resorting to language
analogous to that used by whites: *scum, criminals, loafers, riff-raff, lazy,
shiftless, overdemonstrative, undesirable.* Himself a southern migrant,
Fortune wrote an editorial trying to dissuade those who hoped to come
north. "New York is a good place to shun unless you have plenty of
money or a position secured before coming," he warned, adding that it
was not "simply a paradise where employment of all kinds can be had
for the asking."[15]

Attitudes were more complicated, however. One Philadelphia observer insisted that it was just as natural for blacks to associate with
their own class as it was for whites. "It is the prerogative of every man to
select his own company," he wrote to the Philadelphia-based *Christian
Recorder,* "but it is not considered the proper thing for those filling the
highest positions in our society to be accepting the hospitality of bootblacks." Making a racial uplift argument similar to Crummell's, he went
on to argue that the standards of social behavior set by the elite would
"benefit the masses and inspire young men and women to seek the best
associates." A New Yorker claimed the exact opposite. "Our aristocracy,"
he declared, "is at present more hurtful than helpful, because it stands
with frowning face and open sneers at the threshold and sends shivers
down the spine of the working middle class."[16]

And reality was more complicated. The plain fact was that class in
the black community was fluid, and a fair measure of social mobility did
exist. Consider the following biographies of some of the younger members of Brooklyn's elite.

Portrait of T. McCants Stewart, from *Men of Mark: Eminent,*
Progressive, and Rising, by William J. Simmons (Manuscripts, Archives
and Rare Books Division, Schomburg Center for Research in Black Culture,
The New York Public Library)

Born in Charleston, South Carolina, T. McCants Stewart came
from a relatively privileged background. As a child, he received the
benefits of private schooling, then attended Avery Normal Institute.
Determined to study law, he enrolled at Howard University in Washington, D.C.; he met Charles Sumner and helped lobby for the passage
of his civil rights bill. Stewart then returned to his home state to finish
his law studies at the University of South Carolina at Columbia, which
had opened its doors to all students regardless of race in 1868; he received his bachelor of law degree in 1875. Contemplating a career in the
ministry, he entered Princeton Theological Seminary, but left before obtaining a degree. By 1880, he was in New York City.[17]

T. T. Fortune, artist unknown (Manuscripts, Archives, and Rare
Books Division, Schomburg Center for Research in Black Culture,
The New York Public Library)

T. Thomas Fortune was born, not into privilege, but into slavery
in rural Florida. After emancipation, his father moved the family to
Jacksonville and served as a state senator during Reconstruction. The
young Fortune availed himself of the limited schooling offered by the
Freedmen's Bureau, but also gained a more practical education by ob-
serving his father's political career and working as an assistant printer
for local newspapers. Like Stewart, he headed north to attend Howard
University, while also working for the *People's Advocate* where he was
introduced to men like Crummell and Frederick Douglass. Fortune left
Howard after a couple of semesters and arrived in New York around the
same time as Stewart.[18]

    Unlike Stewart and Fortune, Samuel Scottron's father was not ori-
ented toward higher education. He moved his family from Philadelphia
to New York when Samuel was still a child. According to Booker T.
Washington, Scottron senior insisted that his son work with him on a

Hudson River steamer before the Civil War and as a sutler during the war. After the war, Scottron settled in Brooklyn with his mother and sister. Free to pursue his own interests, he attended Cooper Union and received a degree in algebra in 1875. His mother advertised for boarders in the pages of the *Weekly Anglo-African* while his sister promoted herself as a dressmaker. Scottron went on to become an inventor, devising gadgets of all kinds, most notably the adjustable mirror. Much like his father, he was always on the move, traveling far and wide to sell his products.[19]

My grandfather, Jerome B. Peterson, was a native New Yorker. All I know about his parents is that his father hailed from Maine and worked as a barber on a ship, while his mother was the daughter of a South Carolina slaveholder and one of his slaves. Educated through high school in New York's public schools, my grandfather then took a job as errand boy at the Freedman's Bank. After the failure of the bank, he worked as a clerk in a brokerage business and law office before joining Fortune at the *Freeman* and *Age*.

So I would emend Fortune's dictum to read as follows: New York could be a paradise (relatively speaking) where employment of all kinds, plenty of money, and a secure position could be had for the *working*. Those who undertook this task, however, would need the "hardy muscle" and "strong fibre" that Crummell feared were weakening.

Men of Business

In its March 27, 1888, issue, the *Freeman* saw fit to reprint a speech that an obviously disgusted black businessman had recently delivered to an audience of his peers.

> Knowing as we do that the avenues of trade and commerce are almost closed against us, this should tend to make us more economical and educate ourselves as much as possible in any commercial line we are employed, so as to be able to strike out for ourselves at some future date. But do we do it? I know young men who have gotten good situations, getting

good salaries, yet they are entirely ignorant of the business they are in outside of their own immediate duties. They look well, dress well, and have a good time socially.

While I believe that society to a certain extent is good, yet, when we, who can so ill afford it, make social pleasure the main object of our life, instead of trying to accumulate some money with which to embark into some business, I feel that we are doing that which is detrimental both to ourselves and our posterity.[20]

The speaker was clearly worried that the younger generation had lost the energy and will to work for the economic betterment of the race and had instead become distracted by the pursuit of aesthetical culture. Had he wanted to offer models of emulation, he could have pointed to four men in my family—the three Peters (Ray Sr. and Jr. and Guignon), and Philip White—who were still actively engaged in their line of business. To buttress his case, he could have quoted from an earlier article in the *Freeman* that had singled out Philip White and Peter Guignon, among others, for praise: "We have traversed Broadway from Central Park to Bowling Green, and all their confluent streets, and we have not discovered one colored man engaged in any business requiring $5,000 capital—except indeed, the wholesale and retail drug business of Dr. Philip A. White, whose eminent success is particularly gratifying. . . . In Brooklyn we have three colored druggists—Mr. Kissam and Mr. Douglass, and Peter Guignon."[21] To the names of Peter Guignon and Philip White could be added those of Peter Ray, father and son.

PETER RAY, LORILLARD
FACTORY SUPERINTENDENT

Peter Ray had crossed the East River in 1867 and settled in Williamsburgh on South Second Street, not far from his son and son-in-law's drugstore. Even though he was in his seventies, Ray was doing extremely well thanks to the continued patronage of the Lorillards. "Four generations of the Lorillards have known his active services," Ray's obituary writer observed, "from the grandfather of the present head to his two sons, who often found it useful to consult a man of his long experience." When the Lorillards decided to expand their business after the Civil War, they built a factory in Jersey City and rewarded Ray with the position of superintendent, which he held until three weeks before his death in January 1882.[22]

This was quite an accomplishment for a black man who had started with the company as an eleven-year-old errand boy. The Jersey City factory was a vast enterprise occupying an imposing red-brick structure that covered a full city block. Its army of workers was divided into different departments headed, according to one commentator, by a superintendent "whose experience has won him the position"; Ray was one of them. In turn, the departments were overseen by a supervisor "who requires a strict accounting from his various subordinates, and the great works are operated like a clock." They needed to. Tobacco manufacturing was increasingly mechanized. To make plug tobacco, a plug-making machine cut the dried tobacco into the exact size required; hydraulic presses then smoothed the plugs into the finished product. For making chewing or smoking tobacco, the prepared leaf was placed in a trough on a long conveyer belt where it was cut by a knife at 1,200 revolutions per minute. Mechanization increased productivity. In 1883, the Jersey City factory employed 3,500 workers (men, women, and children), dispensed $35,000 a week in wages, manufactured over 25 million pounds of tobacco a year, collected approximately $10 million in annual sales, and paid $32.5 million in federal taxes over a sixteen-year period.[23]

But there were certain things the Lorillards did not change. They still relied on Peter Ray's expertise. They continued to take good care of their workers. Following industry practice, they employed women and children whose small hands were particularly adept at smoothing the tobacco leaf to be placed in troughs. I suppose the Lorillards would have been truly progressive if they had refused to use child labor. But at least they made sure that their employees were well housed, in contrast to the typical tobacco workers who often lived and worked in one single room where, according to one observer, "the tobacco was stored about everywhere, alongside the foul bedding, and in a corner where there were scraps of food."[24] In addition, Lorillard workers had their own doctor, Leonard Gordon, who was also the company's chemist. Interested in more than just their physical health, Gordon opened a night school for the 250 children in the company, a sewing school for young women, and a library for all who wished to further their education. The Lorillards' book collection became the foundation of today's Jersey City Public Library.

PROFESSIONAL NETWORKS:

PHILIP WHITE, PETER GUIGNON

I wondered how the pharmacists in my family had fared in business after the Civil War. Uncertain how to proceed, I turned back to re-read each man's obituary. Emphasizing Peter Guignon's moral virtues, Crummell had absolutely nothing to say about his old friend's work as a pharmacist. White's obituary offered only the vaguest of statements: "Dr. White was also a member of various societies connected with his profession." Peter W. Ray's obituary, however, did note that he had been a member of the Kings County Pharmaceutical Society founded in 1877 (as well as its much later teaching arm, the Brooklyn College of Pharmacy). I decided to investigate.

I spent many hours calling historians of American pharmacy around the country, none of whom were much help. Finally, after warning me that I would probably come up empty-handed, one suggested that I browse through the *Druggists' Reference Register,* an annual credit rating publication of pharmacists, and the monthly *Druggists' Circular and Chemical Gazette,* one of the field's most important trade magazines, published in New York but with a national reach. The front section of each issue, he informed me, contained scientific articles on the practice of pharmacy, but the back portion had news items about the country's many pharmaceutical associations as well as several pages of advertisements.

On a hot summer day, I trudged up to the New York Academy of Medicine on Fifth Avenue, a few blocks north of Mount Sinai hospital. The reading room was dim, musty, and exceedingly hot. A sign alarmingly informed visitors that the library would close once the temperature reached ninety-nine degrees (air conditioning has since been installed and the thermostat seems fixed at a chilly sixty-nine degrees). The stack attendant brought me twenty years' worth of large folios of the *Druggists' Circular*, each about the size of today's *New York Times*, bound in volumes about two inches thick. They were dusty and dirty and looked as if they hadn't been touched in more than a hundred years.

But my diligence was rewarded. I never came across Peter W. Ray's name, but I did find Peter Guignon's in several reports of meetings of the Kings County Pharmaceutical Society. So he too had been a member of this association, although I don't know when he was admitted. As stated in its constitution, the society's goals were networking, development of pharmaceutical knowledge, regulation and enforcement of the practice of pharmacy, and honesty in business. The society was active. Members met monthly to conduct business and listen to erudite papers on different pharmaceutical topics. Most notably, in its early years the society lobbied successfully for the passage of a countywide pharmacy law that would raise the occupation's standards "from a mere trade to that of a profession."[25] Those seeking to become practitioners would be required to graduate from a college of pharmacy (hence the eventual founding of the Brooklyn College of Pharmacy) or pass an exam administered by the County Board of Pharmacy.

My efforts to find information about Philip's professional affiliations were less systematic, and my discoveries totally serendipitous. I had traveled to the Wisconsin Historical Society seeking definite proof that Philip had attended and graduated from the College of Pharmacy of the City of New York. I had found what I was looking for in the March 1844 minutes of the Board of Trustees. But the April and May minutes informed me that while two members of Philip's class had been proposed and accepted for membership in the college a mere month after graduation, my great-grandfather had not. I assumed that it was case closed, and idly started reading through the printed reports of the college's Alumni Association stacked chronologically in a folder. The association, it appears, was founded in 1871 with only the vaguest of goals in mind: "the advancement of the interests of the College and of the Profession generally and to bring its Graduates into closer fellowship with each other." This sounded like a fancy way of saying "network-

ing," and I wasn't sure that the invitation to "closer fellowship" extended
to Philip. So I was delighted to see his name on the list of association
members in its very first year, and even more thrilled to discover that he
was elected second vice president in 1874. Although I was disappointed
to find that he never achieved a higher office (president, for example), I
decided that second vice president was a significant honor, and certainly
much better than exclusion.[26]

I had one folder left to look at. That's where I found a scrap of
paper on which the following was written:

> The undersigned appointed as a committee on the qualifica-
> tions of Mr. P. A. White for membership of this College re-
> spectfully report that Mr. White is a graduate of this College
> of the class of 1844—that he has been in business for him-
> self in the "Swamp" since 1845 and in addition has recently
> been elected a Vice President of the Alumni Association.
> This leaves no doubt about his qualifications and we there-
> fore cheerfully recommend for election to membership.

On the bottom right of the page were the signatures of George Close
and David Hays, and on the bottom left, in parentheses, the single word
"elected." The note was dated March 19, 1874.[27] Philip had become a
member of the college even though it had taken him, not two months,
but thirty long years!

Armed with this information, I decided to return to the New York
Academy of Medicine to take another look at the *Druggists' Circular* and
the *Druggists' Reference Register*. Here's how I pieced together my version of events.

By 1870, Philip had made it professionally. Every month from 1870
to 1886, he placed an ad in the *Druggists' Circular*. The text was always
the same:

P. A. WHITE

Wholesale Dealer in Drugs, Chemicals, Perfumery,
Fancy Articles, etc., cor. Gold and Frankfort Sts, N.Y.
Sole proprietor of

CHARLES' IODINE LINIMENT
Also, Sole Manufacturer of
BADEAU'S STRENGTHENING PLASTER

The ad told me that Philip had added a wholesale department to his retail business. He was no longer advertising ethnic hair products but rather everyday items, a disinfectant cream containing iodine, plaster for making casts for broken bones, stiff backs, and sprained ankles or wrists. In 1871, the *Druggists' Reference Register* gave Philip a credit rating of B, or "respectable," which was indeed noteworthy since few druggists received an A rating (superior) and most had to content themselves with a C (limited) or D (credit fair for small amounts).[28]

I think a combination of factors enabled my great-grandfather to get this far: methodical procedures, frugality, an uncanny sense of the market, and unofficial networking. My guess is that the men in his profession who knew him personally admired his knowledge and skill and didn't much care about his race. They wanted him to become a member of the college and, to strengthen his candidacy, got him elected second vice president of the less prestigious Alumni Association.

Membership in the Kings County Pharmaceutical Society and the College of Pharmacy of the City of New York gave Peter and Philip heretofore unheard-of access to professional and even maybe social contacts with their white counterparts. First and foremost among them was Edward Squibb, eminent doctor and pharmacist, who was a member of both Peter's and Philip's professional organizations. Squibb began his career as a surgeon with the U.S. Navy, then moved to the Naval Hospital in Brooklyn, where he set up a laboratory to manufacture unadulterated medicines for U.S. seamen and embarked on his lifelong obsession: drug standardization. In 1858, he opened his own laboratory from which he launched a highly successful drug company and taught at the New York College of Pharmacy from 1869 to 1871.

An extraordinary scientist, Squibb possessed a strong sense of ethics in his professional dealings, which must have made him all the more admirable to Philip and Peter. He refused to withhold any of his innovations as professional secrets, shared his working plans with competitors, and rejected patents on any of his inventions. Scrupulously honest, he was the first to admit a mistake and retract it publicly whatever the cost to his bottom line or reputation. He was dedicated to helping other pharmacists, especially the younger generation, and went out of his way to encourage and mentor them.[29]

Although he stood alone at the top, Squibb had many colleagues who had equally high professional and ethical standards, including tolerance in racial matters. Born and trained in Germany, Frederick Charles Chandler taught at the New York College of Pharmacy during the same years as Squibb; I found a photograph of him taken in 1870 standing behind a table of chemical apparatuses with a dark-skinned black student.[30] John Milhau, the trustee who had signed the minutes granting Philip his diploma in 1844, still held membership in the college and attended its monthly meetings until his death in 1874. George Close, the first graduate of the college, a co-founder of the Alumni Association, and one of the two men who pressed for Philip's election to the college, was also a member of the Kings County Pharmaceutical Society. Not only were these men among the most brilliant pharmaceutical minds of the era, but to all appearances they put scientific knowledge and professional rectitude above race.

Although I don't have any firm evidence, it seems inevitable that Peter and Philip must have met these men at one or another of the organizations' gatherings. Maybe Peter was at the July 1880 meeting of the Kings County Pharmaceutical Society when Squibb rebutted a recent accusation that his stock of subnitrate of bismuth contained an excessive amount of arsenic (almost as much as the French!) by explaining how he had reexamined all of his samples and describing in detail his method for removing all traces of the poison. Perhaps Squibb and Close were among those at the June 1882 meeting who "favorably received" Peter's proposal for "the erection of a Pharmacy Hall in Brooklyn to be owned by the members of the Society and to be kept for their benefit."[31] Or maybe they were present at the March 1884 meeting at which Peter, evidently undamaged by the abortion case of the 1860s, was elected to the society's Board of Censors, charged with handling cases of unethical behavior.

The same possibilities existed for Philip. Was he in the audience when Squibb delivered a paper on another one of his great inventions:

distilling and obtaining pure acetic acid from wood by heating the wood to just below the temperature of carbonization? If so, he might have been among those who took away as a souvenir a "small billet of wood" that had been subjected to seven days' distillation in Squibb's apparatus. Or maybe because New Yorkers loved to mix business and pleasure, Philip attended some of the college or Alumni Association dinners, held regularly at New York's most fashionable dining spots like Martinelli's or Delmonico's. He might have attended the Alumni Association's annual dinner at Martinelli's in April 1887, when at the end of the evening "coffee appeared and the smoke of fragrant Havanas began to rise." Against background music, those assembled first toasted the college before proceeding to honor the venerable George Close by rising and drinking to his health.[32]

St. Philip's

If Philip was dedicated to his profession, he remained equally devoted to his church. A second poem pasted on the scrapbook page with his obituary gave me another clue to the importance of St. Philip's in my great-grandfather's life. "To Trinity" depicts the parish's spiritual mother as "an oasis left there by the desert of trade / In a spot that belongs to God," and invites the visitor to come "through the half-open door and sit down / In an old fashioned pew to dream" and pray.

THE NATIONAL EPISCOPAL CHURCH

The racial politics of the national Episcopal Church made it difficult for black worshipers to sit back and dream, however. In matters of religion, Philip and his friends were once again called upon to exercise their "hardy muscle" and fight for racial equality. The status of black parishes nationwide was dismal. It's true that St. Philip's had finally gained admission to the New York Diocesan Convention in 1853, and that Philip had been one of the delegation's members. In the postwar years, this honor was passed on to other family members: Peter Guignon, who served as delegate from 1877 until the year of his death, followed by Peter Williams Ray and Jerome B. Peterson.

The admission of St. Philip's to the convention was a clear and open acknowledgment by the New York Diocese that this black church stood on equal footing with all of its parishes. Many other black churches throughout the country never received such recognition, however, especially those in the South. Unlike other denominations, the Episcopal Church did not split along sectional lines during the Civil War and, after the end of hostilities, openly embraced the prewar southern church hierarchy. Essentially, the denomination turned a blind eye to issues of race, allowing dioceses in southern states to continue excluding black parishes from their conventions. Increasingly emboldened, southern bishops conspired to enforce their racial policies at the national level. Meeting in Sewanee, Tennessee, in 1883, they voted to urge the General (national) Convention to establish separate missionary districts for black parishioners that would be placed under the control of individual dioceses. Simply put, the "Sewanee Canon" was the Episcopal version of states' rights: maintain racial segregation by placing authority in state dioceses rather than in the national body.

The plan failed because of the perspicacity of one man: Alexander Crummell. As soon as he heard of the southern bishops' efforts, Crummell called together a Conference of Church Workers Among Colored People, which met in New York in the home of the aging John Peterson. Composed of black clergy and laity from across the country (and later friendly whites), the conference quickly formed itself into a united front against the Sewanee Canon and managed to get it defeated at the General Convention later that year. The status of black parishes remained in limbo, however, so the Conference of Church Workers became a permanent organization, meeting once a year to continue the struggle for equality within the denomination.[33] Peter represented St. Philip's at the 1884 conference, and Philip in 1885.

Perhaps because its editor T. Thomas Fortune was a devoted member of St. Philip's, the *Globe* followed these events closely. Initially, the newspaper tried to put a positive spin on the proceedings. An article on the Sewanee Convention chose to "pass over its questionable terms" in favor of praising "southern white clergy, whose hearts were moulded amid slavery and attuned to race domination of the worst kind [for] now honestly trying to cut themselves loose from the trammels of caste in the interests of the church, and to leave her free to develope [*sic*] herself on those catholic apostolic lines which are organically hers." An account of the General Convention of 1884 seemed satisfied with the mere fact "that the advisability and necessity of more vigorous work among our people formed one of the principal topics" and with the agreement that more funds should be appropriated for that purpose.[34]

Truly, there was not much cause for optimism. The Conference of Church Workers eventually reached a compromise. It accepted the Sewanee Canon proposal that the General Convention would be allowed to establish a separate district for missionary work among black parishioners, but insisted that the district be placed under the authority of the national church and permitted to vote in the General Convention. States' rights did not prevail, but segregation did. By the time St. Philip's hosted the 1889 Conference of Church Workers Among Colored People, not even the *Age* was sanguine. The newspaper reported that one speaker delivered a paper posing the question, "Shall Expediency Take the Place of Christian Duty in the Church's Work Among the Colored People?" and urged that the answer be no. Meeting the following week, the General Convention thought otherwise. "The majority report, exceedingly kind and courteous," wrote George Bragg Jr., Episcopal minister and church historian, "diplomatically evaded the point at issue" and refused to intervene with the southern dioceses.[35] Black Episcopalians would continue the struggle until well into the 1960s.

PHILIP WHITE: SENIOR WARDEN

If the national prospects of black Episcopalians were bleak, the fortunes of St. Philip's were contrastingly bright. Much of this was due to my great-grandfather's drive and determination. As Maritcha remarked, Philip put "the stamp of his individuality" on every aspect of church life. Read through the church vestry minutes and you'll see how many prominent positions he was elected to in these later decades: senior warden in 1875, 1879, 1880, then from 1884 until his death in 1891; delegate to the Diocesan Convention in 1875 and 1889; delegate to the Conference of Church Workers Among Colored People in 1885. Philip obviously commanded the respect of his fellow parishioners. But then look at the time gaps and read through the minutes once again: Philip resigned from the vestry in 1875; although a candidate, he lost the elections of 1882 and 1883. And when a special election was held in 1883, he garnered only one measly vote as opposed to the other candidate's twenty. It appears that Philip's own fortunes within the church swung from favor to disfavor and then back again.

I can only surmise that Philip was a controversial figure at St. Philip's. Maybe it was this aspect of her husband's character that Elizabeth was alluding to when she wrote the vestry thanking them for their expressions of sympathy at the time of his death. "Impetuous in action and strong in personality," she wrote, "he often differed from his colleagues in method of work, but the labour accomplished, and the welfare of the object once attained, the desire paramount in his mind was that a feeling of good-will and harmony should exist between himself and associates."[36] Here's how I think of Philip: he still proceeded in his same methodical fashion when determining the best interests of his church. But he took counsel only with himself, and once convinced of the rightness of his position could become imperious, pursuing his goals with little regard to the opinions of others. He was intolerant of all opposition, and when others prevailed, he could become angry and petulant. In 1875, for example, he resigned from the vestry in a huff when it refused to reconsider the appointment of the new sexton, whom Philip no longer supported.[37]

On balance, however, Philip's business acumen overcame whatever reservations his fellow parishioners might have had about him. The role of the vestry, led by its senior warden, was to oversee the secular interests of the church and ensure the smooth functioning of all its activities. It worked on behalf of the church community without necessarily concerning itself with broader social or political issues (with the exception of events transpiring in the national Episcopal Church). Philip proved to be masterful at making decisions and implementing them. In the process he centralized power in the hands of the vestry and its senior

Dr. Bishop with the wardens and vestrymen of St. Philip's Church, 1890.
In the front row, Philip White is at left and Dr. Bishop is in the center. In
the second row, Jerome B. Peterson is second from left and Peter W. Ray is
third from left. (Manuscripts, Archives and Rare Books Division, Schomburg
Center for Research in Black Culture, The New York Public Library)

warden, bringing under their control entities as diverse as the music association, the allotment of pews, the cemetery, the Sunday school, and,
most importantly, the church's finances and choice of minister.

After Hutchins C. Bishop was appointed rector in 1886, the two
men went toe to toe over who had final authority in financial matters.
Disclaiming "any desire to be autocratic" or to "exceed his authority,"
Bishop nevertheless maintained that "all societies in the Church are
under control of the rector and funds raised by them do not come under
the jurisdiction of the Vestry." Philip begged to differ, insisting that it
was the vestry's right to "control all sources of revenue." I'm sure you can
guess who won. A month later, the vestry decided that given St. Philip's
current financial state the rector needed to bring all fund-raising efforts
in the church before the vestry.[38]

But Philip could be collaborative. In the postwar period, he and his vestrymen began to give women parishioners a more substantial role in church affairs. Cornelia Guignon was one of them. Although her sphere of action remained circumscribed, it went far beyond what had been permissible in earlier decades.

The vestrymen's minutes make it clear that they considered the projects of church women to be ancillary to their own and to fall under their purview. In 1875, while Philip was still senior warden, Cornelia and her friend Elizabeth Graham (the now married Elizabeth Jennings who had successfully sued the railroad company in the 1850s) wrote an exquisitely polite letter to the vestry stating that they had started the Women's Missionary Association of St. Philip's. With its explicit missionary purpose of sending aid to churches in Haiti and Africa, this female association stood in stark contrast to the vestry's single-minded focus on building up the parish. With considerable rhetorical skill, Cornelia and Elizabeth proceeded to "most earnestly and affectionately desire your honorable body to extend to them your hearty cooperation and spiritual supervision in every direction that may tend to make their enterprise useful and successful." Instead of help, however, the two women received a stern reprimand for having organized the association without the vestry's "sanction or approval." The women's response was a masterpiece of diplomacy: they began by reaffirming the importance of missionary work, offered profuse apologies for neglecting to obtain the vestry's approval, and concluded by requesting ratification of the organization, since "consent cannot be consistently asked for that which is already in operation."[39] The vestry relented, and the association proceeded with its fund-raising efforts.

Maybe the vestry caved in because, as a correspondent to the *Age* later observed, "every day it becomes more evident that women are the life of our churches." This was especially true in the area of fund-raising. Peruse newspapers or vestry minutes and you'll come across mention after mention of church women's fund-raising activities, each more novel than the last: a performance of the comedy "Married for Money," by the same Charles Mathews who had mocked James Hewlett's acting abilities decades earlier, followed by a "handsome supper" prepared under Cornelia's supervision; "an artistic needlework and Apron Bazaar" sponsored by the Ladies' Sewing Circle, with a "bonafide Gypsy skilled in Palmistry" thrown in for good measure; the making of an "Autograph Quilt" to help pay off the debt on the church's organ.[40]

Despite St. Philip's conservatism on issues of gender, there was one project in which the church's men and women operated as equals, indeed in which women took the leading role: the St. Philip's Parish Home. In 1870, the Sisterhood of St. Philip's proposed establishing a place that would "provide a Comfortable Home for the Aged, infirm and destitute members of St Philip's Church." To that purpose, an independent society, composed of a board of twenty-two managers, was incorporated a year later. Almost half of the managers listed in the certificate of incorporation were women. Next to the names of Philip White, James Mars, and Peter Ray, I found those of Cornelia and Philip's wife, Elizabeth.[41]

Cornelia was responsible for much of the parish home's success. Taking the lead, she and the other managers attended to both the spiritual and the temporal needs of its five to ten impoverished occupants living in the home at 127 West Thirtieth Street. John Peterson conducted services on the premise every Friday evening, while Cornelia concocted entertainments of all sorts. A tradition particularly popular with the "old ladies" of the home was a "Lady Washington Tea Party" in which a woman manager played the part of Lady Washington by powdering her hair and serving tea to all assembled.

Over time, Cornelia took on more onerous duties. Quite amazingly, she was appointed treasurer of the society. As an independent corporation, it received no regular stipend from St. Philip's but relied exclusively on voluntary contributions. Cornelia scrounged for funds and resorted to every tactic she could think of. She regularly appealed to the vestry for help in paying the interest on the lease. She raised money using the pages of the *Freeman* and the *Age* to ask for donations. One of her appeals involved a promotional scheme developed by the soap manufacturer Charles Higgins, who had promised to distribute thirty-five thousand dollars to charitable institutions of New York and Brooklyn in the following manner:

Each cake of German Laundry Soap is wrapped in a blue
wrapper, and printed on each is the name of Chas. S. Higgins's
German Laundry Soap, encircling a trade mark, "Colored
Woman at Washtub." The consumers of the soap can send
the wrapper to the institutions they may select, where they
will be taken care of, and at the end of the year, the wrappers received at the different institutions will be counted by
a committee of three citizens (selected by the Mayor of each
city). These gentlemen will appropriate the amount as per the
number of wrappers held by each institution.[42]

It's hard to keep from wondering what the "Colored Woman at Washtub" looked like. Was she the laundress version of Aunt Jemima? A
more virulent caricature? A more benign image? Did Cornelia have to
swallow her pride to benefit a cause so dear to her heart? In any event,
she made a forceful appeal to readers of the *Freeman* and the *Age* to send
their wrappers to the parish home. I don't know how many of them did,
but the incident shows how creative she could be in the name of a mission she considered important.

THE SALE OF THE MULBERRY STREET CHURCH: CATHARINE LORILLARD WOLFE

Hoping to improve St. Philip's financial situation, in 1877 the vestry
decided to invest in real estate. It purchased a property on West Thirtieth Street, "good for tenements, stables and manufacturing," and persuaded Trinity Church to hold the mortgage. Some months later, the
St. Philip's property committee shamefacedly admitted that "in the
transaction attendant upon the negotiation of the loan and purchase of
lease-hold, there may have been displayed a lack of business knowledge
necessary for the consummation of such business satisfactory in all its
detail."[43]

Philip possessed that business knowledge and stepped to the fore.
"In matters concerning finances," Maritcha wrote in her memoir, "he
was an authority. His associates on the property committee gave him

the credit of the wise oversight and judgment that planned, elaborated and made operative a scheme by which certain lands in the city, the gift of Trinity Corporation have become pecuniarly productive."[44]

The most important scheme was the purchase of a new church building. In 1881 St. Philip's was composed of a respectable number of 150 families and 500 individuals, but the vestry continually worried about a fall-off in attendance. As early as 1875, it had decided that "the usefulness of this Parish would be vastly increased by changing the location of its place of worship to a more northerly or westerly part of the city."[45] As in the earlier move from Centre to Mulberry Street, St. Philip's could ensure its survival only by following the intracity migration of black New Yorkers. As Italians streamed into the Mulberry Street area, blacks spread farther north and west.

On July 13, 1886, St. Philip's sold its Mulberry Street church building to Catharine Lorillard Wolfe for forty-five thousand dollars. Once again, a Lorillard was involved in a real estate transaction with my family's church. Catharine Wolfe was a granddaughter of Peter Lorillard, the very same man who had hired young Peter Ray as an errand boy in his downtown factory many decades earlier. His daughter, Dorothea Ann, married John Wolfe, and Catherine was their only daughter. A New York merchant who had made his fortune in the hardware business, Wolfe retired at an early age to devote himself to philanthropic causes, giving liberally to Episcopal institutions in particular—parishes, schools, colleges, benevolent societies. At her parents' death, Catharine came into a vast fortune that brought together the Lorillard and Wolfe estates. Never wed, she was often referred to as "the richest unmarried woman in the world."[46] Catharine took after her father, using her inheritance to carry on his philanthropic activities. Her greatest acts of charity were to her own church, Grace Episcopal Church, but they also included handsome donations to hospitals and institutions for New York's poor.

Preoccupied with the plight of Italian immigrants, Catharine Wolfe established a private mission, the Italian Episcopal Mission of San Salvatore, in what had been St. Philip's Church. In his book *The Battle with the Slum*, published in 1902, Jacob Riis vividly portrayed the historical shifts of Mulberry Street's inhabitants and their impact on the neighborhood's buildings. The church, he maintained, abutted "Cat Alley," which

> was not an alley, either, when it comes to that, but rather a row of four or five old tenements in a back yard that was reached by a passageway somewhat less than three feet wide between the sheer walls of the front houses. These had once had pretensions to some style. One of them had been the parsonage of the church next door that had been by turns an old-style Methodist tabernacle, a fashionable Negroes' temple, and an Italian mission church, thus marking time, as it were, to the upward movement of the immigration that came in at the bottom, down in the Fourth Ward, fought its way through the Bloody Sixth, and by the time it had traveled the length of Mulberry Street had acquired a local standing.[47]

Rummaging through a newspaper clipping file at the Museum of the City of New York, I found a newspaper article from the 1890s describing Catharine Wolfe's Italian mission in some detail. The San Salvatore congregation included physicians, shoemakers, barbers, stone masons, as well as a few bootblacks and pushcart vendors. The minister hailed from Naples and conducted the entire service in Italian. His aim, he insisted, was to turn his parishioners into "good American citizens as well as good Christians." To that end, he offered classes instructing the young men "in the manner and significance of voting, and in the duties of good citizenship."[48] Their place of origin and language certainly differed, but I wondered how dissimilar their commitment to Christianity and citizenship was from that of the congregation that had preceded them.

THE WEST TWENTY-FIFTH STREET CHURCH

Let's join Philip and his family as they attend services one Sunday morning in 1889. By dint of hard work and perseverance, Philip and the vestry managed to purchase the former United Presbyterian Church building at 161 West Twenty-fifth Street for forty-eight thousand dollars. Outside, the building was a plain "red brick structure with brown stone coping and a mansard roof." But the church's interior and its services are truly breathtaking, living up to St. Philip's reputation as the wealthiest and most fashionable black church in the entire metropolitan area. The service begins with an imposing procession: Sunday-school children enter carrying banners, and following them come the wardens, the vestrymen, and then the clergy as the choir sings the processional hymn, "Holy, Holy, Holy," in clear, ringing tones. Rev. Hutchins Bishop delivers a powerful sermon and the service concludes with the recessional hymn, "Gloria in Excelsis."[49]

As we listen to the choir's magnificent singing, we let our eyes wander and are struck by the extent to which the White, Ray, and Guignon families have put their stamp on the interior of the new church building. On an earlier visit, we had already admired St. Elizabeth's Chapel on the lower level. Philip had created it as a memorial in honor of his recently deceased niece Bessie Thompson, a devoted parishioner and church organist, and had adorned it with a cross consecrated to his daughter who had died in infancy and an altar-rail dedicated to one of his sisters. But this Sunday morning we gaze in awe at the church's new altar, a gift from Cornelia and her brother Peter Williams Ray in honor of their parents, Peter and Ann; it still graces the church sanctuary today, in its present location on 134th Street in Harlem. Designed in accordance with the denomination's High Church aesthetics "in perpendicular Gothic style," the New York *Sunday Recorder* deems it "one of the finest altars of its kind in New York or elsewhere." The *Age* offers a fuller description:

> From the richly molded base of the altar rise fourteen pinnacle buttresses forming ten bays and a canopied central recess which contains in a deep niche the Agnus Dei and resting on the Book of Seven Seals. The bays are filled with delicately executed tracery divided in two sections by moldings. The top of the altar is supported by a bold cornice enriched with a carved grapevine in conventional treatment. In

its execution, as well as in the substantial proportions of the different sections, the altar is conceded to be one of the best pieces of high art work in marble ever seen.[50]

At St. Philip's, Cornelia had successfully pushed for a greater role for women in church affairs. At the same time and in much the same way, Maritcha Lyons and her friends of the younger generation were breaking new ground in the larger arena of social activism.

CHAPTER ELEVEN

New Women, New Men at Century's End

AS THE CENTURY DREW TO a close, many black elite families continued to prosper, but across the nation the racial landscape was increasingly grim. The demise of Reconstruction in the late 1870s ushered in a period often referred to as the "nadir" that brought home the hard fact that emancipation was no longer the promise of a brighter future but a faded hope of the distant past. A virulent resurgence of white supremacy spread across the nation taking different guises: ideologies of Negro inferiority even cruder than what John Van Evrie had penned in the 1850s; the repeal of the Reconstruction civil rights laws; the retreat of the federal government from protecting black citizens; the rise of black codes, especially in southern states; disfranchisement; economic disempowerment; the increase in white mob violence, especially lynchings. Although their lives were secure, my family, their friends, and their acquaintances refused to sit back and passively watch the achievements of Reconstruction evaporate before their eyes. Far from being white-washed blacks, they followed Crummell's advice to develop the hardy muscle and strong fiber needed to engage in the stern battle for racial justice. Philip was at the forefront of many of these battles, stimulating his friends, as the *Eagle* put it, with his progressive spirit. His activism extended well beyond St. Philip's to endeavors that spread out in concentric circles from community institutions to city affairs to national politics.

New Women

Philip's collaborators included a growing number of women who were mostly of Maritcha's generation. These younger women were fast becoming a force to be reckoned with, making their voices heard both in venues heretofore reserved for men and in organizations of their own.

THE BETHEL LITERARY ASSOCIATION

In the 1880s, black elite men and women came together in two recently formed literary societies: New York's Bethel Literary Association and the Brooklyn Literary Union. These organizations were similar to those of earlier times in their emphasis on education and intellectual development. But they differed sharply in other respects. First, men and women were no longer divided into separate societies but attended the same meetings together. Second, even though these associations continued to advance a racial uplift agenda, there was an increasing sense of shared knowledge among members. Third, conversation tended to focus on contemporary political issues rather than on specifically literary matters. These discussions made clear that members were definitely *not* indifferent elites who had turned their backs on the less fortunate of their race; rather, they were defiant race men and women committed to racial justice for all blacks.

Since T. Thomas Fortune was intimately involved with both organizations, it's not surprising that the *Globe,* the *Freeman,* and the *Age* reported extensively on their activities. It was Fortune who at the beginning of 1883 called for the formation of the Bethel Literary Association and became its first president. Women filled the position of secretary and sat on the committee of rules and regulations alongside my grandfather, Jerome Bowers Peterson.[1]

Hewing to a traditional format, Bethel Literary offered lectures similar to those of the Philomathean Society in the 1830s and 1840s. Some of the speakers were the same. Shortly after the association's founding, Charles Reason delivered a paper on "Material Educa-

tion" before a packed audience that included Peter Guignon. Aware of
the few opportunities for advanced studies, Reason encouraged young
men to persevere in "those branches of industrial education that go far
toward furnishing him with a means of support outside the professions."
To emphasize his point, Reason offered his brother's career as a model,
rehearsing Patrick's rise from apprentice in New York to prominent jew-
eler in Cleveland. He concluded with an eminently practical proposal:
the formation of a committee that would keep a book listing and up-
dating job openings.[2]

Even more popular than the Bethel Literary Association's lectures
were its debates. Topics were announced in advance as were the debaters, two arguing in the affirmative, two in the negative. They centered on hotly contested issues raging in the larger black community,
many of them echoing the later controversy between Booker T. Washington and W. E. B. Du Bois. Washington sought compromise, acced-
ing to demands that blacks abandon political agitation and access to
higher education in favor of manual training and labor in order to improve race relations with white southerners; but he also championed
the development of black community businesses. While never denying
the dignity of black labor, Du Bois insisted that without political rights
and higher education blacks stood no chance of becoming citizens on
a basis equal to whites. Hence, subjects debated at Bethel Literary included "Shall we support separate schools?"; "Resolved, that we need
wealth more than we do education"; "Resolved, that we should encourage western emigration"; "Labor is a greater power than capital"; "That
we owe no party a debt of gratitude"; and "That we need industrial
more than academical education." The answers were not always clear-
cut. School integration was desirable, but how would black children fare
in a majority-white classroom led by a white teacher? Was economic
development a more productive path to racial equality than education?
Which made more sense under present conditions, industrial or higher
education? Would blacks be better off if they left overcrowded eastern
cities to occupy vacant land in the West? Should they stick blindly with
the Republican Party despite its failed promises?

Most astonishing to me was the presence of female debaters. Not only did women now share a public venue with men, but they argued with them over policy on equal terms. And they were taken seriously. A Miss Crawford and a Mrs. J. L. Grant ably presented each side of the wealth versus education debate. A Mrs. Thompson stood on her own to promote western emigration, overwhelming her audience with statistics and compelling arguments. In contrast, her male opponent "failed to make a point and became hopelessly demoralized before the expiration of his ten minutes."[3] Times had indeed changed.

Bethel Literary lasted less than a year. The newspapers offered no explanation for its demise. I hoped women's increased participation and visibility weren't the reason.

THE BROOKLYN LITERARY UNION

A few years later, black Brooklynites established the Brooklyn Literary Union and elected T. McCants Stewart president. Once again, women held positions as secretaries and served on the Board of Managers. Membership was open and free; theoretically at least, anybody could attend meetings.

Philip White was not involved in the Bethel Literary Association, but he took an active role in the Brooklyn Literary Union. He attended meetings regularly, was a featured speaker, and gave sizable financial contributions. When president Stewart asked at the end of a meeting for a collection to support the free lecture course, he turned first to Philip, who made out a check that covered the cost of the entire evening.[4]

Unlike Bethel Literary, the Brooklyn Literary Union favored the lecture format over debates. Much like its predecessor, the union's lecturers were exclusively male and covered similar topics. The most frequent, and popular, speakers were Philip, T. McCants Stewart, T. Thomas Fortune, and George Downing. Occasionally, whites were invited to speak. In 1887, former Brooklyn mayor Seth Low delivered a paper on the politically safe topic of "Libraries—Ancient and Modern." In contrast, Philip and his friends addressed politically controver-

sial subjects. My great-grandfather adopted the Washingtonian position that favored black economic development, arguing that "the Negro
must work out his future on race lines, organizing and sustaining his
own enterprises." To do so, Philip argued, black businessmen needed to
adopt the standpoint of capital and protectionism over labor and free
trade, both of which Fortune strongly backed.[5]

You'll notice that I haven't yet mentioned the names of any
women. That's because at the union their voices were hardly heard.
Actually, that's not quite accurate, because women provided musical
entertainment at meetings. In the 1880s, classical musical education was
increasingly part of the Colored Public School curriculum. Eager to
provide further musical opportunities for young and old alike, Philip
and his friends founded the Mendelssohn School of Music, where his
oldest daughter Ellie was a teacher. A popular composer in the United
States at the time, Felix Mendelssohn gave his name to New York's most
renowned choral society, the Mendelssohn Glee Club. Yet even though
Ellie, Maritcha, and her good friend Dr. Susan McKinney were assiduous members of the Brooklyn Literary Union, they were encouraged
to display their musical talents only: Susan organized musical events,
Maritcha conducted choral singing, and Ellie played the piano.

I have no explanation for the diminished role of women in the
Brooklyn Literary Union, but it must have been galling to them. Eventually, however, change did occur. In early 1891, a journalist and social
activist, Victoria Earle Matthews, spoke on the topic of "Stoic Philosophy." She was followed a few months later by Fannie Jackson Coppin,
an Oberlin graduate and principal of the Institute for Colored Youth
in Philadelphia, who gave a lecture on "Labor and Education" moder-
ated by Susan McKinney. In December, at the conclusion of a paper on
"Digestive Ferments" delivered by Dr. W. A. Morton, Susan McKinney
rose to challenge him, complaining that he should have "treated the
subject physiologically rather than pathologically." A year after that the
venerable Frances Harper stood on the union's platform to deliver a
paper on "Enlightened Motherhood." "The novelty of the occasion," according to the *Age*, was not so much Harper's presence as the fact that
"a lady, Miss M. R. Lyons, presided."[6]

MARITCHA LYONS:
STUDENT, EDUCATOR, MENTOR

Examine the photograph of Maritcha Lyons taken sometime after she was named assistant principal of Public School 83 in Brooklyn. She's matured into a large-bosomed, imposing, almost regal woman. She's gazing beyond the camera with a determined and purposeful look. She appears self-possessed, even self-satisfied.

I'm finally able to turn to Maritcha's memoir, not to ferret out information about "the gentlemen in black" as her father called his generation, but to glean what she had to say about her own life, aspirations, and achievements. The result is a portrait of a "new woman" emerging from the black community at century's end.

By the time this photograph was taken, Maritcha had fulfilled her childhood ambition to become a first-class teacher, building on a long tradition of black schoolmarms beginning with Rebecca Peterson, Sarah Ennalls, Eliza Richards, Fanny Tompkins, and others. In her memoir, Maritcha went to great lengths to give credit to all the mentors who helped her at every step of the way. In childhood, there were her parents, who "made over a sickly, peevish, unproposing [*sic*] girl into a woman with a new lease on life"; they sacrificed so that she could "attain what was regarded in my youth as a liberal education for a woman." Later came her teachers. Maritcha paid special tribute to Charles Reason, who gave her an education that was exceptional for women at the time. Strict and "intolerant of mediocrity," Reason, Maritcha asserted, demanded that his students submit to his way of teaching and thinking. Those who did developed "a love of study for study's sake. . . . Whoever could be trained to enjoy what he enjoyed in the way it pleased him had measureless content as complete as exceptional."

By Reason's side, Maritcha placed three of his female colleagues. The first two were Helen Appo and Mary Anderson, assistant teachers who ensured Maritcha's "steady, systematic advance" as a student. The third was "Reason's most gifted and brilliant pupil," Mary Eato, who, Maritcha intimated, fulfilled obligations well beyond her job description without ever receiving recognition. As Reason's assistant, Eato

Maritcha Lyons, circa 1900, by an anonymous photographer
(Photographs and Prints Division, Schomburg Center for Research
in Black Culture, The New York Public Library)

functioned as de facto principal when age slowed down the venerable old man, and "shouldered the responsibility of conserving the reputation and service of the institution in which formerly a pupil, she had become a teacher."[7] After Reason's death, however, she was denied the official position of principal.

The same year of her high school graduation, Maritcha applied for a position in Brooklyn's public school system. Even then she continued to be mentored, as "neophytes in teaching" were encouraged to take private classes. Unlike Brooklyn's public schools, which were still segregated, these courses, because private, were integrated. Taught by seasoned educators, they covered such subjects as elocution, arithmetic, geometry, voice culture and oral reading, and psychological studies.

Classes in the natural sciences were held Saturday mornings at the Natural History Museum.

Throughout her long career, Maritcha devoted herself to elementary education. She began at Colored School number 1, later P.S. 67, where Charles Dorsey, another member of Brooklyn's black elite, was principal and the much admired Georgiana Putnam was assistant principal. There, Maritcha progressed from teaching the lowest primary grade to instructing the graduating class. Ten years later, she was hired as the assistant principal of P.S. 83 under Frank Harding, a "skilled trainer of teachers" whose further mentoring helped her become, in her own words, "useful and efficient."

By the time she wrote her memoir in 1928, Maritcha had developed a well-defined set of teaching principles. Grounded in her long years of experience, they are a paean to the possibilities offered by what she called the "Little Red Schoolhouse of Greater New York." Recognizing that elementary education was the full extent of what the majority of children—black or white, native born or immigrant—would receive, Maritcha saw herself as providing "the education of the masses rather than of the classes." But she never thought of the masses in the way the trustees of the African Free Schools had in bygone years. To her, the masses were made up of individual students, each one of whom needed nurturing rather than disciplining. In Maritcha's view, there were three essential components to their education: information, which included not only book knowledge but also critical thinking; elevation, or moral development and the formation of personality; and the cultivation of the mind-body connection, in which control over muscles would lead to greater mental readiness and concentration.

In her capacity as assistant principal, Maritcha honored those who had mentored her by becoming a mentor herself. She was put in charge of training students in "practical schoolroom responsibility," and had the pleasure of seeing "my girls" obtain permanent teaching positions. "The success of the last two decades," Maritcha wrote, "is in no small measure due to their intelligence and whole-souled devotion to striving to visualize and realize what is the ultimate aim of proper teaching."[8]

I mark 1892 as the year Maritcha moved beyond the female sphere of elementary school teaching into political activism. That was the year she debated Ida B. Wells and, in her own words, "won the plaudits of the members of the Brooklyn Literary Union."[9] I wish she had said more about the event. Although Maritcha described Wells as "the afterwards famous lecturer against lynching," she never specified the topic debated or her line of argument. Instead, Maritcha focused on two, perhaps more feminine, issues: the "valued friendship" that subsequently arose between the two women and the mentorship in "extempore speaking" that she extended to Wells.

Wells was the galvanizing force that propelled Brooklyn's black women into public activism. Her story is well known. Originally from Mississippi, Wells moved to Memphis in the early 1880s and embarked on a career in journalism. In 1889 she became editor and partner of the *Free Speech*, publishing militant editorials against the practice of lynching that was sweeping the South and praising those blacks who resisted. In 1892, lynching hit close to home. Three of Wells's Memphis friends opened a grocery store, which was ordered closed after it started taking business away from a white grocer across the street. When deputies arrived to enforce the order, a group of black men defiantly defended the store; in the melee that ensued, one of the deputies was shot and seriously wounded. Scores of blacks were rounded up and jailed, while the three grocers were lynched. Wells wrote a series of angry editorials condemning lynching. Provoked into a fury, the local newspaper, speaking on behalf of Memphis's white citizens, called for *her*—or, since they assumed she was a man, *his*—lynching. It was necessary, the paper insisted, to "brand him in the forehead with a hot iron and perform upon him a surgical operation with a pair of tailor's shears."[10]

Wells, however, had left town and headed north. Reaching New York, she was met by my grandfather and Fortune, who invited her to continue her anti-lynching campaign in the pages of the *Age*. Brooklyn's women joined in. "Two colored women," Wells recalled in her memoir, "said they thought that the women of New York and Brooklyn should do something to show appreciation of my work and to protest the treat-

Ida B. Wells-Barnett, journalist and civil rights activist, photograph by
Oscar B. Willis, 1893–94 (Photographs and Prints Division, Schomburg
Center for Research in Black Culture, The New York Public Library)

ment which I had received."[11] These two women were Maritcha and
Victoria Earle Matthews. Bringing their friends and acquaintances
together, they decided to raise money so that Wells could start her paper
again.

To that end, the women organized a testimonial dinner for Wells
that was held at Lyric Hall on October 5, 1892 (probably around the
time of her Brooklyn Literary Union debate with Maritcha). More than
two hundred attended; they were, according to Wells, the "best woman-
hood" of New York and Brooklyn, joined by friends from Boston and
Philadelphia. No expense was spared. An electric light at the back of
the platform spelled out Wells's pen name, "Iola." The programs were

miniature copies of the *Free Speech*. Ushers and committee members wore white silk badges lettered with "Iola." Floral arrangements included a horn of plenty.[12]

In her memoir, Wells spent several pages reminiscing about the event. Barely commenting on the content of her speech, she simply mentioned that she told the story of her friends' lynching and attempted to account for the "cause of the trouble at home." She dwelled at much greater length on the emotions her speech stirred up in both herself and her audience. Giving in to "woman's weakness," she wept until tears coursed down her cheeks, causing her an embarrassment that doubled once she realized she was without a handkerchief. But it was this very display of emotion, audience members later told her, that "did more to convince cynical and selfish New York of the seriousness of the lynching situation than anything else could have done." For Wells, the event was a financial success; the organizers raised five hundred dollars on her behalf and also presented her with a gold brooch in the shape of a pen, "an emblem of my chosen profession." But it was also a professional success, launching Wells's career as a public activist and speaker.

The testimonial dinner was a triumph for its organizers as well. "It was the real beginning of the club movement among the colored women in this country," Wells wrote in her memoir. "The women of New York and Brooklyn decided to continue that organization, which they called the Women's Loyal Union."[13] Maritcha, Victoria Earle Matthews, Sarah Garnet, and Susan McKinney were among the club's founders.

We've come to know Maritcha, but what of the others? To this day, they stand in the shadow of better-known men. We need to credit Maritcha for much of our information about these women, since she proved just as determined to preserve the memory of her friends as of her family. When Hallie Quinn Brown, a professor of rhetoric at Wilberforce University, published a biographical collection of black women activists, *Homespun Heroines and Other Women of Distinction*, in 1926, Maritcha was one of the main contributors, memorializing several heroines in her short sketches.

Sarah Garnet was the oldest child of a large and prosperous Long Island family. A student in the New York public school system, at age fourteen she was appointed monitor under the supervision of John

Peterson. Like Maritcha, she spent her entire career in education; she was the first black woman appointed principal of a Manhattan grammar school. Married to the widowed Henry Highland Garnet, she separated after a year of marriage, thereafter devoting herself to feminist causes. In the late 1880s, Garnet founded the Equal Suffrage Club, which she kept going until her death in 1911. At the end of her teaching career, she joined other women of her grade in the school system to fight for "equal pay for equal work."[14]

Garnet's younger sister, Susan McKinney, was equally energetic and ambitious. Admitted to the New York Medical College for Women, a homeopathic school founded by a wealthy white abolitionist woman, Clarence Sophia Lozier, McKinney graduated as class valedictorian in 1870. She established a medical practice, treating both blacks and whites, and specializing in childhood diseases such as marasmus (a wasting away of the body). McKinney did so well, the *New York Sun* reported, that she had "a handsome bank account and lives well [in the] fashionable quarter of the hill." Given that homeopathy was much more liberal than traditional branches of medicine, McKinney was welcomed by its professional associations and became a member of state and county homeopathic societies. Unlike her sister, she successfully combined marriage and feminism. In her sketch, Maritcha insisted that McKinney's "message to the world is that no normal woman should neglect to seek opportunity for self-betterment," while emphasizing that McKinney was also an "all around woman," trained in *both* the routine of business and as manager of a home.[15]

Written by someone other than Maritcha, the sketch of Victoria Earle Matthews in *Homespun Heroines* is fascinating for its omission of biographical facts that author, subject, and readers perhaps felt were best left unsaid: that Matthews was born out of wedlock to a Georgia slaveholder and one of his female slaves; that her mother escaped north during the Civil War, returning after emancipation to claim her children. What the sketch does tell us, however, is that by 1873 the family had settled in New York, where Matthews attended grammar school before family finances obliged her to go to work. Engaged as a servant in a white household, she was given free access to her employers' library, beginning a lifelong career of self-improvement. Matthews is best known for her settlement activities among poverty-stricken blacks in the New York area, similar to Jane Addams's work with immigrant families in Chicago. Matthews taught the women under her care how to keep house and established a center to train black girls in domestic work. The culmination of her career came in 1897 when she founded the White Rose Mission to rescue black women recently arrived from the South from the lures of urban life, especially seduction and prostitution.[16]

Matthews was the driving force behind the 1892 creation of the Woman's Loyal Union and instrumental in founding the magazine *Woman's Era* a couple of years later. Although many issues have been lost, it's still possible to trace through it the development of black women's clubs emerging in cities across the country. According to the *Woman's Era*, Matthews was president of the Woman's Loyal Union the first year it was established, and Garnet and Maritcha were first and second vice president, respectively. "The object of the Woman's Loyal Union," the mission statement insisted, "shall be the diffusion of accurate and extensive information relative to the civil and social status of the Afro American, that they may be directed to an intelligent assertion of their rights, and to a determination to unite in the employment of every lawful means to secure and to retain the unmolested exercise of the same."[17]

Accounts of the union's activities in the *Woman's Era* make clear that Maritcha and her colleagues understood the importance, first, of gathering accurate information, and, second, of distributing it to both blacks and whites. They followed the example set by Wells, who pursued the true facts about the lynchings of black men with grim determination and then disseminated them to a wide readership. In that spirit, the Woman's Loyal Union devised a questionnaire to send to black ministers, schoolteachers, and other public-minded leaders to investigate charges of black immorality in the South, "elicit the true statistics of our people," and correct existing misperceptions. The women also wrote leaflets on such topics as "Parents and Guardians" and the "Sanctity of Home" to circulate among the masses, hoping that a wider print distribution would "do more effectual good than spoken words to the few." Aware of the importance of a good education in acquiring knowledge, they boldly ventured into the wider public arena to lobby for passage of the Blair bill, intended to provide federal aid to public schools.[18]

Yet club life was not all work. Each issue of the *Woman's Era* featured a gossip column titled "Social Notes." I'm a little embarrassed to say that that's where I found repeated mention of the women in my family, the newly widowed Elizabeth White, a member of the Woman's Loyal Union, and her three daughters, Ellie, Cornelia, and Katherine, who were now courting, marrying, and having babies. These gossip items included: Elizabeth as a patroness of the upcoming Bachelor's Ball, in the company of the "most prominent ladies of the inner circle of society's exclusive and smart set"; Elizabeth at the ball, "in every way a patrician in a regal costume of gray, her bright black eyes and lovely silver-colored tresses making her look like a daughter of the Revolution"; Elizabeth and her youngest daughter, Katie, summering at Asbury Park; Katie courted by the newly widowed Charles Lansing and the announcement of their wedding day; Ellie's new baby girl; Cornelia's recovery from the death of a stillborn baby.[19]

Amusing as all this was, I wanted Elizabeth and her daughters to be more than society girls and matrons. I wished they were more like Maritcha. So I was relieved to read that Elizabeth was considered one of the "large number of women of means and a larger number of women with brains, who give the support of their intelligent sympathy and money to the work laid out for them by their energetic leader." The energetic leader was of course Victoria Matthews, and their task was the creation of additional chapters of the Woman's Loyal Union in the greater New York area.

Yet another article in the *Woman's Era* informed me that Elizabeth was also a member of the King's Daughters, and president of its "Willing Workers Circle."[20] Ignorant of this organization, I decided to investigate.

Interracial Relations

Up until now, the picture I've painted of Brooklyn's black elite is one of a tight-knit social circle within the black community that, except for the men's business dealings, interacted little with whites. That's not the case. As in the days before the Civil War, the black elite had contacts of all kinds with whites, some predictable, some not.

GENDER NOT RACE: THE KING'S DAUGHTERS

Tracking Elizabeth's involvement with the Willing Workers Circle led me to a relatively unknown history of black and white clubwomen at century's end, that of the Order of the King's Daughters.

The conventional history of black clubwomen goes something like this. In the late nineteenth century, white women founded clubs across the country that they brought together in a federation. At the same time, black women established their own clubs—the Woman's Loyal Union, the Colored Woman's League in Washington, D.C., the Woman's Era in Boston, and many others. Eager to participate in the white women's club movement, black women, however, faced intense racial prejudice; Fannie Barrier Williams was prohibited from joining a white club in Chicago, as was Josephine St. Pierre Ruffin in Boston. Convinced that strength lay in numbers, in 1896 black women formed their own umbrella organization, the National Council of Colored Women.[21]

The King's Daughters was an organization founded by white women. In 1886, ten New York women joined forces under the leadership of Margaret Bottome to create the order. Explicitly religious in orientation, this "sisterhood of service" operated to stimulate Christian activity among "rich women." Their badge was a little silver Maltese cross; their motto, "Look up and not down, / Look forward and not back, / Look out and not in, / And lend a hand." Their watchword was "In His Name" and their text "Not to be ministered unto, but to minister." The order grew quickly, becoming national and then international. Made up of circles of ten women (in emulation of the original New York group), it soon contained hundreds of them, many with fanciful names like "Whatsoever," "In as Much," "Here a Little—There a Little."[22] Elizabeth's circle was named the Willing Workers.

The circles were not integrated, but integration of a kind did take place in which gender trumped race. Let's follow the story through

the pages of the *Brooklyn Daily Eagle*. In the late 1880s, at the urging
of Margaret Bottome herself, the white women's Lower Light Circle,
followed by the Thoughtful Circle, adopted the Zion Home for the
Aged in Brooklyn as its Christian charity. The home was a black community institution, housing approximately twenty impoverished old
people. Dismayed by the building's state of disrepair, the white women
set about cleaning it. "Putting aprons on and gathering together brooms
and swabs and scrubbing brushes," the *Eagle* reported, "they made an
attack on the place and astonished even themselves at the good work
they did." They also raised funds, holding fairs and strawberry festivals,
with the goal of purchasing a new building.[23]

Who were these white women? What were their motivations? The
Eagle doesn't tell us. Their names do not appear on the rolls of activists of the period, so I'm left to speculate that they were simply "rich
women" of Brooklyn. Perhaps their actions were condescending, perhaps their events just an excuse to show off their social status, perhaps
their benevolence a form of social control. But the fact remains that
they did improve conditions at the home and, quite amazingly, happily
collaborated with Brooklyn's black women. As president of the Willing
Workers Circle, Elizabeth joined white women on the Board of Managers, eventually rising to the position of second vice president. Susan
McKinney was the home's doctor, and her sister Anna Rich was also
involved.

The history of the Zion Home for the Aged might remind you of
the old Colored Orphan's Asylum. But the earlier institution never put
black women on its Board of Managers as members, much less as officers. Moreover, this interracial coalition of women prevailed. In August
1892, the home, renamed the Brooklyn Home for Aged Colored People,
moved to a new location on Atlantic Avenue. In June 1899, the corner-
stone for an entirely new building was laid on Douglass Street, at the
corner of Kingston Avenue.[24]

Despite the dismal state of race relations at the nadir, interracial
cooperation could still happen.

RACE NOT GENDER: THE NEW ORLEANS
WORLD'S INDUSTRIAL AND COTTON
CENTENNIAL EXPOSITION

A few days before Christmas, 1884, the New Orleans World's Industrial and Cotton Centennial Exposition opened to great fanfare. One in a series of expositions held in select northern and southern cities following the Civil War, it was the biggest to date. Covering 247 acres, it contained well over twenty exhibition buildings in addition to several smaller structures. The main building was said to be the largest edifice in the United States at the time. Every state was represented as were several foreign countries, notably Mexico and Brazil. Approximately 6 million visitors came during the nine months that the exposition was open. It took four full days to cross the grounds.

Black Americans were invited to submit items for display, but were told that they could not be part of the state exhibitions. Instead, they were segregated in a Colored People's Department, which housed contributions by Native Americans and Eskimos as well. People of color simply did not fit into the grand vision of the exposition's creators, the National Cotton Planters' Association, which had decided to hold the exposition on the centennial anniversary of the first shipment of cotton from America, and to locate it in New Orleans, the South's principal city at the time. The organizers' stated goal was "the upbuilding of the vast southern section of the United States, the development of the great agricultural and mineral wealth of this neglected and apathetic region, the uniting of the two sections of the country divorced by civil war, and the final triumph of the entire United States in the peaceful struggle for the commerce of Central and South America."[25] Translation: they hoped to promote southern agricultural and manufacturing resources, entice investment by northern capitalists, effect sectional reconciliation, and open up new markets in nations to the south.

To the organizers, blacks could never be principal actors in this new imperialism, but they were still necessary to its implementation. E. A. Burke, the unreconstructed southerner appointed director of the exposition, explained the role he envisioned for blacks. Management, he opined, was striving to "reach out our hand to our brother in black

. . . and implant in him the desire to come out of the slough of ignorance and make a manly effort to occupy with us the improved farm, the
workshop, and the factory."[26] Translation: with benevolent concern, the
exposition was making every attempt to teach blacks the importance of
manual labor, to which they were obviously most suited.

Insulted by attitudes like Burke's, blacks were divided over whether
to participate in the exposition or not. For Philip White and Peter W.
Ray the decision was clear: in the fall of 1884 they accepted appointments as commissioners representing New York's blacks. They probably
didn't go as far as a correspondent to the *Globe* who called the exposition
a "special and providential means for the elevation of the Negro race,"
but they must have been pleased by management's initial promises of
exhibition space and funds. Even after the exposition reneged and some
black commissioners resigned, White and Ray remained convinced that
this was an unequaled opportunity to prove to the nation, indeed to the
world, what black Americans were capable of.

To showcase "colored talent, ingenuity and industry," black men
and women joined together to pool energy and resources. According to
the *Freeman*, Philip sent a case of pharmaceutical preparations; Albro
Lyons, a copperplate engraved by Patrick Reason; and Samuel Scottron, several of his inventions, "shade ruler, blackboard table, adjustable
mirror, improved adjustable mirror, ladies' toilet case and linen keeper."
Sarah Garnet submitted examples of her students' work, "chip frames,
wire work, books of composition, each one containing a public building of New York City, specimen cards with State, municipal and educational offices upon them." Other women exhibited quilts and needlework in the form of lace, embroidery, crochet, and braid work.[27]

The commissioner for New Jersey's blacks wrote a retrospective
summary for a new monthly magazine, the *A.M.E. Church Review*.
Commenting on the varied nature and quality of the contributions, he
asserted that these were determined more by region than by race, and
that in his opinion "wherever the characteristics of the negro, as a race,
may appear, it was certainly not visible in their exhibit." Talent, from his
point of view, resided in material conditions rather than in any putative
racial traits. He reserved his highest accolades for the domestic arts of

black women: "The women's work compared favorably with that of their white sisters, so much so that it was hard to tell where the one ended and the other began."[28]

New Men

NATIONAL POLITICS: BLACK REPUBLICANS AND BLACK DEMOCRATS

Beyond expositions like the one in New Orleans, black Brooklynites fought to make themselves seen and heard on the national stage. In contrast to earlier decades, they now had a greater voice in party politics. Inevitably, dissension broke out in their ranks: while the majority of black Brooklynites (indeed of all black Americans) remained staunch Republican, some declared themselves Democrats, while still others became Mugwumps (Republicans who abandoned their party during the election of 1888 and sided with the Democrats). Yet they all shared a common goal: full equal rights for all black Americans.

Like most of the black elite, the men in my family—Philip White, Peter Guignon, Peter Williams Ray, and Jerome B. Peterson—remained loyal to the party of Lincoln despite its less than perfect record on black civil rights. The newspaper trail of their activities is scant. But I do know that in 1872 Philip, Peter, and others got together to endorse the reelection of President Grant, whose administration had facilitated passage of the Fifteenth Amendment. Some ten years later, a group that included Charles Reason and Charles Ray created the Aggressive Radical Republican League and adopted a series of resolutions, one of which was a call for the nomination of a black for "presidential elector," or delegate to the Electoral College. In 1887, black Republican ward clubs united to form the Colored Citizens Central Republican League of Kings County, to which Philip belonged. After the election of Republican presidential candidate Benjamin Harrison in 1888, several members attended inaugural events in Washington, D.C., sponsored by that city's black elite; Philip was there accompanied by Elizabeth and Ellie.[29]

Echoing the prewar skepticism of editor Thomas Hamilton, not all members of the black elite lined up blindly behind Republican candidates. During the 1872 meeting, my great-great-grandfather suggested withholding support of Grant and waiting until after the Liberal Republican Party held its convention. "There were men in that Convention," Peter declared, "who had been friends to the colored men before General Grant." Black Brooklynites, he warned, needed to be careful "lest they should get themselves into a snarl." The friend Peter alluded to was none other than Horace Greeley, still a maverick and still impossible to label. During the Civil War, Greeley had defended the right to secession, and in its aftermath had promoted amnesty for Confederate veterans and sectional reconciliation. At the same time, he spoke out against the Ku Klux Klan and insisted on the federal government's obligation to guarantee free elections in the South. Disenchanted with Grant's first administration, its dependence on big business, its protectionist stance, and its massive corruption, Greeley decided to make a run for the presidency. Amazingly, he was nominated by both the Liberal Republican and Democratic Parties. Although most prewar abolitionists were disgusted with him, Charles Sumner eventually threw him his support. Nevertheless, Grant won with 56 percent of the vote.[30]

The men at the 1872 meeting summarily dismissed Peter's proposal and sent up three cheers for Grant. Some ten years later, however, it was impossible to ignore such dissenting views. George Downing was among the first seriously to question blacks' blind loyalty to the Republican Party, and was soon joined by T. Thomas Fortune and T. McCants Stewart. With the editor's blessing, Downing took to the pages of the *Globe* and *Freeman* to express his views at great length. Echoing the rationale behind his friend Charles Sumner's endorsement of Greeley, Downing argued that no political party should take the black vote for granted: "I desire a division of the colored vote, because I believe it will be better to have more than one party anxious, concerned, and cherishing the hope that at least a part of that vote may be obtained; because a division would result in increased respect from all quarters, and create general competitive concern." Most were horrified, but Fortune took Downing's side. The country needs to understand, he declared in a *Globe* editorial, that "we are not as sheep led to the slaughter, but are men mindful of the blessings of economical and honest administration of the government [who] demand our full share of consideration from the parties with which we affiliate."[31]

Neither Downing nor Fortune was as yet prepared to vote the Democratic ticket, but they were vociferous in their criticism of recent Republican administrations. During the 1884 presidential campaign that pitted Democrat Grover Cleveland against Republican James Blaine, the *Globe* reluctantly supported Blaine; but soon after Cleveland's election Fortune began praising the new administration as liberal and progressive.[32] His enthusiasm for Cleveland was shared by T. McCants Stewart. Both men were impressed when Cleveland made good on his promise to appoint blacks to federal positions.

By the next election, all three men had solidified their position as black Democrats. Fortune and Stewart actively campaigned for Cleveland even though the *Age,* now under the stewardship of my grandfather, remained staunchly Republican and endorsed Benjamin Harrison. Black Republicans' delight with Harrison's victory was short-lived. Under his administration, the Lodge federal election bill, mandating federal supervision of congressional elections to protect black voting rights, and the Blair education bill, providing federal aid to public schools, went down to defeat; blacks in Mississippi were disfranchised; and white violence against blacks rose dramatically in the South. But neither could black Democrats gloat for long over Cleveland's re-election in 1892. During his second administration, Cleveland abolished black patronage, and worse still, maintained a deafening silence over lynching, disfranchisement, and mob law in the South.[33] Downing, it turned out, was wrong. The black man's vote still counted for nothing.

LOCAL POLITICS: BLACK DEMOCRATS
AND BLACK REPUBLICANS

It's been said that all politics is local. Fortune agreed with this adage, repeatedly arguing that a divided black vote was as necessary in local elections as in national ones. Since Brooklyn was a Democratic stronghold, from a local perspective it made sense that its black population would affiliate with the Democratic Party.

If the Democratic Party dominated Brooklyn politics, Boss Hugh McLaughlin dominated the Democratic Party. Although the only elected position he ever held was that of registrar early in his career, by 1873 McLaughlin was the undisputed boss of Brooklyn's Democratic Party. He dispensed patronage in the form of jobs, contracts, and charity, asking for votes in return. He selected all his party's candidates, in particular the city's mayors; once elected, he demanded full subservience. During his tenure, Democratic mayors paraded through City Hall one after the other with few Republican interruptions. They served McLaughlin rather than the citizenry. And whether they started out with good intentions or not, they inevitably gave in to the corruption that plagued the city in the areas of public health, tax collection, and the granting of contracts.[34]

Implementing their theory of a divided black vote, in 1887 Fortune and Stewart worked actively not only for Cleveland but also for Alfred C. Chapin, McLaughlin's mayoral candidate. Stewart became wildly popular among Brooklyn's white Democrats, addressing rallies numbering in the thousands. Although Cleveland lost the national election, Democrats prevailed locally. Chapin was sworn in as mayor and was reelected two years later.

Stewart's and Fortune's involvement in local Democratic politics galvanized black Republicans into action, resulting in the formation of the Colored Citizens Central Republican League of Kings County. At a mass meeting attended by Philip, Peter W. Ray, and Jerome B. Peterson, the league, according to the *Age*, nominated James W. Mars, its president (and commodore of the Ugly Fishing Club), as Republican candidate for alderman-at-large. None too pleased with the nomination of a black man, local Republican officials dragged their feet. But worried about the defection of black voters, they relented and agreed to run Mars as assemblyman for the Third District. Since this ward was the richest in the city and virtually all white, the election was entirely bogus.[35]

Local party politics was all about garnering votes for the candidate and gaining influence in return. I wondered how Brooklyn's black men benefited.

LOCAL POLITICS: MAYOR SETH LOW,
PHILIP WHITE, AND THE BROOKLYN
BOARD OF EDUCATION

"Last evening," a report in the *Brooklyn Union* informed its readers on June 13, 1884, "Mr. White's house was invaded by about fifty of his neighbors and friends." They had assembled to honor my great-grandfather's service as a Brooklyn citizen and public official. Taking the floor, James Mars reminisced about how some two years earlier a subcommittee of the Colored Taxpayers' Committee had called on then mayor Seth Low and requested him to appoint Philip to a vacant seat on the Brooklyn Board of Education. "The mayor looked upon us suspiciously," Mars continued; "he seemed to think the act an intrusion—at least, so it seemed to us. But, to our astonishment, after a while Mr. White got the appointment."[36]

As Brooklyn's Republican mayor from 1882 to 1886, Seth Low was one of the very few local politicians who successfully managed to break Boss McLaughlin's iron grip over the city. In background, upbringing, and temperament, Low was the exact opposite of McLaughlin. His ancestors had come from England on the *Mayflower;* in the early nineteenth century, his grandfather, Seth, had settled in Brooklyn, where he acquired considerable influence in civic affairs. Gaining substantial wealth by trading all over the world, Seth Low was embraced by Knickerbocker society. His son, Abiel, expanded his father's business and founded the family firm, A. A. Low and Brothers. To a certain extent, Abiel was civic minded: he was a member of the Union League Club at the time of the draft riots and worked with it to advance the Union cause. Yet he remained primarily preoccupied with his mercantile interests.

Mayor Seth Low took after his grandfather, who was said to have whispered to him with his dying breath, "Be kind to the poor." After a stint in his father's firm, Low left to pursue a life of public service and joined the Republican Party. In 1882, he was elected mayor of Brooklyn, defeating McLaughlin's candidate. Unlike the Democratic mayors, Low was hard working, efficient, and honest. He went after delinquent taxpayers; modernized the police force, fire department, and sanitation services; overhauled procedures for granting contracts; improved the school system. True to his word, he rejected partisanship and patronage. He became unpopular. By the time he left office, he had alienated just about everybody, Republicans and Democrats, politicians and citizens alike.[37]

I don't know what convinced Low to appoint Philip to the Brooklyn Board of Education. It obviously wasn't patronage. Did the two men know each other? Low was a speaker at the Brooklyn Literary Union in 1887, and it's quite possible that his ties to Brooklyn's black community reached far back in time. Or Low might have been aware of Philip's reputation and liked what he heard. After all, the terms my great-grandfather's obituary writer used to describe him—studious, temperate, pursuing the ends of a noble manhood, with a punctilious regard to truth and fairness—applied equally well to Low. Above all, the two men shared a common goal: improving the city's public schools for all young people regardless of race or ethnicity.

Second only to St. Philip's, education was Philip's life passion. For years, he had been the secretary of the Society for the Improvement of Education Among Colored Children and an active member of its Ridgeway School Prize Committee. And the anonymous scrapbook keeper who pasted several poems next to Philip's obituary included one titled "Why Johnny Failed: Good for a Boy to Read." Some of the lines read:

> At school, the teacher tried her best
> To give him facts and rules
> Of every hopeful sort—but no,
> For Johnny hated school.
> . . .
> So when the day of manhood came
> When Johnny searched his mind

But still and ever it played him false
And nothing could he find
But worthless trash and ugly thoughts
And lo, he failed alas!
Is any other boy who reads this
Coming to Johnny's pass?

Philip did not want any other Johnnies to fail.

It was not at all clear, however, how best to help the Johnnies who happened to be black and living in the United States in the 1880s. By law, Brooklyn's school system was still segregated, although, through another operation of the rule of whimsy, black children were scattered throughout many schools without major repercussions.[38] I traced Philip's course of action through the minutes of the Brooklyn Board of Education as well as Fortune's newspapers.

As usual, my great-grandfather proceeded cautiously. Only a few months after taking his seat, he proposed that the board consider "the desirability either of enforcing the attendance of all colored children upon colored schools, or of adopting some plan of reorganization by which colored children may attend any school within their districts to the end that a uniform system may be adopted."[39] Translation: enforce the current segregated system or move to integration. The response was silence.

As the board member in charge of Brooklyn's three colored schools, Philip began by pursuing the first option. He was particularly concerned about the deplorable conditions of Colored Grammar School No. 1. Throughout 1883, he repeatedly requested items big and small for the school—new furniture, a set of maps, two clocks, a piano. Most important, he helped push through a resolution to buy a plot of land to erect a new building.

The new school opened November 19 of that year to great fanfare. The building itself was a substantial brick structure that cost $25,000. It housed 450 students divided between a primary school on the ground floor and a grammar school on the second. Several men from the black community, Philip included, addressed the audience. In their remarks, they rehearsed the history of black education in the state beginning with

the African Free Schools; named the great men—the Reasons, Crummell, Garnet, McCune Smith, Rays, and Downings—who had benefited from its instruction; and praised the efforts of Charles Dorsey, the
new school's principal, and the teachers who worked under him, among
them Maritcha and her good friend Georgiana Putnam. Finally, Mayor
Low rose and gave "an excellent address, in which he compared the
school house to a fortress and the children to its army, ready to protect
the citadel, ready to sally forth for the attack, as well as to stand for its
defense." He concluded by endorsing the suggestion of an earlier speaker
who had recommended that "the word 'colored' should be erased from
this beautiful building."[40]

Philip, it turned out, had similar ideas. When the Board of Education met on December 11, he introduced the following resolution: "Resolved—That the Principals and Heads of Departments of the schools
under the control of the Board of Education are hereby directed to receive all colored children that may apply for admission on the same
terms that they do white children." The resolution passed. Jubilant, the
black community heaped praise on Philip. One writer to the *Globe* compared him to a medieval knight. To those who expressed surprise at "the
intrepidity, the coolness and the *élan* with which Dr. White carried
the bulwarks of caste," he invited them to look back at history. Peruse
the old *Anglo-African Magazine,* he suggested, and you'll find proof
of his mettle in the 1857 report he and Charles Ray wrote on behalf of
the Society for the Improvement of Education Among Colored Children protesting the treatment of black students in New York's public
schools.[41]

In fact, although Brooklyn's black community was committed to
the principle of integration, it was less sure about the practice. Fortune
neatly summed up the ambivalence in a *Globe* editorial. "What we contend for, and what Dr. White and every other colored man of sense con-
tends for," he wrote, "is, not that colored schools should be abolished,
but that no more inhibitions should rest upon colored children than
upon white ones, that the same laws which govern one class of citizens
should govern every other class, that discriminations should not be applied to one class while another is allowed every immunity." The prin-

ciple behind school integration was important: equality before the law. But so was that behind segregation: black control over education. This latter claim in fact exactly replicated the policy of separate institutions of the 1830s. In separate schools, black teachers, who understood the needs of black children and were sensitive to parental concerns, would be kept on. In contrast, in an integrated system, one injustice, as Fortune put it, would replace another. Black students would benefit, but black teachers, deemed unfit to instruct white children, would lose their jobs. Fortune in fact was convinced that integration was nothing more than a "transparent subterfuge" cooked up to get rid of black teachers.[42]

In point of fact, nothing much changed. The three colored schools continued to operate as before and Philip renewed his commitment to Colored School No. 1 (later renumbered 67). Several times a year, the school held elaborate public exercises, reminiscent of the earlier Ridgeway School Prize Committee ceremonies, covered extensively by Fortune's newspapers. There were declamations, class recitations, choruses, and solos by the students, the best of whom received medals and books. Charles Dorsey was regularly praised for his excellent stewardship of the school, as were Georgiana Putnam, the head of the Grammar Department, and Maritcha, the assistant. They were all showered with gifts; some, like a silver pitcher, fruit dish, or lamp, were quite extravagant; others, the complete works of Washington Irving, for example, were of a more serious nature. Presiding over all the festivities was Philip, whose "suavity and fatherly tenderness" made him enormously popular with the students.[43]

In addition, racist attitudes still prevailed. In the late 1880s, white schools continued to reject black students, claiming that the Board of Education's integration legislation was a one-year law and had long since lapsed. Yet black schools could not refuse white teachers. When Philip, with the backing of three different superintendent reports, recommended the dismissal of two white teachers from Colored School No. 2 on grounds of incompetence, his request was summarily rejected. Although upset, he acquiesced. But not even the diplomatic Philip could contain himself during the ruckus that ensued after he requested a pay raise for Georgiana Putnam as head of department. The board dallied, and agreed to the raise only after passing an obnoxious rule that excluded all the colored schools from general legislation and placed them in a separate category. An angry Philip resigned, returning only after Alfred Chapin, recently reelected mayor by Democratic voters, begged him to do so.[44]

LOCAL POLITICS: T. McCANTS STEWART AND THE BROOKLYN BOARD OF EDUCATION

After Philip's death in February 1892, Mayor Chapin rewarded T. McCants Stewart for his support by appointing him to succeed Philip on the Board of Education. Skilled in legal argument and always spoiling for a good fight, Stewart was the perfect candidate to finish the work Philip had started and create a truly integrated school in Brooklyn. Yet his efforts exposed deep divisions not only between blacks and whites but also within the black community.

Here's what happened. At its May 1892 meeting, the Board of Education decided to reverse a previous decision and give a new building designed for black children to the white P.S. 83. An angry Stewart rose to remind his colleagues of the history of the building. It was Philip White, he declared, who had persuaded the board to build the new schoolhouse for the colored P.S. 68 in Weeksville. Now that the area was becoming increasingly white, the board was reneging on its promise and catering to white parents. A compromise was eventually reached. The approximately 150 black students from P.S. 68 and their five teachers moved into the first floor of the building, while the much larger white P.S. 83, with its 500 students and many teachers, occupied the second floor. Sensing that the battle was half won, Stewart continued his push for a fully integrated school, proposing at the March 1893 board meeting that P.S. 68 be absorbed into P.S. 83. A hue and cry broke out. Whites complained that the presence of black students would lead to "deteriorating influences" and that it was impossible to "force acquiescence." Georgiana Putnam, who by then had been appointed principal of P.S. 68, also voiced her opposition, fearing it would cost black teachers their jobs.[45]

In retaliation, Stewart, backed by the board, tried to get Putnam fired and replaced by a white woman. A fierce battle erupted within the black community. Fortune sided with Stewart and was almost beaten when he brought up the controversy during a meeting. Susan McKinney stood by Putnam, complaining that Stewart had "gone out of his way to do an injustice to one of his race, ... a finely educated and highly cultured woman." Harsher still, Samuel Scottron accused Stewart of "hiding behind a mask of virtue and devotion to the public welfare" when in reality he had shown himself quite willing to betray his race.[46] Surely this kind of bickering would not have broken out had Philip still been alive.

The story has a happy ending. Both Stewart and Georgiana Putnam got what they wanted, as did the black and white children of Weeksville. P.S. 68 merged with P.S. 83 without incident. Putnam became head of department, and after being promoted to principal of a primary school was replaced by Maritcha, who remembered with fondness her many years teaching "all the varied nationalities to be found in a cosmopolitan city."[47]

THE AFRO-AMERICAN LEAGUE

Determined to move beyond local politics and take their struggle to the national level, in 1889 Philip, Fortune, and Stewart, with other like-minded black men, founded a national organization, the Afro-American League. Promising to "ignore all partisan politics," the league pledged to work to "to secure passage of such laws . . . as shall prevent discrimination in any and every form on account of race, color, condition or religion, and to bring and prosecute in the courts actions for the redress of wrongs against their civil rights." Philip was named treasurer and Stewart counsel.

As the league's counsel, Stewart scored one great victory representing T. Thomas Fortune in a civil rights case. In June 1890, Fortune was refused service and ejected from the bar of New York's Trainor Hotel, and then jailed for disorderly conduct. Although the case was dismissed, Fortune decided to sue the owner for ten thousand dollars and appealed to the league to help support his case. Members responded by holding "indignation meetings," and both money and sympathy poured in. At trial a year later, the jury decided in Fortune's favor and awarded him damages and costs totaling one thousand dollars.

But there were no larger victories. At regular intervals, Stewart submitted a civil rights bill prohibiting discrimination in public places to the state legislature in Albany. In 1887, it was set aside; in 1890, it was voted down; in 1895, it passed. But by that time it really didn't matter. Whites in power simply began reclassifying public accommodations as private, or ignored the law knowing full well that there would be no consequences. And by then the Afro-American League no longer existed.[48]

Philip White and Highbrow Culture

In these later decades, Philip had indeed become a race man publicly committed to fighting for racial justice. But with money and leisure time, he could now pursue his love for the arts. From the 1850 census, I knew that he owned a piano, and from more recent newspapers that he helped found the Mendelssohn School of Music. From his work with schools, I deduced that he was an avid reader of books. From his obituary, I discovered that he had been a member of the Metropolitan Museum of Art. In solidarity with W. E. B. Du Bois, Philip seemed determined to enjoy on equal terms with whites the cosmopolitan high culture that was emerging in the nation's urban centers after the Civil War. He fully endorsed Booker T. Washington's call for the development of black business and entrepreneurship. Yet he also stood in awe of the gifts of mind and spirit that were the hallmark of all humanity and nourished what Du Bois called "the sovereign human soul that seeks to know itself and the world about it; that seeks a freedom for expansion and self-development."[49]

THE METROPOLITAN MUSEUM OF ART:
CATHARINE LORILLARD WOLFE

On December 18, 1888, the Metropolitan Museum of Art threw a lavish reception to inaugurate the opening of the new south wing that had been added to its decade-old building on Fifth Avenue. The mayor, representatives of the Park Department, and museum trustees sat on the platform; the Mendelssohn Glee Club, selected to provide music for the occasion, stood in the north gallery; and crammed into the halls were ten thousand invited guests, many of them from the upper rungs of New York high society. The new wing had been necessitated by the Met's vast holdings, which, as one newspaper report put it, had been expanding at a rapid rate ever since Catharine Lorillard Wolfe's bequest at her death in 1887 had "broken forth . . . the flood-gates of personal generosity."[50]

At the opening, Wolfe's portrait painted by Alexandre Cabanel in 1876 was prominently displayed. According to one reviewer:

> There is something inexpressively lovely about the expression of her face that marks her as one of nature's queens. Through all her life she scattered along her pathway the golden sheaves of charity and blessing, and now, though the gentle heart is still and her tongue is silent, yet each day, in a language, more eloquent than words, she speaks to the thousands who, visiting this splendid collection, have cause to bless her memory and her bounty.[51]

Catharine Lorillard Wolfe was more than nature's queen. Incredibly wealthy, she gave generously to many causes. Her greatest sacred charity was Grace Episcopal Church, but her secular passion was art and its altar the Metropolitan Museum, which she was intimately involved with from its inception.

Composed of 120 paintings and 22 watercolors, Wolfe's collection was almost exclusively European, drawn primarily from the French Academic, Munich, and Dusseldorf schools with some representation

Catharine Lorillard Wolfe (1828–1887), painting by Alexandre Cabanel,
1876 (Collection, Bequest of Catharine Lorillard Wolfe, 1887,
The Metropolitan Museum of Art, New York)

from the Barbizon painters. As the daughter and granddaughter of merchants, Wolfe was savvy enough to spell out the terms of her donation,
setting a precedent that continues to this day: the Met was to designate
her artworks as "the Catharine Lorillard Wolfe Collection," and "provide and set apart exclusively for said collection a suitable, well-lighted
fire-proof apartment, gallery, or separate space." In return, Wolfe left
the museum an endowment of $200,000, the interest on which would
be used to preserve the collection and also purchase "modern oil paintings either by native or foreign artists."[52]

I wondered whether even this late in the century I had come across yet another example of an interaction between a Lorillard and a member of my family.

FOUNDING THE MET

The Metropolitan Museum was the brainchild of John Jay II, the very same abolitionist activist who had helped St. Philip's gain admission to the Episcopal Diocesan Convention in the 1850s and who, as a member of the Union League Club, had rushed to the defense of New York's black population during the draft riots. In the museum's Act of Incorporation in 1870, Jay and the other founders wrote of "establishing and maintaining in said city a museum and library of art" that would encourage the serious study of the fine arts while also offering "popular instruction and recreation."[53]

The undertaking cost money, so the trustees launched a subscription campaign to raise (a paltry) $250,000. Inviting New York's elite to become members of the museum corporation, they appealed as much to the pride of potential subscribers as to their pocketbooks: "Think of it, ye millionaires of many markets," trustee Joseph Choate perorated,

> what glory may yet be yours, if you only listen to our advice, to convert pork into porcelain, grain and produce into priceless pottery, the rude ores of commerce into sculptured marble, and railroad shares and mining stocks—things which perish without the using, and which in the next financial panic shall surely shrivel like parched scrolls—into the glorified canvas of the world's masters, that shall adorn these walls for centuries.

One hundred five men and one woman answered the trustees' call. The one female subscriber was Catharine Lorillard Wolfe, who gave $2,500.

The Met's first buildings were located downtown and its first collections were of European masters. Soon thereafter, it acquired the Cesnola Collection of Cypriote Art. From an impoverished but distinguished northern Italian family, Luigi Cesnola had immigrated to the United States in 1860. He served in a New York regiment during the Civil War, then promptly left to become U.S. consul in Cyprus. There he became obsessed with classical archaeology, digging whatever he could, accumulating approximately 10,000 items, which he then sold to the Met for the inflated sum of $110,000. The price tag appeared even more excessive when Cesnola was later charged with fakery—attaching unrelated hands and heads on torsos to make statues appear whole.[54]

If the Met was to continue turning pork into porcelain at such a rapid rate, it needed a new and permanent building. With the help of the Park Department, the trustees settled on the present Fifth Avenue site, which at the time was little more than a semi-rural suburb. Then they addressed the question of fund-raising.

Financing the museum had been an ongoing worry. From its inception, the Met had decided not to charge admission but to rely on its members as well as an annual appropriation from the Park Department. But when those funds proved insufficient, the museum began charging an admission fee. These were paltry measures, so in 1875 the trustees implemented a new membership category. For an annual fee of ten dollars a subscribing member received the following privileges: entrance (with family and friends) to the museum on days closed to the public (Mondays and Tuesdays); ten complimentary tickets for Monday and Tuesday visits to distribute to others; invitation to all receptions given by trustees; tickets to all lectures sponsored by trustees; copies of annual reports; a set of handbooks published by the museum; the privilege of becoming a fellow.[55]

The annual reports list Philip as a subscribing member from the first year it was offered until his death in 1891. The trustees' minutes made no mention of his admission. Was it an issue? Did they care? Had he met Catharine Lorillard Wolfe by 1874, and had she put in a good word for him and smoothed his way? Or perhaps it was John Jay? I found no evidence of either, but it's hard to believe that two members of the Lorillard, Wolfe, and Jay families, who had been directly or indirectly tied to the fate of St. Philip's parishioners, would not have been aware of Philip White's application for Met membership. Certainly after his admission there would be many opportunities for all to meet: receptions in the spring and in the fall, openings for collections on loan, for new acquisitions, for the move from downtown to Fifth Avenue in 1880, and more.

PHILIP WHITE AT THE MET

Philip's annual membership would have included an invitation to the opening reception of the Met's new wing, so I want to imagine that he attended, accompanied by Elizabeth and perhaps his oldest daughter, Ellie. The Met was now filled with so many treasures that it was impossible to see everything. Philip and his family started with the collections in the new wing, proceeding first to the Wolfe Collection. Pausing to admire her portrait, Philip must have silently thanked the woman who had made St. Philip's move uptown possible. The Whites then stopped to examine Camille Corot's *Ville d'Avray* and Pierre Cot's *The Storm*. In a nearby gallery, they chanced upon many objects from the Cesnola collection, and spent considerable time tracing the development of Cypriote art from the late Bronze Age to the archaic and classical periods, and finally to the Hellenistic and Roman eras; they might even have looked for the controversial statues on which it had been whispered that Cesnola had glued a random head or hand. Then they wandered into the old building in search of American art—paintings from the Hudson River school, copperplates engraved for Audubon's *Birds of America,* and the like. To end the evening, they returned to the new wing to look at the Met's latest acquisitions: Henry G. Marquand's gift of Old Masters (and some more recent ones) that included paintings by Van Dyck, Franz Hals, Manet, and Turner, as well as works attributed to Rembrandt, Rubens, and Gainsborough.

My great-grandfather's membership in the museum was certainly an anomaly, but what was *not* anomalous about the Met in those early days? In a way, Philip's presence illustrated the very tensions that existed among the museum trustees and between their stated mission and actual practice. To begin with, the Met sat uneasily on the borderline of public and private institution. Although it received substantial funds from the city government, it was run like a private club or, as the *Tribune* put it, "an exclusive social toy" of the city's elite.[56] When the trustees deemed it necessary to emphasize the museum's public nature, they proclaimed loud and wide their goal of uplifting the lower orders—especially the mass of immigrants streaming into America's cities—by "furnishing popular education and recreation." Such a civilizing process, they claimed, would assimilate immigrants into their new country and produce a new kind of citizen—middle class, educated, respectable—and a new national unity formed around common cultural values. The United States would finally be able to prove to the rest of the world that it had at last fulfilled its own self-civilizing mission and now stood on a par with the European nations from which it descended.

Yet, in an era of increasing nativist sentiment, New York's ruling class could not rid itself of its firm belief in "Anglo-Saxonism," its conviction that white Protestant elites were meant to rule the nation and define its identity. The Met's trustees really didn't think the masses could be civilized and really didn't want to try; the museum, they were convinced, was their domain. Proof of this attitude was the long war they waged against both city government and public opinion to keep the Met closed on Sundays, the one day working people could visit. Their excuses—the need to preserve the Sabbath, the fear of loss of donors, and so forth—rang hollow. When Sunday openings finally became a reality in 1891, Cesnola lamented that the new visitors entered as they would a dime museum on the Bowery, "fully expecting to see freaks and monstrosities similar to those found there." Many, he went on to complain, had gone "to the length of marring, scratching, and breaking articles unprotected by glass" and some had even proved to be pickpockets.[57]

Ironies abound. Many of the trustees, Cesnola included, were themselves of recent immigrant stock. None were aristocrats (in the European sense) but, just as in the 1850s, constituted a class of shopkeepers who had made their fortunes in tobacco, varnish, hardware, and so on. Despite their much-vaunted Anglo-Saxonism, they still felt the need to prove to Europe (especially France and Italy) that the United States was a civilized nation whose citizens were capable of achieving high culture. And until the late 1880s, their taste was uncertain, unformed; all too often they put quantity over quality.

How different was New York's black elite? They too were a shopkeeping aristocracy. They too relied on "civilizationist" language to prove to white Americans that they were capable of uplifting themselves, achieving high culture, and assimilating into the national body politic. In addition, some (like Crummell) advanced nativist, anti-immigrant arguments, even going so far as to adopt the appellation "black Saxons."

I was left with one question. Why did the Met's trustees accept Philip as a member? I'm convinced that here class did indeed trump race. Philip was a prosperous businessman, monied, educated, cultured, and well-mannered; he was not an immigrant and, while "colored," so light-skinned that the trustees could claim him as white. Maybe some even understood how little difference there was between them.

Undoubtedly aware of all these ironies, Philip must have smiled to himself and enjoyed the social joke. I'm sure he felt fully entitled to the Met's privileges. And he certainly didn't need any lectures on the significance of high culture. From his many years of study and observation, Philip was able to draw his own conclusions. Claiming a dual British and African diaspora heritage and living among individuals who were also of diverse multiracial, multiethnic backgrounds, he must have looked askance at notions of "purity"—whether of races, cultures, or nations. In the early 1850s, he had followed the debates among Communipaw, Ethiop, and Cosmopolite in *Frederick Douglass' Paper* asserting that cultures, like races, were forms of "mingling." In the 1870s, he heard his good friend Alexander Crummell apply the same concept to the great civilizations of Greece and Rome, referring to their creators as "cosmopolitan thieves" who "stole from every quarter." So Philip was not about to listen to assertions of a pure European culture or a pure Anglo-Saxonism that were the sole property of one people, one race, or one nation. No indeed, civilization derived from everywhere and belonged to everyone.

PHILIP WHITE: MUSIC, LITERATURE

"I sit with Shakespeare," Du Bois wrote in *The Souls of Black Folk*, "and he winces not. Across the color line I move arm in arm with Balzac and Dumas, where smiling men and welcoming women glide in gilded halls.

From out the caves of evening that swing between the strong-limbed earth and the tracery of the stars, I summon Aristotle and Aurelius and what soul I will, and they come all graciously with no scorn nor condescension."[58] I don't know whether Philip ever sat with Balzac or Dumas, but he did live in the company of Shakespeare, and Dante, and Mendelssohn.

When I helped my mother clear out her house in the summer of 2001, she asked me to leaf through every volume on her bookshelves. I'm not sure what she expected, but among the treasures that had lain there forgotten for years, I found two books with Philip's signature on the title page: an 1857 edition of Mary Cowden Clarke's *Complete Concordance to Shakspere* and the first volume of Henry Wadsworth Longfellow's 1867 translation of Dante's *Divine Comedy*. In addition to art, Philip was drawn to literature, and since he owned a piano for decades, it's evident that he loved music as well. I'm surmising that Mendelssohn was a particular favorite: the composer wrote multiple pieces specifically for the piano; Philip and his friends named the music school they established after him; and last, I remembered that Mendelssohn had been one of my father's favorite composers and that, according to my mother, he had courted her to the sounds of the Italian Symphony.

Shakespeare, Dante, Mendelssohn. Together, they add up to a well-defined fin-de-siècle sensibility: highbrow, nicely adhering to the prevailing aesthetic taste of the times while carefully eschewing the radical and the avant-garde.

Early in the century, Shakespeare's plays had been intensely popular. Whether rendered as serious drama, as burlesque, or as episodes in dime novels, they appealed to a broad cross-section of Americans in search of entertainment. But, with the increasing consolidation of class distinctions after the Civil War, Shakespeare became an author reserved for the elite. *Author,* because it was now fashionable to assert that the bard was at his best when read, not staged. Performance "materializes Shakespeare," one critic maintained, "and in so doing vulgarizes him. Intellectual good taste outside of the theatre spiritualizes him."[59] In contrast, Dante had initially been the exclusive province of American academics (Longfellow was a Harvard professor), who translated his works, critiqued each other's translations, and published essays in scholarly journals. It was only toward of the end of the century that the Italian poet filtered into the ranks of America's reading public.

For his part, Mendelssohn entered the country's—and New York's—canon of classical music early in his career. It was his name that graced the choral society that performed at the Met's opening in 1888. Putting politics aside for the moment, George Templeton Strong turned to music criticism. Inveighing against composers he found too newfangled, Strong insisted that "Wagner writes like an 'intoxified' pig," and Berlioz "like a tipsy chimpanzee." But he placed Mendelssohn in the company of Handel, Beethoven, Haydn, Mozart, and Weber, confessing that his enjoyment of their music was "among the greatest of earthly blessings."[60]

Philip's membership at the Met, his appreciation of Shakespeare, Dante, and Mendelssohn, put him on a par with men like Strong. My great-grandfather could justifiably lay claim to being socially elite, culturally highbrow, broadly cosmopolitan, and an active participant in the formation of the United States' new postwar national identity. But these were mere external identifiers that couldn't begin to account for the deeper meanings the arts must have had for him. Even more than art appreciation, reading and music were solitary activities cultivated mainly in the privacy of home. I imagine Philip's soul thrilling as he played selections from Mendelssohn's *Lieder Ohne Worte* on his piano. I feel him inspired by Mary Cowden Clarke's comment in the preface to her *Concordance* that reading Shakespeare was a path to true self-development. And how could my great-grandfather not have identified with the narrator-protagonist upon turning to the first page of Longfellow's translation of Dante's *Inferno:*

> Midway upon the journey of our life
> I found myself within a dark forest,
> For the straightforward path had been lost.
> . . .
>
> I cannot repeat how I entered there,
> So full was I of slumber at the moment
> In which I had abandoned the true way.

But after I had reached a mountain's foot,
At that point where the valley terminated,
Which had with consternation pierced my heart,

Upward I looked, and I beheld its shoulders,
Vested already with that planet's rays
Which leadeth others right by every road.

Epilogue

COMMEMORATIONS

ON A BALMY JUNE DAY several years ago, I boarded the J train to Cypress Hills Cemetery in Brooklyn. Armed with a map provided by the front office, I went searching for the graves of my forebears and their friends. The White family plot lay on flat land near a broad path surrounded by tall leafy trees. According to the printout, Philip purchased the plot in 1850, undoubtedly in anticipation of his mother's impending death in 1853. Buried next to her were her children: Sarah Maria, Mary Thompson and her family, and Philip and his family. Others lay close by: the Hewlett/Lyons/Williamsons—Elizabeth, Albro, Mary Joseph, Maritcha, Harry Albro, but not Rebecca—as well as Crummell, Charles Ray, James McCune Smith, and their loved ones. Crossing the path and walking up a hill, I found the land that St. Philip's had bought for its parishioners in the late 1850s. The Ray family plot, which included Peter Guignon, was notable for a tall obelisk that jutted skyward. Peter Williams was buried nearby in an imposing mausoleum.

In the waning years of the nineteenth century, New York's black elite reunited in this burial ground. Their graves were physical reminders of their lives and commemorations of their deaths. More than the passing of individuals, however, they constituted the passing of an entire community and indeed of an era. Reading through documents of this end-of-century period, I felt a tremendous sense of nostalgia sweep over the still-living. In myriad ways, they were seeking to make the past come alive by celebrating the achievements of those not yet gone and commemorating the struggles and triumphs of the dead as a legacy for future generations.

As if fearful of forgetting, the black elite cultivated the past with great determination. An 1889 article in the *New York Age* praised the revival of old customs—the return of the spinning wheel, the reproduction of Grandmother's home cures, the restoration of quaint tapestries, rugs, and furniture. Families and community members paid homage

George Downing and family
(Museum of African-American History, Boston)

to those still alive. Every March, John Peterson's former students—
and there were many—held a birthday dinner in his honor. They also
sought to give the dead a place among the living. In 1890, Albro and
Mary Joseph Lyons celebrated their golden wedding anniversary, where
they made sure to honor the memory of their best man, James McCune
Smith, by placing his portrait in a conspicuous place for all to see.[1] An
undated photograph of the Downing family depicts George Downing,
now the patriarch of the family, seated in a parlor surrounded by three
female family members. Every inch of the room, the walls, the tables, is
taken up with portraits of those loved ones no longer—and yet still—
with them.

 Indeed, members of the black elite knew that their greatest responsibility was to preserve the memory of events long since over and
people long since dead. They looked back on the nineteenth century
from a broad historical perspective, eager to compile, analyze, and record

the history of Africans in America. Writing from Baltimore, Bishop Harvey Johnson informed readers of the *Freeman* of his city's creation of a "race Historical Society" where "race relics and works" would be kept for reference and sale. New York's black elite was keenly aware of how many relics had already been lost. In his 1865 sketch of Garnet's life, James McCune Smith had lamented that the mayhem of the draft riots, "among other disasters, has caused the destruction of nearly all the printed minutes of conventions—our Alexandrine library—from which some of the noblest pages in the history of our people could have been selected."[2]

Undaunted, black Americans proceeded to record their history. The *Globe* gave extensive coverage to George Washington Williams's magisterial *History of the Negro Race in America* published in 1883. In his review in the *Age*, my grandfather Jerome B. Peterson emphasized the book's vast sweep. Beginning with early African civilizations, Williams's history continued to the present, and included biographical sketches of contemporary eminent black men and women. As editors of the *Age*, Peterson and Fortune repeatedly advertised the sale of "race literature, old and new"; in addition to Williams's volume, these included Frederick Douglass's *Life and Times*, Garland Penn's *The Afro American Press and Its Editors*, Crummell's *Africa and America*, Booker T. Washington's *Future of the Negro Race*. Alongside book titles, Peterson and Fortune also listed paintings of deceased activists; one of the most popular was a life-size bust portrait of Douglass.[3]

The black elite commemorated in forms other than the printed word. This meant holding ceremonies to honor past institutions and events: annual celebrations of the founding of the African Society for Mutual Relief; commemorations of Emancipation Day and the adoption of the Fifteenth Amendment; observances for past abolitionists and their achievements. Whites who had helped in the cause were not forgotten. Portraits for sale of John Brown and Harriet Beecher Stowe hung next to Frederick Douglass. When Henry Ward Beecher died in 1887, black Brooklynites thronged to a memorial service at the Bridge Street A.M.E. Church. Philip was chairman of the event and, seemingly forgetful of his former indifference to the antislavery cause, commemorated Beecher with stirring words. "We have met to mourn the

loss of one of the great men of the world," he declaimed. "The older people here will remember that when Mr. Beecher presented himself to the people of Brooklyn there was only one thing in the minds of the American people, and that was slavery. The man who took the highest ground on that question was Henry Ward Beecher."[4]

Aware of the evanescence of rituals as well of the word, whether spoken or printed, the black elite turned to more durable forms of commemoration. Some efforts were successful, others not. George Downing's suggestion to erect a monument in memory of John Brown came to naught. Honoring President Grant, who died in 1885, was another matter. Black New Yorkers gathered for a memorial service. T. McCants Stewart delivered a long oration in which he rehearsed the late president's life from his humble beginnings to his generalship and presidency, comparing "our Great Commander" to the biblical David, Oliver Cromwell, Toussaint L'Ouverture, and George Washington. But the black elite also participated in a more permanent memorial to the president. Grant had asked to be buried in New York, and the city's white elite took on the challenge of erecting a "grand memorial temple" in his honor patterned after Hadrian's tomb. A Grant Monument Committee was formed, and black Brooklynite Richard Greener was made secretary. Greener raised substantial funds among the black community and, after twelve years of building, Grant's tomb was opened in 1897.[5]

It was, however, the death of beloved friends and family members that affected the black elite most profoundly. Some occurred close to home, others in faraway places. The venerable patriarch Thomas Downing died shortly after James McCune Smith in the city where he had made his fame and fortune. In a moving tribute written some twenty years later, George Downing recalled how his father had been honored by a large funeral procession, which "spoke of the universal esteem in which he was held." It was composed, Downing continued, of "fellow-citizens from all classes . . . with humility upon their countenances, to pay respect to the generosity, virtue and general goodness that was true of him whose death they mourned, for he had a kind heart for all." Philip Bell died on the other side of the continent, in San Francisco, where he had settled in 1857 and founded his own newspaper, the *Elevator*. Even in the 1860s, Bell seemed nostalgic for the old days and filled his newspaper with articles about the antislavery struggles of yore. Despite the distance and the lapse of time, when Bell fell sick in 1888 and found himself in dire need of money, the African Society for Mutual Relief answered his call and took up a subscription for him. He died the following year.[6]

The farthest away, Henry Highland Garnet, found death in distant Liberia. Forgetting past political differences, the black elite hoped to erect a bronze statue in his honor and got the parks commissioners' agreement to place it in Central Park. But Garnet was not Grant, and funding lagged. An exasperated reader wrote to the *Freeman* angrily complaining that "the race is devoid of public spirit. Education," he continued, "should teach us to perpetuate in brass or bronze the memory of those men, who, by their noble achievements, have done much towards liberalizing public opinion." "We must learn to honor our own," he concluded, "if we desire to leave a legacy in the form of worthy examples to future generations" and encourage others to "be more disposed to honor us than they are at present."[7]

The writer's judgments were perhaps somewhat harsh. It takes a lot of money to perpetuate in brass or bronze. The black elite did what it could. Newspaper obituaries commemorated the many who died in rapid succession throughout the 1880s. Although simply words on a page, they were comprehensive, wedding historical significance to character sketch. Peter Ray was remembered for his improbable rise from errand boy to general superintendent of the Jersey City Lorillard tobacco factory. Peter Vogelsang's obituary extolled his service with the Fifty-fourth Massachusetts and his elevation to the rank of lieutenant at war's end. Whenever possible, commemoration went beyond the short obituary. After Charles Ray's death, his daughters published a loving tribute to their father, *Sketch of the Life of Rev. Charles B. Ray,* in which they detailed his antislavery activity, work with the New York Vigilance Committee and the Underground Railroad, and, in conclusion, provided moving testimonies from friends; a copy of it is preserved in the manuscript room at the Schomburg Center. John Peterson was memorialized in print as "a prince among his people" and his long service to New York's black community duly noted. Alexander Crummell officiated at an elaborate memorial service held in his honor at St. Philip's.

Tributes to John Peterson had in fact started well before his death in the
annual dinners celebrating his birthday, and continued for many years
thereafter. As if material objects would ensure that he would not be forgotten, Peterson directed in his will that his most prized possessions be
distributed to various members of the black community. He bequeathed
Philip his copy of the American Encyclopedia.[8]

My great-great-grandfather was among those who died in the
1880s. Unlike the others, Peter had not participated extensively in public
events and left his mark on the course of history. But Crummell seized
the occasion of his death to recall the early days of the Mulberry Street
School, and noted the deep and lasting impression Peter had made on
all those he had come in contact with from his boyhood years until the
moment of his death:

> Without ostentation, without any prominent position, he
> possessed such peculiar mingled and superior qualities that
> every one will say: 'We ne'er shall look upon his like again.'
>   How deep was the impress of those qualities; how this
> true and singular character was prized, was evident at the
> funeral which took place at his old home. There, in that large
> assemblage of friends could be seen one and another and an-
> other, nay very many of his schoolmates, now gray-haired
> men and women, who had known and loved and played with
> him in the old school house in Mulberry street; and who
> sought the satisfaction of dropping a tear upon the bier of a
> dear friend.[9]

A decade younger than his father-in-law, Philip lived until 1891,
when he died of phthisis, or what we now call tuberculosis. Although I
knew how eminent he had become, I was astonished at the degree to
which he was commemorated in print, ceremonies, and stone by both
the black elite and the white community. The major Brooklyn newspapers all took note. Short obituary notices appeared in the *Brooklyn
Daily Eagle,* the *Standard,* and the *Daily Times.* The *New York Times*
published an appreciative biographical sketch, while the *Brooklyn Citi-*

zen gave an elaborate account of Philip's funeral service and reprinted George Downing's eulogy in its entirety.

No newspaper, however, could outdo the *New York Age* in the lengthy and heartfelt tributes it paid to my great-grandfather over the course of several months. On February 21, the paper published an account of Philip's life and death followed on February 28 by coverage of his funeral at his home and internment at Cypress Hills Cemetery, attended en masse by members of the black elite—among them the Downings, Albro Lyons, T. McCants Stewart, T. Thomas Fortune, Charles Dorsey—as well as members of the Brooklyn Board of Education. On March 7, the *Age* took out a supplement, in which it printed resolutions by the three institutions to which Philip had been especially devoted, St. Philip's, the New York and Newport Ugly Fishing Club, and the Brooklyn Board of Education; Alexander Crummell's funeral sermon; and a special tribute by Horace Dresser, a white member of the Board of Education. But that was not all. On March 21, the *Age* published resolutions taken by one of Brooklyn's most prominent black churches, the Concord Baptist Church of Christ, as well as an account of a commemorative ceremony held by teachers and students of Colored Public School 67. Still more memorial services were yet to come: on March 28, one at St. Philip's; on April 4, another at the Concord Baptist Church held under the auspices of the Brooklyn Literary Union and attended by Brooklyn's top officials, with Mayor Chapin presiding; and on April 11, yet another service organized by the Brooklyn Literary Union, this time exclusively for the black community. Finally, in a short piece in its May 11 issue, the *Age* took note of a tree-planting ceremony in Philip's honor at Colored Public School 67.[10]

Beyond print and ritual, Philip was commemorated in stone. The Brooklyn Board of Education named a school in his honor. St. Philip's placed a plaque on a wall in recognition of his service, one of the very few accorded to a layman.

As I read through these accounts, I was struck by several facts. One was the interracial nature of the tributes paid to Philip. Both black and white newspapers gave extensive coverage to his death. Both blacks and whites gathered together to mourn him at his funeral and then at the Concord Baptist Church memorial service. And almost all of the newspaper accounts emphasized the two events that underscored Philip's successful negotiation of race relations: the saving of his property during the draft riots and his appointment to the Brooklyn Board of Education. For blacks and whites alike, his life stood as a singular model for the possibilities of racial cooperation.

I was also touched by the outpouring of admiration and respect extended to Philip by the black elite. However much they might have been dismayed by his early lack of progressive spirit, they now took full and appreciative measure of the man. Alexander Crummell put it most eloquently in his funeral oration, which he built around the concept of character. "We are here tonight," he proclaimed, "to manifest our respect for the character of our departed friend—Philip A. White." All the printed resolutions agreed on the three areas in which Philip had best exhibited his character. The St. Philip's tribute laid them out neatly. First was Philip's devotion to his church: "From early childhood to ripe manhood and through declining years, Dr. White was connected with our venerable parish. . . . To whatever position he was called he brought to it his best energy, his most lively interest, his most painstaking effort, and above all, the spirit of consecration to his work." Second was his business acumen: "In his business relation he was eminently successful. By close application, untiring industry and exact business methods, he built up a standing in business circles which brought him the respect and confidence which only such qualities beget." And third was his love of family: "In his home life he was an affectionate husband, and a devoted father; thoughtful always of those intrusted to his care."[11]

I pulled out the scrapbook page that had started me on my quest. I now recognized that it was a perfect memorial in miniature. The obituary was a portrait of my great-grandfather's life, from poverty and adversity to prosperity and giving back to the community; one poem pasted on the page underscored Philip's commitment to education; another paid homage to St. Philip's mother church, Trinity; and a third praised his love of home life. But as I read more closely, I realized that no amount of spilled ink would ever reveal the full story of Philip's life. A fourth poem, "If Only We Understood," hinted at secrets Philip took with him to the grave. The second stanza goes as follows:

> Ah! We judge each other harshly,
> Knowing not life's hidden force;
> Knowing not the fount of action
> Is less turbid at its source;
> Seeing not amid the evil
> All the golden grains of good;
> And we'd love each other better
> If we only understood.[12]

As Toni Morrison noted, the "unwritten interior lives" of nineteenth-century black Americans have been buried with them.

As the decades passed, time buried even the public lives of nineteenth-century black New Yorkers. Peter's and Philip's contemporaries, and even members of the black elite born one or two generations later, had desperately tried to preserve their nineteenth-century history; among them were members of my family, Albro Lyons, his daughter Maritcha, and her nephew Harry Albro Williamson. Yet this history was all but forgotten by those who came of age in the twentieth century. Perhaps this new generation could not understand the past in the same ways as those who had lived it. Perhaps they saw only degradation, humiliation, and shame rather than the dignity of struggle and resistance, and so the trauma of remembering became too much to bear. Or maybe with the entry into a new century and the proclamation of a new modernity, they were determined to leave behind what they deemed old-fashioned. Or maybe it was the geographic dispersal from Lower Manhattan to Brooklyn to Harlem and beyond that contributed to the weakening of their will to remember. Within my own family, it might have been generational conflicts too great to bind the younger generation to the older.

But forgetting is not the same as erasing, destroying, obliterating. The past has survived, if only in the form of scraps. The archives in their many guises became a place for safe keeping, for storing memories of the past that were simply waiting to be brought back to light and life in the ripeness of time.

Notes

PROLOGUE

1. Freeman Collection, Box 7.
2. Hodges, *Root and Branch,* 194.
3. Du Bois, *Souls,* 86; Du Bois, "The Talented Tenth," 43–44.
4. Cantwell and Wall, *Unearthing Gotham,* 281–88.
5. Crummell, "New Ideas and New Aims," 123.
6. Early histories of black New Yorkers are James Weldon Johnson, *Black Manhattan* (1930); Kenneth Clark, *Dark Ghetto* (1965); and Roi Ottley, *The Negro in New York* (1967). More recent studies include George E. Walker, *The Afro-American in New York City, 1827–1860* (1993); Sherrill D. Wilson, *New York's City's African Slaveowners* (1994); Rhoda Golden Freeman, *The Free Negro in New York City in the Era Before the Civil War* (1994); Graham Hodges, *Root and Branch* (1999); Shane White, *Somewhat More Independent: The End of Slavery in New York City, 1770–1810* (1995) and *Stories of Freedom in Black New York* (2002); Craig Wilder, *A Covenant with Color: Race and Social Power in Brooklyn* (2000) and *In the Company of Black Men: The African Influence on African American Culture in New York City* (2001); Leslie Harris, *In the Shadow of Slavery: African Americans in New York City, 1623–1863* (2003); Leslie Alexander, *African or American? Black Identity and Political Activism in New York City, 1784–1861* (2008).
7. Crummell, "New Ideas and New Aims," 121–23.
8. Heslin, "John Pintard," 30–39; Burrows and Wallace, *Gotham,* 378; *New York Herald,* February 12, 1805.
9. Johnson, *Black Manhattan,* xvii; *Along this Way,* 4–5.
10. Johnson, *Black Manhattan,* xvii, xviii; Sinnette, *Arthur Alfonso Schomburg,* 43, 32, 134, 141.
11. Williamson Papers, Genealogical Records, reel 1; "Folks in Old New York and Brooklyn," 1.
12. Lyons, "Memories of Yesterdays," n.p.
13. Morrison, "The Site of Memory," 111.
14. Hodges, *Root and Branch,* 279–80.

CHAPTER ONE
Collect Street: Circa 1819

1. *Brooklyn Daily Eagle,* January 5, 1885.
2. R.C. Church of St. Peter's Marriage Records, April 22, 1811.
3. A. Jones, *Pierre Toussaint,* 130–36.
4. *Minutes of the Common Council,* 9:509; Manhattan Tax Assessment Records, Sixth Ward, reels 27 and 28; Lyons, "Memories of Yesterdays," 1–3.
5. Lepore, "The Tightening Vise," 79; Blackmar, *Manhattan for Rent,* 156.
6. Moses, *Alexander Crummell,* 11, 12.
7. Boylan, *Origins of Women's Activism,* 35; Van Doren, *Correspondence,* 97; Nell, *Colored Patriots,* 316.
8. Hoff, "Frans Abramse Van Salee and His Descendants," 65–67.
9. Lyons, "Memories of Yesterdays," 1–2.
10. White, *Stories of Freedom,* 79, ch. 3.
11. Depons, *Travels in South America,* 1:168–82, 346–65, 2:275–85.
12. Gross, *What Blood Won't Tell,* 17–20, quoted in Pratt, *Imperial Eyes,* 32.
13. Lyons, "Memories of Yesterdays," 39, 72; Townsend, *Faith in Their Own Color,* 14–16.
14. Trinity Vestry Minutes, II: April 13, 1795; November 17, 1817; June 25, 1818.
15. Patterson, *The First Four Hundred,* 112; Scoville, *The Old Merchants,* 1:14.
16. Irving, *Salmagundi* 2: nos. 17, 20.
17. Dunkak, "The Lorillard Family of Westchester County," 51–57.
18. Farrow et al., *Complicity,* 13–23; Patterson, *The First Four Hundred,* 44; Matson, *Merchants and Empire,* 202–3, 184; Bagnall, *Sketches of Manufacturing Establishments,* 89.
19. Gately, *Tobacco,* 136–40; Matson, *Merchants and Empire,* 262; Bishop, *History of American Manufactures,* 1:85.
20. Scoville, *The Old Merchants,* 1:252, 259.
21. Blackmar, *Manhattan for Rent,* 44, 30.
22. Smith, ex dem, v. G. & P. Lorillard; Cantwell and Wall, *Unearthing Gotham,* 278–79.
23. Quoted in Wilson, *New York City's African Slaveowners,* 48.
24. Lepore, *New York Burning,* 227; Alexander, *African or American?* 4–5; Cantwell and Wall, *Unearthing Gotham,* 277–90.
25. Lepore, *New York Burning,* 227; Moss, *The American Metropolis,* 2:361.
26. Burrows and Wallace, *Gotham,* 386–87.
27. Patterson, *The First Four Hundred,* 119; Hone, *Diary,* 657; Strong, *Diary,* 4:153.
28. Ford, *Slums and Housing,* 1:59; Duffy, *History of Public Health,* 180–91, 177.
29. Ford, *Slums and Housing,* 1:62.

30. Quoted in Koeppel, *Water for Gotham*, 11, 52.
31. Koeppel, *Water for Gotham*, 117; quoted in Ford, *Slums and Housing*, 1:87.
32. Condran, "Changing Patterns of Epidemic Disease," 30–31.
33. Ford, *Slums and Housing*, 1:61–62.
34. Duffy, *History of Public Health*, 238, 124; Ford, *Slums and Housing*, 1:65–68.
35. Duffy, *History of Public Health*, 171, 168.
36. *Minutes of the Common Council*, 2:123, 15:510, 12:271, 11:301, 16:117.
37. Ford, *Slums and Housing*, 1:86.
38. Duffy, *History of Public Health*, 182–83.
39. Burrows and Wallace, *Gotham*, 371–74, 37–89, 554; Hodges, *Root and Branch*, 194.
40. Bagnall, *Sketches of Manufacturing Establishments*, 87–95; Scoville, *The Old Merchants*, 1:265.
41. Blackmar, *Manhattan for Rent*, 84; Thorburn, *Fifty Years' Reminiscences*, 106.
42. Francis, *Old New York*, 150.
43. *Brooklyn Daily Eagle*, January 30, 1882.
44. Berrian, *Recollections of Departed Friends*, 78; *Colored American*, September 29, 1838.

CHAPTER TWO

The Mulberry Street School: Circa 1828

1. Dickens, *American Notes*, 36.
   Material in chapters 2, 4, 5, and 6 appeared in an earlier essay, "Black Life in Freedom: Creating an Elite Culture," in *Slavery in New York*, edited by Ira Berlin and Leslie M. Harris (New York: Free Press, 2005).
2. Lyons, "Memories of Yesterdays," 2.
3. Zuille, *Historical Sketch*, 5, 23, 26.
4. J. M. Smith, "Freedom and Slavery for Afric-Africans," 270.
5. *Freedom's Journal*, November 27, 1827.
6. Harris, *In the Shadow of Slavery*, 56–62, 70, 65–66; Andrews, *History of the African Free Schools*, 18–24.
7. Teasman, "An Address Delivered in the African Episcopal Church," 7.
8. Williams, "An Oration on the Abolition of the Slave Trade," 347–49.
9. Williams, "An Oration on the Abolition of the Slave Trade," 352.
10. Hamilton, "An Oration Delivered in the African Zion Church," 100.
11. Harris, *In the Shadow of Slavery*, 103, 122–27.
12. J. M. Smith, "Sketch of the Life and Labors of Henry Highland Garnet," 24, 25.
13. Hamilton, "An Oration Delivered in the African Zion Church," 101, 102.

14. Andrews, *History of the African Free Schools,* 57, 25.

15. *Freedom's Journal,* December 21, 1827; Alexander, *African or American?* 65–68.

16. Andrews, *History of the African Free Schools,* 45; Harris, *In the Shadow of Slavery,* 65; Andrews, 70–71.

17. *Freedom's Journal,* December 21, 1827.

18. J. M. Smith, "Sketch of the Life and Labors of Henry Highland Garnet," 21–22; Crummell, "Eulogy on Sidney," *Black Abolitionist Papers,* reel 3:0478.

19. Finkelstein, *Governing the Young,* 207; *Frederick Douglass' Paper,* March 18, 1852.

20. Harris, *In the Shadow of Slavery,* 142–43.

21. *New York Freeman,* March 2, 1885.

22. *New York Freeman,* January 31, 1885.

23. *Manual of the Lancastrian System of Teaching,* 5–8; African Free School Papers, vol. 2.

24. Andrews, *History of the African Free Schools,* 139–43.

25. Andrews, *History of the African Free Schools,* 52.

26. J. M. Smith, "Sketch of the Life and Labors of Henry Highland Garnet," 22; African Free School Papers, vol. 2.

27. J. M. Smith, "Sketch of the Life and Labors of Henry Highland Garnet," 22; *Freedom's Journal,* October 3, 1828.

28. Andrews, *History of the African Free Schools,* 103; Freeman, *Father's Legacy to His Children,* 3–12.

29. McHenry, *Forgotten Readers,* 97.

30. J. M. Smith, "Sketch of the Life and Labors of Henry Highland Garnet," 22; Andrews, *History of the African Free Schools,* 22, 87–88, 91, 98–101.

31. Andrews, *History of the African Free Schools,* 59; *Freedom's Journal,* May 23, 1828; "Questions and Answers on the Island of Hayti," African Free School Papers, vol. 3.

32. Lloyd, *Travels at Home,* 1:9.

33. Leonard, *Literary and Scientific Class Book,* 113, 236.

34. *Freedom's Journal,* January 11, 1828.

35. Andrews, *History of the African Free Schools,* 109–10; J. M. Smith, "Sketch of the Life and Labors of Henry Highland Garnet," 22.

36. Andrews, *History of the African Free Schools,* 60–68, 35; Thurston, "Ethiopia Unshackled," 218.

37. Andrews, *History of the African Free Schools,* 122; J. M. Smith, "Sketch of the Life and Labors of Henry Highland Garnet," 22.

38. Quoted in Barnett, *Education for African Americans in New York State,* 21.

39. J. M. Smith, "Sketch of the Life and Labors of Henry Highland Garnet," 23–24.

CHAPTER THREE
The Young Graduates: Circa 1834

1. Hone, *Diary*, 185–86, 188, 191; Burrows and Wallace, *Gotham*, 601.
2. Hone, *Diary*, 66.
3. Burrows and Wallace, *Gotham*, 456–58, 475.
4. Ford, *Slums and Housing*, 1:93.
5. Condran, "Changing Patterns of Epidemic Disease," 30; Rosenberg, *Cholera Years*, 66–67; Hone, *Diary*, 71; Condran, "Changing Patterns of Epidemic Disease," 31.
6. Rosenberg, *Cholera Years*, 59–61; Blackmar, "Accountability for Public Health," 51–53.
7. J. M. Smith, "Sketch of the Life and Labors of Henry Highland Garnet," 27.
8. Crummell, "Eulogium on Henry Highland Garnet, D.D.," 275–76; J. M. Smith, "Sketch of the Life and Labors of Henry Highland Garnet," 25–26.
9. Hone, *Diary*, 134.
10. Harris, *In the Shadow of Slavery*, 170–71, 176, 188–89, 192.
11. Hewitt, *Protest and Progress*, 45.
12. "Riots Target Black New Yorkers & Abolitionists," *New York Divided: Slavery and the Civil War*, exhibition, New-York Historical Society, 2006–7; Tappan, *Life of Arthur Tappan*, 214; Anbinder, *Five Points*, 10–11.
13. "Riots Target Black New Yorkers & Abolitionists."
14. Hewitt, *Protest and Progress*, 41.
15. Townsend, *Faith in Their Own Color*, ch. 5; Williams, "To the Citizens of New-York," 630; Moses, *Alexander Crummell*, 24.
16. Albro Lyons obituary, *New York Age*, January 9, 1896; J. M. Smith, "Sketch of the Life and Labors of Henry Highland Garnet," 22.
17. *New York Freeman*, March 7, 1885.
18. Andrews, *History of the African Free Schools*, 132; Porter, "Patrick Reason," 517–19.
19. Crummell, "Eulogium on Henry Highland Garnet, D.D.," 278, 279–81; *Liberator*, July 25, 1835.
20. J. M. Smith, "Sketch of the Life and Labors of Henry Highland Garnet," 31–32.
21. Crummell, "Eulogium on Henry Highland Garnet, D.D.," 279, 287–88, 282.
22. Lindsley, *This Planted Vine*, 124–25.
23. Townsend, *Faith in Their Own Color*, 66–67, 61–62.
24. Jay, *Caste and Slavery*, 15–16.
25. Townsend, *Faith in Their Own Color*, 69; *Colored American*, December 7, 1839; Jay, "Caste and Slavery," 9.

26. Du Bois, *Souls*, 236.

27. St. Philip's Vestry Minutes, October 10 and 13, November 14, 1843.

28. *Colored American*, December 7, 1839.

29. Lyons, "Memories of Yesterdays," 75; Lindsley, *This Planted Vine*, 114–29.

30. Morgan, "The Education and Medical Practice of Dr. James McCune Smith," 606.

31. *Colored American*, November 11, 1837.

32. Stauffer, *Black Hearts of Men*, 88; Morgan, "The Education and Medical Practice of Dr. James McCune Smith," 608.

33. *Colored American*, February 17, 1838.

CHAPTER FOUR
Community Building: Circa 1840

1. McHenry, *Forgotten Readers*, 88–114.

2. Genealogical Records, Williamson Papers, reel 1.

3. Lyons, "Memories of Yesterdays, 74.

4. Williamson Papers, reel 1.

5. *Colored American*, September 9, 1837.

6. Harris, *In the Shadow of Slavery*, 115–19; Freeman, *The Free Negro in New York City*, 93.

7. Alexander, *African or American?* 40–43.

8. *Colored American*, September 2, 1837.

9. *Colored American*, August 25, 1837.

10. *Colored American*, November 17, 1838, July 27, 1839.

11. *Colored American*, August 8, 1840, August 15, 1840.

12. *Colored American*, February 13, 1841.

13. *Colored American*, October 30, 1841.

14. *Colored American*, July 14, 1838, September 2, 1837.

15. *Colored American*, September, 5, 1840.

16. Porter, "Organized Educational Activities," 565–66.

17. *Colored American*, May 2, 1840.

18. *Colored American*, January 27, 1838.

19. *Colored American*, August 7, 1841.

20. Harper, "Chit Chat, or Fancy Sketches," 342.

21. J. M. Smith, "Destiny of Our People," 8; "Freedom and Slavery for Afric-Americans," 280.

22. J. M. Smith, "Destiny of Our People," 10, 6, 7, 15.

23. J. M. Smith, "Lectures on the Haytien Revolutions," *Colored American*, September 25, 1841.

24. J. M. Smith, "Freedom and Slavery for Afric-Americans," 279–80.

25. *New York Freeman*, July 18, 1885.

26. Wilder, *In the Company of Black Men*, 114; Brooks, *Official History and Manual*, 12–34.

27. Wilder, *In the Company of Black Men*, 113, 117; Brooks, *Official History and Manual*, 219; Grimshaw, *Official History of Freemasonry*, 9.

28. Brooks, *Official History and Manual*, 221, 222.

29. *Frederick Douglass' Paper*, October 21, 1853.

30. *Frederick Douglass' Paper*, March 24, 1854; Boylan, *Origins of Women's Activism*, 35, 41, 129–30.

31. *Colored American*, March 4, 1837.

32. M. S. Jones, *All Bound Up Together*, 51–57; *Colored American*, August 7, 1841.

33. *Colored American*, September 23, 1837.

34. Boylan, *Origins of Women's Activism*, 221–23.

35. Crummell, "Letter from Alexander Crummell," 94.

36. *Colored American*, December 30, 1837; Harris, *In the Shadow of Slavery*, 202–6.

37. Public School Society Annual Reports, February 1, 1833, May 1, 1835, May 13, 1836, May 4, 1838.

38. Minutes of the Manumission Society Papers, vol. 8, 1829–1849, November 1, 1838.

39. *Colored American*, April 12, 1838, December 12, 1840, September 14, 1839, September 18, 1841.

40. Barnett, *Education for African Americans in New York State*, 36–37; *Colored American*, June 1, October 19, November 9, 1839.

41. *Brooklyn Citizen*, March 27, 1891.

42. Lyons, "Memories of Yesterdays," 80.

43. Public School Society, Record Book, vol. 62, January 25, April 28, 1840, June 11, 1841.

44. Lyons, "Memories of Yesterdays," 49.

CHAPTER FIVE

A Black Aristocracy: Circa 1847

1. *Colored American*, October 24, 1840.

2. Peter Ray obituary, *Brooklyn Daily Eagle*, January 30, 1882.

3. "Receipts, chiefly for curing tobacco and preparing snuff," Arents Collection, New York Public Library, n.p.

4. Robert, *The Story of Tobacco in America*, 77–81, 63–69; *Minutes of the Common Council*, 13:679.

5. Downey, *Lorillard and Tobacco*, 11–13; Gately, *Tobacco*, 117–21.

6. Fox, *The Lorillard Story*, 19, 24–30.

7. Robert, *The Story of Tobacco in America*, 66.

8. Thorburn, *Fifty Years' Reminiscences*, 144–45; *Liberator*, March 14, 1856.

9. Fox, *The Lorillard Story*, 22; Tobacco Institute, *New York and Tobacco*, 17.

10. A. Jones, *Pierre Toussaint*, 130–67, 194–96, 272–75.

11. Letter, Cornelia A. Guignon to Albro Lyons, December 14, 1854; Letter, Harry Albro Williamson to Mrs. Granger, June 20, 1957, Williamson Papers, reel 1.

12. *Colored American*, November 18, 1837; Morgan, "Education and Medical Practice of Dr. James McCune Smith," 610.

13. Harris, *In the Shadow of Slavery*, 145–57.

14. *Colored American*, April 29, 1837, January 19, 1839; Harris, *In the Shadow of Slavery*, 165–67.

15. *Brooklyn Citizen*, March 27, 1891.

16. Higby, *In Service to American Pharmacy*, 40–41; Wimmer, *The College of Pharmacy of the City of New York*, 14; Cowen and Helfand, *Pharmacy*, 123–34.

17. A. Miller, *Shaker Herbs*, 14–15, 29–30.

18. Parrish, "Relations of the Several Classes of Druggists and Pharmacists," 482; Wimmer, *The College of Pharmacy of the City of New York*, 14.

19. *Brooklyn Citizen*, March 21, 1891; Fields's lecture was later published as an essay under the title "Now or Never," *Anglo-African Magazine* (February 1860): 61–62.

20. Philip White obituary, *New York Age*, February 21, 1891.

21. Wimmer, *The College of Pharmacy of the City of New York*, 20–21.

22. *New York Tribune*, August 25, 1847, June 11, 1845.

23. Parascondola, *The Development of American Pharmacology*, 13–15.

24. Charter and By-Laws of the College of Pharmacy of the City of New York, 9–10.

25. College of Pharmacy of the City of New York, Trustees' Minutes, March 14, 1844; Members' Minutes, March 21 and 28, 1844.

26. *North Star*, December 3, 1847.

27. *Frederick Douglass' Paper*, May 27, 1852.

28. *North Star*, February 11, 1848; *Frederick Douglass' Paper*, April 22, 1852.

29. Foster, *New York Naked*, 63.

30. Lyons, "Memories of Yesterdays," 59, 2, 44–45.

31. Beach, *Wealth and Pedigree of Wealthy Citizens*, 49; Freeman, *Free Negro in New York City*, 205–8.

32. Peter Guignon obituary, *New York Freeman*, January 31, 1885; Lyons, "Memories of Yesterdays," 27–28, 79.

33. *Colored American*, March 28, 1840; De Costa, *Three Score and Ten*, 29.

34. Lyons, "Memories of Yesterdays," 72.

35. Lyons, "Memories of Yesterdays," 75.
36. Lyons, "Memories of Yesterdays," 28, 45.
37. Dunbar, *Fragile Freedom*, 122–25.
38. Rebecca Peterson entry, "To Martina," July 16, 1840, p. 46; Rebecca Peterson entry, "On My Lady's Writing, July 11, 1840, p. 35.
39. Charles Reason entry, "True Happiness Has No Localities," 1838, p. 57; Patrick Reason entry, "The Wife," January 1839, p. 25; James McCune Smith entry, "To the River Clyde," August 1833, pp. 39–40; Isaiah DeGrasse entry, "Religion," July 19, 1836, p. 26.
40. *Frederick Douglass' Paper*, February 26, 1852.
41. Bobo, *Glimpses of New York*, 126; *Colored American*, December 9, 1837.
42. Genealogical Records, Willliamson Papers, reel 1.
43. McAllister, *White People Do Not Know How to Behave*, 43, 56, 92–97.
44. White, *Stories of Freedom*, 93–95.
45. McAllister, *White People Do Not Know How to Behave*, 81.
46. White, *Stories of Freedom*, 131–32, 115–18, 135–36, 174–77, 182–85.
47. Foster, *New York by Gaslight*, 122–26.
48. Burrows and Wallace, *Gotham*, 678; *New York Tribune*, November 18, 1851.
49. Burrows and Wallace, 883.
50. Scoville, *Old Merchants of New York City*, 1:258–80.
51. Philip White obituary, *New York Times*, February 18, 1891.
52. Wimmer, *The College of Pharmacy of the City of New York*, 121–22; Parrish, "Pharmacy as a Business," 61; Higby, *In Service to American Pharmacy*, 43.
53. Rosenberg, *Cholera Years*, 105–14.
54. Scherzer, *Unbounded Community*, 31, 66.
55. *North Star*, February 11, 1848.
56. G. Downing, "Sketch of the Life and Times of Thomas Downing," 405–6.
57. Dayton, *Last Days of Knickerbocker Life*, 104.
58. *Frederick Douglass' Paper*, January 6, 1852; *National Anti-Slavery Standard*, November 21, 1850.
59. *Colored American*, June 26, 1841.
60. Foster, *New York in Slices*, 9, 8.
61. Domesh, *Invented Cities*, 52–56; Burrows and Wallace, *Gotham*, 437; Lyons, "Memories of Yesterdays," 44.
62. Homberger, *Mrs. Astor's New York*, 75–81.
63. Gilfoyle, *City of Eros*, 120–23.
64. Homberger, *Mrs. Astor's New York*, 83–89; *New York Tribune*, December 29, 1847.
65. *North Star*, April 27, 1849.

CHAPTER SIX
Whimsy and Resistance: Circa 1853

1. Quoted in Frederickson, *The Black Image in the White Mind*, 78, 86, 83; quoted in S. M. Smith, *American Archives*, 33.
2. Van Evrie, *Negroes and Negro Slavery*, 2, 22.
3. *Frederick Douglass' Paper*, May 11, 1855.
4. Bobo, *Glimpses of New York*, 126.
5. Lhamon, *Raising Cain*, 35–42, 186–88, 154–64, 29–31, 157–59, 47–49.
6. Lyons, "Memories of Yesterdays," 6; *Liberator*, October 12, 1855; Morgan, "The Education and Medical Practice of Dr. James McCune Smith," 609.
7. *Colored American*, September 23, 1837; Alexander, *African or American?* 125–30.
8. *Frederick Douglass' Paper*, March 16, 1855, April 20, 1855.
9. *Frederick Douglass' Paper*, July 22, 1853; Lyons, "Memories of Yesterdays," 43.
10. *Frederick Douglass' Paper*, April 8, 1853; *Liberator*, April 8, 1853.
11. Lyons, "Memories of Yesterdays," 77.
12. Alexander, *African or American?* 89–92; Harris, *In the Shadow of Slavery*, 210–14.
13. *National Anti-Slavery Standard*, October 10, 1850.
14. *North Star*, May 16, 1850; *Liberator*, May 31, 1850.
15. Harris, *In the Shadow of Slavery*, 220–24.
16. Harris, *In the Shadow of Slavery*, 276; Stauffer, *Black Hearts of Men*, 134–46.
17. Letter, James McCune Smith to Gerrit Smith, February 6, 1850, *Black Abolitionist Papers*, reel 6: 0380.
18. Barkan, *Portrait of a Party*, 464–65; Williams, *Horace Greeley*, 29–32.
19. Garnet, "An Address to the Slaves of the United States," 231; Garnet, *Impartial Citizen*, December 5, 1849, *Black Abolitionist Papers*, reel 6:0235.
20. Stauffer, *Black Hearts of Men*, 20–25.
21. *Frederick Douglass' Paper*, July 15, 1853.
22. Moses, *Alexander Crummell*, 81.
23. Schor, *Henry Highland Garnet*, 161; Pasternak, *Rise Now and Fly to Arms*, 89–90, 100–103.
24. Pasternak, *Rise Now and Fly to Arms*, 100; Schor, *Henry Highland Garnet*, 158.
25. Pasternak, *Rise Now and Fly to Arms*, 90; Moses, *Alexander Crummell*, 94–97, 131, 176, 108–9, 116–17, 138, 188–89.
26. Barkan, *Portrait of a Party*, chs. 2–6; *Frederick Douglass' Paper*, August 6, 1852.
27. *Frederick Douglass' Paper*, May 27, 1852, May 18, 1855.
28. *National Anti-Slavery Standard*, May 22, 1851; *North Star*, May 19, 1848.
29. *New York Tribune*, February 21, 1850; *North Star*, April 17, 1851.

30. Freeman, *Free Negro in New York City*, 245, 257; "Communication," 223–24.
31. *Weekly Anglo-African*, October 22, 1859.
32. *Brooklyn Daily Eagle*, November 28, 1886.
33. *Frederick Douglass' Paper*, April 29, 1852, March 24, 1854.
34. Harper, "Colored People in America," 53.
35. "Report: Committee on St. Philip's," 75.
36. Lawrence, "The Episcopate of Bishop Benjamin Tredwell Onderdonk," 18–21.
37. Strong, *Diary*, 1:250.
38. St. Philip's Vestry Minutes, January 14, 1845; Townsend, *Faith in Their Own Color*, 120–21.
39. Lindsley, *This Planted Vine*, 133; Strong, *Diary*, 1:253.
40. St. Philip's Vestry Minutes, May 13, 1845.
41. "Report: Committee on St. Philip's," 73.
42. Townsend, *Faith in Their Own Color*, 184–87, 191–92.
43. St. Philip's Vestry Minutes, October 11, 1853; Strong, *Diary*, 2:131.
44. Letter, James McCune Smith to John Jay, September 18, 1853, *Black Abolitionist Papers*, reel 8:0442; *Frederick Douglass' Paper*, October 7, 1853.
45. *Frederick Douglass' Paper*, May 4, 1854.
46. St. Philip's Vestry Minutes, June 10, 1856.
47. Rev. William Morris Ecclesiastical Trial files.
48. St. Philip's Vestry Minutes, February 8, 1859, June 14, 1859.
49. *Frederick Douglass' Paper*, March 18, 1852.
50. *Frederick Douglass' Paper*, January 8, 1852, March 25, 1852.
51. *Frederick Douglass' Paper*, March 16, 1855, April 20, 1855.
52. Irving, *Diedrich Knickerbocker's History of New-York*, 52–54, 59, 68.
53. *Frederick Douglass' Paper*, March 25, 1852.
54. *Frederick Douglass' Paper*, August 6, 1852, March 18, 1852.
55. *Frederick Douglass' Paper*, January 12, 1855.

CHAPTER SEVEN

The Draft Riots: July 1863

1. Strong, *Diary*, 3:335; Bernstein, *New York City Draft Riots*, 18–19; *Bloody Week*, 2.
    An earlier version of this chapter appeared as an essay, "Reading Contested Spaces in Antebellum New York: Black Community, City Neighborhoods and the Draft Riots of 1863," in *"We Shall Independent Be": African American Place-Making and the Struggle to Claim Space in the United States*, edited by Leslie M. Alexander and Angel David Nieves.

2. Burrows and Wallace, *Gotham*, 881–84, 870–71.

3. Bernstein, *New York City Draft Riots*, 20–26; Strong, *Diary*, 3:340, 337.

4. McCague, *Second Rebellion*, 94–95.

5. Scherzer, *Unbounded Community*, 51, 95.

6. Freud, *Civilization and Its Discontents*, 65–69.

7. *Report of the Committee of Merchants*, 15–18; Bernstein, *New York City Draft Riots*, 28–29; Cook, *Armies of the Street*, 141–42.

8. Burrows and Wallace, *Gotham*, 865, 874–77, 866.

9. Williams, *Horace Greeley*, 210–19.

10. *Weekly Anglo-African*, May 5, 1860.

11. Dodson et al., *Black New Yorkers*, 83.

12. Moses, *Alexander Crummell*, 135–44.

13. *Weekly Anglo-African*, March 17, 1860.

14. *Liberator*, January 16, 1863; *National Anti-Slavery Standard*, January 10, 1863.

15. Harris, *In the Shadow of Slavery*, 167–68.

16. *New York Times*, June 15, 1878; *National Anti-Slavery Standard*, October 5, 1855; *Weekly-Anglo African*, March 24, 1860.

17. *New York Tribune*, July 14, 1863.

18. Smith, "Sketch of the Life and Labors of Henry Highland Garnet," 58–59.

19. *National Anti-Slavery Standard*, July 27, 1851.

20. Foner, "William P. Powell," 103.

21. *Liberator*, July 24, 1863.

22. Alexander, *African or American?* ch. 7.

23. *New York Herald*, July 25, 1863.

24. Lyons, "Memories of Yesterdays," 46: Ray, *Sketch of the Life of the Rev. Charles B. Ray*, 45–46.

25. Lyons, "Memories of Yesterdays," 9.

26. Manhattan Tax Assessment Records, Fourth Ward, 1860–1876, reel 19.

27. Letter from Sargeant John W. Rode to Albro Lyons, July 17, 1863, Williamson Papers, reel 1.

28. Philip White obituary, *New York Times*, February 18, 1891.

29. Philip White advertisements, *Weekly Anglo-African*, December 21, 1861.

30. Philip White advertisement, *Weekly Anglo-African*, July 29, 1865.

31. *New York Tribune*, July 23, 1863; St. Philip's Vestry Minutes, May 16, June 14, 1859.

32. St. Philip's Vestry Minutes, August 4, 1863.

33. St. Philip's Vestry Minutes, November 5, 1863, January 9 and June 20, 1866, July 18, 1871; De Costa, *Three Score and Ten*, 39–40.

34. Stoddard, *Volcano Under the City*, 120–22.

35. Ray, *Sketch of the Life of the Rev. Charles B. Ray*, 48–49.

36. *New York Tribune*, July 18, 1863.

37. *National Anti-Slavery Standard*, July 25, 1863; *Report of the Committee of Merchants*, 7; Lyons, "Memories of Yesterdays," 10.
38. *Weekly Anglo-African*, August 8 and 15, July 25, September 5, 1863.
39. Burrows and Wallace, *Gotham*, 897.
40. *National Anti-Slavery Standard*, July 25, 1863; *New York Tribune*, July 20, 1863.
41. *New York Tribune*, July 25, 1863.
42. Draft Riots Claims, "List of Draft Riot Damage Claims Considered Fraudulent," Box 2; Rejected Claims, Box 3.
43. *Report of the Committee of Merchants*, 4, 35–36, 9, 3.
44. "Schedule of Property Destroyed or Stolen by a Riotous Mob," July 12, 1864.
45. *Report of the Committee of Merchants*, 37.
46. *Report of the Committee of Merchants*, 32–34.
47. Strong, *Diary*, 3:342–43.
48. Foner, *Business and Slavery*, 122–23, 235; Irwin, 12–25.
49. *Weekly Anglo-African*, July 10, 1862.

CHAPTER EIGHT

Union and Disunion: Circa 1864

1. *Report of the Committee on Volunteering*, 13–14, 35–38; J. M. Smith, "Sketch of the Life and Labors of Henry Highland Garnet," 57–58: Strong, *Diary*, 3:347, 411.
2. *New York Tribune*, March 6, 1864.
3. Union League Club, *Report of the Committee on Volunteering*, 17; *Weekly Anglo-African*, August 20, 1864, February 20, 1864.
4. Union League Club, *Report of the Committee on Volunteering*, 17; *Weekly Anglo-African*, January 30, 1864.
5. Duncan, *Where Death and Glory Meet*, 68, 79–88.
6. Duncan, *Where Death and Glory Meet*, 107–16; *Liberator*, August 22, 1863.
7. Reid, *Freedom for Themselves*, 22–31; Humphreys, *Intensely Human*, 74, 67, 95, 124–41.
8. Assistant Surgeon John DeGrasse, Proceedings of General Courts-Martial, RG 153.
9. Letter, Daniel Mann to Major Horace R. Wirtz, October 22, 1863; Letter, Major Horace R. Wirtz to Major General Gillmore, November 20, 1863.
10. Letter, Colonel James Beecher to Brigadier General Edward Wild, December 4, 1863.
11. Rugoff, *The Beechers*, 452–57.
12. Rugoff, *The Beechers*, ch. 24.
13. Stauffer, *Black Hearts of Men*, 277; *Weekly Anglo-African*, November, 25, 1865.

14. *Proceedings of the National Convention of Colored Men, Syracuse, 1864,* 9, 13; Pasternak, *Rise Now and Fly to Arms,* 118.
15. *Proceedings of the National Convention of Colored Men, Syracuse, 1864,* 19, 26–28.
16. Garnet, "Memorial Discourse," 85, 89.
17. *Weekly Anglo-African,* April 22, 1865.
18. *Christian Recorder,* July 15, 1865.
19. Pasternak, *Rise Now and Fly to Arms,* 148–49, 130–44, 153–54.
20. *Christian Recorder,* February 17, 1866.
21. *Frederick Douglass' Paper,* July 27, 1855.
22. Lyons, "Memories of Yesterdays," 12, 14.
23. *New York Freeman,* March 7, 1885.
24. *New York Freeman,* January 2, 1886.
25. Johnson, *Black Manhattan,* 58–60.

CHAPTER NINE
Peter Guignon's Private Wars: Circa 1862

1. Wilder, *Covenant with Color,* 9–15, 37; Livingston, *President Lincoln's Third Largest City,* 25.
2. Miller and Miller, "Brooklyn, 1476–1976," 39; Livingston, *President Lincoln's Third Largest City,* 91–97; Wilder, *Covenant with Color,* 54–58; Merlis, *Brooklyn's Williamsburgh,* 25.
3. Swan, "Black Belt of Brooklyn," 99–111.
4. *Forty-fourth Circular of Castleton Medical College,* 9.
5. Connolly, *Ghetto Grows in Brooklyn,* 23–24.
6. *Frederick Douglass' Paper,* November 29, 1861.
7. Wilder, *Covenant with Color,* 77–78.
8. Roff, "Brooklyn's Reaction to Black Suffrage," 30, 33.
9. Minutes of Stone Square no. 6 Lodge, March 5, 1862, Williamson Papers, reel 1; Williamson, "History of Freemasonry," n.p.
10. Scheiner, *Negro Mecca,* 23.
11. Armbruster, *Brooklyn's Eastern District,* 286.
12. Johnson, *Along this Way,* 48.
13. Livingston, *President Lincoln's Third Largest City,* 23; Williamson, "History of Freemasonry," n.p.
14. *Brooklyn Daily Eagle,* August 5, 1862.
15. *New York Tribune,* August 6, 1862.
16. *Brooklyn Daily Eagle,* August 12, 1862.
17. *Brooklyn Daily Eagle,* August 8, 11, 12, and 14, 1862.

18. *Brooklyn Daily Times*, August 6, 1862.
19. Wilder, *Covenant with Color*, 92, 94, 95.
20. Applegate, *Most Famous Man in America*, 284, 316.
21. *Brooklyn Daily Times*, August 8, 1862.
22. Livingston, *President Lincoln's Third Largest City*, 150, 151; *Brooklyn Daily Times*, July 16, 1863; Swan, "Some Historic Notes," 124.
23. *Brooklyn Daily Times*, August 4, 1862.
24. *Brooklyn Daily Times*, August 4 and 5, 1862.
25. *Brooklyn Daily Times*, August 4, 1862.
26. *New York Tribune*, August 4, 1862; *Brooklyn Daily Eagle*, August 4, 1862.
27. *Brooklyn Daily Times*, August 5, 1862.
28. *Brooklyn Daily Times*, August 5, 1862; *Brooklyn Daily Eagle*, July 30, 1862.
29. *Brooklyn Daily Eagle*, July 30, 1862.
30. *Brooklyn Daily Eagle*, August 5, 1862.
31. Hazelton, *Boroughs of Brooklyn and Queens*, 3:1421.
32. *Brooklyn News*, July 10, 1862.
33. Peter Guignon obituary, *New York Freeman*, January 31, 1885; Lyons, "Memories of Yesterdays," 16.
34. Peter Guignon Jr. obituary, *New York Tribune*, July 29, 1865; *Weekly Anglo-African*, August 5, 1865.
35. Fletcher, *History of Oberlin College*, 1:35–39, 146–47.
36. Fletcher, *History of Oberlin College*, 2:524, 526.
37. *Lorain County News*, August 8, 1865.

CHAPTER TEN
Philip White in Brooklyn: Circa 1875

1. Stiles, *History of the City of Brooklyn*, 2:489; Green, *History of the New York and Brooklyn Bridge*, 10.
2. Buttenwieser, "Exalted Spaces," 23–25; Seim, "To Those Who Lived Below," 23.
3. Livingston, *President Lincoln's Third Largest City*, 41–42; Stiles, *History of the City of Brooklyn*, 3:943–44.
4. *New York Freeman*, March 13, 1886.
5. *New York Freeman*, December 31, 1887.
6. *New York Globe*, September 1, 1883.
7. *New York Globe*, July 12, 1884.
8. *New York Freeman*, January 10, 1885.
9. Lyons, "Memories of Yesterdays," 55–56; Gatewood, *Aristocrats of Color*, 233.
10. Lyons, "Memories of Yesterdays," 55.

11. Crummell, "Attitude of the American Mind," 205–6; "Destined Superiority of the Negro," 50–51.
12. Crummell, "Destined Superiority of the Negro," 51; "Civilization," 198; Crummell, "Right-Mindedness," 154.
13. Patterson, *The First Four Hundred,* 76–87.
14. Sacks, *Before Harlem,* 9; Connolly, *Ghetto Grows in Brooklyn,* 21; Wilder, *Covenant with Color,* 138; Lyons, "Memories of Yesterdays," 28.
15. Quoted in Sacks, *Before Harlem,* 27.
16. *Christian Recorder,* November 23, 1882, quoted in Gatewood, *Aristocrats of Color,* 188.
17. Swan, *T. McCants Stewart,* ch. 1.
18. Thornbrough, *T. Thomas Fortune,* ch. 1.
19. Booker T. Washington, *The Negro in Business,* 150–58.
20. *New York Freeman,* March 27, 1888.
21. *New York Freeman,* March 27, 1885.
22. Peter Ray obituary, *Brooklyn Daily Times,* January 30, 1882.
23. McClean, *History of Jersey City,* 442; "Tobacco Manufactories of Brooklyn," 224; *Industries of New Jersey,* 886.
24. Tobacco Institute, *New York and Tobacco,* 16–17.
25. *Brooklyn Daily Eagle,* February 12, 1890.
26. *Fourth Annual Report of the Alumni Association,* 1874.
27. Records of the College of the Pharmacy of the City of New York, Box 9.
28. *Druggists' Circular,* January 1882, p. 27; *Druggists' Reference Register* 7 (January 1871): 13.
29. Worthen, *Heroes of Pharmacy,* 201–6.
30. Wimmer, *College of Pharmacy of the City of New York,* 127.
31. *Druggists' Circular,* July 1882, 107.
32. *Druggists' Circular,* January 1883, 12, June 1887, 142.
33. Bennett, "Black Episcopalians," 238–40.
34. *New York Globe,* September 8, 1883; *New York Freeman,* January 17, 1885.
35. Bennett, "Black Episcopalians," 240–41; *New York Age,* September 28, 1889; Bragg, *History of the Afro-American Group,* 153.
36. St. Philip's Vestry Minutes, April 14, 1891.
37. St. Philip's Vestry Minutes, July 8, 1875, June 17, 1875.
38. St. Philip's Vestry Minutes, May 13, June 10, 1890.
39. St. Philip's Vestry Minutes, April 13, May 11, 1890.
40. *New York Age,* November 3, 1888; *New York Globe,* December 22, 1883; *New York Age,* April 14, 1888; St. Philip's Vestry Minutes, February 10, 1880.
41. St. Philip's Vestry Minutes, July 12, 1870, Certificate of Incorporation of St. Philip's Parish Home, June 18, 1871.
42. *New York Freeman,* February 12, 1887, May 28, 1887.

43. St. Philip's Vestry Minutes, December 17, 1877, April 17, 1878.
44. Lyons, "Memories of Yesterdays," 79.
45. St. Philip's Vestry Minutes, August 10, 1875.
46. Fox, "Wolfe, Catharine Lorillard," 2:641.
47. Riis, *Battle with the Slum*, ch. 12.
48. "Mulberry Street," Print Archives, Museum of the History of New York.
49. *New York Age*, February 23, 1889; *New York Freeman*, April 17, 1886; St. Philip's Church, news clipping file.
50. Lyons, "Memories of Yesterdays," 80; *New York Age*, June 20, 1891.

CHAPTER ELEVEN
New Women, New Men at Century's End

1. *New York Globe*, January 20, February 3, 1883.
2. *New York Globe*, April 7, 1883.
3. *New York Globe*, February 24, March 3, 10, and 17, 1883.
4. *New York Freeman*, June 18, 1887.
5. *New York Freeman*, May 28, 1887, October 30, 1886, April 24, 1886, February 19, 1887.
6. *New York Age*, January 24, April 25, and December 20, 1891, November 19, 1892.
7. Lyons, "Memories of Yesterdays," 5, A, 49, 6, 50.
8. Lyons, "Memories of Yesterdays," 17, 20-22.
9. Lyons, "Memories of Yesterdays," 32-33.
10. Holt, "Lonely Warrior," 42-43.
11. Duster, *Crusade for Justice*, 78.
12. Duster, *Crusade for Justice*, 79; McMurry, *To Keep the Waters Troubled*, 171.
13. Duster, *Crusade for Justice*, 79, 80, 81.
14. Lyons, "Sarah S. J. Garnet," 110-12.
15. *New York Sun*, June 5, 1877; Lyons, "Susan Steward," 162-63.
16. Frances R. Keyser, "Victoria Earle Matthews," 208-13.
17. *Woman's Era*, March 24, 1894.
18. *Woman's Era*, May 1, 1894, August 1895, November 1894, December 1894.
19. *Woman's Era*, September 1894, December 1894, April 1894, May 1895.
20. *Woman's Era*, September 1894, December 1894.
21. *Woman's Era*, August 1895, February 1896, January 1897.
22. Gugle, *History of the International Order of the King's Daughters and Sons*, 21-23.
23. *Brooklyn Daily Eagle*, April 13, 1891.
24. *Brooklyn Daily Eagle*, April 18, 1891, June 25, 1899.

25. Fairall, *World's Industrial and Cotton Centennial Exhibition*, 10.

26. Rydell, *All the World's a Fair*, 82.

27. *New York Globe*, November 8, 1884, September 20, 1884; *New York Freeman*, March 14, 1885.

28. Herbert, "The New Orleans Exhibition—Colored Department," 190.

29. *Brooklyn Daily Eagle*, May 3, 1872; *New York Globe*, September 27, 1883; *New York Age*, March 6 and 9, 1889.

30. *Brooklyn Eagle*, May 3, 1872; Williams, *Horace Greeley*, 292–305.

31. *New York Globe*, May 12, August 4, 1883.

32. Thornbrough, *T. Thomas Fortune*, 86.

33. Swan, *T. McCants Stewart*, ch. 7.

34. Syrett, *The City of Brooklyn*, 1865–1898, chs. 5, 6, 10, 12, 13.

35. Swan, *T. McCants Stewart*, ch. 4; *New York Age*, November 5, 1887.

36. *Brooklyn Union*, June 13, 1884.

37. Kurland, *Seth Low*, 11–38, 39–49.

38. *New York Globe*, January 27, 1883.

39. Brooklyn Board of Education Minutes, October 10, 1882, p. 772.

40. *New York Globe*, December 1, 1883.

41. Brooklyn Board of Education Minutes, December 11, 1883, p. 683; *New York Globe*, January 19, 1884.

42. *New York Globe*, December 22, 1883, January 17, 1883.

43. *New York Globe*, July 5, 1884; *New York Freeman*, June 20, 1887; *New York Age*, December 22, 1888; *New York Freeman*, February 13, 1886.

44. *New York Age*, September 15, 1888; *New York Freeman*, September 25, 1886; *New York Age*, March 15, 1890, April 5, 1890, June 14, 1890.

45. Brooklyn Board of Education Minutes, May 3, 1892, p. 339, March 7, 1893, pp. 183–86.

46. *New York Times*, June 28, 1893; Swan, *T. McCants Stewart*, ch. 6.

47. Lyons, "Memories of Yesterdays," 20.

48. Swan, *T. McCants Stewart*, ch. 10; Thornbrough, *T. Thomas Fortune*, 117–19.

49. Du Bois, *Souls*, 138.

50. *New York Tribune*, December 19, 1888.

51. *Lehighton Advocate*, January 5, 1889.

52. Metropolitan Museum of Art, *Catharine Lorillard Wolfe Collection*, 6–18; Tomkins, *Merchants and Masterpieces*, 71–72.

53. Lerman, *The Museum*, 16.

54. Tomkins, *Merchants and Masterpieces*, 23, 50–57, 62–67.

55. Tomkins, *Merchants and Masterpieces*, 45; Lerman, *The Museum*, 26.

56. Tomkins, *Merchants and Masterpieces*, 59.

57. Howe, *History of the Metropolitan Museum of Art*, 244.

58. Du Bois, *Souls*, 139.

59. Quoted in Levine, *Highbrow/Lowbrow*, 73.
60. Strong, *Diary*, 4:116, 463.

EPILOGUE

1. *New York Age,* April 6, 1889; *Brooklyn News,* November, 15, 1890.
2. *New York Freeman,* July 16, 1887; J. M. Smith, "Sketch of the Life and Labors of Henry Highland Garnet," 34.
3. *New York Globe,* March 10, 1883; *New York Age,* January 5, 1900.
4. *Brooklyn Citizen,* April 1, 1887.
5. *New York Freeman,* August 15, 1885; *New York Times,* April 25, 1897.
6. Downing, "Sketch of the Life and Times of Thomas Downing," 410; New York African Society for Mutual Relief Records, September 10, 1888.
7. *New York Age,* June 16, 1888.
8. *Brooklyn Daily Eagle,* January 30, 1882; *New York Freeman,* April 9, 1887; *New York Freeman,* July 25, 1885; *New York Freeman,* August 8, 1885.
9. Peter Guignon obituary, *New York Freeman,* January 31, 1885.
10. *New York Age,* February 21 and 28, March 7, 21, and 28, April 4 and 11, May 16, 1891.
11. St. Philip's Vestry Minutes, March 7, 1891.
12. Philip White obituary, *New York Age,* February 21, 1891.

Bibliography

An Act to Incorporate the New-York Society for the Promotion of Education Among Colored Children. Laws of the State of New-York, Passed at the Special Meeting of the Seventieth Session of the Legislature. Vol. 2. Albany: Charles Van Benthuysen, 1847.

Alexander, Leslie M. *African or American? Black Identity and Political Activism in New York City, 1784–1861.* Urbana: University of Illinois Press, 2008.

Anbinder, Tyler. *Five Points: The 19th-Century New York City Neighborhood that Invented Tap Dance, Stole Elections, and Became the World's Most Notorious Slum.* New York: Free Press, 2001.

Andrews, Charles W. *History of the New-York African Free Schools.* New York: Mahlon Day, 1830.

Applegate, Debby. *The Most Famous Man in America: The Biography of Henry Ward Beecher.* New York: Doubleday, 2006.

Armbruster, Eugene L. *Brooklyn's Eastern District.* Brooklyn, N.Y., 1942.

Bagnall, William. *Sketches of Manufacturing Establishments in New York City, and of Textile Establishments in the United States.* 4 vols. Washington, D.C.: Carnegie Institution, 1908.

Barkan, Elliott Robert. *Portrait of a Party: The Origins and Development of the Whig Persuasion in New York State.* New York: Garland, 1988.

Barnett, Enid Vivian. *Education for African Americans in New York State, 1800–1860.* Kingston, Ohio: Harbinger, 2003.

Beach, Moses Yale. *Wealth and Pedigree of Wealthy Citizens of New York City. Comprising an Alphabetical Arrangement of Persons Estimated to Be Worth $100,000, and Upwards, with the Sums Appended to Each Name. Being Useful to Banks, Merchants, and Others.* 3d edition. New York: The Sun Office, 1842.

Bennett, Robert A. "Black Episcopalians: A History from the Colonial Period to the Present." *The Historical Magazine of the Protestant Episcopal Church* 43 (September 1974): 221–45.

Bernstein, Iver. *The New York City Draft Riots: Their Significance for American Society and Politics in the Age of the Civil War.* New York: Oxford University Press, 1990.

Berrian, William. *Recollections of Departed Friends.* New York: Stanford and Swords, 1850.

Bishop, J. Leander. *A History of American Manufactures from 1608 to 1860.* 3d ed.,

revised and enlarged with an introduction by Louis M. Hacker. 3 vols. New
York: A. M. Kelly, 1966.

Blackmar, Elizabeth. "Accountability for Public Health: Regulating the Housing
Market in Nineteenth-Century New York." In *Hives of Sickness: Public
Health and Epidemics in New York City.* Edited by David Rosner. New
Brunswick, N.J.: Rutgers University Press, 1995.

————. *Manhattan for Rent, 1785–1850.* Ithaca, N.Y.: Cornell University Press,
1989.

*The Bloody Week: Riot, Murder, and Arson, Containing a Full Account of This
Wholesale Outrage on Life and Property, Accurately Prepared from the Official
Sources by Eye Witnesses, with Portraits of "Andrews," the Leader and "Rosa,"
His Eleventh Street Mistress.* New York: Coutant and Baker, 1863.

Bobo, William M. *Glimpses of New-York, by a South Carolinian (Who Had Nothing
Else to Do).* Charleston: J. J. McCarter, 1852.

Boyd, W. H. *New York City Tax Book, Being a List of Persons, Corporations, and
Co-Partnerships, Resident and Non-Resident, Who Were Taxed, According to the
Assessors' Books, 1856 and 1857.* New York: Wm. H. Boyd, 1857.

Boylan, Anne M. *The Origins of Women's Activism: New York and Boston, 1797–1840.*
Chapel Hill: University of North Carolina Press, 2002.

Bragg, George. *History of the Afro-American Group of the Episcopal Church.*
Baltimore: Church Advocate Press, 1922.

Brooks, Charles H. *The Official History and Manual of the Grand United Order of
Odd Fellows in America.* Philadelphia: Odd Fellows' Journal Print, 1902.

Brown, William Wells. *Sketches of Places and People Abroad.* 1854. Reprint,
Freeport, N.Y.: Books for Libraries Press, 1970.

Burrows, Edwin G., and Mike Wallace. *Gotham: A History of New York City to
1898.* New York: Oxford University Press, 1999.

Buttenwieser, Ann L. "Exalted Spaces: Recapturing the Glorious Underpinnings
of the Brooklyn Bridge." *South Street Seaport Museum Magazine* (Fall 1983):
22–29.

Cantwell, Anne-Marie, and Diana di Zerega Wall. *Unearthing Gotham: The
Archaeology of New York City.* New Haven: Yale University Press, 2001.

Charter and By-Laws of the College of Pharmacy of the City of New York. New York:
R & G. S. Wood. 1832.

City Directories. Brooklyn. Hearnes, 1850-1854. Hope and Hendersons, 1857–
1867.

City Directories. New York City. Longworth, 1796–1842. Doggett, 1842–1850.
Trow, compiled by Wilson, 1851–1878.

Clarke, Mary Cowden. *The Complete Concordance to Shakespere: Being a
Verbal Index to All the Passages in the Dramatic Works of the Poet.* New and
revised edition. Boston: Little, Brown, 1857.

"Communication from the New-York Society for the Promotion of Education Among Colored Children." *Anglo-African Magazine* (July 1859): 222–24.

Condran, Gretchen A. "Changing Patterns of Epidemic Disease in New York City." In *Hives of Sickness: Public Health and Epidemics in New York City*. Edited by David Rosner. New Brunswick, N.J.: Rutgers University Press, 1995.

Connolly, Harold X. *A Ghetto Grows in Brooklyn*. New York: New York University Press, 1977.

Cook, Adrian. *The Armies of the Street: The New York City Draft Riots of 1863*. Lexington: University Press of Kentucky, 1974.

Correspondence of Aaron Burr and His Daughter Theodosia. Edited by Mark Van Doren. New York: Covici-Friede, 1929.

Cowen, David L., and William H. Helfand. *Pharmacy: An Illustrated History*. New York: Harry N. Abrams, 1990.

Cox, Joseph Mason Andrew. *Great Black Men of Masonry, 1723–1860: A Sourcebook*. New York: Blue Diamond, 1982.

Crummell, Alexander. "The Attitude of the American Mind Toward the Negro Intellect." In *Civilization and Black Progress: Selected Writings of Alexander Crummell on the South*. Edited by J. R. Oldfield. Charlottesville: University Press of Virginia, 1995.

———. "Civilization, the Primal Need of the Race." In *Civilization and Black Progress: Selected Writings of Alexander Crummell on the South*. Edited by J. R. Oldfield. Charlottesville: University Press of Virginia, 1995.

———. "The Destined Superiority of the Negro." In *Civilization and Black Progress: Selected Writings of Alexander Crummell on the South*. Edited by J. R. Oldfield. Charlottesville: University Press of Virginia, 1995.

———. "Eulogium on Henry Highland Garnet, D.D." In *Africa and America: Addresses and Discourses*. Springfield, Mass.: Willey, 1891.

———. "Eulogy on Sidney." *Black Abolitionist Papers*. Reel 3:0478.

———. "Letter from Alexander Crummell." In *Maria W. Stewart, America's First Black Political Woman Writer: Essays and Speeches*. Edited by Marilyn Richardson. Bloomington, Ind., 1987.

———. "The Need of New Ideas and New Aims for a New Era." In *Civilization and Black Progress: Selected Writings of Alexander Crummell on the South*. Edited by J. R. Oldfield. Charlottesville: University Press of Virginia, 1995.

———. "Right-Mindedness: An Address Before the Garnet Lyceum, of Lincoln University." In *Civilization and Black Progress: Selected Writings of Alexander Crummell on the South*. Edited by J. R. Oldfield. Charlottesville: University Press of Virginia, 1995.

Dante Alighieri. *Inferno*. Translated by Henry Wadsworth Longfellow. Boston: Ticknor and Fields, 1867.

Dayton, Abram C. *Last Days of Knickerbocker Life in New York*. New York: George W. Harlan, 1882.

De Costa, Benjamin F. *Three Score and Ten: The Story of St. Philip's Church*. New York: Printed for the Parish, 1889.

Depons, F. *Travels in South America During the Years 1801, 1802, 1803, and 1804*. 2 vols. London: Printed for Longman, Hurst, Rees, and Orme, 1807.

Dickens, Charles. *American Notes for General Circulation*. New York: Harper & Brothers, 1842.

Dodson, Howard, et al. *The Black New Yorkers: The Schomburg Illustrated Chronology*. New York: John Wiley & Sons, 2000.

Domesh, Mona. *Invented Cities: The Creation of Landscape in Nineteenth-Century New York and Boston*. New Haven: Yale University Press, 1995.

Downey, Fairfax Davis. *Lorillard and Tobacco*. New York: P. Lorillard, 1951.

Downing, George T. "A Sketch of the Life and Times of Thomas Downing." *A.M.E. Church Review* (April 1887): 402–10.

Druggists' Reference Register. New York: William G. Stephenson, 1871.

Du Bois, W. E. B. *The Souls of Black Folk*. 1903. Reprint, New York: New American Library, 1969.

———. "The Talented Tenth." In *The Negro Problem*. 1903. Reprint, Amherst, N.Y.: Humanity, 2003.

Duffy, John. *A History of Public Health in New York City, 1625–1866*. New York: Russell Sage Foundation, 1968.

Dunbar, Erica Armstrong. *A Fragile Freedom: African American Women and Emancipation in the Antebellum City*. New Haven: Yale University Press, 2008.

Duncan, Russell. *Where Death and Glory Meet: Colonel Robert Gould Shaw and the 54th Massachusetts Infantry*. Athens: University of Georgia Press, 1999.

Dunkak, Harry. "The Lorillard Family of Westchester County: Tobacco, Property, and Nature." *Westchester Historian* 71 (Summer 1995): 51–58.

Duster, Alfreda M. *Crusade for Justice: The Autobiography of Ida B. Wells*. Chicago: University of Chicago Press, 1970.

Ernst, Robert. "The Economic Status of New York City Negroes, 1850–1863." In *The Making of Black America*. Edited by August Meier and Elliott Rudwick. 2 vols. New York: Athenaeum, 1969.

Fairall, Herbert S. *The World's Industrial and Cotton Centennial Exposition, New Orleans, 1884–1885*. Iowa City: Republican, 1885.

Farrow, Anne, et al. *Complicity: How the North Promoted, Prolonged, and Profited from Slavery*. New York: Ballantine, 2005.

Fields, James. "Now or Never." *Anglo-African Magazine* (February 1860): 61–62.

Fletcher, Robert Samuel. *A History of Oberlin College from Its Foundations Through the Civil War*. 2 vols. Oberlin, Ohio: Oberlin College, 1943.

Finkelstein, Barbara. *Governing the Young: Teacher Behavior in Popular Primary Schools in Nineteenth-Century United States.* New York: Falmer, 1989.

Foner, Philip S. *Business and Slavery: The New York Merchants and the Irrepressible Conflict.* Chapel Hill: University of North Carolina Press, 1941.

———. "William P. Powell: Militant Champion of Black Seamen." In *Essays in Afro-American History.* Philadelphia: Temple University Press, 1978.

Ford, James. *Slums and Housing with Special Reference to New York City.* 2 vols. Cambridge: Harvard University Press, 1936.

Forty-fourth Circular of Castleton Medical College; Being a Catalogue of the Officers of the College and Class of the Spring Session of 1851. New York: Kneeland's Steam Press, 1850.

Foster, George G. *New York by Gas-Light and Other Urban Sketches.* Edited by Stuart M. Blumin. 1856. Reprint, Berkeley: University of California Press, 1990.

———. *New York Naked.* New York: De Witt & Davenport, 1850.

———. *New York in Slices, by an Experienced Carver, Being the Original Slices Published in the N.Y. Tribune.* New York: W. F. Burgess, 1849.

Fox, Daniel M. "Wolfe, Catharine Lorillard." In *Notable America Women.* Edited by Edward T. James. 3 vols. Cambridge: Harvard University Press. 2:641–42.

Fox, Dixon Ryan. "The Negro Vote in Old New York." *Political Science Quarterly* 32 (June 1917): 252–75.

Fox, Maxwell. *The Lorillard Story.* Jersey City: P. Lorillard, 1847.

Francis, John W. *Old New York; or, Reminiscences of the Past Sixty Years.* New York: W. J. Widdleton, 1865.

Fredrickson, George M. *The Black Image in the White Mind: The Debate on Afro-American Character and Destiny, 1817–1914.* Middletown, Conn.: Wesleyan University Press, 1971.

Freeman, Rhoda Golden. *The Free Negro in New York City in the Era Before the Civil War.* New York: Garland, 1994.

Freeman, Russell. *A Father's Legacy to His Children.* Hanover, N.H.: From the Tablet Press, 1806.

Freud, Sigmund. *Civilization and Its Discontents.* Translated and edited by James Strachey. New York: W. W. Norton, 1989.

Garnet, Henry Highland. "An Address to the Slaves of the United States, Buffalo, N.Y., 1843." In Herbert Aptheker, *A Documentary History of the Negro People of the United States,* 1:226–33. New York: Citadel, 1851.

———. Garnet to John Zuille et al. "Impartial Citizen," December 5, 1848. *Black Abolitionist Papers.* Reel 6:240.

———. *A Memorial Discourse by Henry Highland Garnet, Delivered in the Hall of the House of Representatives, Washington, D.C., on Sabbath, February 12, 1865;*

with an introduction by James McCune Smith. Philadelphia: J. M. Wilson, 1865.

Gately, Ian. *Tobacco: The Story of How Tobacco Seduced the World.* New York: Grove, 2001.

Gatewood, Willard B. *Aristocrats of Color: The Black Elite, 1880–1920.* Bloomington: Indiana University Press, 1990.

Gilfoyle, Timothy. *City of Eros: New York City, Prostitution, and the Commercialization of Sex.* New York: W. W. Norton, 1992.

Green, S. W. *A History of the New York and Brooklyn Bridge.* New York: S. W. Green's Son, 1883.

Grimshaw, Wm. H. *Official History of Freemansonry Among the Colored People in North America.* New York: Macoy Publishing and Masonic Supply Co., 1903.

Gross, Ariela J. *What Blood Won't Tell: A History of Race in America.* Cambridge: Harvard University Press, 2008.

Gugle, Sara F. *History of the International Order of the King's Daughters and Sons, Year 1886 to 1930.* Columbus, Ohio: O. Stoneman, 1931.

Hamilton, William. "An Oration Delivered in the African Zion Church, on the Fourth of July, 1827, in Commemoration of the Abolition of Domestic Slavery in this State, 1827." In *Early Negro Writing, 1760–1837.* Edited by Dorothy Porter. Baltimore: Black Classic, 1995.

Harper, Frances Ellen Watkins. "Chit Chat, or Fancy Sketches." [Jane Rustic]. *Anglo-African Magazine* (November 1859): 34–45.

———. "The Colored People in America." In *Poems on Miscellaneous Subjects.* Philadelphia: Merrihew and Thompson, 1857.

Harris, Leslie M. *In the Shadow of Slavery: African Americans in New York City.* Chicago: University of Chicago Press, 2003.

Hazelton, Henry Isham. *The Boroughs of Brooklyn and Queens, Counties of Nassau and Suffolk, Long Island, New York, 1609–1924.* 3 vols. New York: Lewis Historical, 1924.

Herbert, R. Henri. "The New Orleans Exhibition—Colored Department." *A.M.E. Church Review* (July 1885): 189–92.

Heslin, James J. "John Pintard." In *Keepers of the Past.* Edited by Clifford L. Lord. Chapel Hill: University of North Carolina Press, 1965.

Hewitt, John H., Jr. *Protest and Progress: New York's First Black Episcopal Church Fights Racism.* New York: Garland, 2000.

Higby, Gregory J. *In Service to American Pharmacy: The Professional Life of William Proctor Jr.* Tuscaloosa: University of Alabama Press, 1992.

Hoff, Henry B. "Frans Abramse Van Salee and His Descendants: A Colonial Black Family in New York and New Jersey." *The New York Genealogical and Biographical Record* 121 (April 1990): 65–71.

Hodges, Graham. *Root and Branch: African Americans in New York and East Jersey, 1613–1863*. Chapel Hill: University of North Carolina Press, 1999.

Holt, Thomas. "The Lonely Warrior: Ida B. Wells-Barnett and the Struggle for Black Leadership." In *Black Leaders in the Twentieth Century*. Edited by John Hope Franklin and August Meier. Chicago: University of Chicago Press, 1982.

Homberger, Eric. *Mrs. Astor's New York: Money and Social Power in a Gilded Age*. New Haven: Yale University Press, 2002.

Hone, Philip. *The Diary of Philip Hone, 1828–1851*. Edited by Allan Nevins. New York: Dodd, Mead, 1927.

Howe, Winifred E. *A History of the Metropolitan Museum of Art*. New York: Metropolitan Museum of Art, 1913.

Humphreys, Margaret. *Intensely Human: The Health of the Black Soldier in the American Civil War*. Baltimore: Johns Hopkins University Press, 2008.

Industries of New Jersey, Hudson, Passaic, and Bergen Counties. New York: Historical Publishing, 1883.

Irving, Washington. *Diedrich Knickerbocker's History of New-York*. 1854. Reprint, New York: Heritage, 1897.

Irving, Washington, et al. *Salmagundi*. 2 vols. 1808. Reprint, New York: G. P. Putnam's Sons, 1897.

Irwin, Will. *A History of the Union League Club of New York City*. New York: Dodd, Mead, 1952.

Jay, John. *Caste and Slavery in the American Church*. New York: Wiley and Putnam, 1843.

Johnson, James Weldon. *Along this Way, an Autobiography*. 1933. Reprint, New York: Viking, 1968.

———. *Black Manhattan*. New York: Alfred A. Knopf, 1930.

Jones, Arthur. *Pierre Toussaint*. New York: Doubleday, 2003.

Jones, Martha S. *All Bound Up Together: The Woman Question in African American Public Culture, 1830–1900*. Chapel Hill: University of North Carolina Press, 2007.

Joyce, Jeremiah. *Scientific Dialogues; Intended for the Instruction of Young People; in Which the First Principles of Natural and Experimental Philosophy Are Fully Explained*. 3 vols. Philadelphia: M. Carey, 1815.

Keyser, Frances R. "Victoria Earle Matthews." In *Homespun Heroines and Other Women of Distinction*. Edited by Hallie Q. Brown. 1926. Reprint, New York: Oxford University Press, 1988.

Koeppel, Gerard T. *Water for Gotham: A History*. Princeton: Princeton University Press, 2000.

Kurland, Gerald. *Seth Low: The Reformer in an Urban Age and Industrial Age*. New York: Twayne, 1971.

Lee, Henry. "The Most Awful Calamity: The Great Fire of 1835." *South Street Seaport Museum Magazine* (Fall 1990): 28–33.

Leonard, Jonathan Norton. *Men of Maracaibo*. New York: G. P. Putnam's Sons, 1933.

Leonard, Levi W. *The Literary and Scientific Class Book, Embracing the Leading Facts and Principles of Science. Selected from the Rev. John Platts' Literary and Scientific Class Book, and from Various Other Sources, and Adapted to the Wants and Conditions of Youth in the United States*. Keene, N.H.: John Prentiss, 1828.

Lepore, Jill. *New York Burning: Liberty, Slavery, and Conspiracy in Eighteenth-Century Manhattan*. New York: Alfred A. Knopf, 2005.

———. "The Tightening Vise: Slavery and Freedom in British New York." In *Slavery in New York*. Edited by Ira Berlin and Leslie M. Harris. New York: Free Press, 2005.

Lerman, Leo. *The Museum: One Hundred Years and the Metropolitan Museum of Art*. New York: Viking, 1969.

Levine, Lawrence W. *Highbrow/Lowbrow: The Emergence of Cultural Hierarchy in America*. Cambridge: Harvard University Press, 1988.

Lhamon, W. T., Jr. *Raising Cain: Blackface Performance from Jim Crow to Hip Hop*. Cambridge: Harvard University Press, 1998.

Lindsley, James Elliott. *This Planted Vine: A Narrative History of the Episcopal Diocese of New York*. New York: Harper & Row, 1984.

Livingston, E. A. *President Lincoln's Third Largest City: Brooklyn and the Civil War*. Glendale, N.Y.: Budd, 1994.

Lloyd, Charles. *Travels at Home and Voyages by the Fireside: For the Instruction and Entertainment of Young Persons*. 2 vols. Philadelphia: Edward Earle, 1816.

Lorini, Alessandra. *Rituals of Race: American Public Culture and the Search for Racial Democracy*. Charlottesville: University of Virginia Press, 1999.

Lyons, Maritcha. "Georgiana Putnam." In *Homespun Heroines and Other Women of Distinction*. Edited by Hallie Q. Brown. 1926. Reprint, New York: Oxford University Press, 1988.

———. "Memories of Yesterdays, All of Which I Saw and Part of Which I Was—An Autobiography." Harry Albro Williamson Papers. Reel 1. Schomburg Center for Research in Black Culture.

———. "Sarah S. J. Garnet." In *Homespun Heroines and Other Women of Distinction*. Edited by Hallie Q. Brown. 1926. Reprint, New York: Oxford University Press, 1988.

———. "Susan S. McK. Steward." In *Homespun Heroines and Other Women of Distinction*. Edited by Hallie Q. Brown. 1926. Reprint, New York: Oxford University Press, 1988.

Mabee, Carleton. *Black Education in New York State: From Colonial to Modern Times*. Syracuse, N.Y.: Syracuse University Press, 1979.

McAllister, Marvin. *White People Do Not Know How to Behave at Entertainments Designed for Ladies & Gentlemen of Colour: William Brown's African & American Theater*. Chapel Hill: University of North Carolina Press, 2003.

McCague, James. *The Second Rebellion: The Story of the New York City Draft Riots of 1863*. New York: Dial, 1968.

McHenry, Elizabeth. *Forgotten Readers: Recovering the Lost History of African American Literary Societies*. Durham: Duke University Press, 2003.

McClean, Alexander. *History of Jersey City, N.J.* Jersey City: Jersey City Printing, 1985.

McMurry, Linda O. *To Keep the Waters Troubled: The Life of Ida B. Wells*. New York: Oxford University Press, 1998.

Matson, Cathy. *Merchants and Empire: Trading in Colonial New York*. Baltimore: Johns Hopkins University Press, 1998.

Meier, August. *Negro Thought in America, 1880–1915*. Ann Arbor: Ann Arbor Paperbacks, University of Michigan Press, 1966.

Merlis, Brian. *Brooklyn's Williamsburgh: City Within a City*. Brooklyn: Brooklyn Editions and Brooklynpix.com, 1994.

Metropolitan Museum of Art. *The Catharine Lorillard Wolfe Collection in the New Western Galleries*. New York: The Metropolitan Museum of Art, 1890.

Miller, Amy Bess. *Shaker Herbs: A History and a Compendium*. New York: Clarkson N. Potter, 1976.

Miller, Ron, and Rita Selden Miller. "Brooklyn, 1476–1976." In *An Introduction to the Black Contribution to the Development of Brooklyn*. Edited by Charlene Claye Van Derzee. Brooklyn: New Muse Community of Brooklyn, 1977.

Minutes of the Common Council of the City of New York, 1784–1831. Vols. 1–19. Published by the City of New York, 1917.

Morgan, Thomas M. "The Education and Medical Practice of Dr. James McCune Smith (1813–1865), First Black American to Hold a Medical Degree." *Journal of the National Medical Association* 95 (July 2003): 603–14.

Morrison, Toni. *Beloved*. New York: Alfred A. Knopf, 1987.

———. "The Site of Memory." In *Inventing the Truth: The Art and Craft of Memory*. Edited by William Zinsser. Boston: Houghton Mifflin, 1987.

Moses, Wilson Jeremiah. *Alexander Crummell: A Study of Civilization and Discontent*. New York: Oxford University Press, 1989.

Moss, Frank. *The American Metropolis from Knickerbockers Days to the Present Time*. 3 vols. New York: Peter Fenelon Collier, 1897.

Nell, William C. *Colored Patriots of the American Revolution*. Boston: Robert F. Wallcut, 1855.

Parascandola, John. *The Development of American Pharmacology*. Baltimore: Johns
    Hopkins University Press, 1992.
Parrish, Edward. "On the Relations of the Several Classes of Druggists and
    Pharmacists to the Colleges of Pharmacy." *The American Journal of
    Pharmacy* (November 1871): 481–85, 532–35.
———. "Pharmacy as a Business." *American Pharmaceutical Association* (1856):
    59–68.
Pasternak, Martin B. *Rise Now and Fly to Arms: The Life of Henry Highland
    Garnet*. New York: Garland, 1995.
Patterson, Jerry E. *The First Four Hundred: Mrs. Astor's New York in the Gilded Age*.
    New York: Rizzoli, 2000.
Perlman, Daniel. "Organizations of the Free Negro in New York City, 1800–
    1860." *Journal of Negro History* 56 (1971), 181–97.
Peterson, Carla L. "Black Life in Freedom: Creating an Elite Culture." In *Slavery
    in New York*. Edited by Ira Berlin and Leslie M. Harris. New York: Free
    Press, 2005.
———. "Contesting City Space in Antebellum New York: Black Community,
    City Neighborhoods, and the Draft Riots of 1863." *"We Shall Independent
    Be": African American Place-Making: The Struggle to Claim Space in the
    U.S.* Edited by Leslie M. Alexander and Angel David Nieves. Boulder:
    University Press of Colorado, 2008.
Porter, Dorothy. "The Organized Educational Activities of Negro Literary
    Societies, 1828–1846." *Journal of Negro Education* 5 (October 1936): 555–76.
———. "Reason, Patrick Henry." In *Dictionary of American Negro Biography*.
    Edited by Rayford W. Logan and Michael R. Winston. New York: W. W.
    Norton, 1982.
Pratt, Mary Louise. *Imperial Eyes: Travel Writing and Transculturation*. London:
    Routledge, 1992.
Proceedings of the Black State Conventions. Edited by Philip S. Foner. 2 vols.
    Philadephia: Temple University Press, 1979.
*Proceedings of the National Convention of Colored Men: Held in the City of Syracuse,
    N.Y., October 4, 5, 6, and 7, 1864*. Boston: G. C. Rand and Avery, 1864.
"Proceedings of the New York College of Pharmacy." *American Journal of
    Pharmacy* 17 (1846–47): 248–51.
Public School Society of New York. *Manual of the Lancastrian System of Teaching
    Reading, Writing, Arithmetic, and Needle-Work, as Practised in the Schools of
    the Free-society, of New York*. New York: The Society, 1820.
Ray, F[lorence] T., and H[enrietta] C. Ray. *Sketch of the Life of the Rev. Charles B.
    Ray*. New York: J. J. Little, 1887.
Reid, Richard M. *Freedom for Themselves: North Carolina's Black Soldiers in the
    Civil War*. Chapel Hill: University of North Carolina Press, 2008.

"Report: Committee on St. Philip's Church." *Journal of the Convention of New York.* 1846.

Report of the Committee of Merchants for the Relief of Colored People Suffering from the Late Riots in the City of New York. New York: George A. Whitehorne, 1863.

Riis, Jacob A. *The Battle with the Slum.* New York: Macmillan, 1902.

Robert, Joseph C. *The Story of Tobacco in America.* New York: Knopf, 1949.

Roff, Kenneth L. "Brooklyn's Reaction to Black Suffrage in 1860." *Afro-Americans in New York Life and History* 2 (January 1978): 29–39.

Rosenberg, Charles E. *The Cholera Years: The United States in 1832, 1849, and 1866.* Chicago: University of Chicago Press, 1962.

Rugoff, Milton. *The Beechers: An American Family in the Nineteenth Century.* New York: Harper & Row, 1981.

Rydell, Robert. *All the World's a Fair: Visions of Empire at American International Expositions, 1876–1916.* Chicago: University of Chicago Press, 1984.

Sacks, Marcy S. *Before Harlem: The Black Experience in New York City Before World War I.* Philadelphia: University of Pennsylvania Press, 2006.

———. "Re-Creating Black New York at Century's End." In *Slavery in New York.* Edited by Ira Berlin and Leslie M. Harris. New York: Free Press, 2005.

Schechter, Barnet. *The Devil's Own Work: The Civil War Draft Riots and the Fight to Reconstruct America.* New York: Walker, 2005.

Scheiner, Seth M. *Negro Mecca: A History of the Negro in New York City, 1865–1920.* New York: New York University Press, 1965.

Scherzer, Kenneth A. *The Unbounded Community: Neighborhood Life and Social Structure in New York City, 1830–1875.* Durham: Duke University Press, 1992.

Schor, Joel. *Henry Highland Garnet: A Voice of Black Radicalism in the Nineteenth Century.* Westport, Conn.: Greenwood, 1977.

Scoville, Joseph A. *The Old Merchants of New York City.* 5 vols. New York: Carlton, 1864.

Seim, Susan A. "To Those Who Lived Below the Bridge Meant Hope." *Villager* (May 19, 1983): 23.

Sinnette, Elinor des Verney. *Arthur Alfonso Schomburg: Black Bibliophile and Collector.* New York Public Library & Wayne State University Press, Detroit, 1989.

Smith, James McCune. "The Destiny of Our People." 1843. In *The Black Abolitionist Papers.* Reel 3:0799.

———. "Freedom and Slavery for Africans." 1844. In *The Mind of the Negro as Reflected in Letters Written During the Crisis, 1800–1860.* Edited by Carter G. Woodson. Washington, D.C.: Association for the Study of Negro Life and History, 1926.

———. "Lectures on the Haytien Revolutions." *Colored American,* June 5, August 7, August 28, September 18, September 25, October 2, October 9, October 16, 1841.

———. "Sketch of the Life of and Labors of Henry Highland Garnet." In *A Memorial Discourse by Henry Highland Garnet, Delivered in the Hall of the House of Representatives, Washington, D.C., on Sabbath, February 12, 1865; with an introduction by James McCune Smith.* Philadelphia: J. M. Wilson, 1865.

Smith, Shawn Michelle. *American Archives: Gender, Race, and Class in Visual Culture.* Princeton: Princeton University Press, 1999.

Smith, ex. dem. Teller, v. G. and P. Lorillard. Supreme Court of Judicature of New York. 10 Johns. 338; 1813. N.Y.

Stauffer, John. *The Black Hearts of Men: Radical Abolitionists and the Transformation of Race.* Cambridge: Harvard University Press, 2001.

Stiles, Henry R. *A History of the City of Brooklyn, Including the Old Town and Village of Brooklyn, the Town of Bushwick, and the Village and City of Williamsburgh,* 3 vols. Brooklyn, N.Y.: Privately printed, 1867–70.

Stoddard, William Osborn. *The Volcano Under the City.* New York: Fords, Howard & Hulbert, 1887.

Strong, George Templeton. *The Diary of George Templeton Strong.* Edited by Allan Nevins and Milton Halsey Thomas. 4 vols. New York: MacMillan, 1952.

Swan, Robert. "The Black Belt of Brooklyn" and "Some Historic Notes on Black Williamsburgh and Bushwick." In *An Introduction to the Black Contribution to the Development of Brooklyn.* Edited by Charlene Claye Van Derzee. Brooklyn: New Muse Community of Brooklyn, 1977.

———. *Thomas McCants Stewart and the Failure of the Mission of the Talented Tenth in Black America, 1880–1923.* Typescript dissertation, New York University, 1990.

Syrett, Harold Coffin. *The City of Brooklyn, 1865–1898: A Political History.* New York: Columbia University Press, 1944.

Tappan, Lewis. *The Life of Arthur Tappan.* New York: Hurd and Houghton, 1870.

Teasman, John. *An Address Delivered in the African Episcopal Church on the 25th March 1811 Before the New-York African Society for Mutual Relief.* New York: J. Low, 1811.

Thorburn, Grant. *Fifty Years' Reminiscences of New York, or, Flowers from the Garden of Laurie Todd.* New York: Daniel Fanshaw, 1845.

Thornbrough, Emma Lou. *T. Thomas Fortune, Militant Journalist.* Chicago: University of Chicago Press, 1972.

Thurston, Eve. "Ethiopia Unshackled: A Brief History of the Education of Negro Children in New York City." *Bulletin of the New York Public Library* 69 (April 1965): 211–21.

Tobacco Institute. *New York and Tobacco: A Chapter in Industrial Growth.*
    Washington, D.C.: The Tobacco Institute, 1972.
"The Tobacco Manufactories of Brooklyn." *Scientific American* 26 (April 6, 1872):
    224.
Tomkins, Calvin. *Merchants and Masterpieces: The Story of the Metropolitan
    Museum of Art.* New York: E. P. Dutton, 1970.
Townsend, Craig D. *Faith in Their Own Color: Black Episcopalians in Antebellum
    New York.* New York: Columbia University Press, 2005.
Union League Club. *Report of the Committee on Volunteering.* New York: Club
    House, 1864.
United States Bureau of the Census. Historical Statistics of the United States.
Van Evrie, John. *Negroes and Negro Slavery; The First, an Inferior Race—the
    Latter Its Normal Condition.* Baltimore: John D. Toy Printer, 1853.
Walker, George E. *The Afro-American in New York City, 1827–1860.* New York:
    Garland, 1993.
Washington, Booker T. *The Negro in Business.* 1907. Reprint, Chicago: Afro-Am
    Press, 1969.
Washington, S. A. M. *George Thomas Downing: Sketch of His Life and Times.*
    Newport, R.I.: Milne Printery, 1910.
White, Shane. *Stories of Freedom in Black New York.* Cambridge: Harvard
    University Press, 2002.
Wilder, Craig. *A Covenant with Color: Race and Social Power in Brooklyn.* New
    York: Columbia University Press, 2000.
———. *In the Company of Black Men: The African Influence on African American
    Culture in New York City.* New York: New York University Press, 2001.
Williams, Peter. "An Oration on the Abolition of the Slave Trade: Delivered in
    the African Church, in the City of New York, January 1, 1808." In *Early
    Negro Writing, 1760–1837.* Edited by Dorothy Porter. Baltimore: Black
    Classic, 1995.
———. "To the Citizens of New York." In *The Mind of the Negro as Reflected in
    Letters Written During the Crisis, 1800–1860.* Edited by Carter G. Woodson.
    Washington, D.C.: Association for the Study of Negro Life and History,
    1926.
Williams, Robert C. *Horace Greeley: Champion of American Freedom.* New York:
    New York University Press, 2006.
Williamson, Harry Albro, "Folks in Old New York and Brooklyn." Harry Albro
    Williamson Papers. Reel 1. Schomburg Center for Research in Black
    Culture.
———. "A History of Freemasonry Among the American Negroes." Harry
    Albro Williamson Papers. Reel 1. Schomburg Center for Research in Black
    Culture.

Wilson, Sherrill D. *New York City's African Slaveowners: A Social and Material Culture History*. New York: Garland, 1994.

Wimmer, Curt. *The College of Pharmacy of the City of New York*. Baltimore: Read-Taylor, 1929.

Worthen, Dennis. *Heroes of Pharmacy: Professional Leadership in Times of Change*. Washington, D.C.: American Pharmacists Association, 2008.

Zuille, John J. *Historical Sketch of the New York African Society for Mutual Relief*. New York: John J. Zuille, 1892.

MANUSCRIPT COLLECTIONS

Black Abolitionist Papers, edited by George Carter and C. Peter Ripley. Microfilm edition, 17 reels. Ann Arbor: University Microfilms International, 1984.

Library Company of Philadelphia
    Amy Matilda Cassey Friendship Album
    Martina Dickerson Friendship Album

Museum of the City of New York, Print Archives

National Archives, Washington, D.C.
    Descriptive Books, 35th United States Colored Troops, Record Group 94
    Proceedings of General Courts-Martial, RG 153

New-York Historical Society
    New York Divided: Slavery and the Civil War, exhibition, 2006–7
    Records of the New-York African Free Schools
    Papers of the New York Manumission Society
    Public School Society. Annual Reports; Minutes of the Executive Committee; Record Books

New York City Department of Records/Municipal Archives
    Board of Supervisors. New York County Special Commission on Draft Riot Claims, 1863–1865, 3 Boxes
    Manhattan Tax Assessment Records
    Brooklyn, N.Y., Board of Education. *Proceedings.* Brooklyn, 1882–1893.

New York Public Library, Arents Collection. *Lorillard receipt book, 1825–1843, chiefly for curing tobacco and preparing snuff*

R.C. Church of St. Peter's, New York. Marriage Register, 1802–1850

Schomburg Center for Research in Black Culture, New York
    New York African Society Mutual Relief, Records, 1809–1949, 14 microfilm reels
    St. Philip's Episcopal Church Vestry Minutes, 1843–1865; 1865–1875; 1875–1882; 1882–1888; 1888–1894
    Rhoda Freeman Research Collection

Harry Albro Williamson Papers, Reel 1, Schedule of Property Destroyed or
    Stolen by a Riotous Mob
St. John the Divine, Archives of the Episcopal Diocese of New York.
    Parish Records Series: St. Philip's Church, Manhattan—news clippings
        File
    Certificate of Incorporation of St. Philip's Parish Home, June 18, 1871
    Bishop's Papers: Rev. William Morris Ecclesiastical Trial files
    Lawrence, John E. "The Episcopate of Bishop Benjamin Tredwell
        Onderdonk, IV, Bishop of New York." Unpublished paper, 1970.
Trinity Church Archives, New York, Vestry Minutes: Vol. 2, 1791, 1826; Vol. 3,
    1826–1850.
Wisconsin Historical Society, College of Pharmacy of the City of New York.
    Alumni Association Annual Reports, 1872–1880, 1881–1891; Members'
    Minutes, 1829–1886; Board of Trustees Minutes, 1829–1845.

Index

Page numbers in *italics* refer to illustrations